TWO HUNDRED YEARS OF THEOLOGY

TWO HUNDRED YEARS OF THEOLOGY

Report of a Personal Journey

by Hendrikus Berkhof

Translated by John Vriend

GRAND RAPIDS, MICHIGAN
WILLIAM B. EERDMANS PUBLISHING COMPANY

Copyright © 1989 by Wm. B. Eerdmans Publishing Co.
255 Jefferson Ave. S.E., Grand Rapids, Mich. 49503

Originally published as *200 Jahre Theologie: Ein Reisebericht*
© 1985 Neukirchener Verlag

Library of Congress Cataloging-in-Publication Data

Berkhof, H. (Hendrikus), 1914-
    [200 Jahre Theologie. English]
    Two hundred years of theology: report of a personal journey/by
Hendrikus Berkhof: translated by John Vriend.
        p.   cm.
    Translation of: 200 Jahre Theologie.
    Includes bibliographical references.
    ISBN 0-8028-3666-6 — ISBN 0-8028-0473-X (pbk.)
    1. Theology, Doctrinal—History—19th century. 2. Theology,
Doctrinal—History—20th century.   I. Title.
BT28.B44313 1989
230'.09'034—dc20   89-11786
                                                                    CIP

CONTENTS

We have every cause to be cautious in judging whether a given dogmatics has or has not as its standard the revelation of God attested in Holy Scripture. There can be no doubt that in every age men have been much too ready with both positive and negative judgments in the heat of the controversy. It is as well to realize that even when it seems that a verdict can and should be given in a specific case, we can only make, as it were, a judgment for the moment, for to-day, and tomorrow we must give another hearing to find out whether we have perhaps been deceived in some respect and ought thus to alter the judgment. Such judgments, even those that are well-founded, even those that the divided Church has solemnly laid down in its mutually opposed and mutually accusatory confessions, must always be regarded in principle merely as very sharply put questions and not as God's own judgments. But when all this is seen and said, it must also be seen and said that the sword of God's real judgment does hang over our heads —over our own heads as well as those of our heretical partners in the controversy—when we take up and pursue this work.

Karl Barth, *Church Dogmatics*, 1/1:286-87

INTRODUCTION

The task of an author in his introduction is to make clear his aim and the kind of readers for whom he is writing. I must honestly admit that initially I had in mind neither a specific goal nor a specific kind of reader. What lay behind this study and the writing of this book was a certain curiosity. The journey of discovery of which this book is a report is one I undertook for my own benefit, as the style and the relatively loose composition indicate. The majority of chapters can be read separately. Together they do not form the building blocks of a system; rather, they are like coral beads on a string—the string being a question which more or less loosely ties them together.

This question concerns the relationship between the gospel and modern thought. Ever and again and with increasing intensity I asked myself how, speaking generally, these two can coexist, though modern theology in its leading ideas of course presupposes such coexistence both as a possibility and as a reality. Is this assumption well-founded? In view of the essential features of each, must not one assume that the two are radically inconsistent with each other? The gospel, after all, presupposes a personal Creator-God; hence it starts out with a duality of God and world, a view in which God is regarded as a superior, and human beings as dependent on a transcendent being. In addition, the gospel presupposes sin—the radical estrangement of human beings from their destiny. By sin human beings have blocked their own access to the knowledge of God and can therefore, in general, only view themselves and their own achievements with deep distrust. Only within the framework of this situation of estrangement can one understand the person and work of Jesus Christ as "redemption," "liberation," or "salvation." His appearance must be understood as a special manifestation of God's love for humanity, one that has no parallel in human history.

This estrangement as a result of sin is so profound, however, that human beings cannot by themselves grasp this salvation. For that reason a new act of God, a second miracle, must occur: the advent and working of the Holy Spirit which, in conversion and rebirth, effects the radical renewal of human beings. These people are then called together into a new community, a community which lives in exile in the "natural" world and whose life, witness, and service to this world must seem a "stumbling block" and "foolishness."

But diametrically opposed to all this is what we widely regard and practice as modern ideas. These ideas already took root very early in the Christianized European world: they were vigorously at work, not just in the eighteenth century, but already in the Reformation period, and in fact as early as the Averroism of the thirteenth century. In the eighteenth century, however, in the epoch of the Enlightenment, modern thought assumed the position of leadership in European culture. Since then, as "self-evident" truth in cultured circles, it stripped from the Christian worldview its halo of self-evident truth which it had held in Europe for almost a thousand years. The inspired saying in which Kant epitomized the Enlightenment ("Enlightenment is man's emergence from his self-imposed immaturity") makes clear how mutually exclusive these two worlds are: the person of the Enlightenment has come of age, is autonomous, and lives by the light of his own reason. If he speaks of "guilt" at all, he views it as consisting in the fact that for such a long time he permitted his autonomy to be suppressed by heteronomous authorities like God, Bible, and church.

Modern thought, in whatever wide ramifications and inner contradictions it may have taken shape, became and remained conscious of itself, in countless greater and lesser representatives of the either-or situation, in relation to Christianity. Names like Feuerbach, Nietzsche, Freud, Sartre, Bloch, and Fromm may be considered representative of numerous others. One could have expected that a similar consciousness would have developed among the leaders of Christianity, especially since the New Testament, with its antithetical language and its accentuation of the believer as a sojourner, prepared people from the beginning for such a situation. Nevertheless, on the level of theology, the coming to terms with modern thought only seldom took place with this degree of radicalism. This is true not only for the liberal theologians but also for the more conservative. One gets the impression that the majority of theologians, speaking to Christianity's leading "cultured despisers," never really accepted their radical no to the gospel. It would appear that the theologians refused to accept the antithesis. Why? Was it because they had their heads in the sand? Or was it because as university professors (and most leading theologians were and are that) they refused to let themselves, and the gospel, be pushed out of the academic discourse and the world of culture? Did this spring from obedience, or from disobedience, to the gospel?

In only a very few cases will a person be able to answer these questions unambiguously. But we are not interested now in considerations of the psychology of religion. What concerns us is not the reasons but the results. Most of these thinkers tried more or less deliberately to build a bridge between the gospel and their secularized cultural environment, but did they succeed? Were they able to translate the gospel into a modern language such that it could again be heard and understood in intellectual circles and elicit a genuine yes or no? But who is able to judge whether they achieved this goal? We probably cannot say more than this: from where we stand now, this or that attempt seems to us successful or unsuccessful. Such assessment is important, for we are in the same situation and can learn, both in a positive and in a negative way, from preceding generations. It was with this goal in mind that I sounded out the theologians (and a few philosophers) whom I treat in this book. I recognize my own aim in the words of Richard Niebuhr: "All attempts to interpret the past are indirect attempts to understand the present and its future. Men try to remember the road they have traveled in order that they may gain some knowledge of the direction in which it is leading."[1]

When I began thinking of the plan for this book, I remembered that two centuries earlier a book appeared which fundamentally and henceforth changed the discussion between theology and culture: Kant's *Critique of Pure Reason* (1781). It destroyed the harmony which existed between knowledge of the world and knowledge of God; together with the sequel *Critique of Practical Reason* it made theology an appendix of ethics, and to many it seemed even that as a result God had been radically removed from the domain of the knowable. In the face of this challenge, theology could not possibly simply repeat the ambiguous answers it had formulated in the encounter with the empiricism and the rationalism of the Enlightenment—answers of a rationalistic and supernaturalistic stamp. If theology was to exist at all it had to enter upon a new way of doing its work and look for a place to stand—if not within the Kantian framework, at least in a way that gave thorough consideration to the Copernican revolution which Kant had effected in epistemology. Kant and his followers in German idealism were for the most part also part-time theologians and tried therefore to assign to theology a place

1. With these words begins the introduction of H. Richard Niebuhr, *The Kingdom of God in America* (New York: Willett, Clark & Company, 1937), p. 1.

within the new thought-world. We shall therefore also have to occupy ourselves with Kant, Fichte, and Hegel. However, the real theologian in the tradition of idealism, Schleiermacher, sought out other ways. We shall have to deal with him at length. After him, given the progressive secularization of modern thought, the distance between philosophy and theology grew much larger. But they remained within earshot of each other—a situation utilized much more by theology than by philosophy. Theologians needed philosophy as the expression of modern man's understanding of life (*Lebensgefühl*) in order to be able to enter into dialogue with it.

I want to focus on this dialogue, for it is the open or hidden impetus for theology since Kant. My aim is to follow its trail, and thus I have sounded out many theologians. In this pursuit I realized that for this purpose completed systems were often less conclusive than the preceding process of searching and struggling. One tends to learn most from the critical moments, the nodal points, the controversies, and the crossroads where people's ways parted. The result is that the reader will not find much in this book that can also be found in the theological histories of this epoch, while other, less familiar aspects will be given a lot of attention. It is my hope that this approach will lead the readers, as it did me, to surprises and fresh insights.

The peculiar nature of this book will also bring with it, of course, certain additional limitations. I do not at all aim at completeness (cf. E. Hirsch's *Geschichte der neueren evangelischen Theologie*). The entire presentation will be controlled and delimited by the special focus of this book. As a result much more space is devoted to a discussion of liberal theology than to conservative. But this emphasis does not imply a value judgment. It only means—though this is decisive for me—that liberal theologians, in virtue of their liberalism, have done much more with the theme that occupies me than their orthodox colleagues, who aimed more at the exposition of the given content of Scripture or the treasures of tradition. From the perspective of the concerns of theology both, in my opinion, are equally necessary. One must not forget, however, that many conservative theologians, who certainly breathed the air of the modern world, are forced, sometimes consciously and often unconsciously, to take part in a dialogue with the spirit of the times that is similar to the dialogue of their liberal colleagues. Precisely because their concerns are different, conservative theologians may be able in the process to arrive at new and fruitful lines of thought. As representative for many others whom I know and many more with whom I am not familiar, I have devoted a separate chapter to Martin Kähler. And where exactly should we put a certain Karl Barth?! His radical repudiation of his early liberal period belongs to the weightiest, and still not properly assimilated, moments of the modern period.

In addition, apart from the liberal-conservative controversy, many a reader will wonder why I have not included certain important persons and movements in this study. Assuming now that I am familiar with them, my answer is that either they do not share the focus by which I am guided in this book or they treat the question in a totally different framework (as, e.g., the majority of Catholic theologians in this period) or they do not pursue it with the same thoroughness and originality as those whom I have presented here. Of course, this judgment is subjective!

Another limitation springs from the fact that either I am not familiar with the numerous theologians of this epoch or know them too superficially. As a Netherlander I enjoy both a disadvantage and an advantage. On the one hand, I am myself rooted in a well-defined tradition which, moreover, is not accessible to most of my readers. On the other hand, as a schoolboy in the Netherlands one has to take three foreign languages. The result is that we can enter into dialogue with several great theological traditions. I have attempted to utilize this advantage by devoting five chapters largely or completely to theologies not enshrined in the German language. I have not hesitated, however, to write my book originally in German—as a memorial to that theological tradition which by its thoroughness, its keen methods, its broad horizons, and its passionate dedication has in these two centuries taken the leading position.

Yet another limitation of this book is that theologians still living today are often brought into view only incidentally. They are mentioned because and to the extent that they continue to work along the lines of these two hundred years. It is a good thing to define their positions in the light of these longer perspectives. The larger historical framework can perhaps bring with it a new understanding and appraisal. Perhaps also we shall more often discover that the newness of the newest theology is not at all as new as we previously thought. It was only incidentally, however, that I risked bringing my contemporaries into the picture because the distance which lends greater objectivity is still lacking. It is my hope that this book will help the reader to listen to and evaluate these contemporary voices in the context of a much larger chorus.

The genre to which my book belongs is not new in German literature. In it the attempt to come to terms with the past has always played a large role. Unfortunately, too often it was and is limited to German-speaking areas or even to Germany itself. To my knowledge, the European breadth displayed by E. Hirsch's grandly conceived *Geschichte der neueren europäischen Theologie* (5 vols., 1949ff.) has not been attained since. In any case American and Roman Catholic theologies fell outside this purview. Not all the authors in question were as precise as F. Kattenbusch and H. Stephan, who in the title of their book referred to "German evangelical theology." Even P. Tillich issued his posthumously published lectures under the title "Perspectives on Nineteenth and Twentieth Century Protestant Theology," without any mention of British or American theology. In the collection *Die Kirche in ihrer Geschichte*,[2] F. Flückiger treats "Die protestantische Theologie des 19. Jahrhunderts" (pp. 1-97) but restricts himself to the theology that is written in German.

Of the two most recent German histories of theology known to me, that of F. Mildenberger is correctly entitled *Geschichte der deutschen evangelischen Theologie im 19. und 20. Jahrhundert* (1981). I feel a close sense of kinship with it in virtue of my focus on the interaction between theology and modern thought. It deals with a period, however, that ends with the year 1940. Also, the "Decisions" in the closing chapter are descriptions of theologies in vogue between the two world wars. The most recent work, H. Thielicke's *Glauben und Denken in der Neuzeit* (1983), offers a great wealth of information and insight, as one would expect from this author. But it does not offer what the title promises: it deals only with German Protestant philosophers and theologians (with the obligatory addition of Kierkegaard). Ritschl and Herrmann are tucked in between Kant and Hegel as "the theological Kantians." The book ends with Troeltsch and an "epilogue" of eighteen pages about dialectical theology. The reader will understand, I hope, why in view of these facts I held fast to the intention, as did the publisher, to publish this book originally in the German language.

In the First and Third World many theologians are of the opinion that the leadership of Western, and specifically of German, theology is coming to an end. They believe that the force which drives this mode of theologizing stems from the bourgeois-capitalistic culture and milieu produced by the Enlightenment. Theology held this to be the true, "normal" culture and, itself being a bourgeois and university enterprise, related to it much too naively and positively. As a result of not seeing through the basic economic problems, it posed the wrong questions and erected false fronts and became itself part of the problem instead of part of the solution. And now, as we have learned to see through the class-bound character of this theology, its end has come at the same time.

The reader will discern that I differ with this opinion. I take the problems of these two hundred years seriously, not as a reflection of

2. *Die Kirche in ihrer Geschichte,* ed. B. Möller (Göttingen, 1975), vol. 4, fascicle P.

economic relationships, but for their own sake, as an expression of a theological-anthropological problem that was insurmountable in this period of human history. I do believe that social-economic relationships are much more culture-conditioning than we often thought (for thinking was the privilege of the well-to-do classes), but I also believe that fundamentally they are not more influential than so many other elements which together form the infrastructure of our society—like heredity, eroticism, nationality, etc. Conversely, every area of life has its own roots in the structure of our createdness in the image of God.

These areas of life cannot be derived from one another. Religion in particular constitutes a unique dimension which cannot be explained in terms of other dimensions; "religion is itself present at its commencement."[3] The manner in which we reflect on it is doubtlessly also conditioned by numerous nonreligious and nontheological factors. Nevertheless, the same questions and answers arise over and over, however differently colored they may be; they are presented by the object itself—in our case, by the interaction between gospel and culture.[4] An example: later on in this book we shall discover that, in a way which puts German theology to shame, Anglo-Saxon theology displays more sensitivity to the social-economic side of life. As a result, its methodology often gives one a feeling of being closer to everyday reality. At the same time, we observe that in this different kind of setting the basic theological problems which occupy us here remain the same. Another example is the Latin American theology of liberation, which developed in the context of the contrast between oppressors and oppressed but has to proceed from the evangelical concept of liberation or redemption, by way of fresh hermeneutical approaches, to the great classical questions which were characteristic not only for the theology of the first, so-called bourgeois, world but also, for example, for Justin Martyr and for the contrast between Clement of Alexandria and Tertullian. Since no one is able to screen out all the overtones and undertones of theological texts, the only legitimate path which remains to us is to interpret the texts in terms of the meaning and content that the authors consciously intended.[5]

3. Rudolf Otto, *The Idea of the Holy,* tr. John W. Harvey (London: Oxford University Press, 1958), p. 132.

4. Thus an interpretation of German theology in the light of German nationalism would be very revealing! Still, it would not fundamentally alter the given theological problems.

5. In this note I will briefly delineate my position over against the currently influential (semi-)Marxist hermeneutics of theological texts. This hermeneutic brings to the fore certain limited truths, truths which in the final analy-

Meanwhile, I have now repeatedly spoken of "readers," although initially I had not thought of readers at all. But that is how it goes: Once one takes the step from personal inquiry to that of writing, the following and much smaller step is to want to publish. And to desire a book is to desire readers. Though I did not start with them, in the course of writing this work they appeared before my eyes in increasingly clearer profile. I saw before me readers to whom the great names of the history of modern evangelical theology were more or less familiar, yet who had no clear idea what these thinkers could mean for their own questions. Thus, at the same time, I saw before me those who, like myself, struggle with the relationship between the gospel and the modern world and who ask themselves if and how in this world one can ("still," as it is significantly added) be a Christian and with conviction show to others the way to the gospel. Hence I had in mind pastors, teachers of religion, and advanced theological students. In addition, I cherish the quiet hope that other educated people who struggle with the same questions and are familiar with certain aspects of the history of ideas may find some help

---

sis either do not at all, or only marginally, influence the central theological issues. The example of such a hermeneutic best known to me is that of D. Schellong, *Bürgertum und christliche Religion: Anpassungsprobleme der Theologie seit Schleiermacher* (Munich: Kaiser, 1975). The strong side of this compact and substantial little book is its unmasking of the bourgeois spirit of autonomy which seeks to subject the surrounding world to itself as its object. Schellong regards the spirit of the bourgeoisie as incompatible with the gospel. The weakness of the study lies in its lack of clarity about the relationship between bourgeoisie and capitalism: does the first embrace the second or is the reverse true? Schellong seems to lean to the second answer when he speaks of "the capitalistic principle" (p. 27) and describes as the essence of bourgeoisie "the satisfaction of the needs of the individual" (pp. 9, 15). In another passage the "bourgeois subject-will" is considered central, "particularly in its economic components" (p. 31). Also, the assertion that "bourgeoisie can only be made intelligible in terms of economic processes" begs the question (p. 25). This lack of clarity continues to play a role also and especially in the interesting interpretations of many theologians, especially Ritschl and Barth. I proceed from the position that the essence of bourgeoisie consists in a heightened "subject-will" which comes to expression, e.g., in magical words like "freedom," "personality," "self-determination," "morality," etc. Most theologians have rightly seen this stylish terminology as a contrast with the gospel even when (unfortunately) they did not take into their purview capitalistic exploitation as the creation of this subject-will. Had that been the case the discussion would certainly have become sharper but would not, theologically, have fundamentally changed it (as British and American examples show).

here—also because they might have made the discovery that as much as possible I have avoided the jargon of theologians.

I chose as the subtitle "Report of a Personal Journey." An account of a journey presupposes knowledge of the Baedeker. Such an account has a penchant for calling attention to the features about which one does not read in the Baedeker. A travelogue is also much less "objective" than the Baedeker. Aided by my own personal questions, I am making a journey through several landscapes that are part of modern theological culture. I choose the places to visit and there I raise my own questions. I survey the scenes through my own eyes—I have no other. Through these eyes, however, I look at the outside world, toward that which presents itself to me from beyond my own consciousness. I see things which exist apart from me and my seeing them. The resulting report is therefore both subjective and objective.

It would be better to describe the whole experience with the phrase "intersubjectivity as encounter." In a travel report, subject and object work together, and the most successful parts are likely those in which the object presents itself to the recording subject as the true subject, the subject which lays down the law to him who describes it. Aware of the subjective nature of my undertaking, I have tried as much as possible to minimize myself over against the persons to be encountered. I particularly made it my business to bring to the fore their strongest features and to let them speak for themselves before I pointed out their limitations (which sometimes I left out altogether). I did this not only because I learned from Karl Barth to speak about those who preceded us with as much gentleness and understanding as one hopes those who follow will speak about us; I also and especially did this because the weight of the challenge facing theology in the epoch of European-American secularization is so heavy that it will take many and very different shoulders to carry that burden. Here, too, the truth is that one member cannot say to another: "I have no need of you!" (1 Cor. 12:21). We serve one another even with our errors and mistakes. From both a Christian and a scientific perspective, therefore, it is nonsensical to think that within the fraternity of theologians one wins one's own identity only by judging as negatively as one can as many other theologians as possible. It is an optical illusion to believe that one enhances one's own stature when one diminishes that of another. In no way are such inclinations appropriate to a travel report. One reports the things that have enriched oneself in the hope of enriching others. Criticism is not thereby excluded, but it is in order only after one has understood the real concerns of a theologian in their positive intent.

The reader, however, may regard as a disadvantage of this posture the fact that sometimes the question which gives coherence to this project remains hidden or in the background. The manner in which a given theologian views the relationship between the gospel and the modern world cannot in every case be articulated in the same general terminology, and often it can be formulated only with great difficulty if one is not to do the theologian an injustice. Repeatedly, out of respect for the thinker in question, I had to be content to give just a pointer in what I took to be the right direction.

Forming the counterpart to this introduction is the closing chapter, "Backward Glances and Conclusions." There the traveler renders his final account. That, too, is a subjective matter of course, but who could do it otherwise? I must urge readers, however, not to turn to that conclusion, like the impatient reader of a novel. Awaiting them there is not the final unraveling of the riddle. First they will have to make the journey with me. Only then will they be able to understand my final conclusions and compare them critically with the ones they themselves have drawn in the meantime. Only thus will the book have achieved its objective: to make mature readers still more mature.

CHAPTER I

Kant's Four Steps in Theology

Immanuel Kant (1724-1804) studied theology for six years and published theological writings in all three periods of his philosophical labors (the pre-critical, the critical, and the post-critical). At no time was this for him a secondary interest: even in his main philosophical works it is evident that the question concerning God and his knowability was the secret object and driving force of his philosophical thought. One must believe that it was his deepest desire to save God for an enlightened culture and thus to save the Enlightenment itself. Nevertheless, he quite consciously carried out this theological enterprise as a philosopher — with the proud overtones of one who thinks: as a philosopher I know how one can understand theology better than it understands itself; I know how one can at last furnish a foundation for it and practice it with final legitimacy.

We shall pass by the pre-critical writings in which, under the influence of Leibniz and Newton, he attempted to provide a mathematical foundation for metaphysics and offered a new ontological proof for the existence of God. Kant himself rendered these attempts obsolete when at the advanced age of 57 he achieved a complete philosophy of his own with the publication of *The Critique of Pure Reason* (1781).[1] Windelband has correctly called this work "the foundational work of German philosophy." One can at least consider this judgment valid for the whole of continental European philosophy (in the Anglo-Saxon world Kant was never able to push aside Hume); and this foundational work must therefore also be valued as a radical new beginning for evangelical theology. As a result of its appearance, orthodox scholasticism, rationalism, and supernatural-

1. I shall refer to the edition translated by F. Max Müller, *The Critique of Pure Reason* (New York: Macmillan, 1915).

ism found that, at a single stroke, the road forward had been blocked. In addition, the appearance of Kant's *Critique* meant—alongside all else it achieved—the birth of the new theology, or rather: the modern way of posing questions, and modern methodology, in theology.

THE FIRST STEP

Here we shall concentrate entirely on the theological content of *The Critique of Pure Reason* and of other writings of Kant. Long before the middle section, at the point where he moves into "transcendental dialectic," Kant's theological interests and the fundamental theological thrust of the work assert themselves. At first, however, these seem to be of a purely negative kind: the extension of pure reason beyond the experience of space and time is considered "illusion." But Kant immediately adds: "we have here to deal with a natural and inevitable illusion," with a dialectic "inherent in and inseparable from human reason" (p. 242). Hence we are not dealing with illusion in the ordinary, purely subjective sense but with an epistemological and anthropological necessity; one might almost say, with an existential element of existence. Pure reason simply cannot avoid producing transcendental ideas which have no starting point in observation. Indeed, it cannot but think the unity of itself (as soul), of its object (as world), and of all objects of thought in general (as God). Of these pure "objects" of thought we have no knowledge, "but a problematic concept only." "The transcendental (subjective) reality, at least of pure concepts of reason, depends on our being led to such ideas by a necessary syllogism of reason" (p. 275). Kant struggles with the language in order to grasp these syllogisms, "rather to be called sophistical [*vernünftelnde*] than rational [*vernunftschlüsse*]" in both their positive and negative implications.

In the passages concerning the paralogisms and antinomies of pure reason, the negative initially predominates; and we are fully back into "appearance" and "illusion" in the famous sections in which the classical proofs for the existence of God, which meant so much especially for the theology of the Enlightenment, are completely destroyed. This negativity culminates in the third main part, section 7: "Criticism of all Theology based on Speculative Principles of Reason"—in the characteristic statement: "What I maintain then is that all attempts at a speculative use of reason, with reference to theology, are entirely useless and intrinsically null and void" (p. 512). But a few pages later there is a shift in the train of thought. This "transcendental theology," even if it cannot prove what it seeks to prove, may nevertheless serve as a corrective, if one assumes that the concept of a Supreme Being comes to us from another direction: "For the purely speculative use of reason, therefore, the Supreme Being remains no doubt an ideal but an ideal *without a flaw,* a concept which finishes and crowns [!] the whole of human knowledge, and the objective reality of which, though it cannot be proved, can neither be disproved in that way" (pp. 515-16). The transcendental dialectic leads to the conclusion that "human reason has a natural inclination to overstep these limits [the limits of experience] and that transcendental ideas are as natural to it as categories to the understanding." These are strong assertions which at the same time, however, are qualified — or should one say "suspended"? — by words like "deceptive," "unfounded," "appearance," and "illusion" (p. 516).

In my opinion one can explain this ambivalence or this contradiction in Kant only if one assumes that here he attempted to formulate that which we today would call "the questionability of existence," the insight that inherent in human existence is a transcendental question to which there is no corresponding answer. Pure reason reveals generic man as a question without an answer. Hence we find here expressions like "regulative," "asymptotic," "heuristic." In this respect the "Appendix to the Transcendental Dialectic" makes especially fascinating reading. To the question: May we admit a wise and omnipotent Author of the world? Kant answers: "Without any doubt—and not only may we but we must." But a moment later he qualifies it again, repeats it a page later, and finally comes back to the negative aspect.

Kant here finds himself on the heights of speculative reason, in the thin air in which empirical thought pushes against its limits. Thus he arrives at the point people usually describe as the "Prolegomena" of dogmatics, where the question is raised from what realms of experience one may gain a view of the truths of the gospel. Here the philosopher Kant takes his first step into theology. His thinking reminds us of Schleiermacher's introduction to *The Christian Faith* with its "borrowed propositions"; of Paul Tillich's "quest" as ontological fact, or of Karl Rahner's "Transcendentality" as anthropological dimension. In any case we are here dealing with a pointer, an infrastructure, an attempt to define a place —no more, no less.

THE SECOND STEP

That for Kant the "no less" had just as much positive weight as the "no more" had negative can be seen from the fact that in the further development of *The Critique of Pure Reason* he took a second step in theology, again a step in the field of the Prolegomena but this time one that brought him to the boundaries of questions of content. This step occurred in the second chapter of his "Method of Transcendentalism" under the heading "The Canon of Pure Reason." Here Kant seeks to build a bridge from pure reason to practical reason, the reason which can make well-founded statements about God and make clear the inner correlation of the two possible uses of reason. This correlation is of a teleological kind. Pure reason points in preparatory fashion to practical reason. The first defines three limiting concepts: the freedom of the will, the immortality of the soul, and the existence of God. "If, therefore, these three cardinal propositions are of no use to us so far as knowledge is concerned, and are yet so strongly recommended to us by our reason, their true value will probably be connected with our practical interests only" (p. 642). "As this concerns our actions with reference to the highest aim of life, we see that the last intention of nature in her wise provision was really, in the constitution of our reason, directed to moral interests only" (pp. 642-43). At this point Kant sums up his deepest concerns in three famous questions: "1. What can I know? 2. What should I do? 3. What may I hope?" In this connection he remarks that to the first of these questions he has found an answer "with which reason must be satisfied," but "that we remained far removed from the two great ends to which the whole endeavour of pure reason was really directed" (p. 646). As soon as this focus of reason has been discovered and recognized, the horizon of philosophy expands to include "moral theology" and even a "physico-theology" (terms by which Kant anticipates *The Critique of Practical Reason* on the one hand and *The Critique of Judgment* on the other). As soon as reason rises above experience by its engagement with praxis—to which it is fundamentally adapted—its assumptions and content become theological. Their certainty is not of a logical but of a moral nature. It is not for that reason less certain: "I shall inevitably believe in the existence of God, and in a future life, and I feel certain that nothing can shake this belief, because all my moral principles would be overthrown at the same time, and I cannot surrender them without becoming hateful in my own eyes" (p. 664). One must remember that these frequent digressions into theology belong to the essence of *The Critique of Pure Reason* and are treated under the title "The Canon of Pure Reason" ("I understand by a canon a system of principles *a priori* for the proper employment of certain faculties of knowledge in general," p. 639).[2]

Many readers have not taken seriously the positive passages—the passages that led to theology—in the second part of *The Critique of*

2. Whenever the structure of the *Critique* comes up, the comparison with the *Summa contra Gentiles* by Thomas Aquinas suggests itself to me, particularly the relationship of the philosophical books I-III to the theological book IV. Both

Pure Reason; they felt that Kant's real interests were expressed only in the corresponding negative passages, especially in the destruction of the proofs for the existence of God. In my opinion, such a one-sided interpretation of *The Critique of Pure Reason* is intolerable at a later stage. But it is quite understandable that for Kant's rationalistic and suprarationalistic contemporaries his rejection of the proofs for the existence of God was such a hard blow that the positive intent of this negation could hardly be viewed as credible any more. Moses Mendelssohn must have expressed the feelings of many others when, after the appearance of the *Critique,* he spoke of Kant as the "All-demolisher" *(Allzermalmer).* Hence Kant saw himself forced to furnish the second edition (1787) with a long preface whose purpose was to guide the reader through the book. Here occurs the much quoted statement: "I therefore had to abolish *knowledge* in order to make room for *belief."* The statement was not well received, as many people saw in it a less than fully sincere cover under which Kant hid from the attacks of orthodoxy. It sums up precisely, however, what we discovered to be the thrust of the second half of *The Critique of Pure Reason.* One must (something that is usually not done) cite also the line that follows: "The dogmatism of metaphysics, that is, the presumption that it is possible to advance in metaphysics without previous criticism, is the true source of unbelief (always dogmatic) which militates against morality."[3] It was Kant's observation that metaphysical rationalism, instead of supporting the basic truths of religion with its pseudo-proofs, rather effected the opposite and paved the way for atheism. Kant had an inkling of the connection between knowledge and unbelief and sought to guard against it. Faith and knowledge are, to him, complementary. This means that the connection between the two is just as important as their separation. It was Kant's purpose to save religion as well as the Enlightenment: in this double objective, we think, lay his deepest passion as a thinker.

The complementarity mentioned here is also reflected in the relationship between *The Critique of Pure Reason* and *The Critique of Practical Reason.* As we saw, the first already broadly anticipated the second; the

---

thinkers analyze *ratio* in such a way that it emerges as *ratio praeambula fidei,* the reason which precedes faith. Where Kant has "the transcendental dialectic" Aquinas locates *desiderium naturale.* Both thinkers speak of two levels of knowledge. But whereas for Aquinas the *ratio* that is rooted in experience furnishes *proofs* for the existence of God, for Kant it provides only *pointers.* In Aquinas the extension of reason is effected by supernatural power; in Kant such an elevation does not occur, since this extension is given with the nature of reason itself.

3. Translation by J. M. D. Meiklejohn, "Preface to the Second Edition" (London: George Bell & Sons, 1890), p. XXXV.

basic design of the second, in fact, can be fully discerned in the first. It does not surprise us to learn, therefore, that initially Kant had no plans to write the second critique, and he later entertained the idea of incorporating *The Critique of Practical Reason* into the second edition of *The Critique of Pure Reason*.[4] Though it later came out separately (1788), *The Critique of Practical Reason* was nevertheless presented as "an extension of pure reason." As regards the final problems, the two activities of reason relate to each other as question and answer, in which case the answer fulfills the question, but the question limits and purges the answer (cf. pp. 234-43). On a later occasion Kant sharply expresses the ontological superiority of practical reason by saying that in part we have pure reason in common with the animals; by "the coincidence of occasional causes" or "external things" with pure reason the animals are ever only stimulated to a "reaction" but at no time to an independent act; such acts are reserved only to human beings. Hence the conclusion: "Man must be destined for two quite different worlds, for the realm of sense and intellect, hence for the world of this earth; but then also for still another world, one we do not know, a realm of morals" (*Der Streit der Fakultäten*, pp. 69-74).[5]

On account of these and similar statements Kant has sometimes been called a dualist. But that is to misunderstand Kant's concerns. For him intellect, pure reason, and practical reason are the three floors of a building. The windows of these floors offer different views of the outside world. On the first, one sees the world of the senses; on the second, the faraway blue skies. The third opens to a wide landscape. From here one also sees the overall connection with the views of the lower floors.

THE THIRD STEP

The theological prolegomena which surfaced in the second part of *The Critique of Pure Reason*, in the transcendental dialectic, are relieved, so to speak, or sharpened by a further theological step, a step in the domain of ethics this time, in *The Critique of Practical Reason*. Now, through the gateway of freedom, we leave the plains of the prolegomena behind and turn to the contents of faith.

4. Cf. the introduction in K. Vorländer's edition of *Kritik der praktischen Vernunft*, 6th ed. (Leipzig: Felix Meiner, 1915), esp. pp. XI-XVI. In this chapter we shall refer to the translation by Lewis White Beck, *The Critique of Practical Reason* (Chicago: University of Chicago Press, 1949).

5. Here we shall refer to the edition of the Philosophische Bibliothek, vol. 252, *Der Streit der Fakultäten* (Hamburg: K. Reich, 1975).

Man hears within himself the voice of the moral law. As a result he knows that the spatiotemporal world with its chains of causality withholds from him the deepest truth about himself: the freedom by which he, the object of worldly causalities, at the same time becomes the subject of new moral causalities. This free moral will is autonomous.

Kant's notion of autonomy is often misunderstood. One must understand it to mean that the moral side of our existence is not subject to nature with its drives. The moral life requires of all human beings subjection to one and the same categorical imperative: "So act that the maxim of your will could always hold at the same time as the principle of a universal legislation" (p. 142). Thus, this objective anthropological autonomy of moral freedom is completely opposed to the arbitrariness of our wishes and drives, things which from Kant's point of view are considered "heteronomous"—just as he also views many things as "heteronomous" which in the modern usage of language are called "autonomous."

The certainty of freedom as a "postulate" is inseparably given with submission to the categorical imperative: "You can, because you should!" A second postulate, given with the same certainty, is the immortality of the soul. We know of course that during our earthly existence we shall not achieve the perfect fulfillment of the moral commandment: nature and morality do not come into harmony here. Thus for its fulfillment the categorical imperative presupposes an existence that continues endlessly, for with the increase of natural perfection there will be a corresponding increase of duties and the goal of both, blessedness, "which can be contained only in an infinite progress and its totality and thus is never fully reached by any creature" (p. 227, note).

With the same certainty the voice of the commandment implies a third truth: the existence of God. In this broken and often absurd world, not we human beings but only an almighty and benevolent God can guarantee to us that someday the moral will will triumph and find the happiness that is proper to it. This unity of morality and happiness is the "highest good," which can only become reality in the "kingdom of God."

On this basis Kant now attacked "natural theology," by which he means a theology (rationalistic or supernaturalistic) which wants to prove the existence of a perfect author of the world from the state of nature. Our imperfect natural world cannot, with any necessity, be traced to a perfect author.[6] God can only be understood as standing on the side of the moral subject, as the One who can in no way identify himself with the obscuri-

---

6. Already in his pre-critical period Kant had arrived at the conviction that one cannot possibly, with the help of the cosmological proofs for the existence of God, infer a perfect author from an imperfect world. On this subject, cf.

ties and absurdities of the natural world. He is the guarantor that some-day the moral world will conquer and sanctify the world of nature.

Thus, looking through the window of morality, Kant views the world of religion as the world of final truth. In this connection he has in mind, of course, the Christian religion. The Greek ethicists, especially the Stoics, had not discovered the necessity of postulating the immortality of the soul and the existence of the Supreme Being, because they believed that they had no need of happiness and that already in this life they could attain the highest degree of virtue. "But the voice of their own nature could have sufficiently refuted this" (p. 230; see also the note on pp. 230-31). "The doctrine of Christianity . . . gives at this point a concept of the highest good (the kingdom of God) which is alone sufficient to the strictest demand of practical reason" (pp. 230-31). It is also true that "Christian ethics . . . destroyed man's confidence of being wholly ade-quate to it, at least in this life; but it re-established it by enabling us to hope that, if we act as well as lies in our power, what is not in our power will come to our aid from another source, whether we know in what way or not" (p. 231, note).

At the same time, however, we must bear in mind the two re-strictions with which Kant qualifies his theological statements. The first consists in the fact that through the window of morality one can see God and immortality only from one perspective. Indeed, the practical reason provides only a practical knowledge, a knowledge related to free actions. "For we thereby know neither the nature of our soul nor the intelligible world nor the Supreme Being as they are in themselves but have only united the concepts of them in a practical concept of the highest good as the object of our will and have done so entirely a priori through pure rea-son. We have so united them only by means of the moral law and merely in relation to it, with respect to the object which it commands" (p. 236).

Here, too, though in a different sense than in the case of pure reason, we are dealing with limiting concepts. The postulates of practi-cal reason are final concepts, which do not release further possibilities for new developments from within them. They stem from the moral world and serve only that world. For that reason the concept of God must be understood, noetically, as an appendix to human morality and hence as a derived concept. Kant never tires of stressing that religion does not

---

Der einzig mögliche Beweisgrund zu einer Demonstration des Daseins Gottes (1763) and *Untersuchung über die Deutlichkeit der Grundsätze der natürlichen Theologie und der Moral* (1764). In this period, however, he was still involved in developing a kind of ontological proof for the existence of God.

imply any independent knowledge of God but teaches us only to view the moral demands as commandments of God. We must, however, understand that "only" correctly: the case is that in these demands a personal God actually, with postulatory finality, reveals himself. True, his revealed attributes are of a purely moral nature: He is the only holy (as creator and lawgiver), the only blessed (as beneficent ruler and sustainer), and the only wise being (as the just judge) (pp. 233-34, note).

Our knowledge of God has a second restriction, which consists in the fact that—to stay with the analogy made earlier—the panes of the window opening from the moral floor are blurred. They do not give us the same clear view provided by the intellect and the theoretical reason. Here, in fact, not knowledge but moral faith is in command, not a logical but a moral certainty—one that cannot be shaken "because all my moral principles would be overthrown at the same time, and I cannot surrender them without becoming hateful in my own eyes" (p. 664; I am referring to the entire section "Of Trowing, Knowing, and Believing"). In one passage Kant quite clearly expresses the element of indefiniteness there is in moral certainty as follows: "Granted that the pure moral law inexorably binds every man as a command (not as a rule of prudence), the righteous man may say: I *will* that there be a God, that my existence in this world be also an existence in a pure world of the understanding outside the system of natural connections, and finally that my duration be endless. I stand by this and will not give up this belief, for this is the only case where my interest inevitably determines my judgment because I will not yield anything of this interest; I do so without any attention to sophistries, however little I may be able to answer them or oppose them with others more plausible" (p. 245). A bit later, on a more positive note, he says: "it [the faith of practical reason] is itself not commanded. It rather springs from the moral disposition itself. It can therefore often waver even in the well disposed but can never fall into unbelief" (p. 247). Kant continues this line of thought in a short and gripping section: "Of the wise adaptation of man's cognitive faculties to his practical vocation," in which he praises the wise arrangement that "God and eternity in their awful majesty" do not unceasingly and demonstrably stand before our eyes; were this otherwise, we would obey the law from fear and the moral life "would be changed into mere mechanism." It is a good thing that we have only "a very obscure and ambiguous view into the future" and that "the Governor of the world allows us only to conjecture His existence and majesty," allowing us "a view into the realm of the supersensuous, though only a glimpse." Only thus is room created for truly moral character. So we see "that the inscrutable wisdom through which we exist is not less worthy of veneration in respect to what it denies us than in what it has granted" (pp. 247-49).

Hence man lives on earth as citizen of two worlds, as the famous "Conclusion" of *The Critique of Practical Reason* puts it: the starry heavens above and the moral law within. With some measure of justice people have called this Kant's dualism. But, as indicated earlier, one must remember that the knowledge of the lower world is adapted to that of the higher; and that the dualism is abolished when, in virtue of his moral omnipotence, the Governor and Judge of the world unites morality and nature into a harmony of bliss. That "permits hope as genuinely religiously understood hope to become the pivotal concept of Kant's philosophy of religion. For that reason, also Kant's criticism of (Jewish) faith in a Messiah cannot blind us to the fact that his religious understanding of history bears an eschatological stamp."[7]

We need to discuss only briefly the third and concluding Critique of Kant: *The Critique of Judgment* (1790).[8] In it Kant makes a renewed attempt to bridge the gap between morality and nature, between moral volition and rational thinking. Here too, at the end, in the methodology of the teleological judgment, theology comes into play, this time under the name "ethico-theology" (§§ 86ff.), which is opposed to the (false) "physico-theology." God appears here under the aspect of the final moral goal, the moral World Cause which one must postulate (§ 85).

The closing words of the book are noteworthy: "A physical (properly speaking a physico-teleological) Theology can serve at least as a propaedeutic to Theology proper, by giving occasion for the Idea of a final purpose which nature cannot present by the observation of natural purposes of which it offers abundant material. It thus makes felt the need of a Theology which shall determine the concept of God adequately for the highest practical use of Reason, but it cannot develop this and base it satisfactorily on its proofs" (pp. 428-29). This confirms what we observed earlier about the "prolegomena" character of the activity of pure reason. It shows (as does *The Critique of Judgment* generally) to what extent the dualist Kant was a "monist in hope."

---

7. Thus H. Noack in his introduction to *Die Religion innerhalb der Grenzen der bloszen Vernunft* in the series Philosophische Bibliothek, vol. 45, 7th ed. (Hamburg, 1961), p. LXIX. In my opinion, the words "pivotal concept" and "eschatological stamp," though they embody a correct insight, are exaggerated.

8. Here we shall use the translation by J. H. Bernard, *Kritik of Judgement* (New York: Macmillan, 1892).

THE FOURTH STEP

Now, after he has completed his critical labors, Kant must take a new step in theology. He has demonstrated the a priori conditions of the activity of reason, and now, in the post-critical period, he attempts to exhibit the activity of reason, in its legitimacy and concreteness, in the several areas of culture, and to present it in its true nature as being in accord with reason. It is significant for his theological predilection that he undertook this assignment first of all for the area of religion—shortly after the publication of *The Critique of Judgment*. The result appeared in the year 1793 under the title *Religion Within the Limits of Reason Alone*.[9] One may consider the reflections developed there, at least those of the first part, as Kant's fourth step in the domain of religion. Here he is fully involved in the content of the Christian faith and comes to grips with the concepts of inherited dogma.

This step does not mean that Kant is seeking to reach a still higher floor and still wider perspectives. By itself such an attempt would not be inconceivable. For example, he could have written a "Critique of Religious Reason," in which he might have treated religion, in precisely the same way he dealt with knowledge and morality, as an independent dimension of the spirit (*Geist*), "a special province of the mind." Kant blocked off this road, one that Schleiermacher took six years later, by his consistent subordination of religion to morality. There is hardly a hint in Kant's works that he ever considered such a step beyond *The Critique of Practical Reason*. What interested him was not religion but God as guarantor of morality and of the ultimate harmony of nature and spirit (*Geist*).

In *Religion Within the Limits of Reason Alone*, Kant relates his critical-normative discoveries to the world of empirical religion. His question is whether empirical (he has in mind mainly the Christian) religion, in its doctrinal, cultic, and institutional existence, can be considered an expression of the religion of reason developed in *The Critique of Practical Reason*. If so, to what extent? How does one explain and evaluate those elements which cannot be integrated in such a way? In contrast with today's usage, which Karl Barth introduced, Kant calls the normative dimension "religion" and the empirical dimension "faith." Thus, instead of rising higher and seeking new perspectives, he descends, so to speak, to a lower level.

The title of the book might create the impression that here Kant

9. Here we shall refer to the Harper Torchbook edition, *Religion Within the Limits of Reason Alone* (New York: Harper & Brothers, 1934).

is open to new discoveries. If one speaks of "Religion Within the Limits of Reason Alone" one seems at least to allow for the possibility of religion outside these limits and "higher than all reason." Barth, for example, understood this title in that sense.[10] The book itself, however, offers no grounds for this expectation. On the contrary: even if Kant does not exclude the possibility of historical revelations, these have for him no normative standing but only a pragmatic or paedagogical value. They are "means," "vehicles," "husks," or "organs" of the religion of reason. One is reminded of Lessing's "The Education of the Human Race" (1780, posthumous): "There is therefore no norm of ecclesiastical faith other than Scripture, and no expositor thereof other than pure *religion of reason* and *Scriptural scholarship* (which deals with the historical aspect of that religion). Of these, the first alone is *authentic* and valid for the whole world; the second is merely *doctrinal*, having as its end the transformation of ecclesiastical faith for a given people at a given time into a definite and enduring system" (*Religion Within the Limits of Reason Alone*, p. 105). Kant deals quite violently with the historic "ecclesiastical faith." Not that which the texts and dogmas mean historically occupies him (that is the work of scriptural scholarship); he only asks whether one can interpret or reinterpret this ecclesiastical faith in a sense that is in accord with reason—anything else is of no interest to philosophy, as whose representative Kant is speaking here. "Frequently this interpretation may, in the light of the text (of the revelation), appear forced—it may often really be forced; and yet if the text can possibly support it, it must be preferred to a literal interpretation which either contains nothing at all helpful to morality or else actually works counter to moral incentives" (pp. 100-101). In a note subjoined to this statement Kant adds: "I raise the question as to whether morality should be expounded according to the Bible or whether the Bible should not rather be expounded according to morality?"

The result of this approach is that *Religion Within the Limits of Reason Alone*, at least in the second part (we have to talk about the first part later), turned out to be a disappointing and boring book. Kant's hermeneutical starting point made new discoveries impossible. Jesus

10. Karl Barth, *Protestant Theology in the Nineteenth Century* (Valley Forge, PA: Judson, 1973), p. 280. Barth's comment about the "*Parerga* of religion" (pp. 301ff.), which are adjacent to the religion of reason (German *anstossen*, which Barth connects with *Anstoss* as "scandal"), in my opinion has no basis in the text. Kant's own explanation of the title occurs in *Der Streit der Fakultäten* (1798), p. 2, note; it must be understood in the light of his disparagement of every historical revelation.

turns out to be only the great moralist (pp. 109-10); the resurrection is mentioned solely in a footnote (p. 119); works constitute a basis for grace, sanctification is the basis for justification, not the other way around (pp. 107ff.); prayer is a "superstitious illusion" (p. 183); comfort at a deathbed, instead of a moral exhortation, is a sort of opium to the conscience (p. 72, note); etc. Even, and especially, when one admires the consistent moral rigor of Kant, it is still utterly astonishing that this great thinker in the homeland of Luther nowhere shows any sensitivity to the transmoral and anti-moral aspects of the gospel. By means of his enormous powers of thought he attempted to make the gospel understandable in the light of morality and to incorporate it into (practical) reason. But the bridge he built was not adequate. Neither among philosophers nor among theologians did *Religion Within the Limits of Reason Alone* have any real impact. People waited for another "prolegomena"-bridge, one that could link the Christian faith with modern consciousness convincingly.

A FIFTH STEP?

The verdict rendered above relates to the third and fourth "books" of *Religion Within the Limits of Reason Alone.* The first two "books," loosely connected with them, require special consideration. The first is entitled: "Concerning the Indwelling of the Evil Principle with the Good, or, On the Radical Evil in Human Nature." The second reads: "Concerning the Conflict of the Good with the Evil Principle for Sovereignty over Man." The first deals with sin and conversion; the second with the Christ-idea, about Jesus' death, punishment, and substitution. Though connected with the first, the content of the second anticipates, in its violent reinterpretation of the incarnation and atonement, the two following sections. The first section, with its doctrine of radical evil, constitutes a "foreign body" in Kant's philosophy, one that over and over placed interpreters of Kant in an embarrassing position. For here Kant seemed to be on the point of taking a new theological step, a step beyond his a priori moral horizon, in the direction of the classic doctrine of sin and grace. All at once one reads with astonishment that evil in human beings is not a disturbance of moral action caused by their sensuous nature—as Kant had claimed until then—but is rooted in the intelligible world (pp. 30-39). As an act of freedom it is "inscrutable"; it cannot be traced to something else and must therefore be called "radical." At the same time it is something for which the doer is responsible, and as such it is fundamentally surmountable.

"For despite the fall, the injunction that we *ought* to become better men resounds unabatedly in our souls; hence this must be within our *power*" (p. 40). The word *radical* therefore cannot mean altogether evil and without possibility of improvement; that would abolish the responsibility which Kant stressed so much as the corollary of freedom. It is clear that Kant's doctrine of sin has nothing in common with Augustine's teaching but much with that of Pelagius: "even though what *we* are able to do is in itself inadequate and though we thereby only render ourselves susceptible of higher, and for us inscrutable, assistance" (pp. 40-41). But that does not make Kant's teaching any less mysterious. Just what is one to think of this twofold predisposition of human moral reason? And if that condition is in fact conceivable, whence then comes the certainty that the proclivity toward good can be victorious and will overcome? In place of a discussion of the questions arising here, we find already at the end of the first section a retreat from this theme, and in the later sections it disappears almost completely. In later works it never comes back, not even where, as in *Der Streit der Fakultäten,* Kant had good reason to return to it.

From the beginning this erratic block in Kant's work has puzzled people. Goethe's familiar statement to Herder is that, "in order to cleanse his philosophical mantle, which he had worn over a long lifetime, of many foul prejudices, Kant had daubed it with the stain of radical evil in hopes of luring also Christians to kiss its hem." Goethe's explanation, crude as it is, found no approval, but no one has come up with a better one. Or is it the case after all that Kant here really glanced at the classic Christian teaching as a genuine alternative outside the limits of reason alone, as Barth and the school of Ricoeur suggest?[11] In that case one certainly has to say that he swiftly averted his eyes again! I venture to refer to still another possibility.

In 1786, Frederick the Great, the protector of toleration whom Kant so much admired, died. His successor, Frederick William II, was a very different person. His pietistic-orthodox convictions led him to defend the pure doctrine against attacks from the unbelief of the Enlightenment. In 1788 his minister of education and cultural affairs, Wöllner, issued an edict concerning religion together with an edict concerning censure. Soon, as Kant learned, a lecture in Berlin on the subject of *The Critique of Practical Reason* was audited by an informer. The publication of *The Critique of Judgment* (1790), as was to be expected, caused no difficulties. After that he began the work of writing *Religion*

---

11. Barth, *Protestant Theology,* p. 296. O. Reboul, *Kant et le problème du mal,* préface de Paul Ricoeur (Montreal, 1971), pp. XIV, 257-60.

Within the Limits of Reason Alone. In February, 1972, he sent the first part, "Concerning Radical Evil in Human Nature," to the censors in Berlin, who approved the material without hindrance. But their imprimatur was denied the second part, presented for approval in June. Thereupon Kant asked to have his manuscript returned, completed the work, and outside Berlin obtained an academic license to print.[12] This did not, however, prevent the king from threatening, through Wöllner (Oct. 12, 1794), that he would move against Kant if, after the appearance of *Religion Within the Limits of Reason Alone,* he would continue to misuse philosophy "to distort and disparage many of the principal and foundational teachings of Holy Scripture and of Christianity." Kant rejected the accusation but promised to submit. The king died in 1797, and the following year Wöllner was deposed. Kant took his revenge with *Der Streit der Fakultäten* (1798).

His utterances during the Wöllner period strike me as attempts, by way of a mixture of ironic superiority and diplomatic cunning, to escape from a menacing situation. Is it possible perhaps to assess the unusual beginning of *Religion Within the Limits of Reason Alone*—with its doctrine of radical evil—as a political precaution? In any case, with this essay (and only with this essay) Kant managed to pass the scrutiny of the censors. Understandably, this was no longer possible with the second part. However this may be, in *Religion Within the Limits of Reason Alone* there is no question of a serious new step in the domain of theology. Whatever appears as new in this volume disappears in Kant's work as a whole without a trace.

SOME ISOLATED LAST STEPS

The last piece of writing in which the 74-year-old Kant comes to grips with theology, *Der Streit der Fakultäten* (1798), does not, after *Religion Within the Limits of Reason Alone,* seem to offer any new points of view. But it does contain a number of noteworthy sections. The first occurs at the end of II, III. There Kant deals with the correct interpretations of Scripture "according to the principle of the morality aimed at in revelation." Kant explains: "They are really *authentic,* only then; that is, the God within us is himself the interpreter, because we understand no one except the one who speaks with us through our own intellect and our own reason" (p. 44). The expression "the God within us" is quite re-

---

12. On this subject cf. H. Noack's introduction to *Die Religion innerhalb der Grenzen der bloszen Vernunft* (cf. n. 7 above).

markable and contradicts Kant's moral deism. It seems that Kant is taking the step from deism to pantheism. Here practical reason, in fact, does not postulate a transcendent God but is itself the voice of God within us. The words remind us of *Religion Within the Limits of Reason Alone* (p. 103), where moral religion is described as "the Spirit of God, who guides us into all truth." Kant seems to be pointing in the same direction when in *Der Streit der Fakultäten*, in the "Appendix Concerning a Pure Mysticism in Religion," he writes with admiration of a class of people he has met, "who are called Separatists but who call themselves Mystics": "These folks would be (pardon the expression!) true Kantians if they were philosophers." There, as Kant himself indicates, the reference is ostensibly to a group related to the Quakers. They are people who act in accordance with the inner moral law which they "consider an inner revelation and therefore God, definitely, as its author" (pp. 74-75).

The question whether at the end of his life Kant moved from a postulatory deism to an inspiratory pantheism and therefore took an altogether new and fifth step in the domain of theology comes back as one reads the *Opus Postumum*.[13] In connection with the expression "God within us" in *Steit der Fakultäten*, Noack writes: "Mention of 'God within us' may generate doubt whether Kant managed to hold fast to the 'transcendent' existence of God or whether his transcendental-philosophic mode of thinking did not itself imply the final absorption of the existence of God in the necessity of the idea of God as only a symbolic expression of the original and unconditional character of the law of reason."[14] The fragments of the aged Kant present "an unevenness to the point of contradiction."[15] The largest proportion of what we find about God here can be interpreted with little difficulty in the sense of his earlier explanations. From time to time, however, we suddenly encounter (they are mostly loosely connected notes jotted down in preparation for "Transcendental Philosophy") very different phrases or statements, as we also found them here and there in *Steit der Fakultäten*: "Neither gods nor worlds exist but the *totality* of beings is God and world" (21:144, 150). "God is not a being outside of me but purely a thought within me. God is the moral-practical, self-legislative reason—hence only a God within me, for me, and over me" (p. 145).

---

13. Cf. the Academie edition, vol. 21 (Berlin/Leipzig, 1936); and vol. 22 (1938); cf. also what H. Noack writes about "the last writings of Kant," op. cit., pp. LXXIV-LXXXIV (where on p. LXXX n. 20, "XI" must be changed to "XXI").

14. Noack, op. cit., p. LXXVIII.

15. Ibid., p. LXXIX.

"God can only be looked for within us" (p. 150). "What if the idealistic system (that I myself alone am the world) is the only system conceivable by us? Science would not lose anything if that were true" (p. 88). One gets the impression that in the *Opus Postumum* the three regulative ideas of *The Critique of Pure Reason* (World, I, God) have a tendency to flow into each other and to change from regulative into constitutive ideas: "Transcendental philosophy is the principle of the *ideas*, namely, of constituting the self (me) a priori into the object of pure reason (which is the author of its own subject)" (p. 98). Much here reminds us of the idealistic turn which, shortly before, Fichte had given to Kantian philosophy and which drove him also in the direction of pan(en)theism (the subject of the next chapter).

Here and there in Kant's legacy we also run into observations which—we must say this carefully—appear to go, not so much in the direction of pantheism, but more in the direction of atheism: "The proposition 'God exists' does not mean more than that, in the self-determining moral reason of man is a supreme principle to act with unrelenting passion" (p. 146). "The idea that there is a God is a postulate based upon the principle of moral-practical reason because without it human reason cannot be restrained by man. The proposition has a subjective, not an objective, basis" (p. 147). "God, therefore, is not a substance outside of me but merely a moral relationship within me" (p. 149). "God is not something existing outside of me but my own *idea*. It is absurd to ask *whether* a God exists" (p. 153).

One cannot say, therefore, that at the end of his life Kant took a new step in the field of theology. But one does have to grant that, beyond his criticism and the postulatory deism that came with it, Kant entered a region in which he looked to the right, in the direction of pantheism, as well as (by way of exception) to the left, in the direction of atheism. One wonders whether he was aware that his path of criticism had taken him to a crossroads. The absolute idealism, then taking shape and on the march at a point beyond Kant, must have occupied and fascinated him very strongly. His decreasing powers of thought, however, no longer enabled him to take further steps into a new world.

One can understand that in the following years Kant's readers were inclined to reinterpret his great undertaking either in a pantheistic or in an atheistic direction. Fichte was the first to attempt the former. As a harsh example of the latter a statement by Heinrich Heine may serve. He viewed *The Critique of Pure Reason* as Kant's main work, and as its thrust the destruction of the "god" of the deistic Enlightenment by the refutation of the usual proofs for the existence of God. According to Heine, however, Kant figured: "Old Lampe [Kant's faithful servant] must have a God or else the poor fellow can never be happy"; so he wrote *The Critique of Practical Reason* and "reanimated the corpse of deism which theoretical reason had killed."[16]

Though this interpretation is false, there is a grain of truth in it. Kant deeply experienced and took very seriously the atheistic tendencies of his time. It was not, however, Lampe's deep need, but his own and that of his culture that kept him from abandoning the concept of God. We already heard him openly concede that his deepest reason was "that without that [postulate] human reason could not be restrained by man" (p. 147). Without a God above us we would completely fall under the sway of the spatio-temporal and causal reality of our world and, like the other animals of the world, be subject to the absurdities of the course of history until the grave "casts into the abyss of the purposeless chaos of matter from which they came those who had the boldness to believe they were the final goal of creation."[17] The freedom and rule of humanity are guaranteed only by faith in a moral purpose and in an almighty goal-setter. One can imagine that, from 1792 on, the development of the French Revolution (which Kant followed very attentively) greatly strengthened this conviction.

Kant's aim was to save both God and the Enlightenment—both with equal passion, for the two saving acts condition each other, and both are necessary to preserve the *humanum* and thus the future of genuine culture. Kant led the people out of the Egypt of their immaturity into the saving wilderness of criticism. Toward the end of his life he himself had a presentiment that the people had to go forward. And many who had initially followed his leadership with enthusiasm could later on regard the wilderness only as an episode on the way to the promised land of a fuller humanity. The question was: Where is the promised land —to the right or to the left of us?

16. H. Heine, *Religion and Philosophy in Germany*, tr. John Snodgrass (Boston: Beacon, 1959), p. 119.

17. Thus Kant writes in *The Critique of Judgment* toward the end of § 87, where he praises the moral atheist Spinoza, at the same time decisively rejecting his atheism as inconsistent, because compliance with the moral law is not possible without faith in its victory.

CHAPTER 11

Fichte at the Crossroads

We concluded the previous chapter with "the promised land of a fuller humanity." Though it was still future from the vantage point of Kantianism, it was already the thriving present for large groups of the German intelligentsia. Alongside and partly before Kant, a very different experience from that of Kant was uppermost for many people, especially Lessing, Herder, Schiller, Goethe, and the Sturm und Drang period. While Kant, the sober, enlightened analyst, aimed for conceptual explanations, divisions, and boundaries, these others were full of a passion for the unity of life. This is true even for Lessing, who wrote above his garden retreat in Gleims the words *hen kai pan* (the All-One). Here we find the beginnings of Romanticism. For this life in terms of the All-One people drew strength from the newly discovered Spinoza, with his "God or Nature," *deus sive natura*. How different from Kant! Whereas those thinkers and poets experienced humanity as a part of nature, for Kant the human being was a citizen of two worlds, called to rise above nature. Whereas they strove for the harmony and many-sided education *(Bildung)* of human beings, Kant called human beings to their moral duty and to battle against opposing drives. In the future, what will the image of the true, enlightened, and mature human being be like? In the 1780s the various currents flowed more or less next to, or past, each other.

The person most influenced by Kant was Schiller; it is characteristic for him, however, that, in the name of the ideal of the "beautiful soul," he rejected Kant's antithesis between duty and inclination! Kant's dualism must have profoundly annoyed the early Romantics, while Kant was annoyed that "the spirit of thoroughness . . . in Germany . . .

has only been silenced . . . by the clamour of a fashionable and pretentious license of thought."[1]

FROM NATURAL DETERMINISM TO EGO-PATHOS

The man who mediated between the traditions (at first unintentially, we assume) and led them together over into a new epoch was *Johann Gottlieb Fichte* (1762-1814). Although he was the son of a simple weaver, he was able, thanks to the support of a nobleman, to study theology at Jena. During these years he considered himself a Spinozist in the sense of a deterministic naturalism. He also displayed great admiration for Goethe. Since there was no way for him into the ministry of the church, he had to earn a meager living as a private tutor. Restlessly driven from one city to another, in 1790 he came by accident upon the writings of Kant in Leipzig. Reading them gave to his life a radical and ultimately decisive turn. On September 5 he wrote his fiancée in Zurich as follows: "I have gained a nobler morality, and instead of occupying myself with what is outside of myself I employ myself more with my own self. This has given me a peace such as I have never before experienced; amid uncertain worldly prospects I have passed my happiest days."[2] From the time of his encounter with Kant, the turbulent and proud young man no longer regarded himself as a plaything of nature; now, thinking and acting, he took his position within his own self. Today, in the language of Heidegger and Bultmann, we would say: Fichte turned from "absorption in the world" to a "grasp of the existence of the self" (Fichte has in general numerous parallels to existentialism, including that of Sartre). From now on this fundamental distinction governs all his thinking: "Attend to yourself: turn your attention away from everything that surrounds you and towards your inner life; this is the first demand that philosophy makes of its disciple. Our concern is not with anything that lies outside you but only with yourself."[3]

In the 1790s, especially during the years of his professorate in Jena (1794-1799), Fichte passionately promoted this insight in the domain of the theory of knowledge or, as he called it, the science of

1. *The Critique of Pure Reason,* preface to the 2nd ed. (B), pp. xlii-xliii (p. 707 in the Müller edition).

2. Robert Adamson, *Fichte* (Freeport, NY: Books for Libraries, 1969), pp. 21-22.

3. Fichte, "First Introduction" to *Science of Knowledge,* tr. and ed. Peter Heath and John Lacks (New York: Appleton-Century-Crofts, 1970), p. 6.

knowledge. Inspired by Kant, he never tired of stressing "that in all seriousness, and not only in a manner of speaking, the object shall be posited and determined by the cognitive faculty, and not the cognitive faculty by the object."[4] From the period of his Spinozism (which he now called "dogmatism" and "fatalism") he knew that one can also start with the external world. This method, however, represents a lower level of human existence (today we would speak of the "inauthenticity of existence"). As Steffens, the Norwegian student, tells the story, Fichte sought epistemologically to transmit his "grasp of the existence of the self" also to his students. "Gentlemen," he intoned, "concentrate; turn in upon yourselves; we are not talking of anything external but only of ourselves." The students in the lecture hall seemed thus to be summoned really to turn in upon themselves. "Gentlemen," Fichte continued, "think the wall. . . ." Everyone thought the wall. "Have you thought the wall? Now, gentlemen, think the one who thought the wall."[5] The self has to think the self. The self alone is the perspectival point from which the world can be thought, and the Archimedean point from whence it can be changed. The external world is posited by the self as nonself, as its opposite, as the material for its action, in terms of which the self is at loggerheads with and realizes itself, in order thus to arrive at self. That sounds like Hegel. It is not meant, however, in a metaphysical-speculative sense, but as the completion of the Kantian analysis of consciousness. Despite this intent, it brings with it a peculiar pathos which is reminiscent of the words of the spirit chorus in *Faust*, act 1, scene 4:

> Woe! woe!
> Thou hast it destroyed,
> The beautiful world . . .
> Build it again,
> In thine own bosom build it anew!
>
> (Goethe wrote these lines at about the same time
> as Fichte wrote the lines cited above [1797])

At this point one wonders how Fichte's ego-pathos relates to the thinking of Kant, whom he venerated. One can put it this way: Fichte's aim is to combine the yearning for unity of the early Romantics with Kant's criticism. This means that he must attempt to eliminate Kant's offensive dualisms. There are three: (1) The postulate of the thing-in-it-

4. Ibid., p. 4.
5. Heinrich Steffens, *Was Ich Erlebete* (Im Bertelsmann Lesering, 1956), p. 70.

self beyond the reach of perception by the intellect. Some people criticized this postulate as unnecessary and inconsistent. Fichte viewed the empirical world completely as a product of our perception, without the need to reproduce it on the level of the understanding. (2) Thought and action, pure and practical reason. Fichte, for his part, totally subsumes the first under the second. The self-positing self is as such pure act *(actus purus)*, acting, creating, as it thinks. "There is nothing either present or assumed with which the intellect could be set to interact. The intellect, for idealism, is an *act,* and absolutely nothing more."[6] Here, too, we are reminded not of Kant but of Goethe's Faust, who wanted to translate John 1:1 not by "In the beginning was the word" but by "In the beginning was the deed!" (3) Man and God. The reality of the categorical imperative forced moral humanity to adopt the postulate of God as a personal "vis-à-vis." This God-postulate must also have been offensive to Fichte. It took somewhat longer, however, before he drew his conclusions at this point.

The little "correction" which Fichte made in Kant was, in reality, the greatest conceivable revolution. While in Kant reason was kept within bounds, both as a productive and as a receptive faculty, in Fichte it overflows its banks. Instead of being humanly limited, it becomes divinely boundless. It acquires all the attributes which classical theology had ascribed to God: sovereignty, aseity, *actus purus,* the power to create.

Such absolute freedom tolerates no restraining Opposite. Kant's "God," too, had to go. This event was somewhat delayed by the fact that Fichte's first book was of a theological nature. In 1792 he published *Attempt at a Critique of all Revelation.* As a result of an oversight the book made its debut anonymously. Many readers viewed it as Kant's expected philosophy of religion. Once the name of the author became known, numerous admirers suddenly had their reservations, but by then Fichte's renown was established. In this work Fichte is a faithful follower of Kant. In distinction from the latter in his *Religion Within the Limits of Reason Alone,* published a year later, Fichte placed at the center of his reflections not religion but the claim of a universally valid, empirically observable revelation. In the spirit of Kant he destroyed this claim with great acumen. In this undertaking Kant's teaching concerning the postulates of practical reason was his self-evident starting point.

Next come the years at Jena in which Fichte furnished epistemological grounds for, and thought through, his absolute idealism. Initially there was hardly any talk about God—until as a result of a completely

6. Fichte, *Science of Knowledge,* p. 21.

unplanned episode the hour of truth was to strike for Fichte. This "hour" entered the history of philosophy under the name of the *Atheismusstreit.*

THE ATHEISM CONTROVERSY

The issue began harmlessly enough. Fichte was the editor of the *Philosophisches Journal* to which a certain F. C. Forberg, then rector at Saalfeld, submitted an article entitled "Entwicklung des Begriffs der Religion." Fichte regarded Forberg as a dismal rationalist, but since he could not very well reject the article, he sought to undercut its influence by publishing in the same issue an article which he entitled: "Über den Grund unsers Glaubens an eine göttliche Weltregierung."[7] Fichte's starting point was belief in a moral world order as Kant had taught it. His question was: "How does a person arrive at such a belief?" The basis for it can only lie in reason, "in our own inner activity." "I myself and my necessary object are supersensible." Up to this point Fichte still speaks with the voice of Kant. But then he continues: "This is the true belief: this moral order is *the divine* which we accept." Kant (if we ignore some scattered utterances in his later work) could state: "On the basis of this moral order I accept God." But Fichte answers: No, such a duality is unnecessary. "This belief [in a moral order] is faith—whole and complete. That vital and actively working moral order is itself God; we need no other God and cannot comprehend any other. There is no ground in reason why we should leave that moral world-order behind and, with the help of an inference from the grounded to the ground, postulate still another being as the cause of it. The original intellect certainly does not draw this inference and knows of no such being; only a philosophy that does not understand itself makes such inferences." Fichte could hardly have rejected in sharper terms Kant's doctrine of God as a postulate of practical reason. He also shows that for such a being who is distinct from the world one must postulate personality and consciousness. He calls out to his opponents: "Consequently, by the attribution of that predicate you make this being finite, a being like yourselves, and you have not, as you intended, thought God; you have only multiplied yourselves in your thinking." The question "whether God exists" is then answered in two ways: there is a moral world order in which every individual with his deeds and fortunes is sheltered. It is, however, equally sure "that the concept of God as a special substance is impossible and contradictory."

7. *Philosophisches Journal* 8 (1798) 1-20. Repr. in *Ausgewählte Werke,* ed. F. Medicus (Darmstadt, 1962), 3:121-33.

Here Fichte, probably without knowing it, wrote down propositions heavy with content and consequence. Of course, for him they were self-evident inferences from the nature and manner in which he had elevated the suprapersonal Ego to the level of a final and absolute truth. But for many readers these words came as a shock. One may be troubled over the level of the attacks which followed the article; one must not, however, ignore the fact that Fichte's critics assessed the theological and cultural significance of this short article more correctly than those who, with a shrug of their shoulders or out of goodwill, made excuses for Fichte or else ignored the whole matter. Despite his disagreement with the article, the Norwegian Steffens devoted much of his energy to Fichte's defense in the days of the Atheism Controversy. He pointedly formulated the contrast between Kant and Fichte: "The servant of an inscrutable law turns into a titan of self-determination and into the creator of heaven and earth."[8] The truth was that the God of Kant was untenable not only in the light of the gospel but also in the light of modern unitary thinking.

Thinking along ways that went far beyond the critical boundaries Kant had set up, Fichte had to drop God as postulate but in the process also as a personal "vis-à-vis." God is incompatible with absolute idealism. In this way Fichte consciously arrived at the crossroads which Kant, as we saw earlier, viewed from afar at the end of his life. In the process Fichte, with his daring powers of thought, had at the same time looked toward the left and ventured to think the atheistic alternative. His arguments against God as "substance," as an enlarged projection of humanity, sound quite modern. At the least one has the feeling that Fichte here gazes prophetically into the distance beyond the approaching period of metaphysical idealism and anticipates the atheistic turn of the "Hegelian left."

Still, Fichte did not choose this road for himself. Quite to the surprise of his readers he shifted his gaze, on the last page, to the right, to the pantheistic alternative. There he no longer argues; he merely cites "two eminent poets," Schiller and especially Goethe, quoting a passage from the Faust-fragment of 1790, where Faust, in dialogue with Gretchen, speaks in deliberately vague terms about "the All-embracing" and "All-upholding," with this conclusion:

Call it Bliss! Heart! Love! God!
I have no name to give it!
Feeling is all in all:

8. Steffens, *Was Ich Erlebete*, p. 165.

> The Name is sound and smoke,
> Obscuring Heaven's clear glow.

> *Faust,* act 1, scene 16

Fichte was deeply disturbed by the Atheism Controversy which —he could not deny it—he himself had triggered. Quite apart from the quotations at the end, the article could not but leave an atheistic impression. And, one wonders, was the pantheistic alternative then any less radical by comparison with the Christian concept of God as a personal "vis-à-vis" and covenant ally? However this may be, in his *Appellation an das Publikum* (1799), *Rückerinnerungen, Antworten, Fragen* (not completed and unpublished, 1799), *Aus einem Privatschreiben* (1800), and *The Vocation of Man* (1800), Fichte hastened to make clear that he at no time intended to relinquish the vocable and concept of "God." He confronted his opponents with pride and contempt. The train of his thoughts, though illuminating in part, is often veiled. It is significant that he wants to have "Order" understood not as result but as act, as *ordo ordinans.* He does not regard the individual as divine but as a sower whose seed can only sprout in virtue of the soil, that is, in virtue of the moral order which transcends the individual ego. In the inspiring closing pages of *The Vocation of Man,* the monistic passion of his thought issues in an almost mystical panentheism (just to give it a name): "An eternal stream of life and power and action, which issues from the original Source of all life—from Thy Life, O Infinite One; for all life is Thy Life, and only the religious eye penetrates to the realm of True Beauty. . . . [The life of God] is self-forming, self-manifesting Will: this Life . . . flows forth through me, and throughout the immeasurable universe of Nature."[9]

Ten years after Fichte broke with the Spinozism of the *deus sive natura,* he returned, through the door of *deus sive ego,* to the All-One of Spinoza.[10] At that point the intellectual life of Germany and Europe left Kant behind as an episode.

These changes did not occur, however, without intense antecedent birth pangs. Granted, they were not caused by the great decision which was made here; they are attributable solely to the arrogance and tactlessness with which Fichte acted. It was natural for Goethe, who was

9. *The Vocation of Man,* tr. William Smith, 2nd ed. (Chicago: Open Court, 1910), p. 172.

10. "At last that person was seized by the mighty current of esthetic-religious experience itself who until then had been the strongest pillar of ethical idealism and the religion of morality: Fichte" (R. Kroner, *Von Kant bis Hegel,* 2nd ed. [Tübingen, 1961], 2:67).

the minister of education and cultural affairs under the Duke of Sachsen-Weimar, to protect his admirer and intellectual ally at the University of Jena, which was under his jurisdiction. When Fichte began to exert pressure and to threaten to leave, however, Goethe yielded to his feelings of antipathy against Fichte's character and permitted the dismissal to go through. Fichte then made his way to, and was accepted in, Prussia. The reasoning offered by King Frederick William III is well known: "If it is true that there is antagonism between him and the good Lord, I will let the good Lord settle the matter. It is no concern of mine." In Berlin Fichte found a fruitful environment for his work. In 1810 he became the first rector of the newly founded University of Berlin.

At the crossroads of his thinking Fichte had looked to the left and to the right, then chosen the right. The fact that he combined the concept of God with his philosophy of the ego not only changed the concept —it also changed the philosophy. The absolute idealism which had been practiced till then as "Science of Knowledge" now became metaphysical idealism—and that less than twenty years after the appearance of *The Critique of Pure Reason.*

THE WAY TOWARDS THE BLESSED LIFE

During his residence in Berlin, the active spirit of Fichte ranged widely. Once again, for example, he dealt explicitly with religion. In 1806 there appeared in the then customary form of lectures the work *The Way Towards the Blessed Life, or Doctrine of Religion.* The tendency toward a mystical panentheism noted earlier comes to full expression here. The word *blessed* is particularly striking. Blessedness is the expression of the victory over dualism, the unity of the human ego with the universal Ego of God. Just as the thought patterns of the Jena period often anticipate those of existentialism, so the thought patterns of the period after 1800 often recall those of Neo-Platonism and anticipate modern "holistic" thoughts. Of that, too, there had been premonitory signs on the closing pages of *The Vocation of Man* (1800). It would appear as if Fichte's change of residence from Jena to Berlin also meant a move into the sphere of other cultural "powers." Actually, in Berlin Fichte for the first time entered into close contact with the circle of the early Romantics. One must also remember that after the failure of the French Revolution and the rise of Napoleon the word *freedom* had lost much of its magic. It was replaced by words like *personality, individual, universe,* and *love.* Fichte also underwent this change. In *The Way Towards the Blessed Life* the concept of love is central, being identical with universal Unity—that is, God

—and infinitely more true than all the contrasts of actual existence and conceptual divisions. Already at the end of *The Vocation of Man* he erects the bridge: the freedom of the spirit unites us with Universal Life "as the bond which unites spirit with spirit. . . . Borne onward in this stream of light, thought floats from soul to soul, without pause or variation, and returns purer and brighter from each kindred mind."[11] This love, as platonic Eros, reminds us of Schiller's "Hymn to Joy" (1785), with its chorus: "Embrace, ye millions—let this kiss, brothers, embrace the earth below!" (but not the sequel, which is literally: "Beyond the starry tent a good Father must be dwelling," for that is clearly still the theology of Kant's postulates!).

As Kant does in *Religion Within the Limits of Reason Alone*, so Fichte in *The Way Towards the Blessed Life* attempts to present Christianity as the highest expression of his philosophy of religion. But whereas Kant does not trouble himself about the exegetical and historical correctness of his understanding of Scripture (he considers that a matter of importance to scriptural scholars, not to philosophers), in Fichte's case one gets the impression he really believes he is articulating the original intent of the gospel. A further difference is that for Kant the moral element (particularly the Sermon on the Mount) constitutes the core of the New Testament, while for Fichte the prologue of John's Gospel, especially the first five verses, is the real gospel.[12] For Fichte also the historical dimension is much more important than it is for Kant—at precisely this point Romanticism had distanced itself a long way from the Enlightenment. The trend of thought embodied in the well-known sixth lecture, however, remains ambivalent. Only the historical Jesus (meaning the Johannine Jesus) is he who disclosed and realized the absolute unity of human existence with the divine being. Through him we too can and must attain to this unity. Still, our concern is not with the historical but with the metaphysical, the eternal truth which is implanted in every human being. "Only the metaphysical, and in no way the historical, makes a person blessed. The latter only makes one intelligent. If a person is really united with God and in communion with him, it is quite immaterial how he got there; it would be a very unprofitable and wrongheaded busi-

---

11. Fichte, *Ausgewählte Werke*, ed. F. Medicus, 3:412.

12. In Kant also the prologue has special importance (*Religion Within the Limits of Reason Alone*, p. 54), but in a way that is less so, and different from, Fichte's understanding of it. For Kant the Logos is "humanity in its full moral perfection." The Son of God, who is eternally with God, is the idea of practical reason. Being only an illustration of this moral archetype, the historical Jesus is not necessary for us.

ness if instead of living the matter itself one would forever rehearse the memory of how he got there."[13] At the end of the lectures, however, in an appendix to the sixth lecture, he wishes to some degree to rehabilitate the historical: Jesus acquired his knowledge not through speculation but through pure inspiration, "solely out of his own consciousness." The reality of this historical fact cannot be established with metaphysical arguments.

This certainly seems to contradict what we learned in the passage cited above. But that passage in turn is contradicted by the words with which the seventh lecture begins: "We have now completed the presentation of our theory concerning being and life. Now, not at all in order to prove this theory but solely as a comment made in passing, I wish to state that the theory of Christianity about these matters is altogether identical."[14]

PANENTHEISM AS THE END OF THE ROAD

Still, the final conclusion has to be that the historical was totally swallowed up by the metaphysical. Christianity does not reveal anything that the human spirit does not already possess within itself. Jesus is the paradigm of the human ego's mystical experience of unity with the universal life of the divine. That is the Incarnation of the Word, the disclosure of the one (monistic) fundamental truth of the universe.

With these ideas Fichte seems to have become the philosopher of the Romantic movement. In fact, several Romanticists, especially Novalis, received this worldview with enthusiasm as an expression of their own feelings. Others, particularly Tieck, were almost driven to desperation by this monism of the ego, deprived as it was of any personal Other to relate to. Also, Romanticism's deep feeling for nature found no point of contact with Fichte's idealism. Reality was experienced by many in a way that was more abysmal, more divided, more complex, and more dualistic than came to expression initially in Fichte's *Science of Knowledge* and later in his pantheizing monism.

It seems to me that Fichte's lasting merit in theology is that, from a basis in the anthropology he held in common with Kant, he rejected the necessity of Kant's deistic concept of God. He saw that this anthropology could dispense with that concept of God altogether; soon, however, he turned away from this radical insight in order to broaden

13. Fichte, op. cit., 5:197.
14. Ibid., p. 204.

his absolute idealism in the direction of a panentheistic concept of God. As a result he delayed by a number of decades, in the modern (German) world of ideas *(Geistesgeschichte)*, the confrontation with atheism.[15]

15. E. Hirsch's verdict on Fichte's theological significance is very different: "More than any other German philosopher he belongs in the history of Christianity and theology." One wonders with astonishment what the grounds are for this unambiguous judgment (which says more about Hirsch than about Fichte). A few pages later we find the answer. Fichte stated: "The conscience alone is the source of truth." "To develop 'this fundamental moral insight' into a thoroughly constructed whole which sustains all the particulars of knowledge—that is the only way in which white [!] humanity can be saved from a headlong plunge into the subhuman. This was Fichte's view and everything that has happened in the intellectual history of Europe [*Geistesgeschichte*] since then validates his final fundamental viewpoints" (*Geschichte der neuern evangelischen Theologie*, 4:337, 345).

CHAPTER III

Schleiermacher's Direction

Like Kant and Fichte, so also *Friedrich Daniel Ernst Schleiermacher* (1768-1834) started his journey in theology. Unlike them, for all he accomplished and all he was in other ways (and that was a great deal!), he always remained a theologian. The question of God and his revelation was not for him one question among many, as it was for Kant and Fichte, but the all-important one; and the answer to it was not a product of human thought and action but independent of them and utterly essential for our nature and destiny as human beings.

BETWEEN KANT'S POSTULATE AND FICHTE'S EGO

One can say of Schleiermacher, as of Fichte, that the reading of the works of Kant evoked from him his own most characteristic ideas. His encounter with the philosophy of Kant took place when he was a private tutor in the East Prussian town of Schlobitten (1790-1793), and his struggle with Kant's ideas continued during the period in which he was active as minister in Landsberg (1794-1796). In distinction from the majority of the theologians who had been molded by the Enlightenment and its issues, Schleiermacher had no real difficulties with Kant's *The Critique of Pure Reason*. It was and remained self-evident to him that our knowledge is bound up with, and limited to, our experience. To be sure (and that is characteristic), he sought to attach greater weight to the thing-in-itself as the objective "vis-à-vis" of the activity of reason. Against *The Critique of Practical Reason* he had much deeper objections. He did affirm the autonomy of the moral will, but the world of the categorical imperative seemed to him overstrained and abstract. He rejected Kant's dualism of sensibility and morality. Everywhere in life there is constant interaction between freedom and unfreedom, creativity and receptivity. Schleiermacher even spoke of "determinism." Freedom is never an abstraction; it expresses itself differently in every life. He was fascinated by "individuality," "the individual," or "the personality"—a reality for which Kant had no room. Schleiermacher's aim was to incorporate the dimension of freedom and morality in the "totality" of individual personality.

Linked with this way of thinking is Schleiermacher's distaste for the God concept as a postulate of the (abstract) categorical imperative. For him religion is no derivative; on the contrary, it is expressive of the "immediacy of feeling." It springs from a level higher than objectivizing or acting reason—a level where the unity of life is experienced in an inner unity that is prior to the subject-object distinction. These ideas of the young Schleiermacher approach the early Romantic worldview one finds in the tradition of Herder and Goethe. For a time he was also fascinated by Spinoza. In many respects the course of his development away from Kant seems to have been similar to that of Fichte.[1] In his early period we are not surprised to see his intense preoccupation with Fichte, finding many of his own thoughts confirmed in Fichte's works. The language of the works of his youth often reminds the reader of Fichte. Nevertheless, the difference between them was greater than the agreement. For Schleiermacher, Fichte was too "Faustian." The self is too isolated and too unreceptive. Freedom has no "Other" over against it. What Schleiermacher missed in Kant he found even more lacking in Fichte. Fichte also has no room for the uniqueness of the individual. For him human personalities are merely channels through which the absolute Ego expresses itself in a restricted and hence imperfect way.

When the two men met in 1800, after Fichte's expulsion from Jena, the sense of distance in Schleiermacher grew even stronger, also for personal reasons. In the same year Fichte published *The Vocation of Man*, and Schleiermacher wrote a masterful review of it in the periodical *Athenaeum*. In ironic language he both concealed and revealed there his ambivalence toward the great philosopher as well as his resolute rejection of Fichte's philosophy. In the review Schleiermacher acted as a critical questioner, one who is severely conscious of his limitations and incomprehension, and, in reply to fictitious answers, ironically concluded

1. Here one must bear in mind the influence of Friedrich Heinrich Jacobi (1743-1819) on Fichte as well as on Schleiermacher, especially as a result of his rejection of Kant's dualisms in the name of the unity of the activities of the human consciousness. Jacobi's emphasis on the role of intuition and receptivity recurs in Schleiermacher.

as follows: "By this time the whole of his personality has long been lost to him (the individual self); it has become absorbed in the contemplation of destiny; now it considers itself, respects and loves itself, only as one of the instruments of infinite reason's final goal. In this mode of thought alone we can be and remain at one with ourselves and the universe, and take hold of our true being and essence; and invaluable is our merit if we have aided only a few people to do this or confirmed them in doing this."[2]

AS FELLOW MEMBER AND STRANGER IN THE ROMANTIC CIRCLE

In 1796 the court chaplain Sack, a leader in the Reformed church who as patron and benefactor of Schleiermacher had already smoothed his way to Schlobitten and Landsberg, secured for him a post as chaplain at the Charité hospital in Berlin. Soon after his arrival, with the help of Ludwig Tieck, the so-called Romantic Circle was formed around the two friends, Friedrich Schlegel and Friedrich Schleiermacher, who shared living quarters. Educated women like Rahel and Henriette Herz and Dorothea Veit-Mendelssohn also played a prominent role. The sense of life *(Lebensgefühl)* common to the group turned against the rationalism of the Enlightenment and the strong moral commitment to duty which Kant promoted, but also against Goethe's stress on classical form. Pivotal for them was the experience of the unity of life as the harmonious interplay of opposing forces. Life is fluid, dynamic, untamed. One revels in

2. The review was printed in *Athenaeum* 3 (1800) 283-97 (photocopy in Darmstadt, 1960); the quotation is on p. 297. E. Hirsch, *Geschichte der neuern evangelischen Theologie*, offers a very different picture of Schleiermacher's relationship to Fichte: he regards him as Fichte's disciple; and the reservations by which Schleiermacher distances himself from Fichte only serve "to build him up into a fuller and richer figure" (4:511). Hirsch censured the review for "its use of irony which violates the gratitude and respect owing to another" (p. 543). That, surely, is no argument which supports his thesis. I can understand this only in the light of what I quoted in n. 15 of the previous chapter. For Hirsch, Fichte is manifestly the greatest of philosophers and Schleiermacher can only be valued in terms of his being placed in a positive relationship to Fichte. W. Dilthey presents a much more accurate picture of the relationship *(Leben Schleiermachers,* 2 vols. [Berlin: G. Reimer, 1870], 1/1:353-68): "Both had been molded, personally and academically, in the school of idealism. But within this school of character and thought they formed the starkest contrast. . . . To the degree that the situation forced them to be together, an ever deepening antipathy had to develop between them. Corresponding to the personal contrast there was a scientific one, for the worldviews of the two men were the full expression of their respective characters" (p. 355).

nature, feeling, the interior world of the soul, individuality, love. The love between a man and a woman particularly fascinated the members of the group, for here there is a polarity which has to come together and flow into a higher sensual-spiritual unity. In this context the emancipation of women was a primary requirement. The question how such an ideal unity could be realized in this institution of marriage was passionately discussed.[3]

After what we have heard of Schleiermacher's spiritual and intellectual struggles it does not come as a surprise that he could feel quite at home in this circle. He had the same ideals and spoke the same language. Even in the matter of the emancipation of women and relations between the sexes the young Reformed pastor was a passionate defender of Romantic convictions, as his *Idee zu einem Katechismus der Vernunft für edle Frauen* (1798) and his *Vertraute Briefe über Friedrich Schlegels "Lucinde"* (1800) show.

At the same time he must have felt like a stranger in the midst of his companions. This becomes clear in 1799 when his book *On Religion: Speeches to its Cultured Despisers* appeared. These despisers are his closest friends! All of them had turned their backs on Kant and reveled in the All-in-One. In the process they cast glances in the direction of a Spinozistic pantheism and at the same time in the direction of a determined atheism. In the year in which the *Speeches* appeared, the Atheism Controversy was at its height, and all members of the group lined up with warm sympathy on the side of the "persecuted" Fichte. Given the appropriate circumstances, they could be enthusiastic about the "absolute," "the universe," or whatever its name might be, but never about religion as it was taught by the church. Friedrich Schlegel probably expressed the general mood correctly when he wrote: "Religion is usually only a supplement to, or a substitute for, education [*Bildung*]; and nothing is, strictly speaking, religious that is not a product of freedom. Hence one can say: the freer, the more religious; and the more education, the less religion."[4] This was written by Schleiermacher's fellow lodger and closest friend! His friends must have viewed Schleiermacher's ecclesiastical office as unauthentic, a concession to the demands of society. And Schleiermacher must have had the feeling that he could not share

---

3. On this subject, cf. R. Huch, *Die Romantik* (Tübingen: Rainer Wunderlich, 1951), the chapter entitled "Romantische Liebe," pp. 227-52, and the comment on p. 239: "It is amazing how in this period the highest idea of the importance and permanence of love went hand in hand with the most broadminded leniency toward infidelity and all kinds of erotic aberrations."

4. *Athenaeum* 1 (1798) 239.

with his friends that which was most essential and dearest to him. Tension between membership in the group and estrangement from the group must then have become too much for him. Prompted by this inner conflict, he produced the *Speeches* in just a few months (1798-1799).

Already on the first page the author resolutely positioned himself against his friends, tearing open the chasm existing between them. Not for a moment did he count on being successful.

> When you stop to think about it, you realize that faith has never been everyone's affair. Only a few persons have ever seen what religion really is in any age, although millions have variously deluded themselves with the mere trappings of religion—with whatever happened to strike their fancy. But in our day especially, the self-styled life of cultured people hardly yields a glimpse of it. You no longer visit the temples of religion. Indeed, I am aware that for you it is just as passé to worship deity in the quiet sanctity of your hearts. Setting out the clever maxims of our learned men and the resplendent lines of our poets as wall decorations will do very well—but, please, nothing more "sanctimonious" than that! Suavity and sociability, art and learning, have won you over heart and soul—this no matter what little time or devotion you may give to them. These things dominate your lives so completely that no room is left for that eternal and holy being which, in your view, lies "beyond this world."[5]

A little further on, speaking of the true work of religion, he says: "And to the man who has not himself experienced it, would not that . . . be a stumbling block or a folly?"[6] It is too often forgotten that the *Speeches* start out on this bluntly antithetical note and that the author intends thus to set the tone for all that follows.

Nevertheless, Schleiermacher remains one of them. He completely speaks their language, not from a conscious desire to accommodate himself to them but solely because it is his own language. We read of "intuition," "feeling," " the universe," "the World Spirit," etc. At first glance one gets the impression that Schleiermacher, together with his friends, is at the same crossroads at which, in the preceding chapter, we found Fichte, and that it is his aim to direct their attention away from atheism to pantheism, as we saw Fichte attempt to do in the same pe-

5. Cited from the translation by Terrence N. Tice, *On Religion: Addresses in Response to Its Cultured Critics* (Richmond, VA: John Knox, 1969), p. 39. Although we use Tice's modern translation, we retain the traditional title, *Speeches*.
6. Ibid., p. 48.

riod. This is how numerous readers tend to understand Schleiermacher's *Speeches*. People then refer to the Romantic, pantheizing phase in his theological thinking which was later relieved by a more Christian and even ecclesiastical one; and admittedly, Schleiermacher himself furnished some grounds for this misunderstanding.

The second Speech, entitled "The Essence of Religion," is by far the longest. Here one finds almost all the famous quotations which the theological manuals tend to supply to their readers and each other. A second high point occurs in the fifth Speech, "The Religions." It would certainly appear, therefore, that from start to finish we are in the domain of "natural theology." But this perception cannot be accurate, since the fifth Speech constitutes a sharp attack on natural theology as an abstraction and points, in contrast, to the historical, developed, "positive religions" as the only seat in life of true religion, culminating in an account of the Christian faith as the "religion of the religions."[7] This does not prevent the presentation from giving the impression that it proceeds from the general to the specific. The Christian religion would thus seem to be a variety of a pantheizing mystical religion of the All-in-One. This is how the book was interpreted over and over: by D. F. Strauss, the Ritschlian school (with the exception of the study by Otto Ritschl), Dilthey, Troeltsch, Otto, Brunner, right up to Hirsch and others.

We know, however, that this interpretation was not the author's intention. That much is clear from the foreword to the third edition (1821) and from the many explanations added to the text in that edition. In the foreword Schleiermacher mentions "the many misinterpretations," "some of them quite fantastic," which follow from the fact that readers paid too little attention to the circumstances and addressees of the book. Such statements would suggest that, in the twenty years which followed, Schleiermacher had changed a great deal and abandoned his earlier "Spinozism," "mysticism," etc. But that is not so at all. "Except for some further maturing and clarification, at that time my mode of thinking on these matters had already reached the very form in which it has remained to this day."[8] Also, the person who believes that Schleiermacher was himself in part responsible for the "misinterpretations"—an opinion based on the language and layout of the book—nevertheless cannot avoid giving him credence when in the explanations he comments on his earlier statements without, however, taking them back. In addition, when he wrote this foreword his *Christian Faith* was at the point of being published. He himself refers to the fact that, for all the differences be-

7. Ibid., p. 321.
8. Foreword to the 3rd ed., p. 37.

tween the two books in intent, in overall content they are quite parallel.[9] He explains this relation by various references in the footnotes. If one takes these pronouncements by the author seriously, one can, instead of interpreting the second Speech in the light of the fifth, only acknowledge that the *Speeches* belong not to the category of a popular philosophy of religion but to that of Christian apologetic literature.

In the foreword in question one also encounters this proposition: "These misinterpretations . . . are chiefly based on one particular circumstance. The rhetorical form has been almost universally ignored, despite its use throughout the book."[10] Just what does he mean by "rhetorical form"? We are aided here by a note in his diary dated September 29, 1797: "A presentation is *rhetorical* when it is so ordered that the effect of the individual part is determined by its place in the whole—as opposed to the *logical*, where the place of each part is determined by its organic position in a system. The rhetorical is an attribute of arrangement, not dependent on the quality of the several parts."[11] In the composition of the *Speeches*, "rhetorical" could then mean that the most important things were not stated immediately at the beginning but that, step by step, the author aimed at a climax in the light of which all that has preceded acquired its (specific) meaning.

In fact, instead of taking the second Speech as a basic chapter on the philosophy of religion, one can also read it as a clandestine presentation, clothed in general concepts, of "the religion of the religions." Then one must attribute exceptional hermeneutical weight to the concluding pages of the book. When Schleiermacher wished to speak of the religion in which the universe is to be perceived in its highest unity and

9. See n. 5 under the second Speech, ibid., p. 161.

10. Foreword to 3rd ed., p. 37. The term *rhetorical* also occurs in n. 3, first Speech, n. 10, second Speech, n. 16, fourth Speech.

11. In *Die Theologie des jungen Schleiermacher* (Gütersloh: Gerd Mohn, 1960), p. 171, P. Seifert called attention to the importance of this statement for the interpretation of the *Speeches*. This book has exerted a profound influence on the most recent Schleiermacher research. Even if one cannot endorse all its arguments one still has to concur, in my opinion, with the final conclusion: "The speaker of these discourses on religion talks like a preacher; and when he introduces the 'mediator,' develops a doctrine of the church, and clearly commits himself to the absoluteness of Christianity, this was not meant as a digression but rather as the predetermined objective of the entire trend of thought" (p. 197). For this and other insights in Schleiermacher's aim and methods I am much indebted to G. E. Meuleman, "Schleiermacher en de apologie van het christelijk geloof," in the symposium for G. C. Berkouwer, *Septuagesimo anno* (Kampen: Kok, 1973), pp. 152-80.

comprehensiveness, he confessed: "Actually I should speak only of one religion."[12] Here he already described the Christian faith in words which expressed the essence of his later dogmatics: "Corruption and redemption, alienation and reconciliation: these are two inseparably united and fundamental relations that constitute this mode of experience."[13] It is confusing, though appropriate to the "rhetorical" form, that he then posits the possibility that someday Christianity might disappear. Soon, however, this heuristic idea is put aside (especially in the Supplementary Notes and the Epilogue) on the ground that the duality of corruption and redemption will never cease to be a reality. "Every such epoch becomes a palingenesis of Christianity, awakening its spirit in a newer and finer form."[14]

The *Speeches* are a brilliant defense of the Christian faith, totally targeted at a burgeoning new sense of life *(Lebensgefühl)* present among the young German intelligentsia—a sense of life that had quite disappeared, as Schleiermacher observed in the third edition; it seems the detractors and unbelievers had been replaced by the superstitious and fanatic. Schleiermacher's aim was to proclaim the gospel in the emotional idiom of his friends and companions, and he was able to do this because that idiom was his own. As a motto (in the version of the 3rd edition) one can take this statement from the second Speech: "If you regard the world as a universal whole, moreover, can you do this otherwise than in God?"[15] When he speaks of God here, he has in mind the specific understanding of God which we encounter in Jesus Christ. From the vantage point of the *Lebensgefühl* of his circle he sought to let the Christian faith shine out anew; and from the vantage point of this faith he wanted to point the discoveries, feelings, and ideals of his circle to the place where their power to illuminate life could be heightened and preserved.

Schleiermacher did not reach this immediate goal. Novalis was the only member of the circle for whom the *Speeches* meant a burst of illumination which, in the brief time of life still left to him, mightily inspired him in his publications. Friedrich Schlegel, to whom the manuscript was shown beforehand, found, even before he got to the fifth Speech, that the whole thing was "too definite and positive in tone"; he correctly discerned how "Christian" the seemingly indefinite was meant to be. Goethe was elated with the first three Speeches: "Meanwhile, to the degree that style became more careless and the religion more Chris-

---

12. *Speeches,* p. 305.
13. Ibid., p. 308.
14. Ibid., p. 320.
15. Ibid., p. 147.

tian, this effect changed into its opposite and the whole thing finally ended in a healthy and happy aversion." One has to note that both these cultured despisers of religion discovered Schleiermacher's real intention in and behind the rhetorical form. They rejected the invitation the book held out to them, as did the majority of philosophers.[16]

Thus those who caught the intention of the book rejected it. But those who should have gratefully welcomed it in their struggle against unbelief, the men of the church, did not understand this intention and therefore also rejected it. Schleiermacher's benefactor, Sack, the Reformed court preacher, was very upset by the *Speeches*. He was not able to see in them anything more than an ingenious defense of pantheism à la Spinoza. Schleiermacher's reply to him is his first commentary on the *Speeches* and hence important to us. It is disappointing, however, in that he indignantly rejects the accusations rather than refuting them. Characteristically he exclaims: "An apology for pantheism, a presentation of Spinozistic philosophy? Something that came up only in passing on a few pages is supposed to be the main content?"[17]

It was to no avail. As court preacher, Sack "banished" him to Stolp. It is clear from the correspondence that the reason was not just Schleiermacher's heresy but also the immorality of the Romantic Circle. Schlegel's "Lucinde," and even more Schleiermacher's defense of it in his "Vertrauten Briefen" (1800), constituted proof to Sack that corruption in doctrine ever brought with it corruption in conduct.

Meanwhile, owing to a combination of external and internal causes, the Romantic Circle had collapsed. After only three years it succumbed to its own boundless and unstructured individualism. The gap between sensibility and morality, a gap the members of the group sought to bridge both theoretically and practically, demonstrated that it could not be surmounted. They were still a long way from "the unity of life." Could it be that Kant, with his dualism, was right after all? Many Romantics, who on their own had raved about the romanticized Middle Ages, sought in the structures of the Roman Catholic Church the stability and the discipline they had once despised. Others later joined the

---

16. Cf. W. Dilthey, *Leben Schleiermachers*, ch. 10: "The Initial Historical Impact of the *Speeches*."

17. The letter has been made available to a wider public through the excellent Schleiermacher anthology by H. Bolli, *Schleiermacher-Auswahl* (Munich and Hamburg, 1968), pp. 268-73, specifically p. 270. [In English it is now available in *On the* Glaubenslehre: *Two Letters to Dr. Lücke,* tr. James Duke and Francis Fiorenza (Chico, CA: Scholars Press, 1981). This translation is used here. — TRANS.]

evangelical Restoration. Mankind's "emergence from his self-imposed immaturity" (Kant) as the Enlightenment envisaged it required a much longer pilgrimage than people initially thought.

Schleiermacher lost the very circle in which he had received so much and in which at the same time he had never really been completely at home. And the church, which could have been his first spiritual home, rejected him. His attempt to persuade a pastor's wife (Eleonore Grunow) to divorce her husband and to marry him backfired. Dilthey spoke of Schleiermacher as "a person totally isolated from society who, out of the ruins of all his hopes, seems to have salvaged only himself."[18] In his religion, however, he possessed the lodestar which prevented him from losing his sense of direction.

THE FIRST EDITION OF *THE CHRISTIAN FAITH*

The second pivotal point in Schleiermacher's career as a creative theologian became his great work in dogmatics, *The Christian Faith,* whose two volumes appeared in 1821 and 1822 respectively. We already learned how the author, in the foreword and Supplementary Notes of the third edition of the *Speeches* which appeared at about the same time, referred repeatedly to his treatment of the same themes in his doctrine of faith. For him, the two books articulated the same faith. The difference between them consisted partly in that "which the years of each person's life cause to ripen and to clarify" (foreword) but mainly in the different purpose of the two works. The *Speeches* were aimed at non-Christians, particularly the "cultured critics" of religion. The title of this dogmatic work reads: "The Christian Faith, presented systematically according to the fundamental doctrines of the Evangelical Church." At this point we are removed by more than two decades from the circumstances in which the *Speeches* originated. The Romantic Circle had long since disappeared. Tradition, particularly the Christian tradition, was again asserting its prerogatives. The Restoration was celebrating its triumphs. And Schleiermacher, already for many years a professor of theology, not only wished (as he wrote in the first foreword) to make available a manual of theology for those who heard his lectures but also hoped that "many other readers might reach for this book as a public account of my teaching which I had finally submitted to the whole of the theological reading public." As an important parallel aim he mentions his hope that, with this "unified" theory of faith (the first, as he believed in the foreword of the 1st edition), he would be

18. W. Dilthey, *Leben Schleiermachers,* 1:479.

able to undergird dogmatically the union of the Lutheran and Reformed Churches. In conclusion he expressed as his dearest wish and deepest purpose in writing the book that "it may contribute to an ever clearer understanding as to the meaning of our holy faith."

The second preface again picks up this theme. What is clear is that *The Christian Faith* has in view a completely different circle of readers, and pursues a very different goal, than the *Speeches*. The one was intended for people alienated from the church, the other for theologians and church leaders. Schleiermacher knew with what distrust many Restoration and revivalist theologians viewed him. He would have been able to create for himself a much more receptive audience had he, on the occasion of the publication of his main dogmatic work, expressed himself somewhat critically and apologetically about the sins of his romantic youth. But he did not; quite the contrary. In the same year (1821) he reissued his *Speeches,* making emphatic reference to their further elucidation and substantiation in *The Christian Faith.* We simply have to accept his assertion that an understanding of the two works which takes as its point of departure the difference between them instead of their unity is mistaken. The difference between them is not one of belief *(Glaube)* but of genre *(Gattung).* It is the difference between Apologetics and Dogmatics, between the defense of the faith vis-à-vis those outside the church, and systematic reflection on the faith for those inside. The relationship between the two works is comparable to that between the *Summa contra Gentiles* and the *Summa theologiae* of Thomas Aquinas, with this difference: in the case of Schleiermacher the two genres are methodically much farther apart—an indication of how much more acutely the gap between the church and the world was experienced after the Enlightenment.

One has to describe almost as tragic how *The Christian Faith* became the victim of misreadings similar to those which earlier plagued the *Speeches*. From the side of the church the book was charged with a pantheistic denial of the supernatural character of the Christian faith. Of course: this was a way of interpreting Schleiermacher's own emphatic affirmation of agreement between *The Christian Faith* and the *Speeches!* For the second time the author was astonished over so much incomprehension. That astonishment strikes us as a little naive. Just as in the *Speeches,* so here the layout and terminology of the book gave plenty of occasion for misunderstanding, all the more since the method applied was without parallel in the history of theology.

In the first edition[19] Schleiermacher took his point of departure

---

19. This is now completely available again as a result of the meticulous new edition prepared by Herman Peiter, *Schleiermacher: Kritische Gesamtausgabe,*

in "pious states of consciousness" (§ 2), in the "affections of the pious consciousness of the Christian" (§ 3). However, to find the specifically Christian, "we must go and assume a position beyond Christianity in order to compare it with other types of faith" (§ 6; cf. § 7). He then returned to "piety as such" (§ 8) in which "the feeling of absolute dependence" (this word combination occurs for the first time in the second edition) is "the common element in all the affections of piety" (§ 9). On the basis of this general concept he then moved to the different historical communions which he viewed in two ways: as different stages of development and as different kinds (§ 14). In the following sections the viewpoint of development predominates. Even when in this connection Christianity emerges as the highest kind of piety (§ 18), it is nevertheless only one among several (§ 19). The first part of the prolegomena ends with the thesis: "The divine revelation in Christ can neither be something absolutely supernatural nor something absolutely supra-rational" (§ 20).

CRITICISM, DEFENSE, AND REVISION

At first glance the reader may have complete sympathy for the position of the critics. It even seems as if Schleiermacher has fallen back on the first edition of the *Speeches* (to a stage prior to that of his explanations of the *Speeches* dating from 1821) and that the misinterpretations against which in the third edition he lodges a protest are not misinterpretations at all. He cannot escape having to write explanatory commentary on *The Christian Faith* as earlier he had to explain the *Speeches*. But this time he did more. He first wrote his explanations in the form of two letters to his friend, the Göttingen theologian Friedrich Lücke, who published them in his periodical *Theologische Studien und Kritiken* (1829).[20] And, second, he substantially revised the Introduction in the second edition (1830).

    The second letter to Dr. Lücke is one of the most important documents for understanding the basic principles of Schleiermacher's theology. In it he stresses that the Introduction, intended only as "a portal and entrance hall," lies, strictly speaking, "outside of the discipline of

---

Part I, vol. 7, sections 1-3 (Berlin/New York, 1980). In this book I am concerned only with the Introduction; thus I shall quote from Carl Stange, *Schleiermachers Glaubenslehre: Kritische Ausgabe, Erste Abteilung: Einleitung* (Leipzig: A. Deichert, 1910), since this edition (which is not continued after this volume) offers a detailed comparison of the two forms of the Introduction.

20. See *On the* Glaubenslehre (n. 17 above), p. 59.

dogmatics itself" ("and especially from their reading of this first part, some critics have constructed what they regard as my pantheism"). For a long time, in fact, he had toyed with the idea of putting these formal and quasi-speculative considerations at the end, following the treatment of the essential content of the faith. In this connection he writes a most important sentence: "I would have wished to construct the work so that at every point the reader would be made aware that the verse John 1:14 is the basic text for all dogmatics."[21]

Why then did he arrange the book in a way which left it open to so much misunderstanding? The plain but lengthy answer is this: Only the Introduction can correctly bring about the proper separation and connection between faith and learning after the Enlightenment.[22] Here occurs the much-quoted line: "Shall the tangle of history so unravel that Christianity becomes identified with barbarism and science with unbelief?"[23] Also in *The Christian Faith,* even though indirectly, the cultured detractors of religion remain present as important—if not as the most important—partners in dialogue. On the one hand, Schleiermacher fears a Christian obscurantism; on the other, he fears either a quasi-scientific "Ebionitism" for which Jesus is only a wise man whose words serve only as motto for one's own thoughts, or the speculative gnosis of idealistic philosophy. Neither leaves any room for the historical Jesus as our Redeemer. Nevertheless, if only one understands the faith correctly, the modern natural sciences and historical-critical biblical scholarship leave full room for that confession. Schleiermacher does admit that his Introduction leaves an impression as though faith could be derived by merely deductive steps from anthropological presuppositions—at which point, to defend himself, he refers to the 15th question of the Heidelberg Catechism ("What sort of mediator and redeemer must we then seek?"). No: Christianity did not arise from the feeling of dependence. This feeling is the human precondition for it and no more. "Will one also speak in terms of 'deducing,' however, when I say that it was due to the liveliness of this feeling that Christianity arose when Christ appeared and was recognized in his Lordship and power?"[24] In other words, the Christian faith is neither deducible nor provable because it comes to us from history. The Introduction envisages no proof. "In the case of a Christian doctrine of faith, the exposition is at the same time the foundation."[25] Again

21. Ibid.
22. Ibid., pp. 59-68.
23. Ibid., p. 61.
24. Ibid., p. 70.
25. Ibid., p. 78.

we are obliged to accept Schleiermacher's own explanation of what he has written. And we recall that he furnished *The Christian Faith* with Anselm's dictum as a motto: *Neque enim quaero intelligere ut credam, sed credo ut intelligam* ("For neither do I seek to understand in order that I may believe, but I believe in order that I may understand"). As with Barth later, in Schleiermacher reality precedes possibility, not the reverse.[26]

Then what is the purpose of the Introduction? It describes possibility insofar as it resides in humanity. Here Schleiermacher, using the means furnished him by the consciousness-philosophy of his day, sketches what we may call with Kant "the transcendental possibility of faith," or with Troeltsch "the religious a priori," or in Heidegger's language "religion as an existential concern," or with Tillich "the quest of existence." Despite appearances to the contrary, every claim to present a "foundation" is absent here. His concern is rather simply to offer "a specification of the place" of Christianity.[27] Already the first edition stated this point: "The essence of Christianity in and by itself can perhaps be reproduced in a general philosophy of religion and from there, though it cannot be proven in an Apologetic, it can nevertheless be so presented that as a result the specific place of Christianity can be secured."[28] The historical reality of Jesus Christ, as it is mediated to us by the church, is not something that can be derived from a philosophical analysis of existence. Schleiermacher is happy that he has remained faithful to his goal and "to his own philosophical dilettantism," not allowing it "to influence the content of the *Glaubenslehre*."[29] The Introduction only analyzes the domain into which Revelation enters.

While we may accept this explanation, one section still remains obscure. I am referring to § 30 of the second edition—reproduced here in the version of § 34 of the first edition because it states the problem somewhat more sharply: "All dogmatic propositions, in addition to

26. I wish to refer here to the thorough analysis which Doris Offermann presents in *Schleiermachers Einleitung in die Glaubenslehre: Eine Untersuchung der "Lehnsätze"* (Berlin, 1969). In many respects the book parallels that of P. Seifert (cf. n. 11 above). It shows that *The Christian Faith*, too, especially its Introduction, must be read backward. "Our thesis that the borrowed propositions were conceived in the light of the goal . . . as the point of 'departure' viewed precisely from this dogmatic position and to that extent specifically applicable . . ." (p. 330). She refers, e.g., to § 6, where the "feeling of absolute dependence," by its connection with the lower level, had already, a priori, been conceived as Christian.

27. See *On the* Glaubenslehre (n. 17 above), p. 76.

28. *Christian Faith*, § 18.5; cf. C. Stange, *Schleiermachers Glaubenslehre*, p. 123.

29. See *On the* Glaubenslehre, p. 87.

being descriptions of human states of mind, may also be stated in two other forms: as conceptions of divine attributes and as utterances regarding the constitution of the world. And in Dogmatics these three forms have always subsisted alongside of each other." This first formulation clearly expresses the advantage of the first form and thus does not seem to ascribe any fundamental value to the objective content of the emotions of the human consciousness. This is quite openly stated in the explanation of the second edition: "Hence we must declare the description of human states of mind to be the fundamental dogmatic form; while propositions of the second and third forms are permissible only in so far as they can be developed out of propositions of the first form; for only on this condition can they be really authenticated as expressions of religious emotions" (§ 30.2). Does not this formulation open the door to the purest subjectivism? But from what was stated earlier in § 30.2, it is clear that Schleiermacher did not intend to construe a contrast between the subjective (form one) and the objective (forms two and three) but a contrast between a pure expression of the faith and an expression of faith into which convictions of the natural sciences or of metaphysics not deriving from faith might easily creep. In his second letter to Lücke he laments this "almost inconceivable misunderstanding" (namely, the neglect of the historical character of the Christian faith) and states emphatically that "even if all the propositions of faith were given in the first form alone, the place of the historical Christ would be as secure and as certain as ever."[30]

That assertion, too, is one we have to accept from him. In his thinking and language he is intensely concerned to leave behind him both subjectivism and objectivism. Even when he takes his point of departure in human emotions, these emotions are conceived from the very start as relational (object-related). What Schleiermacher attempts to do, even though he does it in formulations frequently open to misunderstanding, is to articulate the concept—a new concept in his day—of intersubjectivity. That is what it says in the concluding sentence of the first Introduction: "it furnishes the advantage that each time something is said of God and of man the one stands in the closest relationship to the other" (§ 35.2). It is, however, a very special intersubjectivity, one in which every reciprocal action is excluded. That is what "the feeling of absolute dependence" is meant to convey. It means that we are conscious "of being absolutely dependent, or, which is the same thing, of being in relation with God" (2nd ed., § 4). Thus Schleiermacher sought to grasp in one statement both the *fides qua* and the *fides quae creditur*, because, in

30. Ibid., p. 72.

fact, in the act of believing they are one. One could also put it this way: he attempted in this way to present God's covenant with human beings both in its two-sidedness and its asymmetry.

If we have correctly understood him so far, then the question arises: Just what is the meaning of that objectivizing second and third forms? Schleiermacher's answer is that without these forms he would not have been understood in the theological world. His first and most essential form is in fact altogether new. To present it as the only one is "still far too early. Moreover, in revising the book, I would run the danger that in this form it would become merely a private work, as it were, a cabinet piece of theological literature. . . . It would lack the proper point of contact."[31] Hence Schleiermacher's point is that in the respective second and third sections of the two parts of which *The Christian Faith* consists he can more fully and thoroughly develop the objective content of what he treats in the first section, and that more nearly in line with the dogmatic tradition and, where necessary, more polemically against that which he regarded as metaphysical and pseudo-scientific error.

Actually, in the second edition Schleiermacher, in keeping with the intention he announced to Dr. Lücke, formulated many things in the Introduction with greater clarity and moderation. To that end the concept of *Lehnsätze* (borrowed propositions) was particularly useful to him. By this means it became unmistakably clear that the Introduction was not a part of the actual dogmatics and only sought to outline the anthropological locus in which redemption in Christ can be personally appropriated. In view of this fact, however, it is remarkable that from the beginning Schleiermacher presented his work as a "Church Dogmatics" (§ 2). True, "church" is initially considered only with the aid of "propositions borrowed from Ethics," and here that means something like philosophical anthropology or the sociology of religion (cf. § 2, Postscript 2): the locus of the community which is called the church is the anthropological "province" called religion. Next follow the "propositions borrowed from the philosophy of religion," which means "the phenomenology of religion" or "comparative religion." By this process Schleiermacher thus introduced the realities that developed historically in order the more precisely to determine the place of the Christian faith. With the help of "propositions borrowed from Apologetics" he then described the specific character of the Christian faith within this place and in its relation to it. This concludes the external prolegomena (§§ 2-14); what follows belongs rather to the internal prolegomena (§§ 15-31). The external prolegomena culminate in § 14: "There is no other way of obtaining par-

---

31. Ibid., p. 72; cf. the 2nd ed., pp. 126-27 (§ 30.3).

ticipation in the Christian communion than through faith in Jesus as the Redeemer."[32] This faith propagates itself through the church, which bridges the historical distance between Christ and us. The church's message makes us contemporaries, so to speak, of Christ. "This, moreover, is what has ever since constituted the essence of all direct Christian preaching. Such preaching must always take the form of testimony; testimony as to one's own experience, which shall arouse in others the desire to have the same experience" (§ 14.1). For the faith and for the church there is no other ground than this double occurrence of experience and preaching.

Schleiermacher's objective can now be clear to us. Another question, one which is equally important, is whether he realized that objective. He correctly concludes the second chapter of the Introduction with the remark that "the method here adopted can only be justified by the finished argument itself" (§ 31, Postscript). He suspected that many readers and critics would not get much further than a (distrustful) reading of the Introduction, but he himself was convinced that the articulation of the contents justified the method.

SCHLEIERMACHER'S IMPACT

One can hardly say that history proved him right. What he took such pains to formulate as the method of theology after the Enlightenment has become, consciously or unconsciously, the common property of the greater proportion of theologians. But there were, and are, only very few "Schleiermacherians." The actual execution of his design has prompted many to admire but few to imitate him. For some it was too radical; for others too traditional; and, of course, both possibilities were inherent in this method. As a result people from both the left and the right could appeal to him as an authority as it suited them, and often also expressed their annoyance at his indefiniteness. This perceived indefiniteness was probably the result of his use of the concept "oscillation" as applied in the "Dialektik" and "Ethik." He did not, like Hegel, operate with sharply defined and dialectically correlated concepts but rather allowed his thoughts to circle around a given theme in a progressive process of ap-

---

32. I owe this insight into the central position of § 14 to D. Offermann, who demonstrates that, just from a methodological point of view, § 14 is the pivotal point of the whole (Offermann, *Schleiermachers Einleitung in die Glaubenslehre*, p. 325). At this point the profoundly churchly character of this dogmatics becomes clear.

proximation. The most responsible verdict on Schleiermacher is perhaps to be found in the five (double) questions which Karl Barth posed toward the end of his life with regard to Schleiermacher's theology. This verdict is a nonverdict: "With regard to this man's basic standpoint, I find myself in a great, and for me very painful, perplexity."[33]

In the framework of the questions raised in this book, however, we may not let it go at that. By comparison with Kant and Fichte we can say a bit more. Like them, Schleiermacher took his point of departure in reason, that is, in the self-consciousness of human beings. In that sense he totally belonged to his own time and to the modern period as it has been stamped by the motifs of the Enlightenment. When it comes to the question of the nature or essence of reason, however, there is a parting of the ways. In Kant, on the lower level of the intuitions and categories, reason is partly receptive and partly creative; and, on the higher levels of pure and practical reason, it is inferential and postulative. In Fichte's case, reason is fundamentally and fully creative. In Schleiermacher reason is also receptive and reproductive on the higher level, and on the highest, that of religion, it is even fully receptive, in the sense of the feeling of absolute dependence. In the Christian faith, this religious reason was nourished totally from without, from history, through the redemption of Christ. That was Schleiermacher's real message, and for most of those who heard him in the Athens of his day that message was a stumbling block and foolishness.[34]

Conversely, for most of his Christian readers his message was

---

33. K. Barth, "Concluding Unscientific Postscript on Schleiermacher," repr. in *The Theology of Schleiermacher: Lectures at Göttingen, Winter Semester of 1923/24*, ed. Dietrich Ritschl, tr. Geoffrey W. Bromiley (Grand Rapids: Eerdmans, 1982), pp. 261-79.

34. Hegel's attack on Schleiermacher in his Foreword to Hinrich's philosophy of religion (*Religion in its Internal Relation to Systematic Knowledge*, 1822) is typical: "If religion in man is based only on a feeling, then such a feeling rightly has no further determination than to be the *feeling of his dependence*, and the dog would then be the best Christian, for the dog feels this most strongly in himself and lives mainly within this feeling. The dog also has feelings of redemption, whenever his hunger is satisfied by a bone. But spirit, on the contrary, has in religion its liberation and the feeling of its divine freedom; only free spirit has religion or can have religion. What is constrained in religion is the natural feeling of the heart, particular subjectivity; what is liberated in religion, and precisely by means of religion, is spirit" (in *Hegel, Hinrichs, and Schleiermacher on Feeling and Reason in Religion, the texts of their 1821-22 debate*, ed. and tr. Eric von der Luft, [Lewiston/Queenston: Edwin Mellen, 1987], p. 260). The gulf which yawns here is unbridgeable.

still too modern, because of his "specification of the place." Can one draw a clear line of demarcation between "relation" and "foundation"? Does not the landing field already determine in part the nature and size of the objects which will land there? Did not Schleiermacher, with his starting point in the modern system of coordinates, already proceed from assumptions which were alien or even hostile to the Christian faith? These questions, which beset our theologizing to this day, could, as far as Schleiermacher was concerned, only be answered in a discussion of the content of the themes of the faith. The answer one gets in each case depends on the kind of person, Christian, or theologian one is.

I wanted initially to title this chapter "From the Younger to the Older Schleiermacher." I discovered, however, that between the *Speeches* and *The Christian Faith* no real change had taken place. Then I chose as the title "Schleiermacher's Point of View," precisely to bring out the consistency of his vision. But I also had to drop that idea because it would suggest a lack of movement in Schleiermacher. The present title speaks of Schleiermacher's *direction*. As a theologian he had a distinct base and goal *(Woher und Wohin)*. The base was the modernity which he totally affirmed. The goal was redemption in Christ, a subject which in his own time he wanted to express in all its fullness. Throughout his lifetime he was on his way from that base to this goal. But he was so strongly bound up with his base that it is questionable whether he really reached his goal.

SCHLEIERMACHER AND BARTH

At this point the obvious thing to do would be to contrast Schleiermacher and Barth as the great antipodes. I cannot do that, however, because, still less than Barth, can I see them as opposites. A great many things could be written about their similarities. Both take their point of departure in John 1:14. Both want to be philosophical dilettantes and eclectics. Both resist the influences of metaphysics and the natural sciences. The object-relatedness of the faith is a concern of both. Both testify to the impossibility of grounding faith in humanity. In their methods both take their cue from Anselm's dictum: "For I do not seek to understand in order that I may believe, but I believe in order that I may understand" *(Neque enim quaero intelligere ut credam, sed credo ut intelligam)*, which Schleiermacher used as a motto for *The Christian Faith* and to which Barth devoted his study *Fides Quaerens Intellectum* (1931) as the methodological basis for his *Church Dogmatics*. Both men wrote a Dogmatics which is at the same time Christocentric and churchly. Both toyed with the idea of structuring their work very differently. Schleiermacher would have liked to dispense with the Introduction and start with the revelation in Christ. He even says beforehand "that sooner or later someone will come who will be in a far more advantageous position to bring the project to a happy and successful conclusion."[35] And Barth, were he to do it a second time, would have structured his theology in terms of the Holy Spirit, "a theology of which Schleiermacher was scarcely conscious, but which might actually have been the legitimate concern dominating even his theological activity."[36] In my opinion they were both in motion from the same base *(Woher)* to the same goal *(Wohin)* (as will be further explained below in the chapter on Barth).

It is only from within this commonality of concern that one can also see the great difference between them. Schleiermacher, on the one hand, was ever conscious of his base and kept looking back to see if he was still in touch with it. Barth, on the other hand, resolutely turned away from his base in order really to reach his goal. Both had to pay a price. It would be natural now to relate the two in some "complementary" fashion and seek to be instructed by Barth's kerygmatic concerns and by Schleiermacher's pastoral and missionary interests. But that would be too simple. Schleiermacher was barely able to maintain the link with the *Lebensgefühl* of the modern period—for the sake of his message he had philosophically distanced himself too far from it. Barth in no way gave up that link; for that he had consciously or unconsciously (as we will see later) incorporated too many elements of his own time in his interpretation of the word of God. Of course, there remains a big difference between them, a difference comparable to that, for example, between Barth and Tillich. In my view Schleiermacher distinguished himself from Tillich by the fact that he had a deeper grasp of the problems involved than Tillich did with his question and response schematism. Hence in Schleiermacher Barth was able to recognize the depth of his own struggle.

It is no accident that suddenly we have moved from Schleiermacher to our own time. As the first to think through so deeply the problems of modern theology, he is just as up-to-date and relevant for us as he was for his contemporaries. Perhaps we have to say: more relevant. For in his day most theologians had as yet no inkling of what the problems were and could therefore lightheartedly shrug off Schleiermacher's answers. The bigger the blueprint, the longer the time before it takes effect.

35. Second letter to Dr. Lücke, in *On the* Glaubenslehre (n. 17 above), p. 59.

36. Karl Barth, *Theology of Schleiermacher*, p. 278.

CHAPTER IV

From Hegel to the Hegelian Left

HEGEL AS THEOLOGIAN

In his relationship to theology, *Georg Wilhelm Friedrich Hegel* (1770-1831) presents a picture similar to that of Kant, Fichte, and other thinkers of German idealism: He started in theology, never lost sight of it, and especially in his later publications returned expressly to it. According to R. Haym, "Theology had been the cradle of Hegel's philosophy. Its boundaries originally formed the boundaries, and its material originally formed the material, of Hegel's philosophical activity. More than that, his interest in theological matters was essentially religious."[1] The second sentence as a judgment concerning Hegel's subjective religiosity is questionable, but not Haym's more objective conviction: "At no point of the intellectual-spiritual [*geistigen*] movement which began with Kant . . . have we come into such close contact with the immediately theological as we do now in the case of Hegel."[2] Hegel, more than Kant and Fichte, pondered the historical components as an essential element of the Christian faith, and he strove to understand and ground it philosophically. This endeavor is already present in a "Life of Jesus"—properly purged by historical-critical methods—dating from 1795 (written for private use in the spirit of the Enlightenment) and in *Der Geist des Christentums und sein Schicksal*, published in the same year in which Schleiermacher's *Speeches* appeared, written this time under the influence of Schelling and Hölderlin in a Romantic pantheistic spirit.

After this initial venture in theology, Hegel began in 1800, like

1. R. Haym, *Hegel und seine Zeit* (Berlin, 1957), p. 397.
2. Ibid.

Kant and Fichte earlier, his long march through the issues of epistemology. In the *Phenomenology of Mind* (also called *Phenomenology of Spirit*), written within this period, he rid himself of the last Romantic eggshells. The ideas concerning "public religion," developed toward the end of that book, later returned in ripened form in his *Lectures on the Philosophy of Religion*, which date from the period of his Berlin professorate. In this period, which covers mainly the second decade of the nineteenth century, Hegel pursued with greater sharpness of observation and more wisdom than before (as far as his system allowed) the concrete realizations of the Idea in nature and history. By this nonspeculative, rather empirical side of his philosophical activity, he himself already paved the way for the "realism" of the young Hegelians. His deepest passion, after all, was to ground the oneness of reality in thought. Also, Fichte's non-Ego, nature, the course of history—they must all be absolutely understood as expressions of the creative Reason in its dialectical movement. That was a colossal and splendid struggle. Hegel believed he would finally succeed in understanding and describing the entire range of multidimensional reality, with its many contradictions, in its ultimate rational unity. In this he believed he was not only bringing philosophy but also theology to its consummation: the insight of the rational omnipresence of God.

From his "Foreword to Hinrichs' Philosophy of Religion" (1822), one can see how Hegel defined his place in the development of theology. There he opposed the predominance of the intellect in the domain of religion as he found it in theological scholasticism, or supernaturalism, and in the Enlightenment; in the end this predominance leads to agnosticism and atheism. With equal sharpness he rejected the predominance of feeling, which can never lead to any objectivity (he mistakenly attributed this notion to Schleiermacher).[3] One should strive for objectivity, not on the level of the understanding but on that of reason. Indeed, God has become manifest, and the Spirit granted to the church does lead into all truth, "just that spirit which, because it is spirit, is not sensuousness and feeling, not a mental imagining of something sensuous, but rather, thinking, knowing, cognizing; and because it is the divine Holy Spirit, is only the thinking, knowing and cognizing of God."[4]

The implications of this statement may be found in his *Lectures on the Philosophy of Religion*, particularly in the passage which deals with

3. See the veiled attack noted in Chapter 3 above, n. 34.
4. Hegel's "Foreword," in *Hegel, Hinrichs, and Schleiermacher on Feeling and Reason in Religion,* ed. Eric von der Luft (Lewiston/Queenston: Edwin Mellen, 1987), p. 267.

the eternal Son of God and the way the historical Jesus relates to him.[5] Already in the *Phenomenology of Mind* Hegel found in the doctrines of the Incarnation and the Trinity—doctrines with which the Enlightenment and until that time also idealism hardly knew what to do—the key to an understanding of the Christian faith and to truth in general. This understanding begins with the doctrine of the Incarnation: in Jesus Christ we are confronted by the unity of divine and human reason. However, Hegel does not wish, in monophysite fashion, to deify redemptive history. One can also view Jesus as a human being. In his teaching we hear the call to turn from the finite to the kingdom of God, that is, that which is universal. This human view of Christ, however, needs completion "through the representation of the divine Idea in his life and fate." Not until the death of Christ is his teaching actualized. In it begins "the reversal of consciousness" (p. 215); "external comprehension" is replaced by "contemplation with the Spirit." Now one no longer sees Jesus in his human finitude; "according to the higher mode of contemplation, the divine nature has been revealed in Christ" (p. 216). Here one sees what God is in and for himself, in his tri-unity, "in which the universal places itself over against itself and therein remains identical with itself" (p. 216). But how can a human—all-too-human—death have so much metaphysical content? Because it is the death of God! But can God die? "The process does not come to a halt at this point; rather, a reversal takes place: God . . . maintains himself in this process, and the latter is only the death of death" (p. 212). This death is "the negation of negation." "The monstrous unification of these absolute extremes is love itself" (p. 202). "Sacrifice means the sublation of natural-ness and other-being" (p. 221). "Through death God has reconciled the world and has reconciled himself externally with himself. This coming back [from estrangement] is his return to himself, and thereby he is Spirit. The third moment, accordingly, is that Christ has risen. Negation is thereby overcome, and the negation of negation is thus a moment of the divine nature. This Son is raised up to the right hand of God" (p. 211). "The reconciliation believed in as being in Christ has no meaning if God is not known as the triune God, if it is not recognized that he exists, but precisely as the other, as self-distinguishing, so that this other is God himself, having implicitly the divine nature in it, and that the sublation of this difference, this other-being, and the return of love, are Spirit" (p. 220).

5. The quotations are from *The Christian Religion, Lectures on the Philosophy of Religion, Part III: The Revelatory, Consummate, Absolute Religion*, ch. IV: "Incarnation and Reconciliation," esp. section 3: "The Passion and Resurrection of Christ," ed. and tr. Peter C. Hodgson, based on the edition by Georg Lasson (Missoula, MT: Scholars Press, 1979).

Here arises the question concerning the relationship between the Universal Idea and the concrete history of Christ. Does one read the Idea from this history? Or, conversely, does one interpret the history in the light of the Idea? It would appear that Hegel tried to hold both trains of thought together. He linked them by separating them, that is, by letting them play themselves out on two different levels. Religious reality is the penultimate stage through which absolute reason passes. Here the Spirit "appears" in historical fact. Jesus really lived and really died. "What must still be added is the return contained herein [of the divine Idea to itself] as a perceptible consummation. With regard to this, I need only to recall the well-known form of this perception: it is the resurrection and ascension. This exaltation [of Christ], like everything that precedes it, has appeared for immediate consciousness in the mode of actuality" (p. 207). This history of redemption in its nonrecurring uniqueness is a reality.

This reality, however, only applies to and operates on the level of sensible representation. For that reason Hegel concluded his reflections on the kingdom of the Son with these words: "This is the presentation of the second [moment of the] Idea, the Idea in appearance, the eternal Idea as it has become [available] for the immediate certainty of man, i.e., as it has appeared. In order that it could become a certainty for man, it had to be a sensible certainty, which however at the same time passes over into spiritual consciousness, and likewise is converted into the immediately sensible, but in such a way that one sees in it the movement and history of God, the life that God himself is" (p. 221).

The historical is a necessary transitional phase in the development of the human race. But it must pass over into a higher destiny and be "sublated"[6] into pure concept. We witness this transition from the domain of sensible representation to the domain of comprehension where the kingdom of the Son emerges as the way to the kingdom of the Spirit, that is, to the formation of the community. "Thus sensible representation includes [the image of] the *return* [of Christ], which essentially is an absolute turning back. But then the transition from externality to internality receives—a Comforter, who can come only when sensible history in its immediacy has passed by. This, accordingly, is the point of for-

---

6. German *aufheben; Aufhebung:* annul, sublate, annulment, sublation (when the double meaning of "annulment *and* preservation or elevation" is clearly intended, the translation uses "sublate," from Lat. *sublatio,* which contains the same double meaning). (From the Glossary in *The Christian Religion* [Missoula, MT: Scholars Press, 1979], p. XXXIII.)—TRANS.

mation of the community; it is the third point, the Spirit" (p. 214). The Spirit guides human beings out of the world of the historical into the truth, truth in the form of the eternal fixity of concept.

Thus the truth of history is the non- and supra-historical, which constitutes its internal side. Hegel therefore considered that "finitude, human nature, and humiliation are posited as something alien to Christ, as they are to him who is strictly God." "This finitude, however, in its being-for-self against God, is evil, something alien to God. But he has taken it upon himself in order to put it to death by his death" (p. 213). "Finitude . . . is a moment in himself, although to be sure a disappearing moment" (p. 220).

One wonders whether in the end Hegel's monism is a dualism of God and the historical world of human beings after all. In Hegel one can find the synthesis of Idea and history but, equally, the depreciation of the finite and its permanent alienation from the Idea. Certainly no one ever made a grander and more comprehensive attempt to capture conceptually the manifold unity of reality than Hegel did with his dialectic. Still, he was not able either to bring together "the rose and the cross"— reason and the recalcitrant reality which reason needs for its actualization—in a genuine synthesis.[7] Also by this failure Hegel himself paved the way toward the Hegelian left and thus to the victory of empiricism over idealism.

THE OPPONENTS: HEGEL AND SCHLEIERMACHER

What about the meaning of these ideas for theology? One is impressed by the apparently or really tireless and organic way in which Hegel designates a place in his system for grand Christian notions like Incarnation, cross, reconciliation, glorification, Spirit, church, and Trinity. Still, Schleiermacher, Hegel's great theological contemporary and fellow townsman, could only read Hegel's thoughts with the utmost aversion. This aversion was mutual and went so far that they were never able to talk with each other face-to-face. Readers had to guess who was meant when they alluded to each other in print.

In his second letter to Dr. Lücke Schleiermacher mentions "speculative theology" as the false alternative to "Ebionitism" (mentioned just before; we would say: theological liberalism). He clearly

---

7. I am referring here in particular to the results of Sander Griffioen's study *De Roos en het Kruis* (Assen, 1976), the evaluation of finitude in Hegel's later thought.

wants to pillory Hegelianism as modern gnosticism. At first, however, he seems to find it attractive. "When I read that this unity of God with man is manifest and real as an actuality in the person of Jesus, I think that it can be a beautiful and true expression of our faith. But when I read that the certitude of this truth is vested in the concept of the idea of God and man, or in knowledge, then, with all due respect to the profundity of this speculation, I must reiterate that I cannot acknowledge that this truth grounds the certainty of my faith. . . . But I could never confess that my faith in Christ is derived from knowledge or philosophy, be it this philosophy or any other."[8] That would be a kind of intellectualism which would subject religion to philosophy and cancel out the independence of the faith as a proper source of knowledge. He (Hegel) threatens the church with "a contrast between esoteric and exoteric teaching," a gulf between those who know and those who "only" believe.

Actually, from the vantage point of reason, Hegel could view religion, considered as a human mode of existence, as the faith "by which" *(fides qua),* only as a preliminary stage to the philosophical mode; only its intellectual components *(fides quae)* possess rational relevance and have it only to the extent that they express the timeless Idea and leave history behind as a disappearing husk.

In his theology Schleiermacher attempted to secure the uniqueness of faith; Hegel sought to embed the faith in the cosmic movement of reason. Claude Welch describes this contrast, one that arises again and again in the history of modern theology, as follows: "Can theology be sustained as a truly independent enterprise, either on the basis of revelation or of feeling, without becoming simply discrete and isolated from the generality of human culture? Or can theology be sustained as a claim to universal truth without being finally subordinate to the other sciences and thus losing its own integrity?"[9] In Hegel's eyes the disjunction seems to have looked different still. Not only did he regard Schleiermacher's "feeling of absolute dependence" as the abandonment of any claim to objectivity (which was a misunderstanding), but he also saw in the word *dependence* the abandonment of that which is most essential and highest in humanity: the free, independent spirit. "Spirit, on the contrary, has in religion its liberation and the feeling of its divine freedom; only free spirit has religion or can have religion. What is constrained in religion is the natural feeling of the heart, particular subjectivity; what is liberated in

8. See H. Bolli, *Schleiermacher-Auswahl,* pp. 62-63.
9. C. Welch, *Protestant Thought in the Nineteenth Century* (New Haven: Yale University Press, 1972), 1:107.

religion, and precisely by means of religion, is spirit [or, in that way comes into being, is the Spirit]."[10]

In these words Hegel, in my opinion, probed the contrast more deeply than Schleiermacher with his repudiation of gnosticism. What divided the two thinkers from the beginning and forever was their respective understanding of the essence of the human spirit. For Hegel the spirit is the divine, autonomous, creative, "masculine" principle. For Schleiermacher, as for Hamann, the word *vernunft* (reason) is derived from *vernehmen* (perceive); it is therefore inherently human, related to that which lies beyond itself, receptive, "feminine" (which may be why Schleiermacher regretted not having been born a woman). For Hegel, the highest attribute of the world and of human beings is freedom; for Schleiermacher, it is dependence.

Still, the deepest theological passion of both is the same. Schleiermacher attempted to save intellectual culture from the agnosticism which threatened it after Kant and the Enlightenment; and against the ascendancy of the intellect and of feeling which leads to atheism or subjectivism, Hegel wanted to let the vocable "God" shine forth again with a new and sparkling rational objectivity. The philosophy of intellect does not allow God to be lifted up, "without any predicates or properties, . . . into the *otherworldly realm* of knowledge, or rather brought down to contentlessness."[11]

With regard to Hegel's concept of God Hirsch correctly states: "In this perspective Hegel appears as one who resisted the threatening collapse of the knowledge of God, if not of faith in God, in the realm of the truth-consciousness of the West."[12] Precisely the same can be said of Schleiermacher. However, in the areas on which the two agree lies also their much larger disagreement. Here one has to make an important choice. For the Christian faith the way of Hegel has been blocked by Genesis 3. His pupil Heine already saw this clearly when he spoke of the snake in Paradise as "that little private tutoress, who lectured on Hegelian philosophy six thousand years before Hegel's birth."[13]

---

10. From the "Foreword" to Hinrichs's philosophy of religion, in *Hegel, Hinrichs and Schleiermacher on Feeling and Reason in Religion*, ed. Eric von der Luft (Lewiston/Queenston: Edwin Mellen, 1987), p. 260.

11. Ibid., p. 253.

12. E. Hirsch, *Geschichte der neuern evangelischen Theologie*, 5:242.

13. In the preface to the 2nd German ed. of Heine's *Religion and Philosophy in Germany*, tr. John Snodgrass (Boston: Beacon, 1959), p. 13.

THE REVOLT OF CONCRETE REALITY

In Hegel's heyday, the 1820s in Berlin, no one could have suspected how close the collapse of idealism actually was, or how in fact Hegel's own thinking would bring it about. This collapse was totally unexpected and came shortly after Hegel's death. Having initially arisen in the form of a clash within the school of Hegel, it has to this day retained a mysterious quality. How was it possible that this unparalleled flowering of German idealism should so suddenly fade and die?

To answer that question I shall attempt to bring together a few essential factors. After Kant, the Achilles' heel of German idealism must be judged to be its depreciation of the phenomenal world. Truth was sought in realms beyond this world. More than other idealistic thinkers, Hegel tried to let the phenomenal world participate in the truth of reason. Still, he did not succeed in bringing about a genuine synthesis between the two. We illustrated this point with the example of his treatment of the kingdom of the Son. The reality of nature and history remains the cross which opposes the rose (of reason). It remains negation, and finds its rational significance only in the fact that reason actualizes itself through the negation of this negation.

The moment had to come in which concrete reality would avenge itself on the Idea on account of this depreciation. Impulses in this direction came partly, and I may say first of all, from without. They were, on the one hand, of a political nature: the time of high ideals, starting from the French Revolution, through the national revival, and extending to the Holy Alliance, had ended with the July revolution in Paris (1830). The cross of reality proved stronger than the rose of the Idea. In addition there was the impulse of the rapid and sensational development of the natural sciences and, in its wake, that of technology and of the first industrial revolution. The Idea simply bore no relationship to that newly created world of phenomena. Before the latter's objective might the Idea had to fade away. Thus a fundamental shift in the European sense of life *(Lebensgefühl)* occurred. Suddenly, from many directions, the question was posed whether the emperor of the absolute Idea had any clothes on. The conviction spread rapidly that the little "worm" called man could not possibly bear the burden of deification.

Paired with these external impulses came the criticism of Hegel's system from within. First of all, in the domain of logic: Can the transition from the conceptual to the many-sided real world of phenomena ever be thought and made convincing? Does consciousness actually condition being, or is the reverse true? If the Absolute appears in no way other than in finite historical forms, is it the Absolute itself that appears? Is what we call *Spirit (Geist)* more than the spirit of the times *(Zeitgeist)*? Second, from the domain of ethics: Now that the Idea has come altogether to itself in Hegel, what is left to us? Hegel himself was markedly conservative. Nevertheless, is all of reality actually as rational as it is claimed in Hegel's much-quoted saying in the preface to his philosophy of law ("What is rational is real and what is real is rational")? However Hegel may have meant this statement (probably only as an incidental tautology), now another concept of reality arose, one that was altogether oriented to sense perception. When Feuerbach writes in the preface to *The Essence of Christianity* (1841), "The method is totally objective—the method of analytical chemistry," one senses with the utmost clarity how thoroughly the point of view and language in relation to reality have changed. It is clear that observation and perception reveal something quite different from "the rule of reason." The world is full of unreason and antireason. Hence it is not enough to explain the world; the world must be changed (Marx).

Thus thought acquires a revolutionary-ethical tendency. This it already had from Hegel, as the reverse of the conservative aspect of the system. The dialectical movement of the Idea also implies a never-ending negation of the existing world, a world which ever evoked its own antithesis. This revolutionary element fascinated the young Hegelians far more than the conservative element, which Hegel himself emphasized. Thus it had to happen that Hegel's synthesis, in the light of advancing history, sank to the level of a thesis.[14]

Once again, in the back-and-forth movement which was so characteristic of the spiritual history of Europe, the pendulum fell back, this time from idealism to empiricism. We know this movement from the contrasting pairs: realism-nominalism, Bacon-Descartes, Hume-Kant, existentialism-structuralism, Neo-Marxism–critical rationalism, and so forth. Often the alternatives stand alongside one another. After Hegel's death, however, an abrupt shift occurred. "Our philosophical revolution is concluded; Hegel has closed its great circle."[15]

THE SHIFT TO ATHEISM

Among the young Hegelians the shift—from a theological point of view —meant a turning to atheism. If "being" is reflected in "consciousness"

14. An excellent initiation to the problems referred to here is furnished by K. Löwith in the introduction to his textbook *Die Hegelsche Linke* (Stuttgart: 1962), pp. 7-38.

15. Heine, *Religion and Philosophy in Germany,* p. 156.

and not vice versa, then man created God in his own image and not vice versa (Feuerbach). Already in Kant and especially in Fichte we perceived the atheistic shadow cast by idealistic thought, a shadow which both thinkers tried energetically to shake off.[16] Hegel believed he had driven this shadow away forever. The Hegelian left, however, discovered in this system in particular the tendency toward atheism. Initially a right-wing Hegelian Christian, Bruno Bauer wrote the anonymous work "The Trumpets of the Last Judgment. Concerning Hegel, the Atheists, and Anti-Christ" (1841) after his conversion to the Hegelian left.[17] Under the mask of a disturbed pietistic theologian, he demonstrates that one can understand Hegel correctly only if one understands him as an atheist. In Hegel he finds "that notion of religion, according to which the religious relationship is nothing but an inner relationship of the consciousness of the self to itself and all those powers which, as substance or as absolute Idea, seem to be distinct from self-consciousness, are nothing but components of it objectivized in the religious imagination."[18] "It is the Absolute Spirit which in finite spirits relates itself to itself, . . . in short, religion is the self-consciousness of the Absolute Spirit."[19] "For philosophy God is dead and only the 'I' as self-consciousness, 'as self placed in opposition to the self-as-such,' only the 'I' lives, creates, works, and is All."[20]

This perspective once again makes us aware how close to each other the hostile brothers, panentheism and atheism, are and how easily the boundaries between the two are crossed. German idealism built a wall between the two, a wall which nevertheless, after a few decades, collapsed. In this movement of thought "God" finally becomes a redundancy. The statement "God is dead," an antithetical truth of transition in Hegel, Bauer, Feuerbach, Marx, and others, became the ultimate truth to

16. If I do not take account, either here or earlier, of Friedrich Wilhelm Joseph Schelling (1775-1854) as the fourth member of the alliance of great German idealists, it is not because, like E. Hirsch (*Geschichte der neuern evangelischen Theologie,* 5:274), I regard him as insignificant and fantastic but only because, with his Romantic-Christian theosophy, he does not fit, in method or content, into the framework of this book. He had left the presuppositions of modern thought (after the Enlightenment) behind him so soon and so thoroughly that he has no place in the tradition we have sketched. From some other point of view, however, he could be very exciting for theology, as one sees, for example, in Paul Tillich.

17. K. Löwith provides a new edition in *Die Hegelsche Linke* (Stuttgart: 1962), pp. 123-225.

18. Ibid., p. 151.

19. Ibid., p. 158.

20. Ibid., p. 169.

which idealistic thought was relentlessly driven. When reason is conceived as self-positing and creative, either it is God himself or it replaces God. These seemingly opposite positions nevertheless yield the same results because they share the same origin. Only Kant stands apart from this movement. The atheistic disciples could do as little with him as their idealistic seniors. Both rejected the way in which Kant restricted reason to the domain between God and the spatiotemporal world. Kant was forgotten; he had to wait.

CHAPTER V

The Aftereffects of Idealism in Theology

Under the influence of idealism at its height, German Protestant theology began to develop in a number of different directions. One can say in general that in European theology, after the relative sterility of the preceding century, the nineteenth century became an epoch of flourishing diversity. In large measure theology owed this new advance to idealistic thought, which in fact seemed to offer a new perspective on religion and on the fundamental truth of Christianity. Still, theology could not and would not unreservedly subscribe to the starting point of idealism: the fusion and continuity of divine and human reason. If theology had adopted this starting point, it would have done violence to its own object.

CONFESSIONALISM AND LIBERALISM

For many theologians the inspiration of idealism meant solely the freedom to address themselves to the Christian tradition with a new language. Out of this tendency came the so-called confessionalism. For this school, idealistic thought was a springboard to be left behind as soon as possible. It often turned sharply against "pantheism," "rationalism," "optimism," etc., so that it seemed to deny or misjudge its connection with this "worldly" mode of thought. Greater historical distance was needed to discover how deeply confessionalism was also influenced by the spirit of the time (*Zeitgeist*).

The purpose of this book prevents us from giving further consideration to the phenomenon of confessionalism. This does not mean that we regard it as unimportant. On the contrary, we view the theology of confessionalism as an alternative to be taken seriously in the period after the Enlightenment. Here, however, we are concerned with those movements in theology for which the *Zeitgeist* was not just a springboard but a challenge with which they constantly had to grapple. That struggle may also have been true for many confessionalists; but confessional theology as such left the challenge behind as a temptation to which it could only relate polemically. For confessional theology the answers were essentially given already; other theologians struggled in the new situation to develop new answers.

Two theological points of view were dominant here. Recall now the quotation from Claude Welch in the previous chapter: One could either, in company with Hegel, look in Christianity for the truth of universal reason (and run the risk of subordinating the gospel to the spirit of culture [*Kulturgeist*]), or one could join Schleiermacher in proceeding from the independent source and nature of the gospel (and run the danger of isolating the gospel from the culture). This contrast led to two distinct theological schools. Since the one attempted to incorporate also the legitimate viewpoints of the other, however, the boundaries between them were not easy to delineate, and in the course of advancing developments they tended increasingly to be watered down. If one could nevertheless make a lasting distinction between the two movements it is that the Hegelian school was representative of liberalism, whereas the school of Schleiermacher, as mediating theology, was closer to classical orthodoxy and more ecclesiastically oriented.

The term "Hegelian school" is usually reserved in theology for a tradition whose beginning and end are marked, respectively, by the names Daub and Pfleiderer. "Speculative" viewpoints were increasingly combined in it with historical viewpoints as well as with the insights of the psychology of religion. Lipsius, usually categorized as belonging to this tradition, was much more oriented to Schleiermacher than to Hegel. But not only the scientific *Zeitgeist* made it impossible simply to follow in the footsteps of Hegel;[1] it is already clear in the case of Daub and Marheineke that the gospel itself also poses a boundary. These theologians, who were unable to adopt Hegel's immanence-thought, confronted it with the idea of "the personality of God." In theology one could not dialectically "sublate" evil as Hegel had done. Also, one had to give greater emphasis to (redemptive) history. The greatest thinker among them, the Swiss *Aloys Emanuel Biedermann* (1819-1885), was unable to view religion as Hegel had done, as the lower knowledge level of "imaginative repre-

---

1. Especially to be mentioned here is A. Trendelenburg, *Logische Untersuchungen*, 2 vols. (Berlin, 1840). This immanent critique of Hegel exerted much influence in theological circles.

sentation," nor to regard it as pure knowledge. At this central point he had to concur with Schleiermacher. But even so the liberal school was suspected by the church of selling the gospel out to modernity. For a growing number of theologians it offered too weak a compromise in both directions. When after 1870 the sun of Ritschl ascended, the stars of liberalism soon grew faint.

THE THEOLOGY OF MEDIATION

A second way of coming to terms with the idealistic *Lebensgefühl* of that day was represented by the so-called theology of mediation, which had its roots in Schleiermacher. In 1827 the theological journal *Theologische Studien und Kritiken* was founded by students and followers of Schleiermacher, among them G. Ch. F. Lücke (the recipient and publisher of the *Two Letters to Dr. Lücke*),[2] C. I. Nitzsch, and others. For over a hundred years the journal exerted much influence in theology and in the church. The catchword mediation was not coined by Schleiermacher, however; it comes from Hegel. In a programmatic article C. Ullmann defined the term as follows: "Mediation is the scientifically executed reduction of relative contrasts to their original unity; as a result an inner reconciliation and a higher standpoint is achieved in which the contrasts are resolved. The resulting scientific state which proceeds from this mediation is the true and sound middle."[3] "This lies in the nature of the case: synthesis ever follows thesis and antithesis; atomistic dispersion ever evokes the need for a gathering in the center."[4] One would think that such a methodological stance would have to lead directly to a Hegelian theology. Though at times the reader may be touching the hands of Hegel —covered with dialectical hair—the voice is nonetheless that of Schleiermacher. This confluence of two language systems only proves that the radicalism of the predecessors had succumbed to eclecticism. At any rate, despite all its vitality, it was a time of epigones.

What the legacy of Schleiermacher came down to may be established from the leading systematic theology of this school, Nitzsch's *System der christlichen Lehre*. Whereas Luther is mentioned in it five times,

---

2. See *On the* Glaubenslehre: *Two Letters to Dr. Lücke,* tr. James Duke and Francis Fiorenza (Chico, CA: Scholars Press, 1981).

3. C. Ullmann, "Ueber Partei und Schule, Gegensätze und deren Vermittelung," *Theologische Studien und Kritiken* 9/1 (1836) 5-61; the quotation is from p. 41.

4. Ibid., p. 45.

and Calvin eight times, Schleiermacher's name occurs thirty-four times. It makes clear that, in method and content, Nitzsch largely followed the anthropologizing tendency of Schleiermacher. But often, as for example in the notion of revelation and in Christology, he stopped where the master went further. Nitzsch tended to remain close to the classical tradition. Characteristic is his treatment of the Virgin Birth, where, partly at least, he follows the line of Schleiermacher.[5] Schleiermacher's kinship with the classical tradition is overemphasized, while his critical and especially his historical-critical lines of thought are soft-pedaled or not considered at all. What fascinated the theologians of mediation was how he theologically affirmed the human dimension (das Humanum), the great concern of the modern period, and accorded it a spacious place in his epistemology and Christology. As Ullmann put it: "[Jesus Christ] is, in the highest sense, the true center between deity and humanity. . . . It is the task of science to develop, unstintingly and correctly, all the elements which lie in this divine-human appearance of Christ, and if it does this, it will have the truth which at its best lies in the middle."[6]

The theology of mediation was a very productive and many-sided movement, one concerning which it is hardly possible to render an unambiguous judgment. If one views it from Schleiermacher's perspective, it is clear that it shared his lifelong concern: "Shall the tangle of history so unravel that Christianity becomes identified with barbarism and science with unbelief?" Its representatives did everything within their power to guard against a hopeless estrangement between the Christian faith and modern, immanentistic, rational thought. Still, the enormous tension, the tension generated by Schleiermacher's struggle with the cultured despisers of religion, was no longer there. Theological thought had become shallower, more cautious and conservative. One seldom senses a genuine relationship to the world. The focus is much more on things within the church. Idealism had become domesticated and been brought under ecclesiastical control.

From this point of view one is inclined to seek the significance of the mediating movement and its energetic activities as an ecclesiastical modality. Part of its program, in fact, was the effort to mediate between theology and the church. It was precisely in that respect that its accomplishments were astonishing. Almost all its protagonists occupied important and influential posts in the church. For almost half a century, with their clear and practically focused ideology, they were the com-

5. C. I. Nitzsch, *System der Christlichen Lehre* (Bonn: A. Marcus, 1829); the improved and enlarged edition is of 1851. Cf. esp. pp. 67, 262-63, 268.
6. Ullmann, *Theologische Studien und Kritiken* 9/1 (1836) 58.

petent church leaders who were able to prevent the church from falling apart into confessionalism and liberalism.[7] In the area of church union and home missions they were also influential supporters and promoters.

The question is whether one should therefore restrict their originality and productiveness to the realm of practical churchmanship; certainly from the perspective of this book that would not be very fruitful. Our question is whether, and if so, how, these theologians established a relationship between the gospel and the secularized culture of their day. One can, from the start, answer that question in the negative: the intellectual world of that day paid as little, or less, attention to this movement as to its "father" Schleiermacher. The extent to which the reason for that lay in Schleiermacher himself or in the theology of mediation can only be discussed later. One can also give a more positive answer, however: this theology, preaching, and teaching definitely enabled many younger theologians and members of the church intelligentsia at one and the same time to participate in their culture and to be Christians with a good conscience: after all, the gospel also speaks of "humanity," organism, development, spirit, idea, history, etc. Granted, the theology of mediation hardly exerted any challenging or recruiting influence externally, but it definitely had a saving influence internally (the same thing can also be said of liberal theology, though to a lesser extent).

One can also state and answer the problem in a different way: from the beginning the gospel was handed down in a variety of forms: the Pauline, the Jamesian, the Johannine, the Lukan, etc. We know that these distinctions relate to the diverse situations, thought-worlds, problems, and language of the people addressed in each case. The mediating theologians, too, became Greeks to the Greeks — which was no great sacrifice: they were the children of their own time — without trying to conceal the trans- and anti-idealistic elements of the gospel. For them the God-man Jesus Christ was the only One in whom the ideal of the philosophy of the day, namely, the unity of idea and reality, was fulfilled. In general, they were more successful in maintaining this double focus than the Hegelians and liberals. But "more" does not mean they actually succeeded. It remains a question whether in the idealistic garments in which they dressed the gospel, the liberating heart of it actually came to expression. And if it did not, or not sufficiently, could they have done better at the time? These are the questions which will occupy us

7. One gets a good insight into the church ideals and problems of the mediation theologians from C. Ullmann, "Vierzig Sätze, die theologische Lehrfreiheit innerhalb der evangelisch-protestantischen Kirche betreffend," *Theologische Studien und Kritiken* 16/1 (1843) 7-35.

throughout the book. At the same time one must ask: Did they do justice to the deepest impulses and highest ideals of their own time? We
shall come back to this question later.

THE TWO DIRECTIONS: ROTHE AND DORNER

In the case of so diverse and differentiated a movement as the theology
of mediation one can hardly give wholesale answers. One has to question
each of the theologians individually. How different the answers may then
turn out to be can best be shown in the positions of the two greatest theologians produced by this movement: *Richard Rothe* (1799-1867) and *Isaak
August Dorner* (1809-1884). Rothe must probably be regarded as the
greatest systematician among his theological allies, and at the same time,
more than the others, sensitive to the spirit of modern secularism.[8] He
sought to claim this entire world for Christ. His passion for a cosmic
philosophia sacra brought him in closer proximity to Hegel than to Schleiermacher. He was emphatically a speculative idealist. At the same time, by
his theory of "pure matter" as the creative basis of "stages growing exclusively out of each other," he anticipated Darwin's theory and the theological discussion of it. He managed theologically to connect the naturalistic
viewpoint with the teleological in a grand way, an achievement which
brings to mind the work of Teilhard de Chardin. With his well-known
ideas about the desacralization and socialization of the gospel and about
the provisionality of the church, and with his struggle against the attempt
to bring life under ecclesiastical control, he seems rather to belong to our
own century than to the previous one. I cannot possibly, as Barth did, regard him as "an end-point, not to say a cul-de-sac."[9]

I can more easily concur with Barth's opening words in his essay
on Dorner, "who," writes Barth, "while standing amidst the problems of
the nineteenth century, points beyond them in his contribution to theological method and poses new questions to us by the new answers that
he gives."[10] In distinction from Rothe, Dorner is not the man of cultural

---

8. Rothe's principal and comprehensive work, *Die Theologische Ethik*,
published first in 3 volumes (1845-1848) and posthumously in a new edition in
5 volumes (1869-1871), is a synthesis of philosophy, natural science, dogmatics,
Christian and general ethics. He himself regarded the whole solely as "theology
or more precisely as theosophy" (2nd ed., 1:XVIII).

9. K. Barth, *Protestant Theology in the Nineteenth Century* (Valley Forge,
PA: Judson, 1973), p. 606.

10. Ibid., p. 577.

breadth but of evangelical depth.[11] He furnished dogmatics with a number of essential new stimuli. His theory of the relationship of the "absolute personality" of God as holy love to the Trinity and its attributes (cf. esp. his fresh development of the doctrine of the immutability of God), his teaching of the impersonal (anhypostatic) humanity of Christ and its historical development, and of Christ as the central individual of the human race—these and other lines of thought, when stripped of their idealistic clothing, remained relevant for succeeding generations right into the present.

In the difference between Rothe and Dorner we rediscover the polarity we found first between Hegel and Schleiermacher and later between the liberals and the theology of mediation. This polarity is fundamental for theology after the Enlightenment. We shall meet it again.

SUDDEN DEMISE

By this time it will be clear that it is hard to furnish a simple characterization of the theology of mediation. The fact that it often turns out to be negative is owing in part to its abrupt decline in the 1870s, when Ritschl conquered the field of theology.[12] Precisely in this and the following decade there still appeared many a mature and comprehensive work from the schools of liberalism and mediation. But they were already outdated on the day of publication.

What explains this sudden demise of the two schools after such a long period of vitality? One can answer: Everything has its day; theological movements are no exception. But why so sudden? Both schools wanted to translate Christian truth into the idiom of modern

11. The recapitulation of his thought appeared shortly before his death in *System der Christlichen Glaubenslehre* (Berlin, 1879; 2nd ed. 1881).

12. A balanced appraisal occurs in H. Stephan and M. Schmidt, *Geschichte der deutschen evangelischen Theologie*, 2nd ed. (Berlin: Töpelmann, 1960), p. 189. These scholars are mistaken, however, when they state: "Its aim was not the conquest of opposites from the vantage point of a new and higher unity but merely mediation." More correct is what occurs a few lines further down: "In the range of their experience, their vision, and their thought, the theologians of mediation were superior to the onesided movements, and accordingly set the highest goal for their theology. But because their creative powers were not equal to the height of that goal, they suffered the tragic fate of mere mediators: to those who did not understand the goal, they seemed to be unclear and vacillating." Cf. also Claude Welch, *Protestant Thought in the Nineteenth Century*, 1:269-91.

consciousness *(Lebensgefühl)*. And for both, this *Lebensgefühl* was un-
questionably the atmosphere created by German idealistic philosophy.
In that regard, however, both were fundamentally wrong. Already
when these schools arose, idealism was close to its demise. Of course,
at the time only a very few (Heine!) saw that with the death of Hegel
and the July revolution a new epoch had begun. But ten, even thirty,
years later matters had hardly changed. Every theology which viewed
itself as timely and up-to-date still related to the thought-world and
cultural climate of idealism. A late idealistic heretic like D. F. Strauss,
accordingly, could remain the main focus of polemics for decades. The
worlds of Feuerbach and Comte, of Marx and Engels, the achievements
of science, technology, and industry, the struggle of the working class,
the "signs of the times" of 1848, and later the German translation of
Darwin's main work (1863)—all these events and influences occurred
out of the hearing range of theological studies and lecture halls. There
were exceptions of course—R. Rothe, for example. But they remained
exceptions because the theologians could not find a point of contact in
the new empiricistic, naturalistic, and atheistic culture of Europe, as
they had found it in the world of idealism.[13] What is said here of theology was generally true of the world of culture and education *(Bil-
dungswelt)* in which the up-and-coming intelligentsia in Germany and
the rest of Europe were educated.

The title of this chapter refers to the aftereffects of idealism. But
seldom did such a "postlude" last so long. I can explain it only from the
circumstance that even "enlightened" members of the educated class
shrank back from this advance of Enlightenment thought. One can
hardly think ill of the theologians for not being more clear-sighted than
other intellectuals. For them atheism was simply a pathological phenomenon. Solidarity with the motives and ideals of culture did not include solidarity with naturalism and atheism but rather excluded it. Behind this attitude lay the conviction that the Christian faith itself bore
not a naturalistic but an idealistic stamp. That is an ancient Christian
legacy which goes back already to the Hellenistic beginnings of church
history. The human race was ever viewed from above, as created after
the image of God (Gen. 1:26-27) but hardly ever from below, as the sec-

---

13. At one point the cultural shift became theologically visible: in the
change of focus from the speculative to the historical, from systematic theology
to historical-critical theology. This shift, however, fit quite well the Hegelian
framework of the relationship between idea and history, as the Tübingen school
of Baur's day proves. Historical developments in theology as such fall outside
the framework of this book.

ond creation account does: as taken from the dust of the earth and related to the animal world (Gen. 2:7, 18ff.). Also, the mandate to exercise dominion over the earth and the powers of nature (Gen. 1:28-29; 2:15; 3:17-19) remained theologically unused. The result was that theologians could not establish a relationship to the new age. Theology and the culture of the Enlightenment, in a long postlude, were allies in a rearguard battle.

RITSCHL: DISCONTINUITY AND CONTINUITY

Albrecht Ritschl was the first to fling a plausible bridge in German theology to the *Lebensgefühl* of realism. Precisely because this "bridge" came so belatedly in the decade of the 1870s, it had an abrupt effect. What many scholars had felt unconsciously came suddenly to the surface: liberal and mediating theology had attempted to relate the gospel to a world that was no longer there. Sharp criticism of the "fathers" set in. The critics were not aware, however, that the same time-bound attitude which separated them from their fathers also united them with their fathers. Both groups sought to make the gospel audible in the modern world. Anyone having that objective must be prepared, as the cultural climate changes, to change also the conceptual apparatus and language of theology. At the same time one must know that, as a result of the dynamics of the modern world, his theological construction will also be obsolete in a few decades. With the modesty produced by this knowledge one can respect the "fathers" and at the same time pursue his own business in his own way.

Ritschl himself had this wisdom. His father had been a well-known cleric in the tradition of mediating theology, and his initial theological orientation (in Bonn) came from C. I. Nitzsch. Next he crossed over to Hegel and the Hegelian school of New Testament at Tübingen, in order, after a decade, as a sober-minded practical theologian, to leave these ranks also. From then on he criticized all inherited directions. At the same time he knew how to value them both historically and scientifically. That was particularly true of the theology of mediation. Ritschl never denied his historical and theological continuity with it. And he was right: as the cultural factors changed, he sought to realize afresh its scientific and ecclesiastical ideals. Hirsch precisely and pointedly expressed it: "At this point Ritschl, viewed from the perspective of the history of theology, is the end of the old and the beginning of a new theology of mediation. His aim was to liberate the theology of mediation both from its speculative and its pietistic presuppositions, and to establish it on a new, positively historical basis, and he largely succeeded."[14]

Does that mean perhaps that "a theology of mediation" is the only legitimate option for theologians who want to remain faithful both to the gospel and to their cultural environment? Or were there alternatives which were overlooked at the time?

---

14. E. Hirsch, *Geschichte der neuern evangelischen Theologie,* 5:558. Cf. also Claude Welch, *Protestant Thought in the Nineteenth Century,* 2:1-30.

CHAPTER VI

Kierkegaard: The Individual

Whether truth is defined more empirically, as the conformity of thought and being, or more idealistically, as the conformity of being with thought, it is, in either case, important carefully to note what is meant by being. And in formulating the answer to this question it is likewise important to take heed lest the knowing spirit be tricked into losing itself in the indeterminate, so that it fantastically becomes a something that no existing human being ever was or can be, a sort of phantom with which the individual occupies himself upon occasion, but without making it clear to himself in terms of dialectical intermediaries how he happens to get into this fantastic realm, what significance being there has for him, and whether the entire activity that goes on out there does not resolve itself into a tautology within a recklessly fantastic venture of thought.

*   *   *   *   *

The fantastic I-am-I is not an identity of the infinite and the finite, since neither the one nor the other is real; it is a fantastic rendezvous in the clouds, an unfruitful embrace, and the relationship of the individual self to this mirage is never indicated.[1]

Who is the author of these two quotations? The student of the period of idealism and post-idealism will not hesitate for a second: we are dealing here with an unmistakable utterance of the Hegelian left, a forceful pro-

---

1. The quotations are taken from Kierkegaard's *Concluding Unscientific Postscript,* tr. D. F. Swenson and Walter Lowrie (Princeton: Princeton University Press, 1944), pp. 169, 176, respectively.

test against the free-floating abstractions of the speculative system, in the name of that which is concrete, in this case of the existing individual who as such finds himself completely outside the universality of the system. The author of these statements must be a thinker "from below," in league with the empirical-scientific and atheistic circles around Feuerbach, Stirner, or Marx.

On the contrary: the author was a Christian, a genuine Lutheran, a theologian: *Søren Kierkegaard* (1813-1855). Still, the association of these statements with the Hegelian left is not wholly mistaken.[2] One should rather say that Kierkegaard was the only theologian who independently helped to give rise to the post-Hegelian movement and who in the process arrived at an independent theological position, a position with which, in his own time and for a long time after, he stood totally alone. It is a question whether that isolation is not permanent, because it is necessarily given with the position itself. Is it perhaps a position that can be held only by individuals? It does, however, present an alternative in the context of the relationship of the Christian faith to post-Enlightenment culture from which, for as long as this period lasts, we cannot detach ourselves.

REVELATION VERSUS HEGELIAN PHILOSOPHY

Kierkegaard's astonishing productivity in barely more than twelve years of writing has manifested itself on so many fronts and in so many forms that we dare not venture a synopsis. It suits our purpose in this book, however, to concentrate on that which he has to say over against Hegel's system as Kierkegaard laid it down particularly in his *Philosophical Fragments*.[3] In this little volume he renders the big decisions relative to the spirit of the times *(Zeitgeist);* and subsequent writings are mostly elaborations of the convictions developed there.

The Hegelian system and the Christian faith, says Kierkegaard,

2. On this point cf. K. Löwith, *Die Hegelsche Linke* (Stuttgart, 1962), Introduction.

3. Often the impression is given that Hegel was Kierkegaard's great and lifelong opponent. That is a serious exaggeration. In fact, Kierkegaard struggled with Hegel especially after 1837 and up until his *Philosophical Fragments* (1844). After that, Hegel's name recedes into the background. By that time, however, as a result of his interaction with Hegel, his message had achieved its clarity and power. Kierkegaard also interacted with Lessing, who played an equally large role in the *Fragments* and an even larger role in the *Postscript*.

are mutually exclusive. Hegelian thought has a profoundly objectivizing tendency: the concrete individual is absent from the system. But that individual is *subject;* as such he lives in "subjectivity," which, accordingly, in Kierkegaard means something different from what it usually means. It is identical with "existence" and "inwardness." By his vocation to exist a person is called out of the world of the universal and away from objectivizing thought. The ethical as well as the religious "stages on life's way" call him to this decision. The result is that opposites arise which cannot be reconciled; Hegel, who wants to mediate between all things, actually has to abolish the essence of human existence. "If our age had not the distinction of simply ignoring the duty of existing, it would be inconceivable that such wisdom as the Hegelian could be regarded as the highest, as maybe it is for esthetic contemplators, but not either for ethical or for religious existers."[4]

In virtue of the nature of his system Hegel left no room for the concrete, the nonnecessary, the individual, "becoming," transitoriness, the moment (as the breaking-in of eternity into time), the "leap" (as a transition from one stage of life into another, a transition not determined by that which preceded). Still, these are the things which constitute reality; Hegel's system operates outside reality.

Part of this criticism could have come from the atheistic post-Hegelians. In Kierkegaard, however, the criticism does not lead to atheism but is grounded in the revelation in Christ which speaks a completely different language from that which Hegel lets it speak in his speculative system. The way Kierkegaard understands the Christian faith, in contrast to Hegel, is sketched briefly but penetratingly in chapters I-IV of the *Philosophical Fragments*. He starts with the "unhappy love" of God: God loves human beings alienated from him, who, being alienated, cannot understand God and his love. This human condition is called "sin." As teacher, God himself had to create the conditions in which he could free us from untruth and open us up to his love. Hence at the same time the teacher must be a redeemer and reconciler. Consequently human beings have to convert. This conversion happens in the "moment" in which one becomes conscious, in sorrow and repentance, of his birth and rebirth. This renewal can only come about as a consequence of the descending movement of the love of God: God the teacher must become the equal of the least of the learners. For that reason he must appear incognito in servant form, "equal to the least through his almighty love." God had to reach humanity through suffering and death. In consequence, human beings face the miracle: they dis-

---

4. *Concluding Unscientific Postscript*, p. 264 note.

cover what they themselves cannot conceive. That is "the paradox of love," the absolutely different, the limit of human thought: a man who is at the same time God.

Here, then, the learner faces the necessity of decision. The sin of his self-love may lead him to a state of being scandalized at the paradox. In this state the paradox is misunderstood and it thrusts humanity from itself. Offended, humanity opts for probability whereas the paradox is the most improbable thing there is. How then is the other possibility realized, namely, that the learner is reconciled with the paradox? That is the "happy passion" of faith. The historical as such cannot arouse faith. It may just as well be the starting point of offense. Only in the paradox of the God-man can one lay hold of the unity of the eternal and the historical; and this paradox is only acknowledged in faith. This faith has nothing to do with one's intelligence or will. It is itself as much a paradox as the paradox with which it enters into a positive and happy relationship. Faith, therefore, is purely a gift received in the "moment" in which the eternal appears in time and by which the learner becomes "contemporaneous" with the teacher. In this contemporaneity, this leap from sinful alienation from God into existence, the historical distance from Jesus, who is now contemporaneous, falls away. In the "moment" the eyewitness has no advantage over those who come later, though the two are also not entirely interchangeable.

Kierkegaard formulated the relationship as follows: "A successor believes, to be sure, on account of the testimony of some contemporary; but only in the same sense as a contemporary believes on account of his immediate sensation and immediate cognition. But no contemporary can believe by virtue of this immediacy alone, and neither can any successor believe solely by virtue of the testimony to which he has access."[5]

Not until after Kierkegaard has given this exposition of the faith does he proceed to discuss Hegel. By this method Kierkegaard makes clear to the reader that revelation is not grounded in speculation but posits itself and the faith from above. In the light of that position he now attacks Hegel's notion of the identity of idea and history, of necessity and becoming. But he undertakes this attack not transcendentally, on the basis of revelation, but in an immanent fashion, in a refined and tireless logical dialectic. (In my opinion this juxtaposition and succession of witness and discussion in Kierkegaard is also for us, in the similar situation in which we find ourselves, exemplary.) Ac-

5. Kierkegaard, *Philosophical Fragments*, tr. D. F. Swenson, rev. Howard V. Hong (Princeton: Princeton University Press, 1962), p. 106.

cording to Kierkegaard, Hegel completely distorted the relationship between revelation and history by his identification of the two. As a result revelation lost its character as paradox; and history was no longer itself when "becoming" was understood as a necessary process. Such a notion rests on an optical illusion: "The past is not necessary, since it came into existence; it did not become necessary by coming into existence (which is a contradiction); still less does it become necessary through someone's apprehension of it. (Distance in time tends to promote an intellectual illusion, just as distance in space provokes a sensory illusion. A contemporary does not perceive the necessity of what comes into existence, but when centuries intervene between the event and the beholder he perceives the necessity, just as distance makes the square tower seem round.)"[6] The anti-Hegelian intent of the *Fragments* was illustrated by the Shakespeare motto: "Better well hung than ill wed."[7] Presumably Kierkegaard meant to say that a risky conflict between revelation and speculative philosophy deserved preference over a false harmony.

SUBJECTIVITY AGAINST CONFESSIONALISM AND MEDIATION

One understands the significance of this conflict if one considers the extent to which the theology of mediation stamped also the life of the church and theology in Copenhagen (Mynster, Martensen). For Kierkegaard, Christianity was not the self-evident datum that should be attuned as much as possible to "the needs and intuitions of the time"; to him precisely his own time was the great threat to true existence and he sought to lead his contemporaries out from under its spell and to the nonself-evident character of faith. This radical repudiation of every attempt at mediation did not mean for Kierkegaard that he should join the ranks of the confessionalists. According to him, in confessionalism the individual was pushed aside just as much by universal and objective truths.

Quite apart from Kierkegaard's important philosophical accomplishments and merits, his witness, considered from the perspective of the history of theology, is already of the highest rank because he chose a

---

6. Ibid., p. 98.

7. This motto stems not from *As You Like It*, as the note suggests, but from *Twelfth Night*, act 1, scene 5, where the Clown says: "Many a good hanging prevents a bad marriage." Presumably Kierkegaard missed the implied obscenity in this statement.

third way: he brought the Christian faith into conflict with the *Zeitgeist*, doing this, however, in the concepts of that time. Having in his language become an idealist to the idealists,[8] he proclaimed to them the faith in a new way so that it no longer appeared to them as something antiquated but as a stumbling block and folly. He did not do this by way of a fresh interpretation of dogma and tradition. He was an orthodox Lutheran and that is all he wanted to be.[9] The new and contemporary dimension consisted in the fact that he focused the whole of revelation on the goal of subjectivity and by that means placed it in a new light. This all-embracing line of vision first occurred in a developed form in Kierkegaard's *Concluding Unscientific Postscript* (a much heftier book than *Fragments* itself, to which it is the postscript), and took further shape in many of Kierkegaard's later writings.

We already learned that Kierkegaard's use of the word *subjectivity* differs fundamentally from the conventional. The statement "subjectivity is truth" in his work means that the hard objectivity of the paradox is acknowledged only where it makes itself real in the inwardness of faith and thus brings one to the paradoxical actuality of one's existence: "Subjectivity is the truth. By virtue of the relationship subsisting between the eternal truth and the existing individual, the paradox came into being. Let us now go further, let us suppose that the eternal essential truth is itself a paradox. How does the paradox come into being? By putting the eternal essential truth into juxtaposition with existence. Hence when we posit such a conjunction within the truth itself, the truth becomes a paradox."[10] Man-in-sin misses out on the saving paradox because he is offended by it; the result is that he frivolously throws away his chance to exist. Everyone who gives himself over to speculation and the mediation which goes with it thereby blocks off his own access to inwardness, to subjectivity, to authentic human existence as an individual.

In all his writings Kierkegaard was imbued with a passion which distanced him from the ranks of professional theologians. By his thinking he aimed to pave the way to the renewal of humanity in true subjectivity. The objective of the Christian faith is certainly not to inform and instruct human beings by means of systematic explanation but to convert them by way of a decision in the face of the paradox.

8. Cf. W. Anz, *Kierkegaard und der deutsche Idealismus* (Tübingen, 1956).
9. His criticism of Luther was that Luther conveyed the discovery of justification undialectically, detached from discipleship in suffering, and that thus pure Lutheran teaching became a means of defense against inwardness.
10. *Concluding Unscientific Postscript*, p. 187.

ANTHROPOCENTRICITY OR PNEUMATOLOGY?

How does this concern of Kierkegaard relate to that which occupied theology before and after his time? Karl Barth has launched the idea that "Kierkegaard was bound more closely to the nineteenth century than we were willing to believe at that time. We may perhaps raise the historically pointed question whether his teaching was not itself the highest, most consistent, and most thoroughly reflective completion of pietism."[11] The parallel does in fact present itself because this seventeenth- and eighteenth-century movement did not at all aim at criticism of the objective content of Scripture and dogma but was totally preoccupied with the appropriation of their content; the whole truth of salvation remains useless, it said, if it does not lead the sinner to regeneration.

The difference between Pietism and Kierkegaard is also clear, however: whereas Pietism presupposed and maintained the orthodox system of doctrine, Kierkegaard made its content existential. In the language of the post-idealistic period he found new formulations and emphases by way of which the reader had to understand clearly that the gospel is totally directed toward his subjectivity as an individual. This thrust toward the individual so pervades the whole of his work that one can understand Barth's suspicion that behind the Pietism there is still something else: "a new anthropocentric systematics" as a possible continuation of Schleiermacher's program, pointing in the direction of the modern existentialist philosophers and Rudolph Bultmann. However, this "suspicion" does not seem to me to do justice to Kierkegaard's concern. His understanding of existence was the reverse side of his understanding of revelation and not intended as *praeambula fidei*. He was hardly aware of such an either-or, however, and was therefore quite able in a carefree manner, as occasion suggested, also to illustrate his discovery with utterances of Socrates and with general psychological lines of thought. He was convinced that revelation discloses as authentic human existence that which is the goal of creation everywhere. "I now resolved to go back as far as possible, in order not to reach the religious

11. The statement was made in a speech delivered on the occasion of the reception of the Sonning Prize in Copenhagen. The speech, entitled "Dank und Reverenz," was published in *Evangelische Theologie* 23/7 (1963); this quotation is on p. 341. [A revised version, which we will cite, was published as "A Thank-You and a Bow—Kierkegaard's Reveille," in *Fragments Grave and Gay,* tr. Eric Mosbacher (London: Collins, 1971), pp. 95-101. The quotation here is from p. 100.—TRANS.]

mode of existence too soon, to say nothing of the specifically Christian mode of religious existence, in order not to leave difficulties unexplored behind me. If men had forgotten what it means to exist religiously, they had doubtless also forgotten what it means to exist as human beings; this must therefore be set forth."[12]

Kierkegaard's real aims have been better understood, I think, by Hermann Diem than by his teacher Karl Barth. Writes Diem: "The unifying link [between philosophy and theology] can only be that it is the same subject of the existential thinker which in its indissoluble self-identity as Christian and as man thinks about its humanity and expresses in its existence the categories flowing from such a process of reflection."[13] Kierkegaard's pivotal focus is "becoming," the "becoming" of existence, the origination of inwardness through paradoxical contemporaneity with Christ, and thus the "becoming" of the truth as subjectivity. In Kierkegaard these are pneumatological categories—even though, as far as I know, he did not use that expression. He attempted to understand the Christian faith anew, not in terms of some anthropocentric system but in terms of the work of the Spirit in the individual. Barth repeatedly tried to interpret Schleiermacher in accord with his deepest motivation by saying that he (Barth) assessed Schleiermacher's utterances pneumatologically. What he thought of Schleiermacher, however, could have been much more appropriately adopted as his opinion of Kierkeaard, based on the whole thrust of the latter's writings. Can one not say even that, fundamentally, Schleiermacher and Kierkegaard aimed at the same goal? Both of them sought to make intelligible for their cultured contemporaries the renewal of humanity through the work of God. The first strove to attain this goal by the way of harmony (though not by that way alone, as we saw); the second by way of conflict (with the tools of contemporary language and psychology). Schleiermacher, and following him liberalism and the theology of mediation, sought to make apologetic use of idealism in order to lead it in priestly fashion to its secret Christian goal; Kierkegaard sought to unmask it prophetically as a form of the never-ending scandal over the paradox of the gospel. In the cultured world of the educated both men remained solitary figures. Schleier-

12. *Concluding Unscientific Postscript,* p. 223.

13. H. Diem, *Kierkegaard's Dialectic of Existence,* tr. H. Knight (Edinburgh/London: Oliver & Boyd, 1959), p. 192. According to Diem, this dialectic has nothing whatsoever to do with the later "existentialism" of Jaspers and Heidegger: "He is not concerned with any doctrine about the right way of being, but with this way of being itself, i.e., the dialectical proceeding by which such a way of being is to be attained and imparted" (p. 216).

macher was adopted, in domesticated form, in the church and assimilated in the theology of mediation. Kierkegaard attacked precisely this theology as the mediating ideology of the church establishment and was, accordingly, rejected also by the church.

ATTEMPT AT APPRAISAL

If we are correct in holding that Kierkegaard's aim was not to emphasize anthropology but pneumatology in theology, and therefore, like Barth, he considered the renewing Spirit as the true answer to the anthropocentric endeavors of the culture of the time, we have also gained the locus from which pertinent criticism of Kierkegaard becomes possible. It is certainly clear that the work of the Spirit does not exhaust itself in that which Kierkegaard unremittingly testifies concerning it. We encounter in him an (pietistic? romantic?) individualism (the "Individual") which does not do justice to certain dimensions of the Christian faith. Here one has to agree with Barth: "What about the individual in whose existence nearly everything seems to be centred for Kierkegaard? Where in his teaching are the people of God, the congregation, the Church; where are her diaconal and missionary charge, her political and social charge?"[14] And no less questionable is that other pneumatological limitation in him: his aversion to justification as "cheap grace," as a soft pillow allowing Christians not to repent, was so strong that justification almost disappeared behind sanctification and the Christian life became an oppressive and unrealizable law. On that score, too, we must concur with Barth: "Was it permissible to make and thus again and again effect the truly necessary *negations* about the subject of theology and thereby to cause the poor wretches who become Christians, or might want to think of themselves as such, to taste again and again the bitterness of the training required? Was that permissible, if the aim was to proclaim and to interpret the Gospel of God and thus the Gospel of his free grace? It is odd how easily one is caught

---

14. Barth, *Fragments Grave and Gay,* p. 99 (= *Evangelische Theologie* 23/7 [1963] 340). One can also think of Kierkegaard's post-Hegelian contemporary Karl Marx to see his limitations. Both men proceed from the self-alienation of man, in Kierkegaard's view as a result of Christianity, and in Marx's view of capitalism. "Marx destroyed the bourgeois-capitalistic world and Kierkegaard the bourgeois-Christian world" (K. Löwith, *Die Hegelsche Linke,* p. 16). But whereas Marx sought the remedy in the consistent socialization of humanity, Kierkegaard sought it in consistent individualization.

in the wheels of a law that can only deaden and make one sour, gloomy, and sad."[15]

Summing things up, Barth says: "I consider him to be a teacher whose school every theologian must enter once. Woe to him who misses it—provided only he does not remain in or return to it."[16] I can concur with the first half of that last sentence, but not with the second. I suppose, however, that Barth's advice not to go back to it is based on his view that Kierkegaard is an anthropocentric thinker. But if one regards that as a misunderstanding, one still has to say that the individualistic and legalistic limitations of Kierkegaard's pneumatology furnish good grounds for the advice not to stay in his school. Many people would only too readily follow that advice because the door of the discipleship of the individual is too narrow for him. Justification by grace as well as the fellowship of the church may, however, lead to a convenient repudiation of one's own responsibility, as the praxis of the church has shown and still shows. For that reason we shall ever have to return to Kierkegaard, or better: to the dimensions of the work of the Spirit he so one-sidedly emphasized. Certainly, Kierkegaard went too far, both for the secular spirit of the time and for conventional Christianity. The person who finds no hearing for his truth is bound to exaggerate. In the first half of our century Kierkegaard found but little hearing and in the second half hardly any at all. He continues to be inconvenient, and therefore relevant, to us. That is particularly true for the theme which occupies us in this book. In the matter of the relationship between the gospel and modernity he thought through, and carried out, the conflict model in a manner both "dialogic" and militant which left confessionalism, to cite one example, far behind. Perhaps the price one has to pay for making such an attempt is that it ever remains fragmentary. Kierkegaard himself believed that "the professor" and "lecturer," in virtue of his occupation, would always objectify his legacy, that is, rob it of its focus on subjectivity and hence destroy it.[17]

Though the method inherent in dogmatics makes this objectifying difficult to avoid, dogmatics is admittedly still an attempt to let the unobjectifiable truth mirror itself in the waters of scientific objectifiability. The fear and trembling which need to go with such an undertaking is something we have to learn from Kierkegaard—something we still

15. Barth, *Fragments Grave and Gay*, p. 99 (= *Evangelische Theologie* 23/7 [1963] 340).

16. Ibid., pp. 100-101 (= p. 342).

17. See the quotations from the diaries in H. Diem, *Kierkegaard's Dialectic of Existence*, pp. 205, 206.

have not learned. We cannot tolerate the tension, anymore than a dog—to use Kierkegaard's figure—can manage for more than a brief moment to stand on its hind legs. Precisely for that reason we shall always have Kierkegaard as much ahead of us as behind us, and we must be concerned to go back to his school![18]

18. With this judgment we are not only taking a position against Barth's view but much more against E. Hirsch, who admittedly deserves much credit for his translation of Kierkegaard into German but whose vast knowledge cannot conceal his inner lack of affinity with Kierkegaard. I am referring particularly to his *Geschichte der neueren evangelische Theologie,* 5:433-91. He is intent on seeing Kierkegaard as a liberal theologian who is "restless in the direction of interiorization" (closing sentence on p. 491). In the process Hirsch turns "inwardness" into a religious-psychological concept. He is aware of the fact that to a large degree this liberalization of Kierkegaard cannot succeed. "He is not able to make clear to himself that a developed church community, adapted to the conditions for continued historical existence, with its existential-dialectical leveling of the Christian faith and its transformation of Jesus into the founder of the church, represents the only possibility of upholding the gospel of Jesus Christ through the ages and letting it become a spiritually formative force" (p. 485). It is as though one were listening to Dostoyevski's Grand Inquisitor! The "hard limitation" to which (says Hirsch) Kierkegaard was subject consists in that he belonged to "the idealistic-romantic type in its extreme form" and hence intelligible, "with all his refinements, only to individual latecomers of this spiritual and mental character. For that reason theology cannot learn from Kierkegaard by simple appropriation of what he teaches but only by a double process of appropriation and rejection" (p. 468). The offense which Hirsch, from within his theology, rightly takes at Kierkegaard, is thus cultural-historically sidetracked—which is to give him a first-class funeral. A person who does not understand Kierkegaard in the light of his passion and his suffering for the sake of the gospel cannot understand him at all. Not till then can one fruitfully raise the question whether and to what extent Kierkegaard allowed his opponents to dictate the themes of his witness and whether Diem is right when he applies to Kierkegaard's relationship to Hegel the dictum *victus victori legem dat* ("the vanquished lays down the law for the victor"; H. Diem, *Kierkegaard's Dialectic of Existence,* p. 191).

CHAPTER VII

The Anglican Pendulum

THE SPECIAL CHARACTER OF BRITISH THEOLOGY

"England is farther away than the moon." Thus did van Unnik, a Dutch theologian, entitle an article about Anglo-Saxon theology. The judgment implied in the title is true for the Netherlands today and was true in the previous century; it applies equally or even more to Germany and to the study of theology (Protestant and Catholic) in many other countries in Europe. The reasons lie within ourselves or are due to the predominance of theology written in the German language. But it also has to do with the situation in England itself. England took another road than continental Europe. Till now theology in England has been done in much greater continuity with its patristic or medieval past. The shaking of the foundations and the theological challenge associated with the Reformation were experienced by the English people from a greater distance.[1] The result was not a deep "separation of spirits" but rather a measure of ecclesiastical and theological pluralism. In this context issues of church organization were at least as weighty as those of the content of faith. Also, the French Revolution and the Napoleonic and post-Napoleonic episodes were experienced in England from some distance. True, England and continental Europe have many points of contact, but our historical experiences are certainly not identical.

There are other differences as well. England is the land of Bacon, Locke, Hume, and so many others who have given to its spiritual and

---

1. Compare how William Temple, Archbishop of York at the time, describes the differences between England and continental Europe in his "Chairman's Introduction" to the Report of the Commission on Christian Doctrine: *Doctrine in the Church of England (1938)* (London: SPCK, 1957), pp. 4-6.

intellectual life an empirical, not to say empiricistic, stamp. We shall leave aside the possibility of an explanation on the level of the psychology of nations. The difference between England and Germany in the areas of philosophy and theology is clear. English expositions very frequently refer to "experience" as a warrant for arguments used in both the first and the last place. In German philosophical parlance numerous more abstract concepts (like category, non-Ego, existence, spirit or mind, universe, etc.) occupy similar key positions. This is not applicable to the entire continent, however. Evangelical theologians in Scandinavian countries are closer, in my opinion, to the English mind-set, while the Dutch and Swiss traditions of evangelical theology occupy a position midway between English empiricism and German metaphysics.

In England scholars have generally followed developments in continental and particularly German theology more closely than vice versa. Influences from the direction of the continent were always assimilated independently, though the end product was hardly considered for possible export. As in the cultures of almost all great countries and language communities, people live their lives autonomously and in isolation. This is especially true for England in its position as an island. An island creates its own cultural climate.

Added to this difference are the differences in the organization of theological study. In Reformed Scotland systematic theology, including dogmatics, is done at the universities. For that reason and through the influence of the Reformed tradition, Scottish theology exhibits greater similarity with continental theology. To a lesser extent that is also true of the Free Church tradition of theological study in England itself. For our purpose, however, this tradition is less interesting than the Anglican. The latter—as the contribution of the leading national church— shifted its attention more energetically to a confrontation with the great ideas of the time and hence with the problems posed by the Enlightenment. In addition, dogmatics as such is not studied at the universities (that subject is left to the church "colleges"). Accordingly, systematic theology done at the universities is overshadowed by a broad range of exegetical and church-historical studies and concentrated mostly on the philosophy of religion, dogmatic prolegomena, and ethics. Besides, in England a student must first have completed a course of studies outside theology. The German often fails to find thoroughness and a rigorous methodology in Anglican theologies. Many an Englishman experiences German systematic theology as abstract and out of touch with the world.

If we turn now to our specific theme and to the nineteenth century, we must note that in the two preceding centuries and in our field, England, France, and from time to time the Netherlands gave direction to German culture. A rapid and radical shift in the cultural balance occurred, however, with the rise of Lessing and Herder, Goethe and Schiller, Kant and German idealism. All at once Germany became the contributing and leading country. When, at the beginning of the nineteenth century, criticism of the Enlightenment—mainly in the form of Romanticism—arose also in England, leading minds took their cues mostly from Germany, in order subsequently to assimilate independently what they learned there.

COLERIDGE

On the threshold of this epoch stands the man whom, with some reservation, one can call the Schleiermacher of Anglican theology: *Samuel Taylor Coleridge* (1772-1834). Like Schleiermacher he sought to oppose the Enlightenment's narrow and shallow notion of reason—or, to put it another way, he tried so to deepen and broaden it that it could also embrace feeling, imagination, religion, and the truths of Christian revelation.

Coleridge was not a theologian. He was a poet, a literary critic, an art theorist, a Shakespeare expert, and a student of political developments. He also took an interest in the relationship between church and state. He was one of the great representatives of English Romanticism. As for Schleiermacher, so for Coleridge the expanse of culture had a theological center, as in recent years the interpreters of his works as a whole have increasingly discovered.[2] From 1824 onward he devoted himself "to what he had long considered to be the great task of his life, the defence of Trinitarian Christianity both as a practical rule for conduct and for politics, and as a necessity of metaphysical thought."[3] In 1825, as the first part of an all-embracing Christian philosophy, his *Aids to Reflection* appeared, a work which initially enjoyed only little notice but gradually gained more attention.[4] The second and concluding volume, which was never published, was intended to deal with Trinitarian metaphysics.

2. See the overview of publications from 1975 to 1979 in Stephen Happel, "Words Made Beautiful by Grace: On Coleridge the Theologian," in *Religious Studies Review* 6/3 (July, 1980) 201-10.

3. E. K. Chambers, *Samuel Taylor Coleridge: A Bibliographical Study* (Oxford, 1938), p. 310.

4. *Aids to Reflection* (1825; 2nd ed. 1831; 3rd ed. 1836; 4th ed. 1839; 5th ed. 1841). The edition used here is that of the Kennikat Press, first published in 1840 and reissued in 1971.

The aim of the book, as the title indicates, was to help people in their reflections. They were to learn to distinguish and employ the several levels and functions of their minds. In this connection Coleridge attributed much significance to insight into the language. It was his intention to construct this theory of reason on a kind of grammar, aiming "to direct the reader's attention to the value of the science of words, their use and abuse, and the incalculable advantages attached to the habit of using them appropriately, and with a distinct knowledge of their primary, derivative, and metaphorical senses" (p. 62). He clearly distinguished the activities of "prudence," "morality," and "religion." "Thus: the prudential corresponds to the sense and the understanding; the moral to the heart and the conscience; the spiritual to the will and the reason, that is, to the finite will reduced to harmony with, and in subordination to, the reason, as a ray from that true light which is both reason and will, universal reason, and will absolute" (p. 87). One can see how language analysis, anthropology, and theology together formed an unbreakable unity. Coleridge was aware that for the distinction between understanding and reason he was dependent on Kant. He also followed Kant in his theory of practical reason. It is striking, however, that the dualistic air of Kantian philosophy is not present in Coleridge. Theoretical reason "is the light of reason in the understanding," whereas "the practical reason alone is reason in the full and substantive sense. It is reason in its own sphere of perfect freedom; as the source of ideas, which ideas, in their conversion to the responsible, will become ultimate ends" (Appendix, p. 353). For real Kantians this kind of talk moves much too quickly. For that reason the German romanticists rejected Kant. The English romanticists had a more homogeneous and harmonious, possibly even a better, understanding of him (cf. Chapter 1 above).[5]

Associated with practical reason, says Coleridge, are "three ultimate facts": the conscience, the will, and the existence of evil. Only the Christian faith does justice to all three. We cannot manage our lives without help from above, from the side of the highest and most perfect reason. Conversely, God presupposes the existence of the faculties he has created within us. We dare not receive as the king's mandates anything that is "not stamped with the Great Seal of the conscience and counter-

5. In this connection it must not be forgotten that this interpretation of Kant was suggested by the preceding influence of the "Cambridge Platonists." For that reason the charge "that he used Kantian language as a cloak for Platonist Doctrine" is not correct. A careful examination of the connection between the two influences is offered by B. M. G. Reardon in *From Coleridge to Gore* (London: Longman, 1971), pp. 69-72.

signed by the reason" (p. 162). These faculties, however, as we learned, point to an absolute source. Universal reason, which is at the same time absolute will, must be a Person. Religion is a relationship of will to will, an interpersonal relationship. That reality comes more clearly to the fore here than, say, in Schleiermacher, whom Coleridge put in second place behind Kant.

The Christian faith is the fulfillment of our deepest nature and our highest ideals. And still, or perhaps because of this, Coleridge knows stringent verification is not possible here. He hears the question of the reader: "How can I comprehend this? How is this to be proved? To the first question I should answer: Christianity is not a theory, or a speculation; but a life; not a philosophy of life, but a life and a living process. To the second: Try it!" (p. 201). As a convinced Anglican, Coleridge had his roots, more than Schleiermacher, in the tradition of the church. In the main teachings of the personhood of God, original sin, redemption through Christ, the Trinity, etc., he found the ultimate truth. Nevertheless, this teaching need not and cannot be imposed on modern people as legally binding. People can and must discover its "plausibility" by listening to their outer and inner "experience." Coleridge was concerned to offer an apologetic not based on abstract and complex philosophical theories, but guided by the voice of "common sense" with "conscience" at its center. The English have a special talent for this kind of apologetic; I have in mind G. K. Chesterton's *Orthodoxy* (1908) and many books by C. S. Lewis, particularly *Beyond Personality* (1944) and *Miracles* (1947). Generally speaking, one can say of Anglo-Saxon theology that its *praeambula fidei* rest on the twin pillars of "experience" and "conscience."

Like Schleiermacher, Coleridge welcomed historical criticism of the Bible and made room for it in his theology. Still, in that connection, he was significantly more conservative than Schleiermacher. That was due to his high estimate of tradition. In all, he was probably closest to the theology of mediation. His *Aids to Reflection* was published a year before the founding of this German school of thought.

In one respect Coleridge was very different from Schleiermacher: his life had roots also outside the contexts of the intellectual and the aesthetic. For a time he was suffering from a dependency on opium; accordingly, words like *original sin, conscience, repentance,* and *redemption* became very real to him. Socially and politically he was also very involved. As we shall see later, among English theologians in the nineteenth century the degree of social awareness and involvement was high—as among their German colleagues it was correspondingly low. That awareness presumably had something to do with their greater emphasis on "common sense" and "experience." At a very early stage already they were conscious of their Christian responsibility vis-à-vis the Industrial Revolution. In my opinion, certain trends in Anglo-Saxon theology are also traceable to this connection.

MAURICE

British theology after the Enlightenment began as a quiet Kant-oriented theology of mediation. This happened at the very time that Kant was being pushed aside by idealistic metaphysics in Germany, and theology had to come to terms with various extremes. Here again there is a typical difference: the extremes are more at home in Germany; in England mediation is. Coleridge decisively influenced several leading theologians of the middle of the century. Here we shall mention only the greatest: *Frederick Denison Maurice* (1805-1872). In a way he too belongs in the context of mediation theology. However, this label means very little when applied to such an original and individual mind. That is also the reason why, in view of our special objective, we shall devote but little space to him.

In his case, the problematics of mediation theology are crowded aside by an all-embracing Christocentrism. He too believes in a point of contact in human beings, an anthropological substratum for redemption in Christ. He calls it "experience" and "conscience" as many other theologians did, but he adds a category of his own: "The Sense of Righteousness in Men." However, he develops this idea not anthropologically but theologically—in the light of Job's struggle with God. And he grounds it theologically on the basis of the preexistent presence of Christ in the world.[6] By doing this Maurice left the method of apologetic discussion behind him. Today he seems to us rather a forerunner of Karl Barth.[7]

6. F. D. Maurice, *Theological Essays* (London, 1853), ch. 4: "On the Sense of Righteousness in Men and Their Discovery of a Redeemer." From the edition with an Introduction by E. F. Carpenter (London: James Clarke, 1957), I cite the following: "You have such a righteousness. It is deeper than all the iniquity which is in you. It lies at the very ground of your existence. And this righteousness dwells not merely in a law which is condemning you, it dwells in a Person in whom you may trust. The righteous Lord of man is with you" (p. 62). "The Righteous one, the Redeemer in whom Job, and David, and the Prophets trusted, the ground of all that is true, in you, and me, and every man. . . . Apart from Him, I feel that there dwells in me no good thing; but I am sure that I am not apart from Him, nor are you, nor is any man" (p. 67).

7. Cf. E. Flesseman-van Leer, *Grace Abounding: A Comparison of Frederic Denison Maurice and Karl Barth*, F. D. Maurice Lectures (London: King's College, 1968).

With this line of thought, however, he had hardly any influence at the time. He developed a consistent theology of love and fellowship which led to a new perspective on the Trinity and Christology, as well as to a strong passion for social concerns. On the basis of the Christian faith he sought an answer to the movements of 1848. He became one of the founders of the "Christian Social" Movement which was opposed both to a-social Christians and to non-Christian socialists. To my mind he brought together theologically the concerns of the two poles of German mediation theology, the poles represented by Dorner and Rothe.

NEWMAN

We shall also bypass the high-churchly "Oxford Movement," which in the 1840s and for a long time afterward held the Anglican church under its fascinating spell. It was interested in intrachurch issues (tradition, succession, devotion), not in a confrontation with the *Zeitgeist*. From this movement *John Henry Newman* (1801-1890), who later became Catholic, came to the fore, a man we mention here because of his *Essay in Aid of a Grammar of Assent*, usually referred to as *A Grammar of Assent* (1870).

In his youth he was influenced by Coleridge, though he considered Coleridge's *Aids to Reflection* as "too speculative and often pagan." Whatever he may have meant by this criticism, from my continental vantage point I see a striking correspondence between the two books in both interest and method. Both authors seek the connection between experience and revelation somewhere between rationalism and irrationalism. Both of them greatly value the wisdom inherent in language, a wisdom which comes out in the appropriate use of language ("Grammar"!). Both distinguish several levels of cognition; both work with "experience" and "existence," and ascribe a key position to "conscience."[8] Both seek to teach people to appropriate the great Christian truths on their own.

Newman struggled with the question how an absolute conviction arises in persons and found it rooted in a "faculty for inference," called the "Illative Sense."[9] In his solution, since he made no use of the

---

8. "Newman, so far as we know, never studied Kant, but in this regard [sc. the moral consciousness] the Kantian bias in his outlook is remarkable" (B. M. G. Reardon, *Religious Thought in the Nineteenth Century* [Cambridge: Cambridge University Press, 1966], p. 28).

9. "The sole and final judgment on the validity of an inference in concrete matter is committed to the personal action of the ratiocinative faculty, the perfection of virtue of which I have called the Illative Sense, a use of the word

proofs for the existence of God and the *motiva credibilitatis* (motives for belief in the traditional Catholic theology), he distanced himself clearly from then current Thomistic intellectualism. From the side of Catholicism he was therefore accused of "subjectivism" and "fideism." The truth is he did not operate in a Latin spirit—separating object and subject—but in the spirit of personalism and encounter-thought which was characteristic for Anglo-Saxon theology long before it became dominant on the continent (after 1920) and in Catholic theology (after 1960).[10]

THE MODERNISM OF *ESSAYS AND REVIEWS*

Around the middle of the century, as naturalistic and deterministic ways of thinking made further inroads, these mediating epistemological and anthropological patterns of thought nevertheless had to come across increasingly as a premature domestication and integration of the secular *Zeitgeist.* Many people saw that the sought-after reconciliation could only be bought at a much higher price.

In 1860, with the appearance of the volume entitled *Essays and Reviews,* a renewed discussion began. In that volume a more radical modernism—radical at least for England at the time—announced itself. It took its starting point in the historical-critical biblical scholarship and on that basis proceeded to undermine the doctrine of inspiration and the authority of Scripture. For England, which tended toward mediating theology, the book was revolutionary. In Germany—which was more radical—people had already experienced such a shake-up at the time of the appearance of Strauss's *The Life of Jesus, critically examined* (1835; 2nd ed. 1836). Looking at its emotional impact from our present historical distance, one marvels at it, not so much because much that evoked offense in the *Essays* is universally acknowledged today, but because since Coleridge critical biblical scholarship had theoretically already been widely accepted at that time. One must remember, however—and this applies to theological dialogue vis-à-vis modern science right up until

---

'sense' parallel to our use of it in 'good sense,' 'common sense,' a 'sense of beauty,' etc.;—and I own I do not see any way to go farther than this answer to the question" (J. H. Newman, *Grammar of Assent* [New York: Doubleday, 1955], p. 271).

10. On the original and difficult position of Newman in Catholic theology, see the "Introduction by Etienne Gilson," in *Grammar of Assent,* pp. 9-21. In 1879 Pope Leo XIII nevertheless appointed Newman a cardinal—another instance of the breadth of vision which distinguished this great pope.

today—that syntheses and reconciliations are always being disturbed by new antagonistic insights from the side of science. Hence theological work must, in the long run, often look as if by a series of movements it falls back upon a shortened front.[11]

The authors of *Essays and Reviews* were so impressed by the natural course of the history of biblical religion that they believed they could rescue the Christian idea of revelation only by means of an altogether radical front reduction. This consisted in accepting a direct separation between the world of the laws of nature and history on the one hand, and the world of spirit and inwardness on the other. This sounds as if they fell back on Kant, interpreted, in distinction from Coleridge's understanding, dualistically. There is, however, hardly any trace of direct Kantian influence. It is worth noting that with this book England not only caught up with Germany but took a position which was not espoused in Germany till ten years later when Ritschl, with the help of Kant, proposed it. Such parallels, of course, have only a limited significance and remain confined to formal categories. Indeed, modernism in Germany was older, and Ritschl was no modernist.

Just what is meant by this separation of nature and spirit in the *Essays* can be ascertained on the first few pages. There Frederick Temple —in his study "The Education of the World"—speaks of the law of cause and effect which would transform the world into a dead machine were it not for the very different law of development in the world of spirits. "Man is a spiritual as well as a material creature."[12] That statement is not elaborated or argued. In his study of miracle Baden Powell writes: "Advancing knowledge, while it asserts the dominion of science in physical things, confirms that of faith in spiritual: we thus neither impugn the generalizations of philosophy, nor allow them to invade the dominion of faith, and admit that what is not a subject for a problem may hold its place in a creed" (p. 143). This means that "outward marvels are needless to spiritual conviction" and that faith triumphs "in the greater moral miracle of a converted and regenerate soul" (p. 144). "The more knowledge advances, the more it has been, and will be, acknowledged that

11. The most thorough and effective essay was probably that by B. Jewett, Regius Professor of Greek at Oxford, entitled "On the Interpretation of Scripture." His solution—"Interpret the Scripture like any other book"—put an end to a comfortable linkage between a doctrine of inspiration and historical research. On him cf. B. M. G. Reardon, *From Coleridge to Gore*, pp. 332-40.

12. *Recent Inquiries in Theology by eminent English churchmen, being "Essays and Reviews,"* ed. Rev. Frederic H. Hedge (Boston: Walker, Wise and Co., 1860), p. 2.

Christianity, as a real religion, must be viewed apart from connection with physical things" (p. 145).

Today all this sounds very simple and dogmatic. It is in fact quite impossible to draw such a clear and convenient line of separation through the universe. For the English, who tend not to think very abstractly, this divorce is even less easy to manage than for German theology, where such a split — from Ritschl to Bultmann — may enjoy a longer life. It certainly limited the influence of *Essays and Reviews*. Still, the shock it produced was enormous. The strength of modernists lay in their attack on the positions of conservatives and mediation theologians. They could refer persuasively to unfounded and even fantastic assertions and analogies or apologetic tricks and devices with which their opponents sought to conjure up harmony between the biblical and the modern world. Thus a premature synthesis was exploded. Then came the second time bomb: Darwin's *Origin of Species* (1859). The *Essays* only once took notice of it, but soon the two effects mingled and reinforced each other. It seemed as if the synthesis was not only undermined but fully destroyed. But one who reaches that conclusion does not know the English mentality very well. Claude Welch cautiously but precisely characterized the effect of the book as follows:

> *Essays and Reviews* certainly worked no universal change in British theology. . . . Yet the book marked a major transition. . . . [It] made impossible a further concealment of the historical question, it greatly broadened the range of permissible religious opinions, it widened the discussion to include the larger public, and it opened the way for acceptance of the work of the rising generation of biblical critics like B. F. Westcott and J. B. Lightfoot — as well as for the reluctant acceptance of writers like T. H. Huxley as serious positivist challengers to narrow biblical belief.[13]

THE INCARNATION THEOLOGY OF *LUX MUNDI*

Still, the aversion to such a split and the search for a synthesis were not eradicated in the leading theological circles of Anglicanism. True, the younger generation took a fairly long time to process the double explosion. Almost thirty years after *Essays and Reviews* a new symposium of

13. C. Welch, *Protestant Thought in the Nineteenth Century* (New Haven/London: Yale University Press, 1972), 1:169.

theological essays appeared, this time under the title *Lux Mundi* (1889). This book originated from within the circles of the Anglo-Catholic Oxford Movement which, in its younger representatives (mostly professors at Oxford), set as its new goal "to attempt to put the Catholic faith into its right relation to modern intellectual and moral pluralism."[14] The editor was Charles Gore (1853-1932), then principal of Pusey House, a man who later, especially as bishop of Oxford, became the leader of Anglican theology, a leadership extending over decades. In his preface he wrote:

> We are sure that Jesus Christ is still and will continue to be the "Light of the world." . . . But we are conscious also that if the true meaning of the faith is to be made sufficiently conspicuous it needs disencumbering, reinterpreting, explaining. (p. VII)

> The real development of theology is rather the process in which the Church, standing firm in her old truths, enters into the apprehension of the new social and intellectual movements of each age: and because "the truth makes her free" is able to assimilate all new material, to welcome and give its place to all new knowledge, to throw herself into the sanctification of each new social order, bringing forth out of her treasures things new and old, and shewing again and again her power of witnessing under changed conditions to the catholic capacity of her faith and life. (p. VIII)

Apart from the spirited warmth of its style, the authors of *Essays and Reviews* could have said something similar. To sense the contrasting nature of its concerns, one must note the subtitle: *a series of studies in the religion of the Incarnation.* The word *Incarnation* not only implies the orthodoxy of the authors and their link with the patristic tradition but also means that Jesus Christ as the incarnate Light of the World illumines and embraces the whole of the cosmos and therefore that there is no dualism of nature and spirit, body and soul, cosmos and humanity. In addition to the "organic" thinking of this period the authors also encountered Darwin's theory of evolution. In the fifth study, "The Incarnation and Development," written by the clergyman J. R. Illingsworth (whose rectory was the annual place of meeting for the *Lux Mundi* group), the convergence of the patristic doctrine of the eternal Word and the cosmic significance of the Incarnation of God with the modern theory of evolution was presupposed

---

14. *Lux Mundi, a series of studies in the religion of the Incarnation,* ed. Charles Gore, 15th ed. (London: Murray, repr. 1913). The quotation is on p. VII of the preface.

and demonstrated: patristic teaching leads one "to view the Incarnation as being the pre-destined climax of creation, independently of human sin" (p. 136). "Now in scientific language, the Incarnation may be said to have introduced a new species into the world—a Divine man transcending past humanity, as humanity transcended the rest of the animal creation, and communicating His vital energy by a spiritual process to subsequent generations of man" (pp. 151-52). Viewed from the perspective of Darwinian theory, however, this synthesis is not so simple. Darwin himself, after all, saw the limitation of his purely deterministic explanation (p. 138). The new insight into the creative forces which uphold our creation also illumines afresh the teaching of the immanence of the Creation-word. The problem of the descent of man is more threatening to theologians. "If we believe, as we have seen that Christian Theology has always believed, in a Divine Creator not only present behind the beginning of matter but immanent in its every phase, and co-operating with its every phenomenon, the method of His working, though full of speculative interest, will be of no controversial importance" (p. 142).

To draw atheistic conclusions is to exceed the boundaries of one's knowledge. The question of miracle and its possibility must be viewed totally in the light of the fusion of spirit and matter. "He who can save the soul can raise the dead" (p. 154). In addition, Christian thinkers take into consideration another fact of experience: moral evil. By the same token, faith does far more justice to "experience" than a scientific theory can ever do. The conclusion of this examination is: "The two conceptions [namely of faith and of science] are complementary and cannot contradict each other" (p. 137).

The other contributions point in the same direction. Thus Aubrey Moore, in his essay "The Christian Doctrine of God," stresses the classic teaching of the immanence of God, which was unfolded, not in deism, but in idealism and the theory of evolution. "And when reason had wandered long, seeking for that which should be Real and yet One, a God Who should satisfy alike the demands of religion and reason, the doctrine of the Trinity is unfolded. It was the gradual revelation of God answering to the growing needs and capacity of man" (p. 76).

This synthesis of the gospel with "experience of the world" elicited widespread approval in England. Despite this approval, it was viewed from two directions as a premature victory. To the modern theologians and philosophers the synthesis appeared to have been bought at the expense of "experience of the world." To the more orthodox and Reformation-minded theologians and believers it was brought about at the expense of the gospel. Although the "hard" aspects of the gospel—sin, atonement on the cross, the conversion of human beings, judgment, etc.

—were certainly not denied (particularly Gore strongly emphasized these aspects), they receded markedly into the background by comparison with the elements that were (really or seemingly) capable of synthesis.[15]

Here, also, theology went hand in hand with the assumption of a social-political position. The unity of the spiritual with the material, as it became manifest in the Incarnation, had to lead to this. Socialism as well as democracy was viewed as an expression of the immanence of the divine Logos. The year in which *Lux Mundi* was published, 1889, was also the year in which the Christian Social Union was founded. In this organization two prominent figures belonging to the *Lux Mundi* group, Charles Gore and Henry Scott Holland (Canon of St. Paul), served as vice-president.[16] Their struggle against injustice in society safeguarded their theology against cheap optimism.

For many decades the fundamental ideas of the *Lux Mundi* group remained characteristic for and dominant in Anglican theology. This is especially true for the evolutionary relationship between Christ and the cosmos, an idea which in our century resurfaces in such eminent theologians as William Temple (*Christus Veritas,* 1924) and Lionel Thornton (*The Incarnate Lord,* 1928), oftentimes with an appeal to the redemptive historical "stages" of Irenaeus.

THE PENDULUM SWINGS BACK TO EMPIRICISM

This form of the typically Anglican theology of mediation, however, sooner or later also had to discover its own limitations. Besides, though it was the prevailing theology, it was never in command of the field. The statement *The Doctrine in the Church of England (1938)* (cited in n. 1 above), together with its introduction by William Temple, makes clear how strong at that time the opposition of modernism still was. From the theology that was shaped by the influence of Karl Barth and Reinhold Niebuhr, Temple himself expected a new shift toward the themes of the Reformation: Redemption, Justification, and Conversion (p. 17). In the years following World War II this shift did occur in part, but looking back one wonders why it was so short-lived. In the 1960s it was inundated by a new wave of liberalism.

15. On the thrust of the movement, the criticism of it, and Gore's own position, see A. M. Ramsey, *From Gore to Temple: The Development of Anglican Theology between Lux Mundi and the Second World War, 1889-1939* (London: Murray, 1960), chs. 1 and 2. The book is an excellent introduction to Anglican theology.

16. Ibid., pp. 12-15.

In accord with the *Zeitgeist*, idealism was replaced by a new empiricism. In England this empiricism clothed itself in the dress of linguistic and conceptual analysis. Again the shift broke into the open with a symposium: *Soundings* (1962). The motto which it bears is characteristic: "Man hath but a shallow sound and a short reach and dealeth only by probabilities and likely-hoods." The editor compared this symposium with the two earlier ones, but described it as more analogous to *Essays and Reviews*.[17] In the following years, an antidogmatic and antimetaphysical modernism became so strong that in 1971 Michael Ramsey, as Archbishop of Canterbury, sought to check its influence with the aid of a theological work group. What was present in his mind might have been similar to what Temple had earlier achieved with his group in *The Doctrine in the Church of England*. The result was the report *Christian Believing* (1976), which was disappointing to many people precisely because it abstained from formulating a common statement of faith and instead proclaimed, as the point of reference for the church, the diversity of belief already present in Scripture.[18] Tradition and the empirical spirit of the times drove the authors far apart (cf. p. 38). Hence the report cannot possibly be understood as a terminal point or new beginning in theological reflection.

This shortcoming is also evident from the fact that soon after the appearance of *Christian Believing*, a new and sensational symposium entitled *The Myth of God Incarnate* (1977) came out, a volume which proves that in England the realization of a new synthesis between Christian tradition and the modernity of the Enlightenment is still a distant prospect.[19] The attack had such a strong effect precisely because it concerned the dogma which had always served as a bridge between gospel and modernity: the doctrine of the Incarnation. According to the seven authors of this volume, however, this doctrine is untenable in the light of the historical development of the Christian faith. That which was held to be a bridge proved to be a myth.[20]

As we saw earlier, the English outlook is well suited to media-

---

17. *Soundings: Essays Concerning Christian Understanding*, ed. A. R. Vidler (Cambridge: Cambridge University Press, 1962), pp. X-XI.

18. *Christian Believing: The Nature of the Christian Faith and its Expression in Holy Scripture and Creeds* (London: SPCK, 1976). Of the 156 pages the common report covers only pp. 3-42!

19. *The Myth of God Incarnate*, ed. J. Hick (London: SCM, 1977).

20. "We have written this book in order to place its topic firmly on the agenda of discussion—not least in England, where the traditional doctrine of the incarnation has long been something of a shibboleth, exempt from reasoned scrutiny and treated with unquestioning literalness" (ibid., preface, pp. X-XI).

tion. As soon as modernity undergoes a change, however, as happened in 1860 and 1960, the synthesis has to collapse. Also, from within the understanding of the Christian tradition, such a collapse can occur, as happened after World War I on the continent. A parallel of similar scope does not present itself in England.

In England the current form of the modern outlook combines positivism, empiricism, historicism, and language analysis. It hardly leaves room for strong expressions of the Christian faith. This challenge is, or at least seems to be, much larger than the ones which came earlier from the side of idealism. England, with its empirical cast of mind, must endure it vicariously for other parts of the Christian church. That same country, however, has a mediating disposition. We may expect that after the second *Essays and Reviews* wave there will be a new *Lux Mundi* movement.[21] In any case, the weak biblical foundation of *The Myth of God Incarnate* encountered thorough opposition from the side of numerous New Testament scholars. And among the members of the younger generation there has already arisen a new demand for the classic content of the faith and for genuine systematic reflection on it.[22]

The pendulum continues to swing. That is all that can be said at the moment. A permanent reconciliation of the gospel and the *Zeitgeist* is not in sight in synthesizing England any more than anywhere else.

21. After reading the proofs of the present translation, Geoffrey Wainwright informed me that he had just edited a book entitled *Keeping the Faith: Essays to Mark the Centenary of Lux Mundi* (Philadelphia: Fortress, 1988).

22. Characteristic in this respect is S. W. Sykes, *The Integrity of Anglicanism* (New York: Seabury, 1978).

CHAPTER VIII

Coming up from Behind in the Netherlands

Whereas in many places in Europe after the Enlightenment theology attempted to determine its position vis-à-vis the new challenges, Dutch theology, exhausted by two hundred years of controversy, slept a deep supranaturalistic sleep. Indeed, Dutch culture as a whole had fallen asleep, at least from the middle of the eighteenth century. Not until after Napoleon, in the period of Restoration under King William I (1813-1840), did the Dutch begin to seek their new identity in a new Europe. Theology then slowly awakened from its slumbers also. Initially, of course, it had to orient itself by what was happening in foreign countries. Among the first to draw the attention of the Dutch was Herder. Lessing and Jacobi also gradually gained recognition. Van Heusde and Hemsterhuis mediated the Romantics. There was little interest in Kant. Schleiermacher's "feeling" was misunderstood, and classic German idealism was much too speculative for the down-to-earth Dutch. The so-called Groningen School was the first conscious attempt to build a bridge, with the aid of the influences just mentioned, between the gospel and post-Enlightenment thought. Today this attempt impresses one as a compromise that had not been well thought through and is even muddled. The Christology is typical: Jesus was a person who, by virtue of his preexistence, had an advantage over us all and was therefore able to become our example. In virtue of divine generation and his own obedience he was superior to us: the Son of God. For a while the ideas prompted by the Groningen School, which was still halfway stuck in supranaturalism, attracted thinking people, but it did not last long.

MODERNISM AS IDEALISM AND EMPIRICISM:
J. H. SCHOLTEN AND C. W. OPZOOMER

In 1840, as the newly appointed dogmatician at the Franeker academy, *Johannes Henricus Scholten*, young and highly gifted, delivered his inaugural lecture in which he attacked the Christology of the Groningen School as being docetic. According to him, it is precisely as a human being that Jesus participates in the divine nature. Scholten's audience and readers sensed the onset of a new epoch, an epoch of radicalism tending toward immanentism and monism, a radicalism nurtured by German idealism. Just where was it headed?

The University of Franeker was dissolved in 1843 and Scholten was called to Leyden. There, in the course of a long and very influential career, his thought came to full fruition (1843-1881). His aim was to construct a more tenable bridge between church tradition and modern thought than the Groningens had built, and to this end he found strong support in Alexander Schweizer, the Swiss theologian of mediation, who in the years 1844 and 1847 had published the two volumes of his *Glaubenslehre der evangelisch-reformierten Kirche.* Scholten, like Schweizer, set out to demonstrate that the theology of the Reformers, or the Reformed confessions, found its fulfillment in idealistic thought. In 1848 (also the year of the victory of liberal democracy in the Netherlands) the first edition of his *Principles of the Doctrine of the Reformed Church* appeared.[1] This book signaled the birth of Dutch "modernism," a term in which people heard the Latin *modo* (just now, today) or the late medieval *via moderna* (as opposed to the *via antiqua*). Scholten intended this book to be a theology for which the Bible had authority, indeed, but which reflected, with equal passion, the desire to think at the highest levels of contemporary scientific culture.

In this book one learns to know the brilliant, congenial, and proud "father of modernism" at his most impressive. The first volume deals, in the manner of Schweizer, with the formal principle of the Reformation, the sole authority of Scripture — a principle which, in the course of a long process of reflection and with an appeal to John Calvin, here dissolved into the doctrine of the *Testimonium Spiritus Sancti internum.* This witness relates not to the historical content of the Bible but to its religious content. At the same time this internal witness must be

---

1. The Dutch title: *De Leer der Hervormde Kerk in hare grondbeginselen.* The two Dutch words *hervormd* and *gereformeerd* both mean literally "reformed." The first can roughly be translated as "mainline evangelical" while the second leans toward "confessionally Reformed" or "Calvinistic."

viewed as the highest and purest form of the natural knowledge of God. In the second volume Scholten dealt with the material principle of the Reformed faith: the unconditioned sovereignty of God as opposed to his absolute causality of the world. In virtue of this rule, expressed most purely in the message of Jesus, God intended that the human world, through a long process of development, would renounce its animal drives, that is, sin; that at the same time it would increasingly follow its true moral-rational nature, that is, the life of God within us, in order thus to arrive at genuine freedom and humanity. Scholten summarized his theology as follows:

> The understanding of God proclaimed by Jesus is: Infinity, omnipotence, or sovereignty, which, however, is the sovereignty and omnipotence of a holy love that unceasingly, by the power of the Holy Spirit, brings into being the kingdom of truth and morality. [This sovereign love], in its unfathomable wisdom, also incorporated sin in its world plan and made the earthly resistance of the flesh serviceable to the victory of the Spirit. Before the eyes of faith, which already see in the present the embryo of the future perfection of the human race, [this love] reveals itself as the eternal and lasting source of light and life in the natural and moral world. In a word, it manifests itself as the love whose purpose it is to glorify itself in the blessedness of all that is called creature.[2]

This much is clear: What we are hearing is the echoes of classic German idealism—though more the rhetorical spirit of it than the assimilated content. A strong sense of freedom reminiscent of Fichte is in the foreground; in the background is a determinism of spirit, a combination of Calvinistic predestination and Hegelian dialectic. Scholten did not wish to be a pantheist: the Author of the entire process must himself be a personal spirit. A more precise determination of the influences of idealism is not very well possible. Hegel and Schleiermacher are quoted five times each; Fichte and Jacobi once each; Kant twice. Thus Kant plays no essential role. In the course of a rapid attempt to catch up, Dutch theology was unable to make use of his contribution. Despite *The Critique of Pure Reason,* Scholten's book was built upon a foundation of speculative reason and the cosmological proof for the existence of God. With its

---

2. J. H. Scholten, *De Leer der Hervormde Kerk,* 4th ed. (Leiden: Engels, 1861), 2:52. This summary does not occur as such in the first edition. Nevertheless, as Scholten himself stresses, there is no significant difference between the two editions. The language became less biblical and more philosophical—that is all.

inspiring flow of thought the book made a very strong impression and quickly conquered many pulpits of the Reformed church. At last an up-to-date interpretation of the gospel, one for which many younger theologians and preachers had been eagerly waiting, had arrived.

But was it really—as people loved to say at the time—up-to-date? In Germany and other European countries, idealism was in retreat in favor of a more naturalistic and empirical view of reality. Shortly after Scholten a second star appeared in the firmament of modernism: the jurist and philosopher *Cornelis Willem Opzoomer* (1821-1892). This highly talented Leyden student was called, at the age of twenty-five, to the chair of philosophy at Utrecht, where to his embarrassment he found several older, and famous, colleagues from the natural sciences in his audience. In view of the rapid development of these sciences by means of experiments and hypotheses, they were looking for philosophical enlightenment. By this confrontation Opzoomer, who initially thought in pantheistic idealistic categories, was converted to empiricism.

Since his interests lay especially in the philosophy of religion, as the second "father of modernism" he became the man who sought to ground religion and theology not in speculation but in experience. Much sooner than Scholten, therefore, he rejected belief in miracles. Reality is known from the observation of experience. There is, in addition, some activity of one's own mind; but this was conceived (contrary to Kant) almost in the fashion of naive realism. Reality as experience lays it out to us is controlled by the laws of nature and is of a deterministic or even— as Opzoomer ventures to put it—materialistic nature. Hence experience and scientific knowledge as such are godless.

There is, however, a second world of experience: that of the (sensuous, esthetic, ethical, and religious) "feelings." These too are sources of knowledge for us. "Religious feeling witnesses just as directly to the existence of God as sense observation does to the existence of the world." Religious feeling witnesses not only to the existence of God (an existence which Opzoomer took to be personal) but also to the fact that the world is constructed purposefully, that it is caught up in an unending process of development, that sin is a purely relative and even subjective phenomenon, etc. These insights which arise from the religious sense complement and correct the insights which arise from observation: the necessities of nature are, in the final analysis, not mechanically deterministic but the expression of infinite love and truth.

From Opzoomer's collection of essays on religion (*De Godsdienst*) we quote the following brief but characteristic statements:

Only modern theology has succeeded in bringing about this higher unity (namely, of deism and pantheism) in a worldview which, while it does not in any way lessen the certainty of the laws of nature, at the same time sees the whole world with all of its laws as no more than an effect, the cause of which is God. The acknowledgement of God as the perfect Spirit is inseparable from the conception that God is perfect wisdom and love. Faith in God's perfect wisdom immediately produces the thought that the world in which it reveals itself is a perfect and harmonious work of art. From faith in God's perfect love emerges [the conviction] that the kingdom of God must come over the entire earth, indeed in each of us, so that our existence cannot end with the decomposition of our bodies. The coming of the kingdom of God only takes place gradually and is not hindered by sin—which indeed is not a power over against God but a phenomenon under God. Despite this, sin may not be allowed to remain, and the more intimately our hearts are united with God—the more firmly our eyes are fixed on that which is perfect—to that degree sin will be resisted by each of us with all the more energy.[3]

These lines of thought exerted a powerful influence on the Dutch intelligentsia of the day. In the 1840s and 1860s the speculative-idealistic sense of life *(Lebensgefühl)* thus receded behind the empirical—behind "the passion for reality," as Allard Pierson described the mood at that time. At a time when, in Germany and elsewhere, idealism was still predominant in theology and the other humanities, people in the Netherlands were ready to make the shift to empiricism. After Hegel's death it became the point of departure for their thinking. Clearly, the shift from being behind to being ahead had occurred very rapidly—as it did in England, where a similar shift happened around a decade later.

For two reasons, however, that statement needs to be qualified. The first is that the polarity in theological modernism between idealism and realism, between the school of Leyden and the school of Utrecht, was never really resolved. The principal reason for this lack of resolution was that, despite their contrasting methodologies, Scholten and Opzoomer arrived at almost the same results. The theo-philosophy of both men can be described in the categories of monism, determinism, and optimism. It is a phenomenon that can be repeatedly observed in the post-Enlightenment period: the theologians fight over method, but their readers tend to observe their agreement in content.

3. W. C. Opzoomer, *De Godsdienst* (Amsterdam, 1864), pp. 345ff.

A second reason why the conflict between idealism and realism remained unresolved must be said to lie in the weaknesses and superficialities of the competing position, weaknesses which the speculative opponents of course eagerly uncovered. In 1849, in the Royal Academy of the Sciences, Scholten and Opzoomer engaged in a sharp polemic against each other. Scholten attacked the narrow "materialistic" concept of science, and in opposition to it stated that experience can lead to knowledge only when combined with reflection and that feelings as such are of a purely subjective nature and can yield truth only when they have a demonstrable objective basis. In time it became obvious to many people that for the foundation of the worldview of modernism Opzoomer's "feeling" (Gefühlserfahrung) was hardly less weak than Scholten's speculation—if for no other reasons, at least on account of the lack of clear definitions.

Let us return once more to Scholten. He would not have been the intrepid thinker "in tune with modernity" if he had not understood the shift to empiricism as a directive for and a challenge to his own method. To remain behind as the cultural currents shifted was for him and his followers the sin against the Holy Spirit. In 1859 he surprised his disciples with the publication of a book on the freedom of the will.[4] In this book he now, as he himself said, set about to tackle on an empirical psychological basis the problem of (in)determinism which he had previously treated dogmatically. People already spoke of the "fundamental shift" that had taken place in Scholten's theology, and in fact the author sometimes gave grounds for this notion. But the reader soon catches Scholten's intent: to show how one should deal with empirical psychological data, namely, with the aid of analytic and synthetic reason which alone is able to raise experience to the level of truth. At the same time he set out to show how experience rightly dealt with is in complete agreement with the truth as apprehended by speculative reason. Hence in the preface to the fourth edition of his Doctrine of the Reformed Church (1861) Scholten could correctly say that between his two main works there was "not the slightest conflict."

That does not, however, convey the whole picture. In 1859 Scholten shifted his emphasis considerably from the ideal to the empirical side of things. The predestination of the omnicausality of God was more firmly combined now with the predominant determinism of the natural sciences. Sin, too, is determined (by our animal situation); it is to be understood, however, as a "not yet" that can and will be overcome by the moral power of God which indwells us. Some years later (1864)

---

4. De vrije wil. Kritisch onderzoek (Leiden: Engels, 1859).

Scholten shifted his interest from systematic theology to the historical-critical study of the New Testament. Under the influence of the Tübingen school, but also independently, he attempted to find "the Son of man," the morally elevated man Jesus, behind the later divinized images of Jesus (especially in John's Gospel). But that study did not bring with it any alteration in his dogmatics. It only meant that its antisupernaturalistic and monistic features were even more sharply—if that is possible—accentuated.

THE PINNACLE AS TURNING POINT:
ALLARD PIERSON AND SYTZE HOEKSTRA

In 1860 modernism reached the pinnacle of its power and influence. At the same time we see the differences between idealism and empiricism weakening in favor of the latter. Still, this development did not lead to a victory for empiricism. Some years later empiricism, and with it modernism in general, was caught up in a deep crisis. Next to the "dogmatic" empiricism of Opzoomer a skeptical empiricism had come into being. Its chief champion was the astute *Allard Pierson* (1831-1896), who on account of his relentless honesty was sometimes called the "enfant terrible" of modernism. As the modernistic pastor of the French Reformed congregation in Rotterdam, he repeatedly raised objections against the leaders of the two main schools. As a dedicated adherent of empiricism, he was unable to find a connection between the self-enclosed deterministic world of experience and the world of religious feeling. He did not have the monistic optimism of Opzoomer. He called himself "a monist in hope." Besides, it became increasingly more intolerable to him to use the institutional church for the propagation of a deterministic humanism (disguised under the name of Jesus) in which there was no room for sin, remorse, forgiveness, prayer, and conversion.

The antisupernaturalism of the modernists, Pierson believed, halted halfway: it denied that God can change water into wine and at the same time proclaimed that God can make a bad person good; it rejected prayer for a healthy body but did pray for a pure heart! Thus it concealed from view the hard fact that Christian faith (as a relation to a personal, living God) and antisupernaturalism are mutually exclusive. Pierson drew his conclusions and in 1865 resigned his office. He was neither the first nor the last modernist to make such a resignation. In 1866 and 1867, however, his apologia unleashed a great deal of excitement among churchgoing modernists and an intense "war of pens," in which

Scholten also took part. Against Pierson's brilliant radicalism, however, the objections had to appear weak.[5] In the eyes of many people the apparent synthesis between gospel and modernity had proved to be flawed and brittle. Whereas in England, as we saw, such syntheses rooted in the theology of mediation had been proven untenable from the side of modernism, in the Netherlands the intellectual honesty which is so essential to modernism turned against its own creations. Both the Bible and the modern experience of reality turned out to be more radical and harder than people had thought and hoped.

In the very year in which the "war of pens" was at its height, 1867, the Reformed Church adopted an addition to its Church Order. The right to appoint a church council and to call a minister was granted to the local church. The result was that in a short time, in most churches, particularly the larger ones, the dominance of modernism was broken. In the 1870s, however, the Leyden theological school continued to flourish. Its influence began to be felt even in other countries. But what was exported was not its obsolete idealistic systematic theology but the findings of its historical-empirical studies, especially Scholten's New Testament research, Kuenen's (Scholten's disciple) Old Testament scholarship, and the research done in the history of religion by C. P. Tiele, who in 1877 was the first in Europe to be appointed to a Chair in the History of Religion.

One may ask whether modernism was not capable on its own of developing an alternative to this optimistic monism, an alternative that could do more justice to the modern experience of reality as well as to the gospel. Actually, in those years that very alternative was available. It stemmed from the Mennonite *Sytze Hoekstra* (1822-1898), professor at the municipal university of Amsterdam. He too was an empiricist, with a special interest in psychological-anthropological experience and developments. These developments, however, pointed not in a monistic but rather in a dualistic direction: The human being is that creature which is at odds with itself. The crises of life, conscience, and the experience of guilt all produce in us a need for redemption. This experience postulates faith in God as saving love.

Hoekstra clearly sought his support in Kant, a philosopher who had otherwise been almost completely neglected in the Netherlands. However, Hoekstra did not wish to restrict the idea of Kant's postulate

---

5. Particularly illuminating from a theological point of view are his brochures: *De Moderne Richting en de Kristelijke Kerk* (Arnhem, 1866); and *Gods wondermacht en ons geestelijk leven* (Arnhem, 1867); the latter was against Scholten's brochure, *Supranaturalism* (Leyden, 1867).

to morality; rather he sought to ground it more broadly in personality and thus to interpret it in a more genuinely religious fashion. Besides, he wanted to complement the transcendental a priori method with a developmental psychological one. Accordingly, in distinction from Scholten's and Opzoomer's work, his work also has genuine room for sin, remorse, grace, and conversion, for the personality of God and of man, and for a relationship between the two.[6] This relationship is so inward, however, and conceived so much in terms of human needs, that for many people he was not able to make a convincing transition from human need to the objective fulfillment of that need. Also, his tedious mode of reasoning prevented him from being more influential. Still, he pointed out a road on which modernism—that brave movement that had gotten stuck— could have escaped the impasse in which it found itself. Hoekstra had many ideas which anticipate what was later developed more persuasively in Ritschl or Herrmann. Not until the renewal of modernism in the Netherlands after World War I (at the time people spoke of "liberal theology") was Hoekstra, as the third father of modernism, esteemed alongside of, or even above, Scholten and Opzoomer. Even then, however, or particularly then, his psychological subjectivism was no longer considered useful as a bridge between gospel and culture.

"TRUTH IS ETHICAL"—THE CONTROLLING IDEA OF MEDIATION: D. CHANTEPIE DE LA SAUSSAYE AND J. H. GUNNING

One cannot help wondering whether the Netherlands had any parallel to the theologies of mediation produced in Germany and England, one that would have been able to bring faith and modernity together convincingly and to avoid the shortcomings of modernism. In fact, there was such a school; but in contrast with what happened in other countries, radical modernism developed a decade earlier than its mediating alternative. Initially, and also later, this alternative was nourished less by Schleiermacher than by the French-Swiss Revival and particularly its theological leader, Alexandre Vinet. It took almost till the turn of the century before it gained a leading role in the life of the church. Between the

6. Cf. esp. his prolegomena to the theory of faith: *Bronnen en grondslagen van het godsdienstig geloof (Sources and foundations of religious belief)* (Amsterdam, 1864). The central thesis is: "All belief in a supersensuous world rests on belief in the truth of our own inner being, of which meanwhile we can only become conscious via our lives in the world of experience and therefore only in connection with, and in the measure of, our experiences" (§ 11, p. 24).

modernism of the theological faculty at Leyden and the supernaturalism of the faculty at Utrecht it first had to win a place for itself in the
years between 1850 and 1870.

That it did win such a place was owing to two prominent ecclesiastical and theological personalities who shaped this new movement.
The founder was *Daniel Chantepie de la Saussaye* (1818-1874; not to be confused with his son, the historian of religion and ethicist, Pierre Daniel).
As pastor of the French Reformed churches in Leeuwarden and Leyden,
as Dutch Reformed minister in Rotterdam, and then as professor in
Groningen for two years, he founded, by means of numerous articles
and brochures, the so-called ethical theology and in the church the ethical movement as an original variety of the theology of mediation. His
younger friend and pupil, *Johannes Hermanus Gunning* (1829-1905), as
pastor in the Hague and later as professor in Amsterdam and Leyden,
promoted the ideas of ethical theology and, by his various talents and
impressive personality, helped to secure for them wide theological and
ecclesiastical influence.

Saussaye came to Leyden in 1848, the year Scholten's main
work in dogmatics appeared. The pastor took up the gauntlet against
the celebrated professor and, in critical but constructive fashion, developed his alternative in a long series of articles under the heading
"Appraisal of Scholten's Doctrine of the Reformed Church" (published in book form in 1859). Later generations are agreed that this answer to modernism was by far the deepest and most thorough. But at
the time its meaning and importance were understood by only a few,
a group to which Scholten himself definitely did not belong. His reply
in the preface to the fourth edition of his work attests with equal
strength to his own incomprehension and his sense of superiority vis-
à-vis his townsman. He could only regard him as inconsistently orthodox. Saussaye's friends, most of them supranaturalists, did not understand him either. His ideas did not seem clear to them. His own
(French or Dutch, mostly the latter) rather ponderous diction was
partly responsible for this impression.

Already his main thesis—"the truth is ethical"—was wide open
to misunderstanding. Many people believed his aim was to emphasize
the ethical implications of the gospel, or to say that only the pure in heart
were able to understand the Word of God. But for Saussaye the word
ethical was not derived from the Greek *ethos* (custom) but from *ēthos*
(character). God's revelation is for him the answer to the deepest needs
and striving of the human personality. "Ethical" meant for him something close to what we mean by "existential." With this thesis he established a front against conservative orthodoxy as well as against modern-

ism. The first negates the deepest concerns of people after the Enlightenment; the second elevates the modern spirit to the level of ultimate truth and norm.

Saussaye directed his energies especially to that second front. Scholten's school proceeds from the Idea; Opzoomer's from the empirical. However, the Idea and the empirical presuppose each other, cannot operate apart from each other. Their fruitless struggle with one another finds its answer and solution in the Christian belief in the Incarnation of God, in the God-man Jesus Christ, in whom the Idea and the empirical are reconciled. This reality must be the starting point both for every modern and for every Christian thinker. Orthodoxy had also been too little aware of this point. It had made too little effort "to liberate the ethical Calvin from the scholastic Calvin" and to make clear the extent to which the great redemptive historical truths of Incarnation, atonement, work of the Spirit, Trinity, etc., all meet "the legitimate demands of modern consciousness," that is, "the unchanging moral needs of human nature." Therefore, as Saussaye put it, the goal of a new theology should be "to humanize the divine without removing its divine character" *(humaniser le divin, sans lui enlever son caractère divin).*

Hence the next question must be of an anthropological nature: What are the deepest needs of human nature referred to here? In this connection Saussaye referred especially (like Vinet) to conscience. In his deepest self man has a sense of duty, on the one hand; on the other, he knows that there is this (for him) insurmountable chasm between "what ought to be" and "what is" which robs him of peace. Only Jesus Christ, the mediator between God and humanity, who reconciles the "is" with the "ought" *(Sollen und Sein),* can overcome this crisis of conscience. The ethical viewpoint is at bottom the Christological one.

Here we shall restrict ourselves to the methodological basics. We must therefore bypass many ideas, for example, his view of Israel's role in the history of redemption, of the self-limitation of God, and of the essence of the church. Having made this reduction one is especially struck by what Saussaye has in common with mediation theologians outside the Netherlands. He himself always strongly emphasized his affinities with Schleiermacher and Vinet. But Schleiermacher tended too much toward subjectivism for his taste, and Vinet too much toward individualism. Philosophically he was probably as close to the dualism of Kant as he was distant from classic idealism. But Kant was too moralistic for him. When it comes to the issues of conscience and human self-transcendence, Saussaye preferred to speak in the manner of Vinet. Much of Saussaye's thinking is reminiscent of German mediation theology, which he followed closely and to which he owed a great deal for the development of his own insights.[7] His work also reveals many parallels with the (later) *Lux Mundi* group, if one ignores for now the influence of the patristics and Darwin among the latter. They, however, were unfamiliar with the work of Saussaye. This should in general serve as a warning to us not to look too much for "dependencies" among European mediation theologians. A common spiritual climate and the estrangement between church and world that came with it drove convinced and at the same time modern Christians everywhere, with inherent necessity, in the same direction.

THE NEO-CONFESSIONAL ALTERNATIVE: A. KUYPER AND H. BAVINCK

In keeping with its nature, mediation theology always suffered attacks from two directions. The liberal groups accused it of interpreting or bending the culture of the day in a Christian direction and thus construing a pseudo-synthesis; we already saw how this objection propelled the history of Anglican theology. In the Netherlands the historical development was rather the reverse. At the cradle of the reawakening of theology stood modernism. Then, because it contradicted the gospel, it was attacked from the right. "Ethical theology" saw itself as the legitimate and appropriate answer of orthodoxy. But when modernism then, especially because of its own inner dichotomy, lost much of its attractiveness, it came to light that for many people in the camp of Reformed orthodoxy "ethical theology" was not representative. After 1870 confessional theology experienced a strong upswing and entered the lists against the mediation theology that had been gaining ground.

In the Introduction above we already explained why we planned

7. On Nov. 4, 1868, on the occasion of the tricentennial of the Convent of Wesel (the synod at which the Reformed Church in the Netherlands was founded), Saussaye gave a speech on the connections between German and Dutch theology: "Over het verband van duitsche en nederlandsche theologie" (*Protestantse Bijdragen* [1872], 3:1-32). It is striking that in this speech he mentions idealistic philosophy only in passing and mediation theology not at all! Only Kant and Schleiermacher were brought to the fore with much praise. Although he could not regard Kant as a Christian, he wrote (significantly for the connection between Kant's philosophy and his own theology): "I believe I can say that in Kant's moralism there is not only a point of contact for the Christian doctrine of sin but also a challenge to the church to enter more deeply into its own mystery and to turn from a rigid scholastic dogmatism to a living conception of the truth of salvation" (p. 14). This speech prompted the theological faculty of Bonn to confer an honorary doctorate on him the same year.

to give only incidental consideration to confessional theology. At this point, however, an exception must be made. Dutch Neo-Confessionalism, one must know, developed in close and frequently existential contact with the two preceding alternatives through the careers of two great leaders, Kuyper and Bavinck (both of them having far-reaching influence, in part through the Princeton theology in America). In common with them it had the conviction that classic orthodoxy had to be further articulated in conscious confrontation with the questions of the modern period.

At Leyden *Abraham Kuyper* (1837-1920) had been the ardent pupil of Scholten, inspired by his knowledge of Reformed theology and his determination to raise it, through fresh interpretation, to "the height of the modern age." As a young pastor he discovered the pietistic-Calvinistic circles of his church, people for whom the Reformed faith still had a very different existential meaning than it did for Scholten and himself. A spiritual crisis and the experience of "rebirth" led him to seek the renewal of Reformational theology along very different lines. For a short period he sought help in the works of Vinet, Saussaye, and Gunning. But because he had in mind a renewal especially of the church and society along Reformed lines, and because the ecclesiological and political thinking of "ethical theology" did not seem clear and vigorous enough to him, he soon turned away from these men, in order to start afresh with Calvin. Soon after 1870 Kuyper devoted his energies to a reformation and reorganization of the Reformed (Hervormde) Church (opposition to the liberals and the restoration of church discipline). As a result he increasingly alienated himself from the (less "juridical" and more "spiritualistic") "ethicals." But he did not, as his social and political ideas and actions show, develop a theology of repristination. Conservative Christians charged that his so-called Neo-Calvinism had hardly anything to do with Calvin anymore. E. Troeltsch billed him as the modernizer of Calvinism.[8] In theology—apart from his broad development of the doctrine of common grace—Kuyper closely followed the Calvinistic tradition, even in its scholastic form.

8. Ernst Troeltsch, *The Social Teaching of the Christian Churches*, 2 vols., tr. Olive Wyon (repr. New York: Harper & Row, 1960), 2:577, 655, 660, 931 n. 414, 934-35 n. 415, 938-39 n. 418, 676. His verdict was that "in all these questions [pluriformity of the church and political tolerance] Neo-Calvinism has drifted far away from Calvin—a fact which Kuyper tried in vain to conceal" (p. 676, more sharply on p. 879 n. 309). The last words are unfair, due to Troeltsch's unfamiliarity with Kuyper's main (Dutch) works in which Kuyper explains his distance from Calvin. Troeltsch took his cue from Kuyper's Stone Lectures, a summary of his views.

Herman Bavinck (1854-1921) belonged to the Reformed Church of the Secession. After his seminary training, he studied in Leyden under the guidance of Scholten—against the prevailing tradition of his church. But he never was or became a follower of Scholten. In his search for the right response to modernism he was fascinated, already in Leyden, by "ethical theology," and its influence always stuck with him. In 1880, the same year in which he founded the Free University in Amsterdam, Kuyper discovered this highly gifted young systematician. Repeatedly but in vain he invited Bavinck to join the faculty (though at last in 1902 Bavinck did become his successor). Kuyper, the strategist, also saw how strongly Bavinck was drawn to "ethical theology." On several occasions, even public ones, he appealed to his young co-religionist to give clearer and more polemical expression to his objections against "ethical" views. Bavinck finally yielded to this appeal but, in Kuyper's judgment, did it much too gently.

Bavinck's lecture to the Reformed Ministers' Conference in 1884, and the expanded version of it which he published shortly after,[9] is a testimony to his great openness and to an appreciation for the deep and often difficult thought-complexes of Saussaye, an appreciation rare among opponents. From his own more classically Reformed viewpoint, Bavinck found in Saussaye's thinking a lack of distance between God and humanity, a deficiency in the sense of the transcendence of God, too little authority and sovereignty, not enough recognition of the transethical elements in revelation and faith, and therefore too much immanence, an excess of "humanizing the divine," of the normativity of the experience of the Christian church, of self-fulfillment at the expense of self-denial. The weakness of Bavinck's presentation and appraisal lay in his idea of the concept of mediation. Bavinck thought that Saussaye aimed at mediation between orthodoxy and modernism; the latter, however, had in view the mediation between God and humanity as it occurs in the God-man Christ and which must be assimilated by us as a basic theological principle.

Bavinck did not rest with this (mild) evaluation but also tried to indicate an alternative. He stressed that he did not want, any more than Saussaye, to return to the sixteenth and seventeenth centuries. The difference between them began with the question of the response to which the modern period, or God through this period, was calling them. Saussaye was struggling to achieve a new Christian-culture synthesis, the reconciliation of faith and science. Bavinck believed, however, that such

9. H. Bavinck, *De Theologie van Prof. Dr. Daniel Chantepie de la Saussaye: Bijdrage tot de kennis der ethische theologie* (Leiden: D. Donner, 1884).

"irenicism" would always be hurtful to the church of Christ. "Could it not be, then, that those are right who say that today the confessors of Christ have to take a different road, namely, the road of self-denial?" We are much too enchanted with the principles of our opponents. First of all we must learn again to reflect on our own cause: "We shall have to practise self-denial to this end that for a certain period we shall have to put up with being called 'unscientific,' to forgo a generally unfruitful and powerless apologetic, and in every area of life to assume the burden of separation."

The concluding paragraph reads:

> Sectarianism is as repugnant to us as it is to de la Saussaye. But it is our judgment that the proper reconciliation of faith and science, of church and theology, can be achieved only by isolation, not by union and a higher synthesis. Thus, whereas he entertains the idea of fighting the enemy on his own ground and with his own weapons, we believe that the Christian can only count on victory if he enters the lists against his enemies in his own armor and in the name of the Lord of hosts whom they have defied. It could be that thus a beautiful day might still dawn upon the horizon for a church and theology in our fatherland! (p. 97)

Those are weighty words. Bavinck decisively rejected repristination and searched for alternatives to modernism and the theology of mediation. Some things in his lecture make one think of Kierkegaard, other things of Barth.

BRIDGE CONSTRUCTION THWARTED

Bavinck was most heavily attacked by Gunning, who defended his late teacher and friend in a book entitled *Jesus Christ, the Mediator of God and Men*, which appeared in the same year as the lecture. In reality Bavinck and Gunning were not at all that far apart, and they both knew it. Gunning addressed the young Bavinck emphatically as his "brother." In regard to church politics, however, they found themselves in opposing camps. Bavinck had opted for Kuyper's strategy and organization, whereas Gunning rejected this strategy as unspiritual. This background gave his book an edge which could not be justified theologically. He rightly attacked Bavinck's mistaken understanding of the notion of mediation. On other points he stressed those elements in Saussaye which were most important to him, without seeing that Bavinck had with equal or more justice put the emphasis on other elements. Whereas Saussaye emphasized especially the harmony between the anguished search of man and the experience of salvation in the church—without denying the break between them—in Gunning the accents have clearly shifted. Much more than Saussaye, he pointed out the discontinuity between flesh and spirit, between church and world. More than the need for redemption he emphasized sin, and over against "experience" he posited faith. His thinking is more personalistic, shaped by the cross instead of the Incarnation, by the eschatological future instead of the presence of the Spirit. Characteristic is the statement that the mediation pursued by ethical theology "is that which follows from afar the mediation between God and world which brought the Savior to the cross" (p. 32). Such sentences, though one reads them in Saussaye's sermons, hardly ever occur in his theological treatises. From this angle one understands that in the Netherlands even today Gunning's works are still much read by theologians. They regard him as a forerunner of Barth's theology. Gunning's thought constituted a bridge from mediation theology to Neo-Confessional theology just as Bavinck's thought was that from the opposing side. Still, no bond was established—it was thwarted by church-political solidarity of each with his own camp.

THE BRIEF TRIUMPH OF NEO-CONFESSIONALISM

Bavinck's hope that "a beautiful day might still dawn upon the horizon for church and theology in our fatherland" if they gave up apologetics and gained the courage to pursue their own cause was actually fulfilled —by himself, in the four volumes of his *Gereformeerde Dogmatiek,* which for many Dutch-reading theologians has remained to this day a mine of information and insight. In 1895 the first volume of the first edition appeared in which the foundations (Bavinck called them *Principia*) of dogmatics were treated. In Bavinck the objective principle of knowledge is primary: the Holy Scriptures, the fruit of the final act of the Spirit in the objective revelation of God. The subjective principle is faith, rather faith's final ground in the testimony of the Holy Spirit which spontaneously communicates to us the certainty of being children of God and, in that context, the divine inspiration of Scripture. Accordingly, Bavinck has to reject (§ 19) "the ethical-psychological method": there is no road from human needs, as man himself senses and interprets them, to the truth as God reveals it to us.

When Bavinck published this volume, the theological dialogue between the "Ethicals" and the Reformed had for a long time already been pushed aside by the church struggle. Bavinck was viewed as the faithful theological partisan and alter ego of Kuyper. In 1902 he yielded to Kuyper's urging of him to leave the Theological School at Kampen and to become Kuyper's successor in dogmatics at the Free University in Amsterdam. There he worked on the second edition of his dogmatics (1906-1911) and wrote a one-volume summary which he called *Magnalia Dei* (1909), a book which enabled many people at home and abroad (it was translated into English)[10] to appropriate his fund of ideas unencumbered by the complicated structure of the main work. Apart from this work, Bavinck produced notably little in the field of dogmatics during these years and almost nothing that was new and original. He felt increasingly that the modern period needed a much more vigorous renewal of theology than he himself had produced or was able to produce. Particularly the issues arising from the historical-critical interpretation of Scripture needed a very different approach.

In his views of the issues at stake he became increasingly more relativistic. Around 1910 he sold a large part of his dogmatic works. During these years the issues posed by culture fascinated him. In this Amsterdam period his most important publications concerned psychology, pedagogics, and politics. Common cultural interests brought him into contact again with the "Ethicals" in the Association for Christian Students (then usually avoided by the Gereformeerden) and in the editorial board of a Christian-cultural periodical.

The title of this chapter, "Coming up from Behind in the Netherlands," applies also to Neo-Confessional theology in the Netherlands. In most European countries such a theology came about as a product of restoration as early as the second and third decades of the nineteenth century. The Netherlands was more than a half-century behind; here this theology was consciously forged, next to and after modernism and the theology of mediation, as a third response to the intellectual challenge arising from the Enlightenment. That is what gave it a vitality and scope which is usually not typical of confessionalism elsewhere. Besides, it was a powerful inspiration in the political and cultural awakening of the Calvinistic segment of the population which in these years achieved a strong position in the modern world.

Still, after 1900 Bavinck increasingly felt that his theological direction was leading to a dead end. Why? Was it only historical-critical research which undermined his earlier certainty? Perhaps Gunning, in his polemics against Bavinck, had revealed a deeper understanding of

10. *Our Reasonable Faith*, tr. Henry Zylstra (Grand Rapids: Eerdmans, 1956).

the problem. For him the difference between Reformed theology and "ethical theology" did not lie in theocentricity versus anthropocentricity but in intellectualism versus personalism: Is faith submission to the authority of scriptural truths or is it the personal encounter with God through the person of Christ by which we are transformed into personalities? Bavinck opted for the priority of the scriptural principle, and in the prolegomena of his dogmatics he threw in his lot (with some Reformed corrections) with Neo-Thomism. For him faith was not in the first place a yielding up of one's life to a Person but intellectual assent and submission to Scripture. Hence Bavinck remained more strongly burdened than he wished by the legacy of the Reformed scholasticism of the seventeenth century and gave up intellectual tools he could not well do without in the continuing confrontation with the modern spirit. It is not surprising, therefore, that in the first three or four decades of the twentieth century Reformed theology fell back on the traditional scholastic elements of Bavinck. This tendency was furthered by the predominance of Kuyper, who in his dogmatics was much closer to the old scholasticism than Bavinck. Not until after World War II did Gerrit Cornelis Berkouwer, Bavinck's second successor, consciously go back to the original, antischolastic lines of Bavinck's thought, while in the 1960s historical research again uncovered his numerous (forgotten) links with "ethical theology."

The years 1848-1884 mark the period of florescence for systematic theology in the Netherlands. Later the various positions stabilize, church conflicts absorb most of the available energy, and in theology the focus shifts to historical studies and particularly to the pros and cons of Bible criticism. In all directions the epigones are in charge. Undoubtedly the most interesting personalities are in the ranks of the "ethical" theologians. It is they who, by a plethora of cultural, biblical, and ethical studies, mediate between gospel and culture. Additions to, or a deepening of, the foundations no longer occur. The tendency to subjectivism which Bavinck feared and pointed out in fact came ever more clearly to the fore after the death of Gunning. Bavinck's warning to the "Ethicals" at the close of his study of Saussaye remains just as relevant as Gunning's warning in his reply to Bavinck and the confessionally Reformed. Not until after World War I do the questions change, and after World War II the answers and the fronts also change. Or is it perhaps the case that only the personalities and the situations change while the questions and the possible answers remain basically the same?

CHAPTER IX

Ritschl: His Design and Its Limitations

THE MECHANISM OF NATURE AND HUMAN FREEDOM

In chapter 5 above, "The Aftereffects of Idealism in Theology," we saw how long idealism in Germany dominated theology (and partly philosophy), even though in England and the Netherlands, for example, empiricism had long since become the unofficial or official partner in dialogue. One has to assume that this situation also had deeper roots in the psychology of the nations. Germany tends to be more at home in the world of images and ideas than in empirical observation. Hence in Germany, in the nineteenth century, empiricism played a less influential and less radical role, and did so later and for a shorter period, than in many other European circles. In time, however, people could no longer ignore the changed world. From 1830 on empiricism had been dominant in the sciences, and from 1860 on the cultural effects were everywhere visible: in steam power and mechanics, in railroads and ocean-going vessels, in the opposition between capital and labor, in imperialism and militarism. Besides, on these waves of "realism" Germany had been lifted to a level of political superiority — through the Prussian victory over Austria (1866), Bismarck's policy of uniting the German states, the founding of the German empire (1870), and the German victory over France (1871). The cultural mood in Germany turned more and more to the world of experience and the natural laws governing it. The reality of space and time gained much more weight and a much clearer autonomy than an idealistically disposed mind could handle. Still, this reality was not experienced in a deterministic fashion. The experience of the mechanisms of nature went hand in hand with a strong sense of progress, of human freedom and power. Humanity is clearly not a product and plaything of the powers of nature but superior to them as their ruler. By utilizing the predictable laws of nature humanity can establish a realm of progress that becomes ever more free.

The philosophy which fitted this double feeling was not the absolute idealism of Fichte or Hegel but the dualistic idealism of Kant. We note how in the 1860s in Germany, following Kuno Fischer, Friedrich Albert Lange, and others, there is a shift back to Kant. Still, while in keeping with the emerging evolutionary thought and the period's sense of harmony, the distinction between "pure" and "practical" reason is accentuated, the opposition between them is not. In this period the transcendental critique of reason advanced by Kant was complemented by a psychology of the development of reason. On the one hand, the rootedness of all reason in the animal and primitive human layers of reality was brought to light, and on the other, people pointed out the teleological tendency of natural complexes toward hominization and freedom. Nature's mechanisms are fully recognized (hence the inherent orderliness and limitation of pure reason and particularly of the natural sciences); from the very start, however, this world is viewed, so to speak, as the necessary infrastructure of a cosmic movement that is teleologically adapted to the highest ideas (freedom, immortality, God) and the highest values (truth, morality, beauty).

The most influential philosopher, one who was at the same time representative for the thinking of this epoch, was *Rudolf Hermann Lotze* (1817-1881). Especially his work *Mikrokosmos: Ideen zur Naturgeschichte und Geschichte der Menschheit: Versuch einer Anthropologie* (1st ed. 1856-1864; 2nd ed. 1869-1872) was widely read. He created the appropriate model in which the experiences of the time found a place—from the deterministic theory of evolution to the theory of the personality of God and the infinite value of the personal minds created by him.

Living and working in this world was the by now matured *Albrecht Ritschl* (1822-1889). In his training and further development he had passed through supranaturalism, the theology of mediation, and the Tübingen Hegelianism of F. C. Baur. After 1846 he turned away from Baur. He mistrusted the a priori scheme into which Baur forced the New Testament and opted for open-minded research in accord with the empirical historical method (which immediately led him to more conservative results).[1] Still, he did not give up his confidence in the rule of Spirit in the world and particularly in the historical process. But for Ritschl this rule could only be established by a long journey through historical studies (he studied biblical theology and the history of dogma

1. A lengthy account of this shift occurs in O. Ritschl (Albrecht's son), *Albrecht Ritschls Leben*, vol. 1 (Freiburg, 1892), chs. IV and V.

throughout his life). Then, in his philosophical orientation, he shifted from Hegel to Kant. And professionally he shifted from New Testament to Dogmatics, in order from that vantage point again to inquire into history. In 1848 as *Privatdozent* (university instructor) in Bonn, he began annually to give lectures in the history of dogma—a new practice. As professor in Dogmatics he worked first in Bonn (1852-1864), then, till his death, in Göttingen (1864-1889).

JUSTIFICATION AND RECONCILIATION

In 1870, an exceedingly crucial year for Germany, the first (dogmatic-historical) volume of Ritschl's *The Christian Doctrine of Justification and Reconciliation* came off the press. The second (biblical) and the third (dogmatic) volumes appeared in 1874. A second edition appeared in 1882-1883, a third in 1888-1889. In each of the two new editions Ritschl introduced significant changes, changes which must be considered not as essential corrections but as important shifts in emphasis. We shall consider a few of them later. A fourth (posthumous) edition appeared between 1895 and 1902, and in 1910 a popular edition in two volumes. That this learned and dryly written work should enjoy so many readers is to be explained by the fact that it was very much in tune with the times and that many people found expressed in it the way they themselves experienced, or wanted to experience, the Christian faith. Ritschl was and wanted to be, heart and soul, a believing Christian, and at the same time belonged with the entire fabric of his life to his own culture and time. He was a down-to-earth, disciplined, and rationally pious "man of duty," of the beginning of the "Wilhelminic" epoch, animated by faith in progress and moral self-confidence. People have sometimes viewed him as the symbol of the bourgeoisie of that time (Emperor William II). In him the Christian and the solid burgher had merged. It is remarkable to see embodied in him such an undisturbed synthesis between biblical faith and a keyed-to-the-times realism—a complete contrast with what we saw in the Netherlands, where the experience of the determinism of nature opened the gap between faith and knowledge and drove pastors out of their ministry. Ritschl had not a trace of such a split. In his worldview he cast his lot with Lotze, whom he had learned to know and value as colleague in Göttingen, and whose *Mikrokosmos* is repeatedly quoted in Ritschl's main work.[2]

2. Hence I cannot agree with Schellong's interesting view that Ritschl's dualism of nature and freedom marked "the beginning crisis of the bourgeoisie" (D. Schellong, *Bürgertum und christliche Religion* [Munich: Kaiser, 1975], pp. 52-

RITSCHL, LUTHER, KANT

This brings us to the question of the ideological and philosophical un-
derpinnings of Ritschl's dogmatics. The question seems to be an easy
one and is usually answered by reference to Kant and Lotze. Both names,
however, play only a more or less marginal role in his works. After all,
Ritschl was by nature a historian, not a philosopher. He devoted but little
attention to the "prolegomena," viewing them as the "court of the Gentiles."[3] His son reports that he only gradually developed his epistemological viewpoints "when he abstracted them basically from his theological understanding as it had already been clearly formulated." After all,
the theory of cognition "concerns only the formal laws of knowledge,
the laws which apply in every science. Hence it is absurd to take its rules
as the constitutive principles of theology."[4] One such line of thought may
remind the present-day reader of Karl Barth! When, shortly before the
appearance of the second edition of his main work, he then published a
book more explicitly on method,[5] it had to be disappointing on account
of its lack of new viewpoints and an excess of polemics.

Despite this shortcoming, however, a lot more needs to be said.
We mentioned Ritschl's orientation to Kant after he turned away from
Hegel. The extent to which this new orientation was based on his own
study, the extent to which he received it secondhand, the extent to which
he absorbed it unconsciously when the shift to Kant was in the air—all
this is hard to ascertain. Clearly, what attracted Ritschl to Kant was the

---

69). His comparison with Schleiermacher only proves that the face of bourgeoisie
had changed, particularly under the influence of technology. If Ritschl saw "a
crisis of bourgeoisie" he saw it arising not from the spirit of the time but from
the gospel.

3. See S. H. Stephan and M. Schmidt, *Geschichte der deutschen evangelischen Theologie*, 2nd ed. (Berlin: Töpelmann, 1960), p. 217. I regard the presentation of Ritschl in this book as exemplary.

4. O. Ritschl, *Albrecht Ritschls Leben*, 2:185-86. In his opinion, psychology meant much more for Ritschl's thinking than epistemology. On Ritschl's rejection of the overvaluation of method, see p. 106, where also the characteristic
quote from a letter to H. Holtzmann occurs: "The folks who keep wallowing
about merely in the prolegomena issues of the subjective locus of religion, of religion in general, of miracle and dogmatic method, remain stuck in the court of
the Gentiles and keep themselves far from the face of God." On Ritschl and
philosophy, see also D. Schellong, *Bürgertum und christliche Religion*, p. 63.

5. A. Ritschl, *Theologie und Metaphysik: Zur Verständigung und Abwehr*
(Bonn, 1881).

latter's focus on morality as the divinely appointed field of human activity. Also clear is that in his reception of Kant there was development. Finally, we see that at crucial points, precisely as a theologian, he decidedly rejected Kant, especially because as a Christian and Luther scholar he emphasized, in his teaching of justification, the independence of religious relationships vis-à-vis the ethical.[6]

We mentioned a development in Ritschl's reception of Kant. This comes out especially in the changes which Ritschl made in § 29: "The so-called proofs of the existence of God" in the third volume of his *Justification and Reconciliation*. In the first edition, Ritschl agrees with Kant's moral proof for the existence of God but rejects his separation of this "practical" proof from the proofs of theoretical reason. "Kant wrongly let himself be persuaded . . . to oppose practical Reason as one species of Reason to theoretical Reason as another." Now the spirit experiences itself as an end while nature is the means. It is "the task of cognition to seek for a law explaining the coexistence of these two heterogeneous orders of reality." "Nothing remains but to accept the Christian idea of God" also as a scientifically valid truth. "To accept the idea of God in this way is not practical faith but an act of theoretical cognition."[7] This opposition to Kant's dualism is completely in agreement with the way people in this period sought to bring together in one conception the mechanical world of nature and the world of spiritual freedom. Ritschl therefore intended, to the same degree, to bring together in one conception theology and philosophy or metaphysics. In succeeding editions, however, he offered a revision of § 29 in which he concurred with Kant's separation of the two modes of cognition. Is it because in these years he is more impressed by the godlessness of the mechanism of nature?

In any case, his faith in "metaphysics" and "natural theology" is completely over. Whether and how that relates to the increasing secularization of his world is nowhere made clear. Ritschl himself explains his new view very differently. New § 29 starts with the sentence: "That religious knowledge consists of value judgments is brought out in a

6. On Ritschl's relation to Kant, see P. Wrzecionko, "Der geistesgeschichtliche Horizont der Theologie Albrecht Ritschls," *Neue Zeitschrift für systematische Theologie* 5 (1963) 214-34.

7. These translations are from the 1st edition, pp. 190-92, cited by the author (Hendrikus Berkhof), which is not the edition translated by Mackintosh and Macaulay, *The Christian Doctrine of Justification and Reconciliation* (Clifton, NJ: Reference Book Publishers, 1966), the translation from which I quote here wherever possible.—TRANS.

felicitious way by Luther in his *Larger Catechism* in the explanation of the First Commandment" (3rd ed., Eng. tr., p. 211). By this statement he means that the knowledge of God is realized only in the act of faith and that faith directs itself toward the saving activity of Christ. Ritschl emphatically states "that I maintain the religious conception of God as conditioned in the way Luther describes" (p. 212). If today such thoughts seem to us self-evident, it is to a large extent owing to the intellectual labor of Ritschl. And he owed it to a high degree to his study of Luther. It is typical for the shift in emphasis in the successive editions of the third volume of *Justification and Reconciliation* in general that the ideological elements yield to the biblical and Lutheran elements and that, in connection with that act, the religious foundation (justification) comes to the fore more strongly alongside the moral goal (reconciliation). For Ritschl the Christian faith increasingly became a special kind of cognition that does indeed wish to be acknowledged as a distinct sphere of experience by theoretical science but does not require its grounding from this direction.

It is clear that for insight into the independence of theology Kant's thinking can render the services of a midwife. The usual assumption is that this was increasingly the case in the successive editions. A comparison of the texts of § 29, however, makes this conclusion doubtful. For, contrary to what one would expect, though in the later editions Ritschl softens his polemic against Kant, he never turns it into consent —as especially the introduction of the concept "value judgment" would lead one to expect. One is astonished to see how most of the quotations we adduced from the first edition return essentially unchanged in the third. Only one sentence has been changed into its opposite: "To accept the idea of God in this way is, as Kant observes, practical faith and not an act of theoretical cognition" (pp. 224-25). It is an enigma how Ritschl possibly conceived the remaining antithetical thoughts to be in agreement with his new statement.[8] At the end, however, he added a page to

---

8. O. Ritschl, *Albrecht Ritschls Leben*, 2:139-40, writes that in the 2nd edition his father still believed that theology was possible as science only if the idea of God was an act of theoretical cognition. "But in the context of his overall theological outlook it made sense for him not to repeat this insight in the third edition but rather to replace it with the opposite judgment. To be sure, this meant the entire section (§ 29) should have been refashioned. Since this was done only in part, the later segments are not in complete agreement with the older ones. Accordingly, the explanations of the earlier editions which remained in the third, require a correction in the sense that a theoretical proof for the existence of God can in no way be given."

guide the train of thought back toward the opening words concerning Luther. Here he emphasizes that only Kant's moral proof for the existence of God can do justice to "the Christian conception of God" and "to his worth for men and in particular his worth for men as sinners. . . . Yet he does not posit this idea—which is an object merely of practical faith, and cannot be proved apart from such faith—as a conception which is theoretical or rational in the sense of general science. On the contrary, he maintains it in its original and specific character." And in the very next sentence he stresses that "it is the duty of theology to conserve the special characteristic of the conception of God, namely, that it can only be represented in value-judgments" (p. 225). It is in such sentences that Ritschl lays bare his very heart. He intends to maintain the uniqueness of the Christian faith as a way of access to the "conception of God" through trust in Jesus Christ—apart from any ground other than that given in the unity of revelation and faith. In that context he utilizes Kant to the extent that Kant is useful, and he is only useful where he seems to point, in philosophical and timely fashion, to that which has already been said before in the New Testament and by Luther.[9]

THE CONCEPT "VALUE JUDGMENT"

This leads us to a more precise consideration of "value judgment," a concept Ritschl introduced as the very expression of his changed view of cognition (2nd ed., § 28: "The peculiar character of religious knowledge"). To this day Ritschl is under a cloud especially in orthodox circles on account of this concept. It was adduced ever and again as proof that Ritschl was an extreme dualistic Kantian who delivered the Christian faith over to pure subjectivism.

9. P. Wrzecionko, *Neue Zeitschrift für systematische Theologie* 5 (1963): 231, offers the following happy formulation: "Just as Luther coming from nominalism overcame the theological metaphysical self-sufficiency of medieval thought by his radical commitment to 'sola scriptura,' as Kant destroyed the logical deduction of rationalistic metaphysics in his critique of reason, so also Ritschl, under the influence of both men, opposed the positive-historical tie to Scripture to the metaphysical autonomy of idealistic thought. The epistemological basis for this, however, comes predominantly from the second." Only the last sentence seems to me to take Ritschl's relationship to Kant more seriously than he himself did (witness the botched revision of § 29 in the 3rd edition). I have come to the same conclusion as J. Richmond, who, in his excellent book *Ritschl: A Reappraisal* (London/New York: Collins, 1978), writes: "It is hard to resist the conclusion that Ritschl has little or no *intrinsic* interest in philosophical issues" (p. 24).

It is not at all easy correctly to interpret the concept of value judgment in terms of origin, content, and function. Kant did not use it. Nor did Lotze, although in this period the word *value* was much in vogue and occurs in his work, in Ritschl, and many others. The word *value* was intended to represent the autonomy of the world of the mind vis-à-vis the mechanism of nature. However, in Lotze's *Mikrokosm* (the only work by him that Ritschl cited), where in connection with religion one would expect the expression "value judgment," other expressions occur, like "experience," "feeling," "ethical core," "mood." Ritschl appeals neither to Kant nor to Lotze, when in the second edition of his main work he develops the concept of "value judgment" in barely five pages. One has no choice but to believe that his use of the word as a technical term was his own invention. The two most significant passages read:

> Religious knowledge moves in independent value-judgments, which relate to man's attitude to the world, and call forth feelings of pleasure or pain, in which man either enjoys the dominion over the world vouchsafed him by God, or feels grievously the lack of God's help to that end. (p. 205)

> In Christianity, religious knowledge consists in independent value-judgments, inasmuch as it deals with the relation between the blessedness which is assured by God and sought by man, and the whole of the world which God has created and rules in harmony with His final end. (p. 207)

Just what Ritschl meant by those statements can only become clear as we study the relationship between divine providence and human dominion over the world. Here we can only note with astonishment the isolated character of these passages concerning value judgments; the whole conveys the sense of an erratic glacial boulder. After these few pages the course of Ritschl's thinking again proceeds as in the previous edition. We already heard that this key expression returns in § 29 but only rarely. This fact again reminds us of Ritschl's struggle in this section to make clear both the autonomy and the objective content of Christian cognition. His aim in the expansion of § 28 must have been the same as that of the expansion and partial correction in § 29; namely, to express the peculiar character of religious knowledge as it became clear to him through the study of Luther, after the appearance of the first edition of *Justification and Reconciliation*.

He used the concept a second time in § 44, which deals with "The Divinity of Christ as religious knowledge." Anger over the term stems almost totally from this Christological application of it. Still, this title (in the

3rd edition) sounds much fuller than it does in the first where it reads: "The specific importance of the founder in the Christian religion." It was precisely from the perspective of value judgment that he was able to appreciate the confession of the deity of Christ more positively than before. Very characteristic is the sentence: "Since the aim of the Christian is to be attained under the form of personal freedom, therefore the twofold significance we are compelled to ascribe to Christ as being at once the perfect revealer of God and the manifest type of spiritual lordship over the world, finds expression in the single predicate of His Godhead" (p. 389).

This statement agrees with the one cited above (from p. 205) to the effect that the religious value judgment relates to man's position vis-à-vis the world and to the help of God he enjoys or has to do without in that context. Faith — as trust in Christ's saving activity — can only indirectly express such a value judgment ("Christ is God") because Christ's being manifests itself only in his works and can only be read from his works. An ontological utterance apart from a functional relationship to God and to Christ who reveals him is in fact not possible. It would transform faith into metaphysics and a purely intellectual affirmation of doctrinal propositions. This, of course, is where we encounter the statement of Melanchthon which was endlessly repeated in the Ritschlian school: "For to know Christ is to know his benefits, not as the scholastics teach, to contemplate his natures, the modes of his incarnation" (*Hoc est enim Christum cognoscere, beneficia eius cognoscere, non quod isti [scholastici] docent, eius naturas, modos incarnationis contueri,* p. 396). Luther is also quoted at length. Question: Does Ritschl, by saying this, make Christ's deity into an attribute of his humanity? His answer: It is an attribute of his working as revelation of God. "If Christ by what He has done and suffered for my salvation is my Lord, and if, by trusting for my salvation to the power of what He has done for me, I honour Him as my God, then that is a value-judgment of a direct kind. . . . The nature of God and the Divine we can only know in its essence by determining its value for our salvation" (p. 398).

This line of thought and its underlying assumptions are so familiar in contemporary theology that one may easily forget it was first formulated clearly by Ritschl and that he was continually and with great severity attacked for that very reason. The word *value judgment*, however, is misleading; it creates the impression that it is solely grounded in subjective human appreciation, as a postulate or projection, without having an objective content. Ritschl's line of thought was not at all intended anthropocentrically but relationally and functionally (not functionalistically!): in the face of the saving encounter with the Christ of revelation a person finds himself forced to make this judgment. "The religious estimate of His Person will stand related to His moral conduct in so far as the latter is the test and counterpart of His own conviction that He enjoys a unique fellowship with God" (p. 413). It remains an enigma nevertheless why all of a sudden, in a few scattered passages, Ritschl introduced this misleading expression to illuminate a line of thought that by itself was clear enough in the work as a whole.[10]

OUR DOMINION OVER THE WORLD AND GOD'S PROVIDENCE

These considerations do not lead to the result that Ritschl, proceeding along the (misconstrued) tracks of *The Critique of Practical Reason*, turned the Christian faith into a purely subjective affair. Still, these considerations and actually all the dogmatic pronouncements of Ritschl point in the direction of anthropology, even if in a different way than Kant. We learned that the value judgment a person makes depends on "his position vis-à-vis the world," and that the value of Christ is to be found in his "spiritual lordship over the world." Ritschl's work is full of similar expressions; for the goal of our world is "practical proof of sonship with God in spiritual freedom and dominion over the world and labor for the kingdom of God."[11] This idea is every prominent in *Justification and Reconciliation* (III, § 62), under the title "Religious lordship over the world not negation of the world." The opening words of this section are: "The lordship over the world possessed by believers, which is the aim of reconciliation with God in the Christian sense . . ." (p. 609). Ritschl has in mind not (only) a technical lordship but in the first place a moral lordship, one that is grounded in a religious attitude. In regard to this religious foundation he thinks of texts like Mark 8:35-37 (the soul as far superior to the world), 1 Corinthians 3:21-23 (all things are yours), and

10. Here too H. Stephan and M. Schmidt strike the right note: "Hence, according to Ritschl, a value judgment does not stand in opposition to an ontological judgment but to a theoretical judgment. The 'value' in question was undoubtedly understood as an objective entity" (*Geschichte der deutschen evangelischen Theologie*, p. 219).

11. Quoted from *Instruction in the Christian Religion*, tr. P. Hefner (Philadelphia: Fortress, 1972), p. 240. This summary of Ritschl's dogmatics greatly contributed, through its five editions, to the spread of his ideas. One must remember, however, that it was written immediately after the 1st edition of *Justification and Reconciliation* and stresses even more than this work the moral goal at the expense of the religious foundations.

Romans 8:38-39 (no creature can separate us from the love of God). Still, the idea remains remarkably undeveloped also in § 62. It is continually presupposed as self-evident, although scriptural proof is needed and Ritschl himself remarks somewhere that even Luther did not know too much about it. For him, however, it was a self-evident Christian principle which he saw expressed and realized especially in the exaltation of Christ. Even or especially the sacrificial death of Christ, as the most perfect expression of his "vocational obedience" (the resurrection plays no role here) signifies the victory over the world. "For through this suffering he transformed the world's opposition to his life purpose into a means of his glorification, i.e., into the certainty of overcoming the world by the very fact of this momentary subjection to its power and assuring the supramundane continuance of his life" (*Instruction,* § 23). Hence lordship over the world has for its foundation and core the reality of Christian freedom as the self-maintenance of the moral subject over against the course of nature and the attraction of evil.[12]

But more than this (moral and by extension technical) lordship over the world—an idea which Ritschl has more or less in common with his time—the question how a person could attain to this position and remain in it occupied him. He did not share with his age its proud confidence in the victorious autonomy of humanity. The idea of lordship over the world can only be realized by a counterweight that comes from without, one which makes possible a feedback reaction to the world by way of a source from which people can draw inspiration and power in order to orient and conduct themselves morally. Ritschl found this source in faith in the providence of God: "Faith in the fatherly providence of God is the Christian worldview in an abbreviated form" (*Instruction,* § 60 [or § 51]).

I know of no other theologian, either classical or modern, who so strongly emphasizes providence as Ritschl. In *Justification and Reconciliation,* after § 62, which we have referred to, comes a far lengthier § 63: "Faith in the Fatherly providence of God," to which the sections on

---

12. "Lordship over the world" often seems to be no more than a fashionable and inappropriate term for what Paul and Luther call Christian liberty, or even for submission to God's will. Technical culture must remain subordinated to the moral culture "if such activities are not to end in antisocial egoism or in a materialistic overestimate of their immediate results. . . . In that case, however, the farthest advance of civilization were likely to bring in its train only moral and intellectual barbarism"(§62). With regard to Ritschl's "lordship over the world" one thinks in turn of Bultmann's "desecularization" *(Entweltlichung)* and Gogarten's "secularization" thesis.

patience, humility, and prayer are then joined. The idea of lordship simply means that man, for all his smallness amidst the often unfathomable powers of the world, is "the final end of the phenomenal world, the end supreme over all nature," and that the Christian view of the world "has for its aim to make possible the supernatural independence of the spirit in all its relations to the world of nature and to society" (p. 615).

The mechanical consideration of the world, if it seeks to extend itself into the realm of spirit, contradicts this teleological view of faith. Faith in divine providence, however, agrees with the essence and tasks of the spiritual life. It is true (though Ritschl does not employ the word here) as "value judgment." Empirically, providence is not provable. Nor is it a matter of universal theoretical knowledge but a truth of personal faith. It means that as a human being I exist as a final goal for God and am treated by him as a final goal.

> Now, in general, the form in which religious lordship over the world is exercised is *faith in God's providence*. For that unified view of the world, the ruling idea of which is that of the supramundane God, Who as our Father in Christ loves us and unites us in His Kingdom for the realisation of that destiny in which we see the final end of the world, as well as the corresponding estimate of self, constitutes the realm within which come to be formed all such ideas as that all things and events in the world serve our good, because as children of God we are objects of His special care and help. (pp. 617-18)

"This truth stands firm only when based upon our reconciliation with God" (p. 625). It is not empirically ascertainable. Nor does it have anything to do with "egotistical dogmatism" which easily enters in. "A religious judgment on our experiences of life is light of touch, tender in feeling, discreet. There are no organs other than those of patience and humility, by which all those experiences of life which lie nearest—those which are most special as well as those which are common—may be comprehended under general faith in God's providence" (pp. 627-28).

Thus faith in providence makes possible the freedom to maintain the moral self against the mechanisms and incomprehensibilities of the world's course. Providence stands in the service of world rule. At this point one clearly realizes the extent to which Ritschl considers the gospel from an anthropological perspective which he not only found in Kant but which he experienced as his own reality as a German around the year 1870. In the battle with the laws of nature and society the moral self can only develop as a free personality when God reveals to him, in the victorious life and suffering of the "vocationally faithful" Jesus,

God's own final goal: the kingdom of God as a fellowship of free spirits; forgives him his sin, and assures him, by his sonship accepted in faith, of God's loving care. By this assurance he is inspired and led to fulfill his moral vocation in neighborly love, in marriage and family, state and society. By nature man already knows his moral vocation and is familiar with the struggle between spirit and matter. In virtue of this knowledge and the implied value judgment one is able to discover in Jesus the revelation of the intention and love of God.

RITSCHL FROM TWO ANGLES OF ILLUMINATION

It is clear that numerous German and other Christians in the age of Emperor Wilhelm II understood and welcomed this presentation of the gospel as moral power. One also knows, however, that others, especially the post–World War I generation, regarded Ritschl's theology as a betrayal of the gospel to the spirit of bourgeoisie. This is the fate of every theology which seeks to articulate the gospel for its own time and culture. In the case of Ritschl, to make a fair appraisal, some things must not be overlooked. With great erudition and—what is more—conscientiousness, in the midst of the many voices of his time, he let the voice of the gospel and the voices of the Reformers speak again. To this end he utilized, eclectically and pragmatically, the thought patterns of his day; and he always consciously did this in such a way that certain elements of the gospel could be set free again, especially those which have to do with the Word of God's relatedness to existence. As a result, concepts like the personality of God, the offices of Christ, and faith as trust began again to come alive. We could show, for example, how Ritschl used the voguish term *experience* in order thus to pull the church into the center as the bearer of the experience of salvation and to counter the tendencies toward individualism. Certainly, he lived and breathed in the atmosphere of the proud moral self-consciousness of his time. Still, in him it was constantly broken: the sense of lordship over the world, by submission to providence; and moralism, by justification as gratuitous imputation.

One can also, however, interpret Ritschl the other way around and say: providence stood in the service of lordship over the world; justification in the service of moralism; God in the service of humanity. In any case Ritschl's limitations are clear: he barely had an inkling of the supra- and anti-moralism of the gospel, and as an opponent of pietism he was averse to its "mystical" aspect. His moralism and rationalism showed him the paths he could travel as well as the limits he had to observe. In this duality he was typical of numerous theologians after Kant who, breathing the atmosphere of their own world, at the same time sought to be faithful interpreters of the gospel for their time. For him and for them all, it is true what Thielicke says so well with regard to Rothe: "His theology is justified, not by what it says intellectually, but by that at which it looks."[13]

ATTACKS ON THE RITSCHLIAN SYNTHESIS

The Ritschlian synthesis of gospel and *Zeitgeist* was attacked from several directions already during Ritschl's lifetime. Especially, of course, from the side of Lutheran orthodoxy, which had little difficulty showing how badly Ritschl had treated (and from his basic positions was able to treat) such themes as "the wrath of God," "the facts of redemption," "vicarious atonement," "eschatology," and others. On the historical front, Ritschl's interpretation of Luther had been rendered fundamentally obsolete by the Neo-Lutheran Theodosius Harnack with his work on Luther's theology,[14] although this only became noticeable later, as the research progressed.

In time, New Testament scholars were also unable to agree with Ritschl. One of his favorite students was Johannes Weiss, who became his son-in-law, and who with his book *Jesus' Proclamation of the Kingdom of God* (1892) joined the just then emerging religion-historical school.[15] Earlier Franz Overbeck had demonstrated that Jesus and early Christianity, with their *Naherwartung* and apocalyptic otherworldly hope, had nothing to do with Ritschl's this-worldly bourgeois moral idea of the kingdom of God. Ritschl had correctly sensed the challenge implied in Overbeck's "Über die Christlichkeit unserer heutigen Theologie" (1873) and had attempted, not unintelligently but very inadequately, to refute it (in *Justification and Reconciliation*, pp. 612-14). How the conversations with his son-in-law on the same theme in the decade of the 1880s went we unfortunately do not know.[16]

13. "Auch seine Theologie ist nicht durch das gerechtfertigt, was sie denkend ausspricht, sondern durch das, worauf sie blickt" (H. Thielicke, *Glauben und Denken in der Neuzeit* [Tübingen: Mohr, 1983], p. 455).

14. *Luthers Theologie*, 2 vols. (repr. Munich: Kaiser, 1927).

15. The English translation by R. H. Hiers and D. L. Holland (Philadelphia: Fortress, 1971).

16. In the triumphalistic collection of essays entitled *Der Protestantismus in seiner Gesamtgeschichte bis zur Gegenwart in Wort und Bild*, ed. C. Werckshagen, 2nd ed., vol. 2 (Cassel/Reutlingen: Enslin & Laiblins, n.d.), I found an article

Of the religion-historical school Ernst Troeltsch became the real dogmatician, or rather the philosopher of religion. His opinion of his former teacher is this: in his relation to history Ritschl remained stuck halfway. In this respect he seems to identify with the historical consciousness which marks the modern mind, though at bottom he is not modern at all but still supernaturalistic. One cannot simultaneously recognize the limited individuality and many-sided dependence of all historical figures on the one hand, and on the other, infer from this historical process the absoluteness of Christianity and its founder (and that without utilizing miracle as a decisive argument).

Thus Ritschl's theology was viewed from many sides not as a splendid synthesis but as a weak compromise. Nevertheless, during the period of the German empire, many theologians remained true to it. These theologians not only dominated systematic theology via their academic posts but also belonged to the most faithful pillars of the monarchy and the empire, a fact to which, at the outbreak of World War I, many names subjoined to the manifesto of the ninety-three intellectuals testify.

After World War I, Ritschlian theology seemed to have collapsed along with the bourgeois world of which it was a part. That situation changed again, however, after World War II. Many elements in the theologies of Bultmann and Gogarten and especially of the Neo-Bultmannians, Fuchs and Ebeling, remind us of Ritschl's basic stance, even if this is not due to his immediate influence, but a result of the revived influence of Wilhelm Herrmann, who was spiritually and intellectually akin to him. This situation may alert us afresh to the ambiguity which is native to all theological attempts at mediation. They can nearly always be interpreted from two sides. The focus one favors depends mainly on whether one views his own position in the history of thought

---

written by Johannes Weiss entitled "Albrecht Ritschl" (pp. 688-92), which shows great respect, admiration, and real understanding. He also states, however: "On the whole he explored history from a distinct point of view, gathering witnesses for his understanding of Christianity . . . out of the fulness of biblical ideas he selected those sequences which seemed to him of direct significance for the church of today . . . while other sections, which are at least of equal importance to the modern science of religion, remain in the shadows. His interpretation is frequently controlled by the overall dogmatic perspective in which he understands the early Christian concepts in a reformational or rationalistic sense. In many details his interpretation must be considered wrong, but whoever studies his biblical work in context will always profit greatly from it."

as related to the life situation of the earlier theologian in question. If one senses no such kinship, then one is apt to oppose the person with biblical arguments.[17]

17. With this presentation and appraisal of Ritschl's theology I distance myself rather sharply from that which Karl Barth writes about Ritschl as a "provisional close" to his lectures (*Protestant Theology in the Nineteenth Century* [Valley Forge, PA: Judson, 1973], pp. 654-61). The loving penetration into the thought structures and the personalities behind them, by which Barth's presentations became such trailblazing and exemplary ventures, seems in this obviously hasty treatment of the last chapter to have left him. Contrasting Ritschl with Schleiermacher, he regards him not as an epoch but as an episode, an interim, a reaction, a falling back into "the completed enlightenment," that is, into the moralism of Kant, after which the next generation (he has in mind especially the "history of religion school") again happily takes up the main line of Schleiermacher and Hegel from which Ritschl departed. In my opinion, such a gap between Schleiermacher's initiative and that of Ritschl does not exist. A return to Kant was necessary and was later more or less attempted by Barth himself. Generally, he has more in common with Ritschl than he is willing to grant. Barth's notion that Ritschl was a brief episode is contradicted by the history up until 1914 and after, as well as by what happened after the appearance of Barth's essay. J. Richmond, *Ritschl,* pp. 33ff., also forcefully and on good grounds rejects Barth's judgment concerning Ritschl, though I cannot agree with his psychological-biographical explanation of this rejection. E. P. Meyering, *Theologische Urteile über die dogmengeschichte: Ritschls Einflusz auf von Harnack* (Leiden: Brill, 1978), pp. 65-69, has demonstrated that Barth had much greater affinities with Ritschl than he himself realized.

CHAPTER X

Conservative Theology: Martin Kähler

VARIETIES OF CONSERVATIVE THEOLOGY

Presentations of modern theology tend to focus on "liberal," "progressive," "modern," "modernistic," and "radical" theologians. The question we have posed in this book takes us especially in this direction. What these thinkers have in common, positively, is their attempt to bring about a reconciliation between the gospel and the spirit of modernity; negatively, their deviation, to a greater or lesser degree, from the classic or traditional teachings of the church. That is what makes their thinking interesting and challenging. In the meantime, we may not forget that the majority of theologians do not belong to these groups. As a rule, they are grouped under the common and slightly disparaging name "conservative." They seem to be much less original and interesting and are therefore dealt with much more briefly than their opponents.

As a wholesale judgment concerning this very diverse group, viewed from the outside under one and the same name, that is very unfair. In the first place, one should take a more careful look at the labeling: *liberal* means to think and stand in (a certain) freedom vis-à-vis tradition; *radical* means to run with this freedom (almost) to the point of rejecting tradition; *conservative* means to stand by tradition (as much as possible). The words in parentheses already indicate the shading that occurs within each group. Having made these distinctions, however, we have hardly said anything about the varying degrees of originality. It is quite possible for a "modern" theologian to follow the spirit of the age to a fault; and as a "conservative" theologian one may actually affirm tradition with a lot of originality. Many modern insights are considered antiquated after a few decades, while many conservative views, after

being rejected by the theological fashion of the day, celebrate their resurrection later. That does not mean, of course, that everything that is
called "conservative theology" has historical value or that, within the
perspective of this book, it has any significance at all. Much that is called
"conservative theology" only serves to explain and maintain certain
ecclesiastical positions. Theologians of this stripe are quite at home in
numerous church-related universities and seminaries. Rather than "conservative" they should be called "status-quo" theologians. Other conservative theologians should rather be described as "confessional" or "con-
fessionalistic." They consciously take their place in a great tradition
which they seek to redefine or develop. Among them the theologians of
Neo-Thomism, Neo-Lutheranism, and Neo-Calvinism are to be
counted. Others reject such confessional ties and are described as biblicistic. But one has to make a distinction here. Fundamentalism is a mode
of thought which, seemingly basing itself on the doctrine of verbal inspiration, disregards the diversity of Scripture and the hermeneutic
problem in general; it belongs to a churchly subculture that is of no interest to us here. There is also, however, a biblicistic tradition which
seeks, on the basis of Scripture, to relativize the confessional distinctions
and point out new directions. The "neo-s" of the confessional theologians, as also the return to Scripture, are often prompted by contemporary questions. These theologies then, despite or in virtue of their conservative orientation, are to be appreciated as genuine contributions to
the understanding of the relationship between gospel and modernity.

From what we have said, it follows that the boundaries between
certain varieties of "conservative theology" and the theology of mediation are fluid. Both took part in a confrontation with the spirit of modernity; and precisely at the point where the conservative school distinguished itself in method or content from that of the theology of
mediation it becomes interesting to us. Although a great deal that is of
interest must be ignored here, I do wish to mention the so-called Erlanger
theology. This theology constituted a Christian answer to the historicizing tendencies of the culture of that time by renewing, at a deep level,
the redemptive-historical method. If we do not deal with it and other
phenomena of equal merit, the reason is that its influence now seems to
us to be over while other conservative thinkers have continued their
work in the twentieth century and still (also side by side with Barth) exert
influence today. As an outstanding example of such an original and influential conservative variety of thought I have chosen the theology of
Martin Kähler.

KÄHLER BETWEEN RITSCHL AND BIBLICISM

Like so many theologians, *Martin Kähler* (1835-1912) was deeply shaped during the time of his studies at Halle by Tholuck, whose assistant and boarder he became. A disciple of Ritschl, in 1864 he became an associate professor in Bonn. Already in 1867 he returned to Halle, where he served first as director of the Student House and later as regular professor (1879-1905). One might expect that Kähler, as a younger contemporary of Albrecht Ritschl and as a leading conservative theologian, would especially define his position over against Ritschlianism. But in his works that is not what happens. He was much too free a man and a thinker for that. A comparison with Ritschl shows how their positions converge. Both came from a Kantian position; both sought to purge theology of metaphysical admixtures; both thought Christocentrically and placed the Bible above experience; for both the concepts of personality and morality were central; both struggled with the relationship between faith and history. It would not be difficult to cite from the works of both men many a passage, in the face of which even experts would hesitate, not knowing to which of the two they should attribute it.

Nevertheless, the differences and contrasts between them are also very obvious. For Kähler justification is the center from which the whole of faith derives, including sanctification. In Ritschl he does not see an ellipsis with two foci but only one single center: the kingdom of God as ethical goal, with that which is religious (salvation) only coming into consideration as a means to an end. Kähler also felt obliged to reject firmly Ritschl's negative attitude toward mysticism and pietism; the same is true for Ritschl's teaching concerning the wrath of God, which underestimates the seriousness of sin. Connected with this is Kähler's opposition to Ritschl's doctrine of reconciliation. Over against Ritschl's Abelardian view, Kähler posed a theory of reconciliation which brought the objective and the subjective, past and present, together in a transhistorical Christ. Thus deep questions which the two thinkers had in common were resolved in opposing ways. Still, in these representatives of opposing camps, "liberalism" and "conservatism" remained within speaking and listening distance of each other.[1]

1. Note the nuanced and respectful treatment of Ritschl in Kähler's lectures: *Geschichte der protestantischen Dogmatik im 19. Jahrhundert* (Munich, 1962), pp. 240-63. When in this book he dealt with the relationship between Christ and history in Ritschl, he excused himself for perhaps reproducing this "related view" too much in his own words (p. 257). His final verdict was nevertheless: "a historically based moralism" (p. 260).

From all this what becomes clear is that Kähler can be described neither as a "confessionalist" nor as a "biblicist." In the foreword to the first edition of his main work, *Die Wissenschaft der christlichen Lehre,* he writes that "the individual proofs from Scripture, the confessions, and the history of doctrine are omitted" because he sought "to place the main emphasis on a closed progressive development from a single source, on the presentation of the unity and coherence of the Christian view and its inexhaustible riches, as also today it can still be offered and as it can be offered precisely in the thought and speech patterns of our day."[2] In the third edition he added lengthy quotations from Holy Scripture, though with some hesitation. "I was concerned that some might confuse the presence of these quotations with a lapse into the conventional proofs from Scripture."[3] Nevertheless, he proceeded to provide them, for, as he once wrote a friend: "in theology I must try—without the ballast of verbal inspiration and legalistic biblicism—not to let the fundamental meaning of God's Word and Scripture slip under the table."[4] Kähler was certainly deeply rooted in the Reformation. At the same time, however, he was strongly influenced by Pietism. Often confessional historians of theology take a negative view of such influence because it diminishes the power deriving from the Reformation. But one can just as well regard Pietism as the form which evangelical Christianity had to take in the post-Cartesian epoch of European culture. Once one has undergone the influence of Pietism one can be alert to further challenges and discoveries. That is also true for Kähler: "I recall with gratitude Tholuck's admonition: 'A Christian should be a person who lives and moves in the present'" ("Der Christ soll ein Mensch der Gegenwart sein").[5]

DIE WISSENSCHAFT DER CHRISTLICHEN LEHRE

Where then lay the starting point and what was the focus of Kähler's thought if it cannot be fixed either in the *Zeitgeist* or in the Bible or in the confession? "The Science of Christian Doctrine, Presented in Outline, in

2. M. Kähler, *Die Wissenschaft der christlichen Lehre von dem evangelischen Grundartikel aus im Abrisse dargestellt, Nachdruck der dritten Ausgabe (1905), mit einer Einführung von M. Fischer* (Neukirchen: Neukirchener, 1966), p. XXXIII.

3. Ibid., p. XXXVI.

4. Letter to A. Bertheau (27-3-1896) in *Theologe und Christ: Erinnerungen und Bekenntnisse von Martin Kähler,* ed. A. Kähler (Berlin, 1926), p. 343.

5. Ibid., p. 333 (letter to his wife, 28-8-1869).

the Light of the Fundamental Evangelical Article," the title of his main work, already seems to give a clear and unambiguous answer: the pivotal point is the doctrine of justification. We already saw how Kähler, proceeding from this starting point, developed his objections against Ritschl. However, from this angle one can still not grasp the totality of his thought; not, in any case, if in this connection one thinks of Luther and Melanchthon—or even of Paul. Kähler is particularly fond of the expression "the state of justification" as a quality of the believing person from which the entire content of the faith can be developed. Everything seems to turn on this state. For that reason it was possible to describe Kähler not as a "biblicist" or "confessionalist" but as a "subjectivist," a "spiritualist," a "theologian of consciousness," and an "Osiandrist." Just as the first criticism ("biblicist") came naturally from the lips of his liberal contemporaries, so the second set of epithets came naturally from the dialectical theologians of the twentieth century.[6] For this second view one can often furnish evidence from his (nineteenth-century) diction. Many expressions which were later discredited must have seemed to him helpful at the time. To understand what motivated him, we shall turn first to the threefold division of his *Wissenschaft:* Christian apologetics, evangelical dogmatics, theological ethics. Kähler offers the following explanation (§ 71, pp. 70-71):

> The new state which begins with faith has its foundation in the content of faith; to its reasoned establishment, however, belongs not only (a) the understanding of this content but also (b) insight in the possibility and motives for such faith within the earlier state on the one hand; and (c) on the other, the conviction that inherent in this faith is the power to overcome the continuing conflict between the new and the old state in one's personal life. From these viewpoints the whole of Christian doctrine can be exhaustively comprehended on the basis of the fundamental evangelical article. Once a unified starting point has been gained

6. Barth remains cautious and questioning. He speaks of the "half-light which pervades it" (namely, the *Wissenschaft der christlichen Lehre*) (cf. *Church Dogmatics*, 1/2:786). In the incidental references to Kähler in *Church Dogmatics*, 4/1, he is mostly in agreement with him. In his thorough study *Gott in der Geschichte: Studien zur theologiegeschichtlichen Stellung und systematischen Grundlegung der Theologie Martin Kählers* (Munich: Kaiser, 1963), J. Wirsching arrived at a sharper repudiation. Because he applied "objective" criteria to Kähler, he had to view him, in a kind of optical illusion, as a "subjectivist" or "Osiandrist" (cf. pp. 58-66, 162-66, 197-206, and esp. pp. 202ff. n. 18). M. Fischer offers a refutation of Wirsching's basic view in his introduction to Kähler's *Wissenschaft*, pp. XXVIff.

with scientific precision in the prolegomena, then justifying faith in the historical-suprahistorical Christ first presents its *presuppositions* in Christian apologetics, its *contents* in evangelical dogmatics, and finally its *operations* in theological ethics.

Of special interest to us is what the "presuppositions" of the state of justification—the presuppositions dealt with in Christian apologetics—could be. On the first page of the first cycle of lectures Kähler speaks of "receptivity," "points of contact," "capacity," and "need." Certainly, justification was proclaimed in a world which needed it. The common ground on which need and offer meet is religion. Then we find, however, that Kähler, deviating from the usual practice in writing prolegomena, does not wish to proceed from a general concept of religion. "One must derive the concept of religion from Christianity" (p. 86), and then take the reverse route: "thus a viewpoint valid for all leads to the uniqueness claimed by Christianity" (p. 87). This uniqueness, however, is to be tested from two sides; on the one hand, by a "theological anthropology" which, coming from the basis of revelation in Christ, illumines man in his twofold character as a religious and moral being; on the other, by a "theological theology" which treats "the doctrine of God in its knowability apart from his revelation in Christ" (p. 87). Hence Kähler, like his liberal contemporaries, wants to relate the gospel to the reality of the human situation. In order to do this, the liberals find their point of contact in an anthropological model that seems to have sprung from some other source. Kähler consciously abstains from doing that. He consistently moves within the "theological circle" and reads from the pages of revelation what needs and calling human beings have apart from revelation. That is both the strong and the weak side of this "conservative" theologian: he refuses to introduce sources and norms for the truth other than those which come from the gospel. The question is whether he is successful, whether his concepts like "personality," "morality," "religion," "conscience," etc., are as purely theological as he believes. It would seem he is no more able than the liberals to establish a connection except by an unclear mixture of evangelical and modern thought patterns.

Still, the result is different. In Kähler the connection is much less harmonious: there is "ungodliness in all God-relatedness," and "God-relatedness . . . is only conceivable and real in a conditional way" (pp. 178-79). Besides, in Kähler religion is much less closely tied in with morality than in Ritschl. The moral consciousness in fact leads into unresolvable contradictions and demands (pp. 137-40). Humanity is dependent on salvation from without. Here, coming as they do from

Luther's concept of law, the thought patterns of Kähler and those of his liberal contemporary W. Herrmann connect.

His apologetics (much more developed here than in the liberal Ritschl) teaches us something essential about the way Kähler thinks. For all that, we have not yet discovered the perspectival point of his theology. Does it lie in a self-contained state of justification characteristic for the regenerate human being? That, in any case, is not the correct way to put it. Kähler never tires of saying: "This state is determined by its relation to God; it is a *religious* state" (p. 73). That is: it is constituted from without and by a relation to that which is without. It is rigorously object-related. It is Kähler's aim to present the Christian religion as relational, as a relationship of intersubjectivity. As a scion of the Reformation, he is concerned to see God as the object of his faith and thought; as a man of his time, he is interested in human consciousness and its renewal. As a biblically thinking person, he finds the unity of the two viewpoints in his favorite expressions "covenant" and "covenant religion" (§§ 214ff.). For that reason he cannot possibly be described as "objectivist" or as "subjectivist," terms which can be applied, generally speaking, to very few nineteenth-century theologians. For Kähler what is important is the relationship between God and humanity, that relationship which totally and exclusively proceeds from God and which is totally and exclusively directed toward the justification of humanity (which, however, is inseparably bound up with ethics). Such a relationship is ever personal: it presupposes God as Person, a Person who renews us into persons in his image. Hence a strong personalism pervades Kähler's thinking. "Person," in Kähler, however, is not the same as "individual"; it means the capacity to take part in the life of others. That is true even and in the first place of God (§ 260).

THE CENTER: "THE HISTORICAL-SUPRAHISTORICAL CHRIST"

Having gone this far, we still have not reached the central focus of Kähler's thought. For God mediates himself through a "covenant." There is something between him and us which is necessary to unite us with him. We heard Kähler speak almost as though he were giving a definition of "justifying faith in the historical-suprahistorical Christ" (p. 71). This last expression is very important to him. It keeps coming back in his books. It proves not only how object-related his justifying faith was but also that in his view of this object he placed the accents differently than he had picked up from the Reformation tradition. He speaks not of the "crucified" Christ, or of the "crucified and risen" Christ, but of the "historical-suprahistorical" Christ. What does he mean with this—often misunderstood and rather misleading—expression? In my opinion, something very plain but also very central: namely, that Jesus Christ is not a figure of the past but one who in the present daily establishes and maintains, in the name of his Father, the covenant relationship between God and humanity. In contrast to the liberals, Kähler cannot view the so-called historical Jesus as the center. The exaltation of Christ is not a plausible or implausible appendix to his earthly life; his earthly life is the launching platform for the work of the exalted Christ and can only become meaningful and effective on the basis of faith in the exalted Christ.

The term *suprahistorical* is not essentially incorrect for Kähler's purpose. He does not mean "unhistorical." As one who is released from and transcendent over history, Christ does in fact affect history. Kähler also writes: "Hence the 'Christ-for-us' remains merely a heightened presentation of the law and remains concealed behind the promise of the new covenant which Christ referred to himself. The Word, however, not only became flesh; the Word also became Spirit. Only through the appropriating reconciliation which the Spirit of Christ accomplishes on the basis of the reconciliation of the world, only through the 'Christ-in-us' does effective inner assent to the law, in the form of the moral courage for progressive conversion, come into being" (pp. 508-9). Those are bold words. One can easily misinterpret them in a spiritualistic direction. But they are statements about the working Christ. Hence the next sentence reads: "This operation of Christ in his Spirit . . . effects itself in constant reference to the historical revelation; and without the clear preaching of 'Christ-for-us,' that which has at times been called 'Christ-in-us' would be, for a person's moral equipment, a phantom or empty cover for arbitrary ideals or so-called moral worldviews."[7] The Christ who is working through his Spirit links us, through the witness of the apostles, through Bible and church, Word and Sacrament, precisely with his historical work, in order by this means to give us the "moral courage for

---

7. In my opinion, J. Wirsching completely misunderstands Kähler's emphasis on the suprahistorical when he writes (quoting the above lines): "The suprahistorical finally possesses no genuine historical reality, but remains on a level of being that exists, prototypically, at some distance from history [*Geschichte*]" (*Gott in der Geschichte*, p. 168). He calls this the "history of meaning, experienced and interpreted history, for which it is essential to have been created by a historical value judgment" (ibid.). "History in which God's revealing action takes place is interpreted history, subjected to a value judgment. Again we hear the echoes of Schleiermacher's consciousness-interpretation" (p. 169). Wirsching seems completely to have forgotten that in Kähler the suprahistorical is a person!

progressive conversion" and to transpose us into the state of justification. Here we also see in Kähler how, and how closely, the personal character of revelation is bound up with its historicity. In § 71, speaking of the "fundamental article" *(Grundartikel)* of justification, he states: "It is the summarizing pronouncement simultaneously of historical and personal Christianity; as the one is summarized in the operative words of the Savior, so the other is summarized in a repentant faith." The history of reconciliation mediated by the exalted Christ is aimed at personal faith; personal faith is generated and nourished by this history.[8]

From what we have developed here it is plain that Kähler could not simply join the then current discussion about "faith and history," about the "historical Jesus," and about "the absoluteness of the Christian religion" in those terms. For him the "basis of faith" finally lay not in history but above it. In the light of this conviction he designed his epoch-making lecture, "The So-called Historical Jesus and the Historic Biblical Christ."[9]

According to Kähler, literary-historical criticism can lead only to a "field of ruins," never to the knowledge of the person who evoked those utterances, and that through the preaching of the crucified and risen One, through faith in the exalted One. It is to this suprahistorical reality that the so-called historical reports testify. They are confessional pronouncements, "proclamations of the messiahship of the crucified Jesus" (p. 83). "Even in their narratives they *portray* the Man in his action and intention" (p. 81). The narratives are "examples of how Jesus customarily acted, what he was like then, and therefore what he is like today" (p. 81). Does this observation make the issue of historical accuracy unimportant?

> Nevertheless, from these fragmentary traditions, these half-understood recollections, these portrayals colored by the writers' individual personalities, these heartfelt confessions, these

---

8. Here, too, Wirsching gives a very one-sided presentation because he does not see that historicity and personality are brought together as the two sides of the same process by the suprahistorical Christ. He regards history in relation to personal renewal only as "occasion," "image," "transparency," and "mediation" (p. 159). True, Kähler often uses expressions which, taken in isolation, are misleading. Wirsching, however, constantly has to qualify his own interpretation on the basis of other expressions.

9. Quotations are taken from M. Kähler, *The So-called Historical Jesus and the Historic Biblical Christ*, tr. and ed. Carl E. Braaten (Philadelphia: Fortress, 1964) (based on the 1896 edition of the original *Der sogenannte historische Jesus und der geschichtliche, biblische Christus*).

sermons proclaiming him as Savior, there gazes upon us a vivid and coherent image of a Man, an image we never fail to recognize. Hence, we may conclude that in his unique and powerful personality and by his incomparable deeds and life (including his resurrection appearances) this Man has engraved his image on the mind and memory of his followers with such sharp and deeply etched features that it could be neither obliterated nor distorted. If we are drawn up short by this mystery, then we must recall that he himself solved it in advance when he said: "When the Spirit of truth comes . . . he will glorify me, for he will take what is mine and declare it to you" (John 16:13a, 14).

There is no one among us who knows the course of this tradition in detail. . . . (pp. 89-90)

The "Counsellor" has guided the evangelists "into all the truth," which is Jesus himself (John 16:13; 14:6, 16). Under the Spirit's guidance they remembered Jesus, his words, his deeds, his life. All the chaff of what is purely and simply historical was sifted by the winnowing fan of this pneumatic hypomnesia (John 14:26), and only the ripened grain of the words and works of the Father in and through Christ was garnered into the granary. (p. 94)

Thus, our faith in the Savior is awakened and sustained by the brief and concise apostolic proclamation of the crucified and risen Lord. But we are helped toward a believing communion with our Savior by the disciples' recollection of Jesus, a recollection which was imprinted on them in faith, renewed and purified in them by his Spirit, and handed down by them as the greatest treasure of their life. From this communion faith draws its resources to overcome all temptations and finds the means to withstand in all situations and circumstances (Heb. 4:15-16). In this communion we grow into an inseparable union with Christ (Rom. 6:5; Gal. 3:1; Phil. 3:10-11), the weakening of which is felt as an attack upon one's very existence. In this communion with Christ we are nurtured—by the picture the Bible paints of him—unto the freedom of the children of God, who still find their treasure to be the abashed, timid, and yet genuine confession: "Lord, you know everything; you know that I love you." (pp. 96-97)

The continuing influence of this booklet to this day we owe especially to Bultmann and his school. In Kähler he again found the conviction that the Gospels are not intended as historical reports but as testimonies of faith, and that not the historical Jesus but the kerygmatic Christ concerns the faith. Nevertheless, this agreement is only superficial. The sharp disjunction which Bultmann, following Kant and Heidegger, made between "history" and "existence" is utterly foreign to Kähler. For him, even the historical "portrayals" were related to faith. He was also far removed from Bultmann's skepticism. For the full, "biblical Christ," the exalted One who works in the Spirit, *is himself the originator of the biblical picture of the Christ*" (p. 87). "Within the circle in which one may assume the presence of Christian conviction, one can face the Gospel reports with much more confidence than happens in the Quest-for-the-Historical-Jesus movement in two-thirds of its participants, but only on one condition. And this one condition is: to be satisfied with what we have before us. And that is, in fact, no poverty, provided a person's concern is the glory of God in the face of Jesus Christ, and not Christological problems in the fashionable form of psychological analysis."[10] What seems to me to be even more essential is the distinction that, whereas Kähler speaks of the "exalted One," of the "suprahistorical biblical" Christ, Bultmann speaks of "kerygma." Bultmann's hermeneutical key is a (philosophically framed) concept; Kähler's is a person.

I believe that, as a result, Kähler has progressed further than Bultmann in understanding the New Testament. For the New Testament witnesses, after all, it was not a concept but "the Lord who is the Spirit" who moved them to preach and report. At the time, however, Kähler's position remained foreign both to his liberal colleagues and to his orthodox brothers.

In this light, one can also understand Kähler's seemingly ambivalent position vis-à-vis "the Bible issue." One can tell at once that he could not possibly have been a "biblicist." One is rather inclined to praise him on account of his "free" position toward the Bible. Still, there was hardly a theologian at the time who devoted himself as tirelessly as he did to the validity of the Scriptures as the Word of God.[11] Obedience and freedom went hand-in-hand in him. His standard was Luther's *Was Christum treibet* ("What puts forth Christ"). His attitude is also reminiscent of Calvin's beautiful definition of Scripture: "the person of the God who speaks" *(Dei loquentis persona)*. Here, too, Kähler's personalism is the key to understanding. Scripture is nothing "in itself"—"dead rock," as he said once. It is the Spirit who in the words of Scripture makes

10. From the German original of the 2nd enlarged edition (Munich: Kaiser), footnote on pp. 68-69.

11. His most important and ever timely publications on this theme were reissued by E. Kähler in *Aufsätze zur Bibelfrage* (Munich: Kaiser, 1967).

audible the voice of Jesus Christ. For that reason and to that extent the Bible has authority—the authority of an instrument. The same is true, in a derivative sense, of the church's preaching and means of grace. Kähler is close to Barth's doctrine of the threefold form of the Word of God (as proclaimed, written, and revealed).

KÄHLER IN HIS OWN TIME

In a period that was anthropocentric in its thinking, Kähler attempted to incorporate this thought (man as justified and sanctified) into the theocentric and Christocentric thought world of the Bible and the Reformation. For him truth was "encounter," and he tried therefore to rescue the intersubjectivity of the covenant of God with man from the dead ends of objectivism and subjectivism. His faith in the "full, biblical Christ" kept him from absolutizing human, historical, or biblical occurrences, without being led in the process into a skeptical direction. His personalism held God and man, Word and Spirit, together. In Kähler a genuine answer was given, strictly from within the gospel, as an offer to the people of the modern world who yearn for real personhood. Was it precisely this conservative who chose the good portion (Luke 10:42)? Was the exalted Christ too speculative for his "realistic" contemporaries, and was the gate of justification too narrow for them?

Alternatives: Herrmann and Troeltsch

HERRMANN AND RITSCHL: AGREEMENT AND DIFFERENCE

Most of those who came away from Ritschl's lectures took other roads than the master. This is true of Ernst Troeltsch, who, no later than the age of thirty, turned his back on Ritschl (1895). The "firstborn" son of the well-known and influential Ritschlian school, however, had never attended Ritschl's lectures. Reading Ritschl became for the 28-year-old Wilhelm Herrmann the discovery of a profound congeniality of spirit and made him into an independent follower of the master—one who, unlike the majority of followers, was comparable in stature to Ritschl.

For as long as thirty-seven years *Johann Wilhelm Herrmann* (1846-1922) was professor in Marburg (1879-1916), where his personality and teaching style brought him numerous devoted students, through whose mediation his influence continues to the present, even among many people who have never read him. What attracted Herrmann to Ritschl was the latter's fundamental theme: the calling of people to relate and conduct themselves as free personalities within a determined world. To that end ethics serves as guide and religion as the source of power. His thoughts circled unremittingly around the relationship between religion and morality. Like Ritschl, Herrmann found the unity of the two in the figure of Jesus; the moral consciousness of people only submits to the perfect moral personality in which they discover the revelation of God. At the same time, however, the morally alive, through their relationship to Christ, discover their own failure. In Christ they find more than the ethical ideal; in and through him they receive the forgiving and redeeming grace of God which alone enables them to live a new life of moral rebirth. What strongly attracted Herrmann to Ritschl and what he expressed already in his early work, *Die Metaphysik in der Theologie,* was the sharp separation between faith and every kind of knowledge. This was the source of his persistent struggle against any form of confusion between a personal faith in Christ and faith in the authority of Scripture, dogma, or creed: they cannot bring about a saving personal encounter; they appeal to our thinking only as law. Religion is a totally independent world, though closely bound up with morality, because it relates us to divine revelation and must be the answer to the misery of our moral condition.

There are also certain significant differences between Herrmann and Ritschl. In the first place, Herrmann was much more concerned than Ritschl with a solid philosophical foundation. He could find his basic theme only in Kant, "whose mighty thoughts emerge increasingly in almost all the domains of human learning as the silent governor of all true research" and which at the same time show a strong analogy to the gospel, especially "because in every connection he has placed the value of faith, its independence from science, in the clearest light." Unfortunately Kant viewed religion as a postulate of morality and not as the independent power "which is given to the morally weak and lost human being in order to save him."[1]

Herrmann had the good fortune to find in Marburg two colleagues in philosophy who as Kantians were occupied with the same questions and as founders of the Marburg school (Marburg Neo-Kantianism) won worldwide fame. One of them, *Hermann Cohen* (1842-1918), had already been active in Marburg for six years when Wilhelm Herrmann started there; the other, *Paul Natorp* (1854-1924), arrived two years later. All three were occupied with the distinction between the rules of (natural) science and the other areas of culture, especially morality. And all three sought to understand the role which religion plays in the midst of, and over against, these cultural values. Particularly the Jewish thinker Cohen made a very intimate connection between religion and morality. Herrmann closely followed the development of the ideas of both men, especially that of Cohen, and repeatedly stated his agreement or disagreement.[2] His main criticism of both philosophers was that for religion they demanded "universal validity" and thus made it into a

1. The quotations are taken from a lecture on "Kants Bedeutung für das Christentum," first published in W. Herrmann, *Schriften zur Grundlegung der Theologie* (Munich: Kaiser, 1966), 1:104-22 (cf. pp. 109, 117, 122, respectively). This edition in two volumes (vol. 2, 1967) appeared at the height of Neo-Bultmannianism, and points up the rediscovery of Herrmann in these circles.

2. Cf. *Schriften zur Grundlegung der Theologie,* vol. 2, the articles "Hermann Cohens Ethik" (1907, pp. 88-113), "Die Auffassung der Religion in Cohens

kind of knowledge or feeling, by which it was robbed of its historical and personal focus.

Also in his formulation of the essence of faith Herrmann deviated from Ritschl. In contrast with Ritschl's dry and rationalistic manner of speaking and writing, Herrmann had warmth and a tone of personal piety. It was not for nothing that he came from a circle that had been stamped by the Revival. In addition, as a student in Halle he had been Tholuck's secretary. All his students praised him for his ardent delivery in the classroom. Of course, this had something to do with his giftedness, but also with the fact that for Herrmann the essential experience in life is the liberating Person-to-person encounter. In comparison with Ritschl, Herrmann's thinking is less "objective" and much more personal: the foundation of our life is the experience of meeting the person of God in the person of Jesus. Jesus makes us into personalities who are able, on their part, by transmission, education, and personal encounter, to evoke personhood in others. In distinction from Ritschl, Herrmann made many of those who attended his lectures into enthusiastic students and followers.

In terms of Dogmatics this meant a more rigorous Christocentrism than there was in Ritschl and an even greater distance from all the cognitive values with which orthodoxy (with its dogmas and creeds) and liberalism (with its historical-critical research) sought to buttress their beliefs. Ritschl, to Herrmann's mind, was still too objectivistic. In time Ritschl's influence on Herrmann declined in favor of Schleiermacher's *Speeches on Religion,* a book in which religion is presented even more in its radical and fiery power to create relationships, also independently of morality. In general it may be said, in the felicitous phrasing of Stephan and Schmidt: "They [i.e., 'the fundamental concepts, especially faith, history, revelation'] become still livelier than they are in Ritschl, still more independent of all theological schematism, still more open to and simultaneously more stable in the face of all historical criticism, still more immediate, more personal, and plainer."[3]

The most important difference between Herrmann and Ritschl, however, lay in the cultural diversity of their *Sitz im Leben.* Herrmann was younger than Ritschl by almost a quarter of a century. Both were

---

und Natorps Ethik" (1909, pp. 206-32), and "Der Begriff der Religion nach Hermann Cohen" (1906, pp. 318-23). Also in his *Ethik* (1st ed. 1901, 6th ed. 1921) he repeatedly interacts with them.

3. Cf. H. Stephan and M. Schmidt, *Geschichte der deutschen evangelischen Theologie,* 3rd ed. (Berlin: Töpelmann, 1960), p. 258.

acutely conscious of the gap between the mechanistic world image of natural science and the conviction, inherited from Christianity and idealism, that man in his freedom and his moral actions is both able and called to transcend the necessities of nature. For Ritschl this gap was still no problem. This duality, in the way Kant and Lotze understood it, was self-evident to him; insofar as one can speak of a gap, it is something man in his freedom and world domination can surmount. But for Herrmann the situation was far more threatening. Over the years the flood of empiricism and determinism, psychologism and historicism, had risen high and threatened totally to overflow the banks of practical reason. The defenders of moral freedom had to move their positions ever further back. Ritschl's triumphalistic offensive had to yield to a reductionist defensive.

THE SECULARIZED WORLD AND "THE INNER LIFE OF JESUS"

When I read Herrmann what emerges in my mind is the image of a rock in the midst of a rising flood. In Ritschl the rock of moral autonomy still had a broad surface. Now, however, with the waves of the flood rising higher and higher, it became much narrower. The parts that are closer to the sea—like corporeality, psychological development, history, social relationships, and the authority of Scripture and Christian tradition—have already been inundated. Herrmann now withdrew to the narrow center, to individual (though conceived as interpersonal) inwardness where the individual is in communion with God through "the inner life of Jesus." With a splendid sort of consistency, he devoted his intellectual powers to the defense of the peak of this rock. Next to him he found, as his great fellow-combatant, Martin Luther, who also (over against Aristotelian scholasticism) in faith accomplished such an existential reduction.

This struggle for a place to stand in the midst of increasing uncertainty shows up especially in his position vis-à-vis historical-critical research. This research can never lead to the certainty of faith, not only because it can only attain probabilities, but also and especially because there is no link between knowledge and faith. Although faith does take historical shape, it is based on something above history and beyond the reach of research, namely, on "the image of his inner life," "the reality of his personal life," in short, on "the inner life of Jesus." This life comes to expression in the narratives about him, the legendary as well as the historical. Through those stories our personhood achieves contact with his "as something presently at work in us," yet without becoming dependent on the details of this history.

For a long time Herrmann assumed an essential connection between revelation and history. Around or after 1910 (the period of heated discussions about the historicity of Jesus), however, he completely divorced personal faith from the results of research into the question of historical trustworthiness. Now the personality of Jesus, active in the past as well as the present, was opposed to the historical Jesus. And presently Kähler's distinction between the *historische* Jesus and the *geschichtliche* Christ was attacked by the Ritschlian school on the basis of very different considerations,[4] and developed into a disjunction by the next generation—the school of Barth on the one hand and that of Bultmann on the other. This distinction, which can only be made in the German language, was very influential. It gained broad acceptance because it promised a separate but peaceful relationship between the gospel and modern historicism which could serve as a bomb-proof bunker for faith in Christ.

THE MAIN WORKS: *ETHIK* AND *DER VERKEHR DES CHRISTEN MIT GOTT*

In conclusion let us turn expressly to Herrmann's two main works. They are *Der Verkehr des Christen mit Gott* (1st edition, 1886; 7th edition, 1927) and *Ethik* (1st edition, 1901; 6th edition, 1921). *Der Verkehr* offers an exposition of the essence of faith; *Ethik* is more explicitly directed toward dialogue with the intellectual *Umwelt*. In keeping with our objective in this book we shall first turn to *Ethik* (though it appeared later) because here a bridge was built between the gospel and the modern world.

In the experience of human encounters which create trust relationships there grows in us the recognition of an "unconditional demand" and a longing to achieve "a different life than nature can furnish us." In his view of this dimension of existence Herrmann joined Kant and Cohen. However, he left their line of thought behind when he wrote: "It is not in enthusiasm for the moral idea already, but in the acknowledgment of his own moral predicament which springs from it, that man takes the direction toward the religious Beyond [*Jenseits*] of a new existence." In religion man is referred to the "inner situation of human individualism" in which "he is placed before a Power before which all

---

4. For a concise and good overview of the development of the contrast between *Geschichte* and *Historie*, see George Rupp, *Culture-Protestantism: German Liberal Theology at the Turn of the Twentieth Century* (Missoula, MT: Scholars Press, 1977), pp. 25-29. (The distinction between *historisch* and *geschichtlich* cannot be rendered in English.—TRANS.)

resistance is excluded because he knows himself to be totally dependent on it in free surrender." "The moral law remains the product of his own thought which alone points the way to authentic intention. But if for him, as the law of liberty, it becomes the law of his God he may perhaps be saved from the danger that now this consciousness of freedom, by the compulsion to condemn himself, might destroy his confidence, that is, the truth and purity of his own life."[5] For Herrmann morality is the *praeambulum fidei* common to all conscientious people, the means by which they are pitched into inner conflict before they can experience the saving encounter with Jesus Christ in religion. He wants to raise the awareness "that God can only reveal himself to those who want to be authentic, and therefore that the moral self-determination to which the superiority of a stronger personal life brings us is also the beginning of a faith of a genuinely religious nature."[6]

Especially *Der Verkehr* describes how the encounter with the superior personal life of Jesus proceeds and effects our inner renewal. Chapter II provides the foundation, chapter III the explanation of our communion with God. We are most interested in the way, according to chapter II, in which the saving experience of the grace of God in the encounter with Jesus comes into being. "A fact of redemption, for a person who wants to escape the bondage of his own powerlessness, can only be that which transforms him inwardly. That, however, is effected only by his own experience, not by that which he is merely told about. Hence we call 'a fact of redemption' the inner life of Jesus which became known to us in contact with the tradition" (p. 65). How does the process of becoming known actually occur? The personal mystery of Jesus is mediated to us through the transmission of his image. In that context we discover that "the Christ of the New Testament displays a firmness of religious conviction, a clarity of moral judgment, a purity and power of will, as they occur together in no other figure of history" (p. 67). Somewhat later Herrmann turns that three-part statement into a two-part one: Jesus is unique, in the first place, in that he is conscious "he does not lag behind

5. W. Herrmann, *Ethik*, 5th ed. (Tübingen: Mohr, repr. 1921); the quotations have all been taken from the basic section § 18, "Sittlichkeit und Religion," pp. 90, 93, 95. The next section, § 19, is called: "Die Erlösung durch Jesus Christus." Next, the sanctification of life, first in its personal, then in its social aspects, is discussed. The preceding sections §§ 1-17 deal with the interconnection and contrast between natural life and moral thought.

6. W. Herrmann, *Der Verkehr des Christen mit Gott im Anschluss an Luther dargestellt*, 6th ed. (Stuttgart/Berlin: J.G. Cottasche, 1908), p. vi, the last pages of the preface to the 4th edition.

the ideal for which he is giving his life" (p. 70). In the second place, he is the man not only of the task but also of the gift. In distinction from Buddha or Socrates he does not modestly conceal himself behind the cause he represents. "[Jesus] knows of no more sacred matter than to point people to himself" (p. 73). Why? "Jesus knew himself capable of letting people know, by the power of his personal life, that God draws near to them and that this alone can save them" (p. 76). The following summary is quite characteristic: "Whoever lets the reality of the personal life of Jesus affect him so that he is moved to trust him, cannot escape the thought of a Power over all things who is with Jesus. In that which he experiences in contact with Jesus he feels himself apprehended by that Power. That this beginning of a religious life should dissolve for him in something purely subjective — that is a prospect from which he is safeguarded by the historical reality which, since he has seen it, cannot again fade from his sight, and by his conscience" (p. 85).

Precisely the addition of the last four words indicates how significant conscience was to Herrmann. Conscience and history are the twin pillars on which the Christian faith rests. Moral sense, for Herrmann, is the point of access to the gospel. However, this sense is purified, refined, and elevated in the encounter with Jesus. In the moral person it goes side by side with a feeling of inner division and impotence, which is overcome only in the experience of the grace of God in Jesus. In this dialectical sense, morality or conscience forms the bridge between our world and the gospel. We are reminded here of Luther with his dialectic of law and gospel. In fact, throughout his lifetime Herrmann had no other goal than to interpret to his contemporaries the existential discovery and liberation of Luther (note the subtitle of *Der Verkehr*). Many of Herrmann's statements have strong associations with Luther; for example: "God takes our self-esteem and creates for us an unbreakable spirit; he destroys our joy in life and makes us blessed; he kills and makes us alive" (p. 94). The difference between him and Luther is that the killing power of the law is also, and in the first place, a natural experience which unites or should unite the Christian and the non-Christian. The law of God coincides with the individual and inward moral sense of educated Europeans around the turn of the century. Within the hermeneutical circle of this sense of life, the gospel can and must come up, complementarily, as God's redeeming answer to our question—a question, however, which is elicited by our Creator.

As in the case of Ritschl, so here too one cannot circumvent the question: Is the God who is complementarily related to our needs still really God? Or is he perhaps only the projected reflection of human ideals and human misery? In the year Herrmann died a book appeared which answered these questions in the affirmative, thus ending one epoch and opening another: the revised edition of *The Epistle to the Romans,* written by an erstwhile, devoted student of Herrmann: Karl Barth.

TROELTSCH: CONFRONTATION WITH HERRMANN

In large measure *Ernst Troeltsch* (1865-1923), professor in Heidelberg from 1894 to 1915, later professor of philosophy in Berlin, shared the worries, the *Lebensgefühl,* and the religious perceptions of his older and much-appreciated Marburg colleague Herrmann. For many years the two were the recognized leaders of German liberalism. However, Troeltsch left this common background behind him and took a very different, even an opposite, direction. He also saw that the rock of ethical freedom and, connected with it, of the gospel was inundated by the deterministic-historical way of thinking in vogue. But he did not believe that he could occupy and hold a small peak as a last resort. He left this tight spot and plunged into the stream. To him an absolute moment in history was a contradiction in terms. For that reason he had to disagree with Ritschl and Herrmann, who sought to lift Jesus out of history with its laws of analogy and correlation. It is true everywhere and for everyone: history is an ever-moving stream in which the movement of each drop is determined by the mass of water that precedes it, and each drop shares in determining the direction of what follows. That is the fundamental view of "historicism," another term for determinism applied to historical reality.

Troeltsch dealt thoroughly and at great length with Herrmann on the occasion of the appearance of the *Ethik.* His essay "Grundprobleme der Ethik: Erörtert aus Anlasz von Herrmanns Ethik" has the length of a book.[7] Immediately at the outset he emphasized the Ritschlian legacy that the two had in common, namely, that "ethics is the higher and most fundamental science. It is within the framework of this science that the science of religion finds its place" (p. 553). Repeatedly he expressed his admiration to Herrmann for the manner in which he seeks to realize their common goal: to establish ethical certainty in the stream of history. "Herrmann's *Ethik* is one of the most mature, thought-out, and intellectually free works of present-day theology" (p. 570). Still,

7. E. Troeltsch, "Grundprobleme der Ethik: Erörtert aus Anlasz von Herrmanns Ethik," appeared in 1902 in *Zeitschrift für Theologie und Kirche* and was included in *Gesammelte Schriften* (Tübingen: Mohr, 1913), 2:552-672. The references here are to the latter.

he considered his attempt unsuccessful because, along with Kant, Herrmann retreated to a position in formal ethics, "indifferent to the determination of all ethical and religious problems by the prevailing condition of objective consciousness" (p. 571). Herrmann believed he was thereby orienting himself to the inner life of Jesus, but falsely so. "Herrmann's program is conditioned above all by the (historically effected) disintegration of the earlier conceptual apparatus of theological ethics" (pp. 572-73). Besides, it is not true that Jesus taught and lived by such a formal ethic. The "golden rule" (Matt. 7:12) is not the center of the ethics of Jesus, but the double commandment of love whose objective goal is "the restoration of a fellowship of all God's children" (pp. 629-31). In the gospel the formal principle of moral autonomy is subordinated to this objective goal. Therefore religion, the relationship to God, is more than merely the authority and guarantee for ethics. "Through their connection with it certain relationships to the deity become the great commandments and the highest goods" (p. 671).

One naturally thinks that Troeltsch considers this material ethic of Jesus time-conditioned (especially because of its connection with the *Naherwartung*) and therefore not binding for us. Here, however, beside the line of historical relativism, another line of thought emerges, namely, that of historical development: the personalistic ethics of love which Jesus taught is the highest stage in the ethical development of mankind. In this way Troeltsch, by way of the detour of historical development, still attains a more or less absolute point, one for which he yearned as much as Herrmann.

The same year (1902), in his book *The Absoluteness of Christianity and the History of Religions,* Troeltsch furnished a deeper foundation for and more comprehensive treatment of the things referred to in the essay.[8] By way of this book Troeltsch exerted great influence. It is rightly regarded as the mature product of his middle period of creativity. Here again the starting point, though no longer his main purpose, is his intent to settle accounts with Ritschlianism. In the same period the lectures of A. Harnack (delivered in 1899/1900), published in 1900 under the title *The Essence of Christianity,* found an enormous response. Harnack sought, along the lines of Ritschl, to demonstrate the absoluteness of Christianity historically. In his book Troeltsch tried to show how untraversable this road was and to take another direction. His point of departure is that

---

8. E. Troeltsch, *Die Absolutheit des Christentums und die Religionsgeschichte* (Tübingen: Mohr, 1902; 2nd ed. 1912). (Here I shall quote from the English translation by David Reid, *The Absoluteness of Christianity and the History of Religions* [Richmond, VA: John Knox, 1971].—TRANS.)

the historical as such can ever have only a relative, never an absolute, significance. But he did not stop there. After 1901 he no longer looked for his philosophical support in a metaphysical psychology such as that of Dilthey and Eucken, but in the Neo-Kantianism of the Baaden school, especially in H. Rickert, who from 1891 on was professor of philosophy in Freiburg-im-Breisgau, and developed his "philosophy of values" there: Whereas the natural sciences look for causality and universality, the science of history looks for the individuality which expresses itself in the realization of transindividual values in history. Troeltsch did not uncritically adopt this idea but supplemented it with Dilthey's psychological method and extended it along ethical and philosophy of history lines—so much so that in this period of his thinking one can hardly call Troeltsch a (Neo-) Kantian, in any case much less than Herrmann.

With this theory of the transhistorical values which are historically realized in the individual, Troeltsch believed he was able to overcome relativism. "It would be highly fallacious to think of historical relativism as if it involved a limitless number of competing values. On the contrary, experience shows that such values are exceedingly few in number and that disclosures of really new goals for the human spirit are rare indeed" (p. 92). Is there a criterion by which these disclosures of values can be compared? In that case, such a criterion would have to be considered as a historically conditioned and future-oriented idea. "We may likewise understand the criterion of evaluation as something that emerges within this movement of life as a result of a universal perspective on the one hand, and involvement in this movement on the other" (p. 96). "The converging lines evident in these basic features suggest, however, a normative, universally valid goal toward which the whole is directed" (p. 98). "It is the concept rather, of a common, orienting goal that may from time to time manifest itself in history in clear and distinct preparatory forms but always remains a goal 'out in front'" (p. 99). At this point Troeltsch moves from the historically empirical to metaphysics:

> This idea [namely, of an absolute goal] requires *a turn to the metaphysical*, a retracing of all man's goals and orientations to a transcendent force that actuates our deepest strivings and is connected with the creative core of reality. The various eruptions, breakthroughs, and manifestations of the higher spiritual life are rooted in the goal-oriented character of this force. It stands over against what is merely given in nature and towers up at different points—here clearly and profoundly, there more weakly and obscurely—till it has found concentrated expression, from that

point on pressing forward to goals that exceed all knowledge and imagination. This is the permanent element in the *concept of evolutionary development,* which in this case signifies not only a postulate that accompanies all faith in the spiritual life but also a fact of experience that has been manifested with some degree of clarity. (p. 100)

From here on it was not difficult for Troeltsch to make plausible, though it could not be proven from the history of religion, that up till now Christianity is the highest level of the human apprehension of truth:

> Only Christianity has overcome this way of looking at things that actually represents a vestige of nature religion. Only Christianity has disclosed a living deity who is act and will in contrast to all that is merely existent, who separates the soul from the merely existent and in this separation unites it with himself. In this way the soul, purified from guilt and pride and granted assurance and security, is set to work in the world for the upbuilding of a kingdom of pure personal values, for the upbuilding of the Kingdom of God.
>
> Thus Christianity must be understood not only as the culmination point but also as the convergence point of all the developmental tendencies that can be discerned in religion. It may therefore be designated, in contrast to other religions, as the focal synthesis of all religious tendencies and the disclosure of what is in principle a new way of life. (p. 114)

It would seem that, with this "absoluteness of Christianity," an "absoluteness" based on historical development (because "absolute truth belongs to the future and will appear in the judgment of God and the cessation of earthly history," p. 115), Troeltsch came very close to a kind of Hegelian pantheism and immanentism. Over against this, however, there is a strong personalism, because for Troeltsch as a modern person it is precisely the personalistic legacy of Christianity which constitutes a cornerstone of culture, individual life, and progress.

This comes to the fore especially in his *Glaubenslehre.*[9] In this volume he opposed the Christian concept of God to "a so-called natural knowledge of God." "Christian faith in God is . . . the religion of perfect personality in contrast with the religions of half-perfect personalities and with the religions of impersonality." "God's essence is will, and as such holiness and love" (p. 128). This leads to a sharp separation of God and

9. E. Troeltsch, *Glaubenslehre* (Munich/Leipzig, 1925).

world: the world is only the means to the self-glorification of God. "This principle of the divine will is, however, something purely irrational. . . . The final ground of all grounds is the total groundlessness of the divine will" (p. 150). Troeltsch's position reminds one of Dutch modernism a half-century earlier. There, too, a passionate search for God within the life of the human spirit went hand in hand with the assertion of his transcendence and personality and with man's personal relation to him (especially in prayer). Here the paths of modern thought and modern Christian theology had to separate. The latter had the suspicion that otherwise it would forfeit not only the gospel but also the future of Western culture, a culture based on personality.

HERRMANN: CONFRONTATION WITH TROELTSCH

Just as in this period Troeltsch reacted to Herrmann, so also Herrmann had to come to terms with Troeltsch. To Troeltsch's broad discussion of his *Ethik* he gave, as far as I know, only an incidental reply in the preface to the third edition of the book, where he mentions that, in view of Troeltsch's objections, he had to reformulate a number of things. He referred, with great courtesy, to that discussion, and to Troeltsch's historical studies as well as his accentuation of the ethics that comes to us from history and its treasures. Then he continued: "But the object [*Gegenstand*] of ethics cannot be these life-forms themselves. They can at any time become the means of selfishness. . . . The object of ethics is only this present, forward-surging life of history [*Geschichte*]. To describe that which came into being in the past is a historical task. I daresay it is impractical to burden ethics with it; it has enough to do as it is" (5th edition, p. XII). Again we sense the contrast which Herrmann's disciples later formulated as the contrast between *Geschichte* and *Historie*. For Herrmann the past is an ambiguous mixture; for Troeltsch it is the bearer of value and meaning.

Herrmann dealt more thoroughly with *The Absoluteness of Christianity*.[10] For all his courtesy he nevertheless charged that Troeltsch wanted to ground faith in the science of history and thus nullified his own certainty and therefore faith. "For that which Christ gives us and we have through him makes it impossible for us to think that after him someone greater than he may come. . . . If therefore we can comprehend

10. In *Theologische Literaturzeitung* 27/11 (1902) 330-34; also printed in *Schriften zur Grundlegung der Theologie,* 1:193-99 (from which the quotations are taken).

moral love, we have the faculty with which to grasp, in the Jesus of the New Testament, the only power of personal life which can fill us with complete confidence and pure reverence. . . . The fact, however, that nothing higher can be granted us is clear to everyone who has become inwardly independent in the understanding of moral love" (p. 199). The inner life of Jesus elevates itself above the laws of historicism: "However much we are convinced of the impossibility of a miracle, we ourselves, in contact with the incomparable nature of this personal life, experience a miracle" (p. 199).

In 1911 Troeltsch published a second essay on the theme of absoluteness: "The Significance of the Historical Existence of Jesus for Faith."[11] Here the issue is whether the Christian church can have a future apart from its being grounded in the historicity of Jesus. He denies it on grounds of social psychology; without a fellowship, a cult, and a historical personality to ground it, only an individualistic spirituality remains. As such a historically based cult community, Christianity can well maintain itself, even by historical-critical norms. "In my opinion the decisive chief facts [Troeltsch has in mind the basic religious-ethical character of the message of Jesus] can here be ascertained with certainty despite all the questions which remain open" (p. 200). So far Troeltsch has come to the same conclusions as Ritschl and Herrmann. But because to him that was a social-psychological and not a dogmatic pronouncement, he could not on that basis conclude that "Christianity itself will remain for ever the religion of humanity unto the end" (p. 205).

To this last lecture Herrmann also responded, this time with unaccustomed vehemence.[12] The explanation for this reaction is that in the lecture Troeltsch had defined his position especially over against that of Herrmann; he had charged that Herrmann, with his claim to absoluteness, had remained stuck in the old orthodoxy. For his part, Herrmann accused Troeltsch of fundamentally sharing the position of modern-apologetic orthodoxy, by which "a tradition, assumed to be certain, is made into the ground of faith" (p. 280). Accordingly, religion and science are confused with each other; the purely experiential character of religion

---

11. This essay is printed in *Die Absolutheit des Christentums* (Munich/Hamburg: Siebenstern Taschenbuch, 1969), pp. 132-62. The English translation from which the quotations are taken is printed in *Ernst Troeltsch: Writings on Theology and Religion,* ed. F. von Hügel, tr. and ed. Robert Morgan and Michael Pye (London: Duckworth, 1977), pp. 182-207.

12. In *Theologische Literaturzeitung* 37/8 (1912) 245-49; also published in *Schriften zur Grundlegung der Theologie,* 2:282-89 (to which the references are here).

threatens to be transformed into an idea. One does not have to rescue, by historical-critical methods, the experience of truth in the person of Jesus; nor desire to crush underfoot in advance the negative findings of this research in a false kind of certainty. Science ever remains relative; faith, however, gives itself over to the life-giving power of experienced reality, also when "we cannot dissolve one point of view into another" (p. 289). Thus the monist (Troeltsch) charged that the position of the dualist (Herrmann) would lead to Christianity's being ignored, and Herrmann charged that Troeltsch's starting point must lead to the dissolution of it.

EXHAUSTION ON BOTH SIDES; TROELTSCH TURNS AWAY FROM HISTORY

After 1910 there are symptoms of exhaustion in both men. For both, though in very different ways, the connection they made with history became problematic. In the case of Herrmann we noted this already earlier on.[13] For Troeltsch too the time came when he no longer saw how he could, with the aid of "values," pull himself out of the quicksand of historicism. Contributing to this was his deep study of sociology which found impressive expression in *The Social Teaching of the Christian Churches* (1912). One of its concluding sentences comes as a surprise: "The truth is—and this is the conclusion of the whole matter—the Kingdom of God is within us."[14]

Increasingly, his faith in the convergence of values in history as a sign of the ultimate unity and the metaphysical foundations of history waned. In the process he became less oriented to the Neo-Kantianism of Rickert. In his place, Hegel, the young Schleiermacher, and especially

13. See the Introduction by P. Fischer-Appelt in *Schriften zur Grundlegung der Theologie,* 1:XLI n. 42: The book *Jesus Christus und die Christliche Gemeinde,* announced in 1914, never appeared. "For the integration of Christology in the late form of Herrmann's thought encounters peculiar difficulties which are not only rooted in the (now apparent) crisis of the Quest-for-the-Historical-Jesus movement but also in the implications of Herrmann's own theological positions. It may be that in view of these difficulties Herrmann's strength finally failed him."

14. Ernst Troeltsch, *The Social Teaching of the Christian Churches,* tr. Olive Wyon, repr. in 2 vols. (New York: Harper & Row, 1960), 2:1013. The closing pages (1010-13) convey a mood of resignation, e.g., "It [i.e., Christian social activity] is problematic in general because the power of thought to overcome brutal reality is always an obscure and difficult question" (p. 1012). In the *Glaubenslehre* he also expressed in strong words his doubt about progress in history (pp. 320-21).

H. Bergson and Leibniz came to the fore. A mighty impulse toward this shift in perspective came from World War I. Troeltsch's faith in European culture as the highest stage of the ethical-cultural development of humanity received a blow from which he never recovered. Universal history, which was once his starting point, now became a question to him. He began to see that even his central idea of "personality" lacked universal historical validity but was typical for one culture—namely, Western culture. Even the basis of his historicism became historicized. Against a boundless relativism he sought shelter in a panentheistic metaphysic, especially with the aid of Leibniz's doctrine of monads: Every spiritual world is a monad which participates, however, in a universal consciousness and, by way of this detour, is capable of osmosis and extension; in this way "a new culture synthesis" becomes possible.

Troeltsch also converted the idea of the renewal and advancement of culture into action. Especially after the war, as a member of parliament in Prussia and as Under Secretary of State for the Prussian ministry of education and cultural affairs, and in his anonymous "Spectator Letters," he devoted his energies to the realization of the ethical and political ideals of the Weimar Republic. In March, 1921, however, he retired from politics and, as thinker and author, resumed the battle against a threatening nihilism on behalf of the cultural legacy of the West and the new culture synthesis. In this last period he still published *Der Historismus und seine Probleme* (1922). Then suddenly, on February 1, 1923, lung embolism ended his life. The lectures he was scheduled to deliver that same year at English and Scottish universities were posthumously published under the misleading title *Der Historismus und seine Überwindung* (see n. 16 below). In these lectures there comes to the fore, more than in his earlier publications, a tendency toward individualism and mysticism, one we saw earlier in the concluding sentence of his *Social Teaching*. In history the individual personality and its connection with the ground of being is the overriding goal. As such, however, it is not attainable within history. Two significant quotations may serve to characterize Troeltsch's thinking in its final phase:

> It is not possible to survey history in the light of "its final eternal goal." That . . . could be the case only for a divine kind of cognition, if such a single overall development exists at all, and the real eternal goal does not rather lie in the perfection of individuals, whose inner history is known tolerably well in a very small way in a few specimens, but which presumably is the real meaning of the whole for God. From his point of view, therefore, it may be altogether immaterial whether this perfection occurs

at the beginning, in the middle, or at the end of the historical process, or wherever.[15]

Troeltsch concluded the first lecture (on ethics and the philosophy of history, intended for delivery before the University of London) with these words:

> It is not for nothing that the religious idea places the individual, his decision and his salvation, in the foreground. He alone transcends history; and the inward union of the devout with one another is a heavenly object of longing or a monastic order, while it is only the ever-recurring mixture of light and darkness which suits earthly history. The kingdom of God, just because it transcends history, cannot limit or shape history. Earthly history remains the foundation and the presupposition of the final personal decision and sanctification; but in itself it goes on its way as a mixture of reason and natural instinct, and it can never be found in any bonds except in a relative degree and for a temporary space.[16]

Those are unmistakable words. In the boundless waters of world history Troeltsch looked in vain for a new rock to stand on. If there is such a thing as an eternal foothold it lies somewhere beyond life and death, a place of which one cannot say anything with certainty. History, which for Troeltsch initially promised the disclosure of the final secrets of the world, now emerges as a final curtain beyond which we cannot see.

One may have the impression that Troeltsch's intellectual odyssey ended in an impasse. His early and sudden death in a period of disillusionment may confirm this impression. One must remember, however, that for a long time already Troeltsch had harbored such thoughts. That is apparent not only from the last sentence of his *Social Teaching*, but also from the entire thrust of that book, which sees Christianity in the modern period developing ever more in the direction of a mystical-individual sectarianism. This is evident also from the *Glaubenslehre* of the same period, a book whose concluding sections know only of an unhistorical final consummation. "The final goal of a

---

15. E. Troeltsch, *Der Historismus und seine Probleme*, in *Gesammelte Schriften* (Tübingen: Mohr, 1922), 3:112. Cf. also p. 199: "This common basis and that common desired goal . . . can never be thought of as a final goal attained on earth; and how the universal and the individual are reconciled in a life after death is as dark a matter as everything else behind the curtain of death."

16. E. Troeltsch, *Christian Thought: Its History and Application*, tr. Mary E. Clarke, et al. (London: University of London Press, 1923), pp. 67, 68.

human life after death can . . . only be the return of the purified and sanctified creaturely being into the deity. . . . For the creature, the world process returns to its beginning . . . , and the transformation of this creatureliness in the total return of the person and the soul (now become spirit) to God is the end of the process. It is a process of emanation and return" (p. 381).

Conversely, it is also true that to the very end, knowing the limitations of human existence and history, Troeltsch, undoubtedly now "a sadder and wiser man," devoted all his intellectual energies to "damming and controlling the stream of historical life" and sought to make precisely this mystical-individualistic love toward the ground of being fruitful for the new culture synthesis.[17] Through his entire career as a thinker runs the thread of concern to save the Western culture of personality from the threatening nihilism which he saw coming, first in determinism, then also in bureaucracy, in capitalism, and in militarism. It is also true, however, that the struggle became increasingly heavy for him. The cruel forces of history drove him back to his final position: "the Kingdom of God is within us."[18]

CONVERGENCE AND CONTRAST

Herrmann and Troeltsch illustrate the two ways in which, while affirming the contemporary deterministic-empirical culture, one can still speak of "the absoluteness" of Jesus or of Christianity. They were two very different personalities. Herrmann was the man of one controlling idea, the one thing needed—a person who drilled to the very depths of existence. Troeltsch was the man of great breadth, a master of multiplicity, with a comprehensive knowledge of the intellectual-spiritual history of hu-

17. Ibid., esp. the three lectures of Section II, pp. 39-129.

18. I am referring here to a contrast in the interpretation of Troeltsch's thought. In the Netherlands it came out in two dissertations. The first: J. Klapwijk, "Tussen Historisme en Relativisme" (Assen, 1970). The author sees in Troeltsch an irreversible movement from historicism to relativism. See the German summary on pp. 469-99. The second: G. W. Reitsema, "Ernst Troeltsch als godsdienst-wijsgeer" (as philosopher of religion) (Assen, 1974). The author, looking at Troeltsch's thought from the vantage point of the middle period, sees it as a consistent whole. He accuses Klapwijk of completely failing to appreciate the continuity (p. 156). True, Klapwijk too sharply defines the divisions in Troeltsch. But Reitsema tends to neglect the importance of the shifts in emphasis whose irreversibility is clearly manifest in the light of the general development of European culture.

manity. They moved along opposite paths and pursued very different goals. Still, they found themselves on the same field of operation. Fundamentally and historically, they shared the same points of departure. There were, as we saw, striking parallels between them. They were motivated by the same concerns and driven by the same convictions.

Both sought to save the faith as well as the culture. They understood Christianity as ethical power, as the only moral power able to save a tired and disoriented European culture. Through the concept of history both wanted to bring the Christian faith into union with their culture. Both started with Ritschl's position and had to abandon his confidence in history. They ended with the young Schleiermacher of the *Speeches*, hence at the point where a century before the great attempt at reconciling gospel and culture had started. By doing this, they both rendered a negative verdict on the subsequent development.

In their attempts at reconciliation neither Herrmann nor Troeltsch could in the end avoid returning to the supernaturalism they despised. In the case of Herrmann, Jesus—with his unique inner life—remained the big exception and the great miracle in the midst of history. Troeltsch radically exposed himself to the temptations of contemporary culture. But for him, too, Jesus remained the hitherto unsurpassed high point in the great movement of the Spirit. For the sake of redemption of the human personality neither was able to abandon faith in the personhood of God. For the salvation of human beings both men reached for a Beyond—Herrmann for the inner life of Jesus beyond observable history, Troeltsch for the kingdom of redeemed spirits, also beyond history.

At bottom, therefore, both had the same faith. In that respect their opposite paths again came together; rather: fundamentally they had never gone separate ways. In one passage Troeltsch described "the essence of Christianity," which was so much discussed at the time, in these words: "The belief of the Christian religion is belief in the regeneration and higher birth of the creatures who were estranged from God in the world through the acknowledgement of God-in-Christ and thereby union with God, and among themselves into the Kingdom of God."[19] This statement is one the Ritschlians and also Herrmann could have fully endorsed.

In the face of so much commonality, what is the significance of the difference? The alternatives, which we observed before (between Schleiermacher and Hegel, and between Dorner and Rothe), are inherent in the very enterprise of reconciling the gospel and modern culture.

19. In "Die Dogmatik der Religionsgeschichtliche Schule," *Gesammelte Schriften*, 2:512.

The gospel cries out for concentration on the one thing necessary, the culture for going out into the broad expanse of the world. One can start out on either side. For one who started on one side it is difficult to do justice to the concerns of one who comes from the opposite direction. On the one hand, as a moral ascetic, Herrmann remained in opposition to his culture. On the other hand, Troeltsch could not do justice to the gospel claim of absoluteness.[20] Still, despite this larger difference, we must nevertheless again stress what they have in common. Both experienced and observed the Christian faith entirely within the framework of the cultural presuppositions of their time. In the case of Troeltsch this is clear. But also for Herrmann the ethical ideal of personality prevailing in his day was the unavoidable presupposition for faith in Jesus. Culture and Jesus belonged together as two sides of one phenomenon. Hence Herrmann, no less than Troeltsch, found his point of departure in the ideas and ideals of the cultured classes of his age.

When at the outbreak of World War I a group of German intellectuals ventured to support the politics of their emperor, their manifesto was also undersigned by Herrmann. That was too much for his young disciple and admirer Karl Barth. It seemed to Barth that the God about whom everyone had always talked now proved to be merely the national God of the German nation, a mirror image of its cultural pride. "A whole world of exegesis, ethics, dogmatics and preaching, which I had hitherto held to be essentially trustworthy, was shaken to the foundations, and with it, all the other writings of the German theologians."[21] Troeltsch's admirer, Freiin Gertrud von le Fort, joined the Catholic church in the very year (1925) that the edition of the *Glaubenslehre* she herself had prepared came out. These two are representative of the many who ran into the limits either of Herrmann or Troeltsch, barriers which could not be crossed from within or by the two systems.

After the crisis of World War I the influence of both men sharply declined. Still, there was an appreciable difference between them.

20. On the last page of his insightful dissertation ("Christelijke Religie en Historie in de Theologie van W. Herrmann" [Utrecht, 1922]), F. W. A. Korff clearly brings out the one-sidednesses and complementarity of the two thinkers. Korff proposed a possible synthesis and subsequently attempted to provide one himself in *Op weg naar een nieuwe levenseenheid* (Amsterdam, 1931). Later, under pressure from the direction of dialectical theology, he saw himself compelled to think through afresh the antithesis between revelation and life.

21. Cf. Eberhard Busch, *Karl Barth*, tr. John Bowden (Philadelphia: Fortress, 1975), pp. 81ff., where Barth's scattered references to the manifesto of the 93 German intellectuals are summarized.

Troeltsch's thinking was so strongly identified with the European culture of the "Wilhelmine" period that after his death, for half a century, his influence was almost nil. Herrmann's influence, in contrast, revived much sooner; in fact, as we shall see in the next chapter, it never really ended, not even after World War I. Neither Barth, nor Bultmann, nor the Neo-Bultmannians are thinkable without Herrmann. Only a rigorous Christocentrism had a message for a culture in crisis. Such a theology, however, can no more succeed in sidestepping the challenge of historicism than Herrmann could in his day. In time, therefore, Troeltsch too had to make a comeback. Pannenberg was the first to revive Troeltsch's concerns and simultaneously to work them out in a more Christ-centered manner. Since then the renewed interest in and grappling with the problems posed by Troeltsch has not stopped. We have still not been able to free ourselves from the choice between Herrmann and Troeltsch. It is a dilemma inherent in the post-Enlightenment theological program.

CHAPTER XII

The Split in the Herrmann School, I:
Bultmann and the Neo-Bultmannians

BULTMANN AS DISCIPLE OF HERRMANN

Rudolf Bultmann (1884-1976), who studied theology in Tübingen, Berlin, and Marburg, was trained as a New Testament scholar in the history of religions school, especially by Johannes Weiss in Marburg. He also had a close association with Weiss's successor, Wilhelm Heitmüller. In systematic theology the young Bultmann was especially fascinated by Wilhelm Herrmann. Thus the foundations were laid for that unique combination of professional exegetical work, the methodology of the history of religions school, an interest in hermeneutics, and systematic breadth which is characteristic for Bultmann's thinking and by which he exerted such strong influence. As a systematician he was a fervent adherent of the liberal theology which flourished at Marburg. He spent a great deal of his time as a student in Marburg in the home of Martin Rade and was a diligent reader of the journal *Die Christliche Welt* in which, in the years 1908-1930, he also published numerous articles and book reviews. In 1912 he qualified at Marburg as a lecturer in New Testament. After brief professorates in Breslau and Giessen he returned, in the fall of 1921, to Marburg ("which is, so to speak, my academic home") as the successor of Wilhelm Heitmüller, and remained to teach till 1951 and to live there till his death.[1]

The special perspective of this book entails that we cannot deal

---

1. The biographical details have been borrowed from Bultmann's brief autobiography printed in *The Theology of Rudolf Bultmann*, ed. Charles W. Kegley (New York: Harper & Row, 1966), pp. xix-xxv.

with the whole of Bultmann's many-sided thought. For us only the systematic side of it comes into view, particularly the question: How did Bultmann, who experienced deeply the chasm between the world of the New Testament and the world in which he himself lived, attempt to bridge it? Our focus forces us either totally to ignore, or only to touch in passing, many an important theme in Bultmann; for example, his view of the historical Jesus, his hermeneutical method, his idea of the kerygma, and his program of demythologization.

The roots of his systematic thought lie clearly in the teaching of his revered teacher Wilhelm Herrmann. But this is not at all as self-evident as it may appear to us in the light of his position in the Marburg tradition. In the New Testament department the history of religions school predominated. Viewed as the systematician of this school was Herrmann's antipode in liberal theology, Ernst Troeltsch. His ideas arose organically from the researches of the history of religions school —something that can definitely not be said of Herrmann's thinking, seeing it rather presupposed, in the person of Jesus, an incursion in the history of religion. The flip side in the case of Herrmann was a profound mistrust of historically ascertainable facts as vehicles of revelation. They are merely, as Bultmann also repeatedly emphasized, "intramundane conditions and occurrences." Bultmann's mistrust of history as means of revelation is even more radical than that of his teacher, as we shall see. Like Herrmann, he objected to Troeltsch that "the world which faith wills to grasp is absolutely unattainable by scientific research." The absolute does not permit itself to be grounded in relativities — which is all scientific research can offer. That which emerges on the basis of Troeltsch's methodology has nothing to do with Christian theology but is a kind of "pantheism of history." The Christian experience of faith is not in a conventional sense "grounded"; it implies a radical release from empirical certitude *(Entsicherung)*.[2]

In these lines of thought, which remained characteristic for Bultmann throughout his life, he is through and through the faithful disciple of Herrmann. However, he took an important step further. In my opinion, that had to do with the conscious or unconscious influence of Troeltsch. The Achilles' heel of Herrmann was, certainly, that for his faith in Jesus he needed a little segment of history, namely, "the inner life of Jesus" or the "secret of his Person," however nonvisual it might be.

---

2. The quoted material occurs in a programmatic article by the young Bultmann: "Liberal Theology and the Latest Theological Movement" (1924), repr. in Rudolf Bultmann, *Faith and Understanding,* ed. Robert Funk, tr. Louise Pettibone Smith (New York: Harper & Row, 1969), pp. 28-52.

Troeltsch did not believe in this rock as a place of refuge to which one could go in the midst of the flood of historical determinism. And Bultmann, as one who practiced the religion-historical method, had to concur here with the opponent of his teacher. However, unlike Troeltsch he did not plunge into the sea, but believed he could find revelation concerning the sea above the inundated rock, in a higher atmosphere which the flood could not reach, in the free air of human existence addressed by God, on a level of reality which can only be reached by a radical detachment from the world. Pure and practical reason were strictly separated here. The historical Jesus belonged to the first domain, the preaching of the crucified Jesus to the second. Only the "that" of the life of Jesus still had weight; the "what," even if it was the inner life of Jesus, was surrendered to the relativization of historical criticism. The only thing that was still valid was the unhistorical, and as such *geschichtliche*, kerygma of the cross, which concerns my existence here and now and calls it to its own "actuality," in isolation from the horizontal powers of world, law, and history. Accordingly, Bultmann wanted to sever the last remaining connection between *Historie* and *Geschichte* in order to protect the faith from any and every critical assault on the part of science. The retreat of the Ritschlian school in the face of the increasing secularization of the prevailing sense of life *(Lebensgefühl)*, in the person of Rudolf Bultmann, advanced by still another final decisive step.[3]

BULTMANN AND BARTH

For a moment it might seem as if by taking that step Bultmann had left the track of the Ritschlian school. That was the case in the period between 1922 and 1925 when Bultmann was strongly influenced by Barth's *Epistle to the Romans* (2nd edition, 1922). With astonishment the theological world took note that the astute liberal New Testament scholar apparently championed the highly personal and muddled ideas of the orthodox Swiss pastor. For some time he seemed to be affiliated with "dialectical theology" and the group around the journal *Zwischen den Zeiten*. That was, however, a misunderstanding destined to be short-lived.

In Barth, himself a product of Marburg and a Herrmann disciple, Bultmann saw a critical extension of liberal theology. Here this theology was being liberated from the dead end of subjectivism and

3. Bultmann clearly formulated his divorce from Herrmann's thinking at this point in "On the Question of Christology" (1927), repr. in *Faith and Understanding*, pp. 132ff.

again made into "speech concerning God"—God as One who is not at our human disposal and with whom faith as trust in the midst of uncertainty enters into a relationship. Herrmann had said the same thing earlier. Did not Herrmann ground faith in the moral consciousness? "The Word of God is a 'stumbling block' for this world and primarily a 'stumbling block' for an earnest mind, for the moral consciousness. Here again Barth and Gogarten state the conclusions which are actually inherent in liberal theology. For who has emphasized more forcibly than W. Herrmann that there is no specifically Christian ethic? And who has shown more convincingly than Troeltsch the problematic character of the relation of the Christian to the world?"[4] For that reason Bultmann can see Barth on the very line that runs from Schleiermacher's *Speeches* directly to Herrmann. "No one in our time has proclaimed with this self-confidence the uniqueness and absoluteness of 'religion' (of faith!) with more clarity than Wilhelm Herrmann, with whom Barth is in complete agreement."[5]

It is striking to what degree, in the review referred to, Bultmann measures Barth by Herrmann. According to Bultmann, Barth essentially reiterates Herrmann's concerns, sometimes remaining behind him and at other times surpassing him.[6] Bultmann believed that, in virtue of the strong object-relatedness which he attributed to faith as trust, Herrmann did not fall under Barth's verdict of anthropologizing the faith and had the same concern as Barth.

However, from the beginning Bultmann could not agree with Barth on two important points. The first is hermeneutics. He charged that Barth "did violence to Romans and to Paul" instead of submitting them to material criticism *(Sachkritik)*. In the review referred to one senses this criticism only in passing in the last point. After the appearance of Barth's study on 1 Corinthians 15, *The Resurrection of the Dead,* Bultmann's criticism in this regard is much sharper: "It is no small matter when *the* ideas of Paul which are particularly plain and which were certainly important to Paul (the whole 'closing scene of history,' for example) are so to speak explained away—whether it be by re-interpretation or by critical analysis."[7] More than with Paul, Bultmann agreed with Barth whose hermeneutic he understood as existential interpretation hence constructed from within a specific anthropological pre-under-

4. *Faith and Understanding,* p. 45.
5. *The Beginnings of Dialectic Theology,* ed. James M. Robinson (Richmond, VA: John Knox, 1968), p. 102.
6. Ibid., pp. 113, 114, 115.
7. *Faith and Understanding,* p. 86.

standing.[8] Bultmann's judgment had an effect on Barth that was the opposite of what was intended: Barth began to criticize, not Paul, but himself. Not his understanding of existence but the objective content of the biblical text was decisive for him. After a brief period of seeming agreement (in which Barth never really believed) their ways separated.

The difference between them was even clearer at another point. Bultmann could only view Barth's understanding of the relationship between revelation and history as contradictory. On the one hand, he agreed that the nonvisual Christ as the proclaimed Word is the living, present revelation; on the other he stated emphatically: "Therefore the years 1-30 are a time of revelation, a time of discovery." Precisely at the point where Bultmann had taken his leave of Herrmann he saw Barth remaining stuck in the half-measures and confusion of their common teacher.[9] Barth refrained, however, from complying with Bultmann's demand and criticism. The difficult question as to how revelation and history are related in Barth is one which will occupy us later.

At this point it is enough to observe that from the beginning Bultmann brought out two important differences between himself and Barth, a hermeneutical difference and a systematic difference. It became evident that the kinship between them did not go deep enough. And when we look back from the later mature positions of the two men and their correspondence after 1952 to the beginning of their relationship, it strikes us that already in his review Bultmann was more interested in Barth's statements concerning the human self, about faith and consciousness, about "the ultimate question concerning the meaning of human existence," hence in the *fides qua creditur,* than in Barth's main concern, the question concerning the deity of God and the objectivity of his Word.[10] With this focus Bultmann was and remained more faithful to Herrmann than Barth was. Already in 1930 Barth correctly wrote: "It might well be that what I understand by the 'Word of God' has never been a concern of yours in this way and that you have developed much more directly than I thought from Herrmann and Otto to the place where you now are, so that our ships were merely ships that passed in the night."[11]

Contact with "dialectical theology" for Bultmann never pro-

8. As he explained in his Eisenach lecture of 1927: "The Significance of 'Dialectical Theology' for the Scientific Study of the New Testament," repr. in *Faith and Understanding,* pp. 145-64.

9. See *Beginnings of Dialectic Theology,* pp. 114-18.

10. Ibid., pp. 104-14.

11. *Karl Barth—Rudolf Bultmann Letters, 1922-1966,* ed. Bernd Jaspert, tr. and ed. Geoffrey W. Bromiley (Grand Rapids: Eerdmans, 1981), p. 50.

duced a shift in his thinking. In dialectical theology he only welcomed
—in a somewhat more modern form—the religious insights he had appropriated in the school of Herrmann.

BULTMANN AND HEIDEGGER

In the very period in which Barth presented for Bultmann a new systematic-theological stimulus Bultmann also had the intensive contact
with Heidegger which in time became of great philosophical importance to him.

Initially *Martin Heidegger* (1889-1976) studied (Catholic) theology
at Freiburg, but soon switched to philosophy. For a time he became an adherent of Husserl's phenomenology. When in 1923, as Natorp's successor, he was appointed full professor in philosophy at Marburg, it seemed
that Marburg's Neo-Kantianism had come to an end. During his professorate in Marburg (1923-1928), Heidegger entered into close contact with
Bultmann, through shared seminars, among other ways. Heidegger was
still theologically interested, and Bultmann soon sensed that for him the
philosophy of existence with which in these years Heidegger occupied
himself in preparation for his *Being and Time* (1927) could be very helpful
as a foundation for his theology. He himself wrote: "In doing so, the work
of existential philosophy, which I came to know through my discussions
with Martin Heidegger, became of decisive significance for me. I found
here the concept through which it became possible to speak adequately
of human existence and therefore also of the existence of the believer. In
my efforts to make philosophy fruitful for theology, however, I have come
more and more into opposition to Karl Barth."[12]

Heidegger analyzed human existence in a way which enabled
Bultmann to illuminate the connection between the Word of God and
our existence. In his opinion this was possible precisely because Heidegger made explicit that image of man which underlies the witness of Paul
and John. Heidegger could therefore become "the philosopher" for Bultmann as Aristotle had been for Thomas — with this difference that
Heidegger was a philosopher *after* Christ, and that on the whole the true
"natural" understanding of man had not been discovered and processed
"without the New Testament, without Luther, without Kierkegaard."
Bultmann therefore had a tendency to Christianize Heidegger's insights.
"For the existential interpretation of human existence says precisely that
the human subject (or human being, I might also say) is not without his

12. From the autobiographical sketch mentioned in n. 1 above, p. xxxiv.

world, nor even without God insofar as the philosopher regards it as legitimate to speak about God, so that self-understanding is *also* understanding of (God and) the world."[13] One may ask whether this sentence could not be understood as "natural theology" just as well as the Christianization of Heidegger. In my opinion the two points of view are fused in Bultmann. In order to see this, one must remember the function which Heidegger's analysis of existence gained in Bultmann. In his well-known study "The New Testament and Mythology" (1941), he clearly expressed himself on the subject: according to Heidegger the "mundaneness of the world" causes people to be satisfied with an illusory existence; as a result they miss out on "the reality of existence." This condition of lostness is what the New Testament calls "sin." According to Heidegger people must now lay hold of existence on their own: Become what you are! "But philosophy is convinced that all that is needed to bring about the realization of our 'nature' is that it be shown to us. . . . Is this self-confidence on philosophy's part justified? In any case, here is its difference from the New Testament." People cannot free themselves from their fallenness, because in their fallenness any movement is a movement of fallen human beings. This laying hold of existence in one's own strength is precisely that which Paul calls the boasting of man who wants to be justified by his own work. This situation leads to the question (which is at the same time an answer): "Does this really settle whether the only appropriate attitude for human beings without Christ is to despair of the possibility of their being?" People must first be liberated from themselves. That happens through the message of Christ, through the forgiveness of sin, by which alone people receive the "freedom for obedience," surrender to the love of God, and therewith the authenticity of their existence.[14]

This means that Heidegger's analysis of existence occupies the same place vis-à-vis the gospel as the law in Luther and the moral idea in Herrmann, both of which lead to moral despair. Of course, that was never Heidegger's own intention. However, Bultmann "uses" Heidegger in the

13. *Karl Barth—Rudolf Bultmann Letters, 1922-1966*, pp. 98-99.

14. R. Bultmann, "Neues Testament und Mythologie," in *Offenbarung und Heilsgeschehen* (Munich: Lempp, 1941), pp. 27-69; repr. in *Kerygma und Mythos* (Hamburg, 1948), 1:15-53. The quotations here are taken from *New Testament and Mythology and Other Basic Writings*, tr. and ed. Schubert M. Ogden (Philadelphia: Fortress, 1984), pp. 21-43. Bultmann's lines of thought here relate particularly to M. Heidegger, *Being and Time*, tr. John and Edward Robinson (New York: Harper & Row, 1962), §§ 54-60. A good account of the agreement and difference between Heidegger and Bultmann occurs in W. Schmithals, *An Introduction to the Theology of Rudolf Bultmann*, tr. John Bowden (Minneapolis: Augsburg, 1968), esp. chs. 3-5.

same way Thomas uses Aristotle and Herrmann uses Kantianism: as "preamble to the faith." Also, Heidegger's dichotomy between world and existence must have appeared familiar to him as a new formulation of the divorce between determinism and freedom. In Heidegger Bultmann found back again, in a more up-to-date formulation, what he had learned from Herrmann's lectures. Later he wrote on this subject: "That W. Herrmann anthropologized the Christian message seems to me to be contradicted already by the role that the concept of trust plays for him. Certainly his conceptuality was inadequate in relation to what he was trying to say. But it was because I learned from Herrmann that I was ready for Heidegger. Heidegger, too, learned from Herrmann and rated him highly (esp., e.g., his essay on the penitence of the evangelical Christian)."[15]

The question whether Bultmann correctly understood (the) Heidegger (of that time) can be left undecided. Very soon after completing his *Being and Time*, Heidegger took totally different directions. He had hoped, on the track of a phenomenology of existence, to solve the question of Being which was central to him but had to acknowledge that this study had led him to a dead end. As a result he shifted to Being itself, a shift to which he gave expression in his *Letter on Humanism* (1947): The real subject is Being itself, which merely is. "But it is by saying its matter" (p. 236). In and through man Being attains language. "Language is the house of Being" (p. 213). And man is the guardian, the watchman, the "shepherd of Being" (p. 221). On the basis of this insight Heidegger now rethinks and redefines the concepts of *Being and Time*. Existence means: "man occurs essentially in such a way that he is the 'there' [*das 'Da'*], that is, the lighting of Being" (p. 205). "Man is, and is man, insofar as he is the ek-sisting one. He stands out into the openness of Being. Being itself, which as the throw has projected the essence of man into 'care,' is as this openness. Thrown in such fashion, man stands 'in' the openness of Being" (pp. 228-29).[16]

15. *Karl Barth—Rudolf Bultmann Letters*, p. 99. Here I may perhaps refer to the fact that in the history of theology theologians have often relied on the authority of philosophers with whom they found themselves in close proximity. That applies to Ritschl (Lotze), to Herrmann (Cohen), to Troeltsch (Rickert), to Bultmann (Heidegger); and on the international scene, to many Anglicans (the philosophy of language analysis); to many Frenchmen (Merleau-Ponty, Ricoeur, and Levinas). One often gets the impression that differences and communication problems between theologians stem more from their philosophical affiliation than their religious convictions.

16. The *Letter on Humanism*, from which these quotations have been taken, can be found in English translation in Martin Heidegger, *Basic Writings*, ed. D. F. Krell (New York: Harper & Row, 1977).—TRANS.

AGAIN: BULTMANN AND HERRMANN

Bultmann never went along with that shift. He never really believed that such a radical change in focus occurred in Heidegger at all. Besides, he could not do anything with this shift from human subjectivity to the objectivity of Being. Heidegger, like Barth, exerted only a temporary influence on Bultmann. What remained was the framework of Herrmann's thought and behind this framework the duality of the two worlds of Kant.[17]

This result is indirectly confirmed by Bultmann's sermons. Although they were delivered in the most tumultuous years of recent German history, they seem oddly timeless. For example, the message given on May 30, 1943, reads: "We must be ready to enter into a solitariness in which the world fades away, in which all relationships, even the most binding and the dearest, are loosed and where we stand confronted by God alone" (though of course this must be proven in one's daily life). One may perhaps hear an echo here of *Being and Time;* it is, however, far more a witness of nineteenth-century individualism and pietism. This comes through also in the authors cited: Tersteegen, Novalis, Hölderlin, C. F. Meyer, Eichendorff, Rückert, Raabe. A few weeks after the defeat of Germany Bultmann preached about 2 Corinthians 4:6-11, stressing that man lives in two worlds, a visible world marked by suffering and an invisible "world of the good, the true, and the beautiful."[18] Bultmann once remarked that the events of World War I did not influence his thinking; it is clear that the same applies to World War II. His thinking developed and matured in the intellectual and religious atmosphere which prevailed before the two great wars.

Apart from his more or less modern terminology, what distinguishes Bultmann from his teachers is the radicalism with which he severed the final tenuous connections between faith and the reality of time and space, existence and world, between *Geschichte* and *Historie.*[19]

17. In his (Dutch) dissertation on Bultmann, "Kerygma" (Assen, 1958), J. M. de Jong correctly writes: "In Bultmann there is really no fundamental dependence on Heidegger; there is on Descartes and Kant, even though these names are rarely mentioned by him, if at all" (p. 61 n. 1). De Jong describes the presuppositions of Bultmann's theology without enlisting the aid of the philosophy of Heidegger.

18. R. Bultmann, *Marburger Predigten* (Tübingen: Mohr, 1956). (The quotations are taken from *This World and the Beyond,* tr. Harold Knight [London: Lutterworth, 1960], pp. 194-95, 211ff.—Trans.)

19. This radicalism works itself out especially in his program of demy-

However, whether he distanced himself from Herrmann as far as he himself believed is a question. At this point we encounter the most difficult questions in the interpretation of Bultmann: theologically, what did the cross mean as the thin thread which connected the proclaimed Christ with the earth and with history? Either nothing—and then Bultmann turned away from the gospel; or it has to mean everything—and then all the attacks which can be directed against the faith from within "the scientific image of the world" come back. We are left with an air of indefiniteness and ambiguity which hangs over Bultmann's presentations. Hence Buri and Jaspers could accuse him of "illiberality" and inconsistency in his demythologizing. Many of his disciples took the opposite course and accused him of undervaluing the importance for faith of the historical Jesus. With that we come upon the phenomenon of the "post-Bultmannians" or rather the "Neo-Bultmannians."

BULTMANN AND THE NEO-BULTMANNIANS

The first and most influential breakaway from Bultmann came from the New Testament scholar *Ernst Käsemann* (born 1906) in his lecture: "Das Problem des historischen Jesus" (The Problem of the Historical Jesus) (1954). In it he explains that the kerygma also presupposes and includes facts. The right road passes between docetism and historicism. The proclaimer and the proclaimed are not only separated by the Easter event but also united. Why else should the inscripturation of the Gospels have been necessary? The historical Jesus is essential to the faith; without him the contingency, the condescension, and also the objectivity (the "extra nos") of revelation would not have remained known. "The question of the historical Jesus is, in its legitimate form, the question of the continuity of the Gospel within the discontinuity of the times and within the variation of the kerygma."[20] From the start Bultmann defended himself

---

thologizing, where one sees the operations the gospel must undergo in order to agree with the existential interpretation. Demythologizing, however, is a consequence of Bultmann's rigorous systematics rather than a point of entry. The central focus is the existential interpretation itself, as a bridge between the gospel and the modern world.

20. E. Käsemann, "Das Problem des historischen Jesus," in *Exegetische Versuch und Besinnungen* (Göttingen: Vandenhoeck & Ruprecht, 1960), 1:187-214. (The quotations here are taken from "The Problem of the Historical Jesus," in *Essays on New Testament Themes*, tr. W. J. Montague, Studies in Biblical Theology 41 [London: SCM, 1964], p. 46.—TRANS.)

against these far-reaching corrections of his theology. He warned Käsemann that with his views he was returning to the hybrid position of Herrmann.[21] To many a Bultmann disciple, however, this position seemed less impossible than the radical rejection of the historical as a category of faith by Bultmann.

With this attack Käsemann rang in the rise of a Neo-Bultmannian school. He himself, however, did not belong to it. The Neo-Bultmannians remained true to the existential interpretation of the kerygma, but Käsemann left that common ground behind. This is particularly evident from two articles: "The Beginnings of Christian Theology" (1960) and "On the Subject of Primitive Christian Apocalyptic" (1962).[22] By way of the misleading concept of "apocalyptic" Käsemann introduces, as keys to the gospel, a series of viewpoints all of which break out of the confinement of the concept of existence: Easter faith, *Geschichte,* future expectation, the not-yet, etc. In doing this, however, Käsemann did not simply work along the lines of classic Lutheranism but made them his point of departure for a new synthesis between the *theologia crucis* and a theology of freedom: Jesus is the God-given bearer of freedom whose life project attains validity forever by the message of the resurrection. It has a contagious effect, leading disciples of the Crucified one on a narrow path between legalism and "enthusiasm" *(Schwärmerei).* From this hermeneutical perspective Käsemann now reads the entire New Testament. In a fascinating little book *Jesus Means Freedom,* Käsemann articulated the views which emerge in the process. Published in the year of the student revolts (1968) this book offers a theology of liberation of far greater biblical depth than what is presented elsewhere under the same or a similar name.[23] Since then the interpretation of the New Testament and a passionate prophetic witness against the establishment of church and state have been one and the same for him. One might perhaps characterize his position as a "political laying hold of existence" *(politische Existenzergreifung)* as a variation within the Bultmann school. It was, however, far removed from Bultmann's "laying hold of existence" as "de-secularization" *(Entweltlichung)* and, in distinction from Bultmann's theology, had no connection any more with the individualistic inward-

---

21. According to an oral communication from Käsemann.
22. In German these essays were repr. in *Exegetische Versuche und Besinnungen,* 2:82-131. Cf. the translation by W. J. Montague, in *New Testament Questions of Today* (London: SCM, 1969), pp. 82-137.
23. E. Käsemann, *Der Ruf der Freiheit,* 3rd ed. (Tübingen: Mohr, 1968). Cf. the translation by Frank Clarke, *Jesus Means Freedom: A Polemical Survey of the New Testament* (London: SCM, 1969).

ness which so marked the piety and theology of the previous century. At the same time he brought to expression, much more powerfully than Bultmann succeeded in doing, the independence and offense-giving character of the gospel.

All these things are very different in the case of the real Neo-Bultmannians, especially the two leading figures of the movement, *Gerhard Ebeling* (born 1912) and *Ernst Fuchs* (born 1903). For both of these men Käsemann's article about the beginnings of Christian theology meant a parting of the ways. Both of them theologize in terms of the polarity of gospel and law in the tradition of Luther and in the fashion of Herrmann and Bultmann. According to Fuchs, "enthusiasm," *Naherwartung,* and Easter faith are peripheral phenomena in primitive Christianity, whereas for Käsemann the precise opposite is the case: the issue of the "law" is only a peripheral phenomenon, one that was made acute by the quick expansion of the mission to the Gentiles.[24]

More important to us are the starting points of Ebeling and Fuchs. What distinguishes them from Bultmann is their recourse to the historical Jesus. What unites them with him is the central position in their thinking of the question of existence as the key to the gospel. However, according to them true existence does not come into being exclusively as a result of the preaching of the crucified Jesus but comes to us primarily through the unique life project of the historical Jesus. This project *(Entwurf)*—to be sharply distinguished from the psychological and biographical data of this life—is referred to, alternatively, as Jesus' "faith," "trust," "conduct," or "love." It is here that the Word-event from God's side comes about. This event breaks through the limitations of the historically conditioned in the resurrection. The resurrection itself is a hermeneutic event which gives worldwide expression to the new existence of Jesus.

This new existence is God's answer to the predicament of human existence. The natural man lives in uncertainty and dread, and is subject to the accusations of conscience and the threat of the law. Jesus is the answer, in the name of God, of forgiveness and love. The dialectic of law and gospel is the true explanation and liberation of human existence.[25]

24. Ebeling responded to Käsemann's essay of the year 1960 with the article "Der Grund christlicher Theologie," in *Zeitschrift für Theologie und Kirche* 58 (1961) 227-44; and in the same issue Fuchs reacted to Käsemann's essay with the article "Über die Aufgabe einer christlichen Theologie," pp. 245-67. Käsemann's second article, already mentioned above, "Zum Thema der urchristlichen Apokalyptik," was the reply to both.

25. Cf. G. Ebeling, *Dogmatik des christlichen Glaubens,* 1/1, "Der Glaube an Gott den Schöpfer der Welt" (Tübingen: Mohr, 1979), where he extends this

THE BACKGROUND AND DEVELOPMENT OF THE STRUGGLE

We must spend a little more time on the question of what caused Bultmann's disciples to move away from him. Up to this point we traced it back exclusively to their stress on the significance for faith of the historical Jesus. However, in theology such shifts never have a merely theological background. Playing a large role here also is a philosophical and cultural shift.

The philosophical shift we have in mind is Heidegger's turnabout. Bultmann ignored it but for Fuchs it was theologically of real moment. Along with Heidegger he made the discovery that *Da-sein*, "eksistence," in itself does not lead us to Being. Our self can also, and that according to the New Testament, be a self-contained world. Precisely the self, however, is put at risk by Being, which is the true "pre-understanding." The liberation of the self by Being comes from without. This Being discloses itself in language. And "the essence of language is permission." The great language-event of Jesus' preaching gives us permission to believe in the love of God.[26]

With these brief suggestions we must let the matter rest. For Fuchs and others it was plain that the objectivity of the Word-event (never denied by Bultmann) as basis for and the counterpole of our act "of laying hold of existence" can be much better discussed with the help of Heidegger after his "turnabout."

The second shift, which we called cultural, is the shift from idealism to empiricism, which, be it under other names, took place again as it had in the previous century. A theological generation grew up for whom the language of the great predecessors was no longer intelligible. However diverse Barth, Brunner, Bultmann, Niebuhr, and Tillich were, their basic concepts like "revelation," "Word of God," "absolute and infinite Being," even the vocable "God," all belonged to a conceptual *Überwelt* which was not open to empirical verification. Also, Bultmann's preaching of the Crucified and his "de-secularization" *(Entweltlichung)* of existence now became intangible and unintelligible. I see no indications that the Neo-Bultmannians consciously involved themselves in this shift toward empiricism. But since 1950 it was in the air, expanded

---

line of thought, e.g., in his treatment of the relationship between faith and religion (cf. esp. p. 139).

26. Cf. esp. Fuchs's contribution to the Festschrift presented to Bultmann on his eightieth birthday, *Zeit und Geschichte,* ed. E. Dinkler (Tübingen: Mohr, 1964), pp. 357-66, under the heading "Das hermeneutische Problem."

rapidly, and manifested itself in many areas. The "shift" from "Christ" to "Jesus" belongs entirely to this new climate. For many during these years it made the gospel credible again to have it anchored in the histori- cal Jesus. And it explains why Bultmann's influence so quickly had to make way for that of his disciples.

This also meant a return to Wilhelm Herrmann. He, too, had at- tempted to interpret the gospel for an empiricistic generation. In the process he found himself entirely on the defensive. But he was never able to give up the connection with the empirical, however tenuous it might be. What he called "the inner life of Jesus" was essentially the same as what the Neo-Bultmannians described as "the conduct" or "the faith of Jesus." It is significant that during the very heyday of the theology of Fuchs and Ebeling, Herrmann's writings were very much in demand again, and that in 1966 and 1967, under the title *Schriften zur Grundlegung der Theologie*, a new edition of Herrmann's less obtainable works again came out.[27]

Bultmann firmly rejected the "corrections" of his followers, giving a comprehensive account of his reasons in the *Heidelberger Aka- demie* essay "Das Verhältnis der urchristlichen Christusbotschaft zum historischen Jesus."[28] He focused particularly on two problem areas: (1) Does the post-Easter kerygma presuppose the proclamation of the historical Jesus? The synoptic reports on this subject are themselves al- ready post-Easter proclamation. Certainly Jesus' preaching had much in common with the post-Easter message (with the exception of Chris- tology). That, however, is a merely historical fact; Jesus' message itself was not an eschatological event. It just makes historically under- standable how the proclaimer became the proclaimed. "Does Jesus' claim to authority, considered as historical phenomenon, reach beyond the time of his work on earth? Do the claim and promise of the histori- cal Jesus, in their immediacy, reach later generations? But that occurs precisely in the kerygma in which not the *historical* Jesus but the *exalted*

---

27. Closely allied with the Neo-Bultmannians was Friedrich Gogarten (1887-1968), for whom also the law-gospel dialectic was decisive and who saw the "turning point of the world" (*Wende der Welt*, according to the title of his work in Christology, 1966) begin with the historical Jesus. Through the relation to God Jesus entered, and in his steps we also enter, upon a new "responsibility for the world" in which one's neighbor is central. Gogarten was no Bultmannian; but with his way of posing the question and its solution he belongs totally to the school of Ritschl.

28. R. Bultmann, "Das Verhältnis der urchristlichen Christusbotschaft zum historischen Jesus," in *Exegetica* (Tübingen: Mohr, 1967), pp. 445-69 (from which the quotations have been taken).

Jesus speaks. . . . The Christ of the kerygma has, so to speak, pushed aside the historical Jesus and now, in the fulness of his authority, addresses . . . every hearer" (p. 458). (2) Fuchs and Ebeling necessarily slip into a historical-psychological interpretation of Jesus and hence into a historicizing grounding of faith. "The Gospels do not speak of Jesus' own faith nor does the kerygma refer back to Jesus' faith" (p. 461).

In a relatively small book, Ebeling replied to Bultmann's counterattack.[29] He answered the first objection by saying that kerygma, besides being an "address to existence," is also a testimony to that which has happened and therefore requires legitimation from history, or else Jesus becomes a myth. One cannot make a disjunction between historical continuity and essential *(sachlicher)* continuity. Ebeling barely entered upon a discussion of Bultmann's second objection, but he did believe that with his reply to the first he had adequately covered it.

In my opinion, the conflict between Bultmann and his disciples has not been resolved. His disciples were stronger in their accentuation of the essential continuity between Jesus and Christ. Bultmann's suggestion that their position was perhaps also "based on certain dogmatic interests" (p. 446) sounds a bit strange because he does not seem to realize to what extent his own sharp disjunction of "History" and existence-related "Kerygma" is based on the philosophical views of Kant and Heidegger respectively. Bultmann's second objection against his disciple-critics is one they could not, in my judgment, invalidate: the post-Easter kerygma is not identical with the message of Jesus and does not (very often—I would prefer to say) refer back to the message and conduct of the earthly Jesus.

This brings up the nature and significance of Easter. In the 1960s, in fact, the discussion shifted to that subject. The Neo-Bultmannians also had to accept a certain historical legitimation for the Easter message, one they found in the resurrection appearances. But by doing so they stepped outside the realm of faith as delimited by the concept of existence. For that reason they could not ground faith in the empty tomb, and the resurrection appearances were viewed, so to speak, as the first stage of the rocket of the kerygma which now dropped, meaningless, into the sea of historical memorabilia.[30] One senses here a Herrmannian continuation and min-

29. G. Ebeling, *Theology and Proclamation: Dialogue with Bultmann,* tr. John Riches (Philadelphia: Fortress, 1966).

30. The classical expression of the Neo-Bultmannian construal of the relationship between the historical Jesus and the post-Resurrection kerygma occurs in G. Ebeling, *The Nature of Faith,* tr. Ronald Gregor Smith (Philadelphia: Fortress, 1961), ch. IV, "The Witness of Faith," and ch. V, "The Basis of Faith," pp. 44-57, 58-71.

imalization of the historical basis of faith. Questions from two sides simply had to erupt at this point. Is the historical necessary to the explanation of the kerygma (Bultmann, Marxsen)? And: Is this minimal history sufficient for the explanation of the kerygma (Künneth)? By answering the first question in the negative one remains strictly within the existentialist framework. By answering the second question in the negative one breaks out of this framework in favor of an ontological mode of thought.

It seems the discussion collapsed the moment these last questions fully surfaced.[31] Here the fundamental decisions were made at a point beyond the intellectual arguments with which the theologians battled each other. But there were also other reasons why the whole discussion became a matter of the past. New stars had appeared on the theological firmament. And the general theological interests had shifted toward the realm of social ethics. For answers to these questions the methodology of the Neo-Bultmannians was as little suited as that of their teacher. Jürgen Moltmann (with the concluding chapter of his *Theology of Hope*, 1964) and the new political theologies, and Käsemann to some extent, offered much richer sources of inspiration for this purpose.

In addition, the theology of Pannenberg — outside Germany more than in Germany — attracted attention. He again picked up Troeltsch's way of posing the issue: the gospel must not be positioned as far from history as possible but be understood altogether as historical power and as answer to the quest for truth in history. It seemed the path of theological development had curved back to where it was in 1910. The alternatives were still the same. Do we now have answers to the questions of that time which are better grounded and more deeply thought through? People may differ about the answer. Whatever the judgment, it will say more about the person making it than about those who are being judged. We are still players in the field, not objective onlookers.

31. The discussion and explanation were more or less rounded off by the disputation which Fuchs and Künneth conducted on Oct. 12, 1964, before more than 2000 people in Sittensen by Hamburg. The documentation may be found in: E. Fuchs and W. Künneth, *Die Auferstehung Jesu Christi van den Toten: Dokumentation eines Streitgesprächs* (Neukirchen-Vluyn, 1973). Characteristic for Fuchs are the words of his thesis: "Whoever speaks of the resurrection must hold to the unity of life and death in love" and "the unity of life and death in love has appeared to the world in the love of Jesus and is experienced and expected by faith in Jesus as the rule of God" (p. 13). Here 1 Cor. 15 is read in the light of 1 Cor. 13!

CHAPTER XIII

The Split in the Herrmann School, II:
Karl Barth

THE FAITHFUL PUPIL

Immediately following his preliminary studies at Bern, the twenty-year-old Karl Barth wanted to pursue his studies at Marburg. But his father, not eager to see him attend that bastion of liberalism, proposed that he go to Halle or Griefswald. In the end they settled for Berlin as supposedly more neutral. There Barth purchased Wilhelm Herrmann's *Ethik* for himself. Later he wrote: "The day twenty years ago when I first read his *Ethik* (Ethics) I remember as if it were today. . . . I can say that on that day I believe my own deep personal interest in theology began."[1] Under pressure from his father he also spent time in Tübingen (1907/1908), but in the end Fritz Barth allowed his son to go to Marburg after all (1908). "I came to Marburg as a convinced 'Marburger.'"[2] "I soaked Herrmann in through all my pores."[3]

In Marburg he soon became the editorial assistant for the journal *Die Christliche Welt* and as such an assistant of Martin Rade and even a friend staying at his home. After his second examination (1908) he quite

1. K. Barth, "The Principles of Dogmatics According to Wilhelm Herrmann," in *Theology and Church,* tr. Louise Pettibone Smith (New York: Harper & Row, 1962), p. 238.

2. Ibid.

3. Eberhard Busch, *Karl Barth,* tr. John Bowden (Philadelphia: Fortress, 1976), p. 45. For Barth's relationship as a student to Herrmann see K. Barth, "The Principles of Dogmatics According to Wilhelm Herrmann," in *Theology and Church,* pp. 238-71; and Busch, *Karl Barth,* pp. 44ff.

definitely did not yet wish to go into parish work. The reason for his reluctance may be found in the article which he published under the title "Moderne Theologie und Reichsgottesarbeit." In it he refers to a familiar circumstance: "It is incomparably more difficult to move from the lecture halls of Marburg or Heidelberg to the work of a pastor on the pulpit, at the sickbed, or the meeting room, than from those of Halle and Greifswald." Modern theology trains its adepts in two basic positions: religious individualism and historical relativism. For an authentic pupil of Herrmann or Harnack the "flight into pastoral work" was not an option. One had to find his own narrow path between "the Scylla of clericalism" and "the Charybdis of agnosticism." "We also apply historical relativism to our own theology and, when we compare ourselves with others, consider it as one form alongside others in which the gospel comes to manifestation." That is our weakness and at the same time our strength. "For us religion is experience understood in rigorously individual terms, and we feel it to be our duty to deal clearly and positively with the general human cultural awareness in terms of its scientific side." That sounds like correct Marburg liberalism. The only thing that may elicit faint surprise is the reference to "historical relativism." Had it not, then, been disarmed in Marburg by "religious individualism"? Apparently that had not been Barth's experience. Although he had decided in favor of Herrmann, Troeltsch's alternative had also more or less become a conviction he owned or a temptation which troubled him. Later too, more than Herrmann, he struggled with the issue of historical relativism.[4]

　　　This short article Barth wrote while still a student set off a reaction which today seems rather strange. Two professors in practical the-

---

4. Cf. K. Barth, "Moderne Theologie und Reichsgottesarbeit," *Zeitschrift für Theologie und Kirche* 19 (1909) 317-21. The quotations occur on pp. 320-21. Barth's later comment on his relationship as a student to the alternative theology of Troeltsch cannot possibly convey the whole truth: "At that time the name of Troeltsch stood in the centre of our discussions; it denoted the point beyond which I felt that I had to refuse to follow the dominant theology of the time" (Busch, *Karl Barth*, p. 50). In his second semester at Marburg Barth copied out "all Troeltsch's lectures on the philosophy of religion from the summer of 1908" (p. 50). And when in Safenwil his preoccupation with the social question perceptibly pushed back his interest in theology, this interest as such "continued to be nourished by eager reading of the *Christliche Welt, Zeitschrift für Theologie und Kirche*, the works of Troeltsch, etc." (p. 69). See also W. Groll, *Ernst Troeltsch und Karl Barth — Kontinuität im Widerspruch* (Munich: Kaiser, 1976), which unfortunately does not deal with the problem of the relationship between revelation and history *(Geschichte)*.

ology, both of them belonging to the Marburg school, felt personally affected by the article and responded accordingly in the same year: E. Chr. Achelis (Marburg) more mildly, to be sure, than P. Drews (Halle). Like Herrmann and against Barth, they both rejected historical relativism as a mark of liberalism and emphasized the object-relatedness of the religion of the individual. In his response Barth repeated and defended his formulations and intent. He was slightly astonished at the excitement and concluded by saying "that a genuinely vital theology not only tolerates but demands that its problems be examined and stated openly." The discussion ends with a concluding editorial comment by Martin Rade in which he defends the inclusion of the article as a human document "which permits us, with admirable straightforwardness, to look into the heart of a wide-awake theologian who is at the point of concluding his studies and entering upon the work of the church."[5]

Barth wrote his reply from Geneva, where on September 26, 1909, he had delivered his inaugural sermon on Philippians 3:12-15. In the sermon he stated emphatically: "Our beginning as well as our goal is Christ." His biographer Eberhard Busch refers to this text as a motto which "set out the intentions with which he was entering his ministry." This motto is actually significant for Barth's entire life — for the later Barth but also for the pupil of Herrmann that he was at the time. It points to a continuity. But at the time it was totally intended in the sense of Herrmann. "And on the day I began my ministry, five minutes before I was to go up into the pulpit, the post brought me the new, fourth edition of Herrmann's *Ethics,* which the author had sent me. I accepted this coincidence as a dedication of my whole future."[6]

Barth's first real theological study to be published was an extended paper for Swiss pastors on the theme "Christian Faith and History." It was read in 1910 and printed two years later. It began with a lapidary opening sentence: "I view the problem which will occupy us here as *the* problem of contemporary Protestant theology." One reads it with expectancy but is disappointed. What is striking in this article is that nothing in it is striking. From beginning to end it offers Herrmannian theology that is true to all its main lines. All the principal dogmas of the Marburg school are bunched together here: the inwardness

---

5. In a letter to Helmut Thielicke dated Nov. 7, 1967, Barth, looking back upon his article, said: "In those essays I simply wanted to state that these were the presuppositions on which *tant bien que mal* I would have to preach and teach" (*Letters 1961-1968,* ed. Jürgen Fangmeier and Hinrich Stoevesandt, tr. and ed. Geoffrey W. Bromiley [Grand Rapids: Eerdmans, 1981], p. 277).

6. Busch, *Karl Barth,* p. 52.

and individualism of true religion, the distinction between faith and the idea of faith, the contrasting ideas of *assensus* and *fiducia*, criticism of Protestant orthodoxy, the practice of seeing Luther and Schleiermacher together in the same perspective. The only new feature is the appeal to Calvin, who here appears explicitly alongside Luther as a herald of true religion. Obviously, during his period as assistant pastor in Geneva (in which he wrote the paper), Barth thoroughly studied the "genius of the place" *(genius loci)*.[7]

Barth's third theological publication, "Der Glaube an den persönlischen Gott," also a paper given before Swiss pastors and published in 1914, is a brilliant and original study which clearly shows that the author was not merely a fellow traveler of the Marburg school but an independently thinking member of it. In addition he proved himself to be intimately familiar with German theology after Schleiermacher. Though Herrmann is not mentioned, the method is totally that of the master. Barth inferred the necessity of attributing personality to God from religious experience. But also the suprapersonal conception of the Absolute or the Sublime is grounded in the same experience. "The religious formula which fits the issue can only be: *uphold* both conceptions but *do not attempt* to combine them in one formula."[8]

The fourth theological article Barth published is "The Righteousness of God," an essay from 1916, which he included as the first in a series compiled in *The Word of God and the Word of Man* in 1924, because he viewed it as being fundamentally one with the following essays. Here we expect at least the announcement of a breakthrough to new insights.

---

7. K. Barth, "Der christliche Glaube und die Geschichte," *Schweizerische Theologische Zeitschrift* (1912) 1-18, 49-72.

8. K. Barth, "Der Glaube an den persönlichen Gott," *Zeitschrift für Theologie und Kirche* 24 (1914) 21-32 and 65-95; the quotation occurs on pp. 94-95. [Cf. also Busch, *Karl Barth*, p. 72.—Trans.] F. W. Marquardt, *Theologie und Socialismus: Das Beispiel Karl Barths* (Munich: Kaiser, 1972), p. 236, refers (pp. 232-34) to the accentuation of the Kingdom of God in Barth's article (pp. 92-94), which ended with the remarkable conclusion: "The idea of personality is no longer adequate to capture this content in words; involuntarily it drives religious thought beyond that notion to new 'material' [*sachlichen*] definitions" (p. 93). That may signify a first step outside the boundaries set by Herrmann. It serves the purpose of according the idea of absoluteness a place on a level with that of personality. Marquardt concludes from this that "the 'absoluteness' of God is an expression of the highest earthly experience and affirmation; or to put it differently: it realizes itself—in a personally radical and social total sense—in societal praxis" (*Theologie und Socialismus*, p. 235). This conclusion cannot be justified from Barth's wording, however, and in my opinion goes beyond the intent of Barth's own thinking here.

But at the outset this does not at all seem to be the case. A voice calls: "Prepare ye the way of the Lord!" "This is the voice of our conscience, telling us of the righteousness of God." "We must let conscience speak." However, we also perceive there is "another kind of will . . . , a will which knows no dominant and inflexible order but is grounded upon caprice, vagary, and self-seeking . . . ; many times the fearful apprehension seizes us that unrighteousness may triumph in the end." But then we hear the assurance of conscience: no, that is not true! People like Moses, Jeremiah, and John the Baptist "uncovered to men their deepest need; they made articulate their conscience within them; they wakened and kept awake the longing within them for the righteousness of God. They prepared the way of the Lord." Unfortunately, "we do not let conscience speak to the end" because of our pride and our despondency which express themselves in our society, our morality, our state, and our religion. "Conscience within us continues to call. Our deepest longing remains unstilled." It is senseless to ask whether God is righteous, "for the living God never for a moment manifests himself in our conscience except as a righteous God." He asks us "if we want to acknowledge him and accept him as he is." We should, however, direct our accusing question to the God of our morality, our state, our culture. "This god is really an unrighteous God and it is high time for us to declare ourselves thorough-going doubters, sceptics, scoffers and atheists in regard to him." "He is an idol. He is dead." If we then become quiet, "if we let conscience speak to the very end," we shall discover, in a fierce inner conflict, the saving righteousness of God, God's will "as a Wholly Other will" which strives to make us new, "embryonically but truly." That is the way of faith in the love of God as it has appeared in Christ as the Son of God. Following him we learn "that the Father's will is truth and must be done."[9]

If we now recall the main ideas of Herrmann's *Ethik* we can easily discern that this essay of Barth still moves within its framework. What distinguishes the pupil from his teacher here (though it does not separate them) is twofold. First, there is the extension of the indictment of conscience to the trans-individual areas of political and social life. Barth refers especially to "capitalism, prostitution, real estate speculation, alcoholism, tax evasion, and militarism." Herrmann hardly looked in that direction.[10] And Barth's negative illumination of "religion" as a

9. K. Barth, "The Righteousness of God," in *The Word of God and the Word of Man,* tr. Douglas Horton (New York: Harper & Row, repr. 1957), pp. 9-27; the quotations occur on pp. 9, 10, 11, 12, 21, 23, 26.

10. In the light of the passages adduced I consider mistaken the attempt

means whereby people shield themselves from the righteousness of God at least contradicts Herrmann's use of the word *religion*. We are now hearing in Barth the new sounds of social prophecy as he learned it from Leonhard Ragaz and even more from Hermann Kutter and finally in still a different way from Christoph Blumhardt.

There is even more tension between Barth and the Marburg tradition at the second point: the question of the accusing human being who impugns the righteousness of God is rejected and countered with the question of God concerning the righteousness of man. As in Herrmann, God is still the fulfiller of human longing as it comes to expression in conscience. At the same time, however, and to a greater extent, God is in opposition to man and his idolatrous religion. The liberal harmony of God with the bourgeois moral values of European man is at the point of collapsing. Herrmann, however, might have anticipated these two shifts of emphasis as befitting the later situation and as representative of his own theology. (Might! Even after he discovered that Barth regarded his nationalism as idolatrous religion?!)

Accordingly, Barth's process of moving away from Herrmann's theology must have been more gradual than is often assumed on the basis of certain things Barth said. In his "Afterword" to a Schleiermacher anthology he refers to the shock produced at the outbreak of the war by "the terrible manifesto of the 93 German intellectuals who identified themselves before all the world with the war policy of Kaiser Wilhelm II and Chancellor Bethmann-Hollweg." Harnack and Herrmann were also among the signatories. "Thus a whole world of exegesis, ethics, dogmatics, and preaching, which I had hitherto held to be essentially trustworthy, was shaken to the foundations, and with it, all the other writings of the German theologians." Soon after this he addressed a sharp inquiry to Herrmann.[11] Still, immediately after the publication of the manifesto,

---

of F. W. Kantzenbach (*Programme der Theologie* [Munich: Kaiser, 1978], pp. 129-33) to attribute to Herrmann a theological-political intention and convergence with the socialist Barth. Concerning the privatization and individualization of social problems in Herrmann and his Ritschlian contemporaries, cf. G. Rupp, *Culture-Protestantism: German Liberal Theology at the Turn of the Twentieth Century* (Missoula, MT: Scholars Press, 1977), pp. 43-51.

11. According to Barth's letter to Thurneysen dated Nov. 5, 1914, the letter to Herrmann contained three inquiries: "(1) about the scholarliness of the German 'bearers of culture'; (2) about war-'experience' as religious argument; (3) about the 'communion of saints' and German self-righteousness as a threat to it" (*Briefwechsel Karl Barth—Eduard Thurneysen*, 2 vols. [Zurich: Theologischer Verlag, 1973-1974], 1:19).

he expressed himself to his friend Thurneysen in a much gentler fashion: "The spiritual situation of our German friends is now more comprehensible to me, even if it is not more congenial . . . . It is truly sad! Marburg and German civilization have lost something in my eyes by this breakdown, and indeed forever."[12] Doubts about Marburg must already have started around 1910, however. When Barth had to teach and preach, the whole theological enterprise seemed somehow alien to him; this was also one of the reasons why his plan to study for a doctorate under Herrmann "never came to anything."[13] Nevertheless, the basic structures of Herrmann's theology were still visible in Barth's thinking in 1916.

THE DETOUR OF THE FIRST EDITION OF *RÖMERBRIEF*

In the same period in which Barth delivered his lecture on "The Righteousness of God," a crucial shift took place in him and in his friend Thurneysen. At the outbreak of the war their experiences with liberal theology as well as Social Democracy (which proved unable to muster international resistance to the war) were very disillusioning to them. They were now looking for a new foothold, being driven to this especially by the predicament of having to preach every week. More decisively than before Barth now devoted his theological interest to interpreting the Bible. He studied the letter to the Romans and, after July, 1916, wrote down in personal notes what he discovered there. This process took two years to complete. With financial help from his friend Pestalozzi he was able to have the book published.[14]

If this commentary had appeared anonymously then or later an "expert" would hardly have credited the book to the pastor of Safenwil. It is the expression of a thought world which was neither prepared for by Barth's development in the years between 1910 and 1916 nor does it

---

12. Letter dated Sept. 4, 1914, in *Briefwechsel*, 1:9-10. [The translation here is from *Revolutionary Theology in the Making: Barth-Thurneysen Correspondence, 1914-1925*, tr. and ed. James D. Smart (Richmond, VA: John Knox, 1964), p. 26.—TRANS.]

13. Busch, *Karl Barth*, p. 58.

14. Ibid., esp. pp. 92-109. The book appeared as follows: Karl Barth, Pfarrer in Safenwil, *Der Römerbrief* (Bern, 1919). An unchanged photomechanical reprint, with a preface by the author, appeared in 1963, published by the EVZ-Verlag in Zurich. [We will refer to this 1st ed., which was not translated into English, as *Römerbrief*; but we will refer to the 2nd ed. as *Romans*, citing from *The Epistle to the Romans*, tr. Edwyn C. Hoskyns (Oxford/New York: Oxford University Press, repr. 1980).—TRANS.]

itself prepare for Barth's development after 1919. Experts would attribute the book to an original, be it a somewhat confused, mind, belonging probably to the "positive" circles of the mediating theologies and influenced on the one hand by Württemberg "Pietism" and on the other by modern evolutionary vitalist philosophy. Just to cite one of many characteristic examples, we shall reproduce a passage from the beginning of Chapter 8 (8:1-11):

> It is certainly not the doctrines of faith and the ideals of life of a new *religion,* but the conditions and foundations of a new *world* under which we as Christians have been placed. For us it can no longer by any means be a matter of *seeking out* (or even first to create) a distant, alien, unknown divine principle but it is a matter of *taking* and *growing* out of the fulness of life that is present. . . . But in Christ the divine that must be manifest in our existence is here: nature, gift, growth. Not a new idea about God, but a whole new divine world, atmosphere, and possibility of being appeared on earth in Christ. . . . But if Christ be "in you" through the "Spirit of life" in whom you share as his, then the redeeming power of God is in you. Proceeding organically, that power changes into freedoms and victories the bonds to which you may now, with the disappearing remains of your merely personal God-alienated existence in the flesh, be still subject . . . , and [the vital powers of the Spirit] will not rest until nothing mortal will be left in you, until your total existence-unto-death be changed in an organism of life. For as sin has devastated not only the soul but nature, so also the end of God's ways is newly created corporeality.

Just how are these pronouncements to be squared with his preceding development? We must not forget that the new orientation Barth longed for concentrated itself in "the radical and deadly serious problem of faith: 'With God or—as so far—without him.'" "For Barth, the question of according God a place of central importance was becoming more and more fundamental. And since he had met Blumhardt, it was very closely connected with the eschatological question of the Christian hope."[15] In this world which is hostile to God, how is the kingdom of God at work and—as Barth presumably believed at the time—visibly and demonstrably at work? In the grip of this question Barth had read Romans with the excitement of a discoverer. For him it became primarily the great witness to the absolute priority of God, visible in the work of

15. Busch, *Karl Barth,* pp. 89, 87.

Christ and the working of the Spirit, the Spirit who in an organic process, on the basis of Christ, transformed creation into the glory of Christ. This working of the Spirit is the inner side—perceptible to the eye of faith—of our secular exterior side. Ontology, objectivity, realism, and universalism—these are the categories which here determine Barth's exposition of Paul.[16] Paul helped him to proclaim the superior power of God in an alienated world and even to make it visible for those to whom this is given.

This discovery at once distanced him by a vast remove from the path of liberalism he had been on till now. It seemed Barth had joined the side of orthodoxy. What he put forth, however, was far removed from the Reformation tradition. He still had no real appreciation for the classic teaching of justification. For him justification meant the disclosure of the true world of God, a disclosure which transforms us—as one can read, for example, in his explanation of Romans 3:21ff. That had nothing to do with Luther and a great deal to do with Osiander. The influence of Christoph Blumhardt, by comparison, is palpable. The interpretation of Romans by the Württemberg scholar Johann Tobias Beck also greatly inspired Barth.[17] His father had been a pupil and admirer of Beck; in this manner the son now also arrived at a new appreciation for his father.

Barth himself later said: "My interpretation was more strongly influenced than I had noticed by Bengel, Oetinger, Beck and even by Schelling (passed on through Kutter). Subsequently this did not prove adequate for what had to be said."[18] Under the influence and particularly the weight of Pauline thought, the two worlds in which he moved

---

16. A good characterization of this 1st edition of *Römerbrief*, in distinction from the 2nd, occurs in N. T. Bakker, *In der Krisis der Offenbarung: Karl Barths Hermeneutik dargestellt an seiner Römerbrief-Auslegung* (Neukirchen-Vluyn: Neukirchener, 1974), pp. 44-72.

17. On the relationship between the influences of these two authorities on Barth opinions diverge. T. Stadtland, *Eschatologie und Geschichte in der Theologie des jungen Karl Barth* (Neukirchen-Vluyn: Neukirchener, 1966), writes: "We consider Beck's influence on R I [the 1st ed. of *Römerbrief*] to be decidedly stronger than that of the Blumhardts" (p. 46; cf. pp. 41-51). E. Busch, *Karl Barth und die Pietisten* (Munich, 1978), believes, however: "What he found in Beck was in fact akin to what he found in the Blumhardts—and he focused (exclusively) on the related material" (p. 43; cf. pp. 39-44). More in a systematic than a biographical vein, E. Jüngel (*Karl Barth: A Theological Legacy,* tr. Garrett E. Paul [Philadelphia: Westminster, 1986], pp. 54-70) regards Overbeck and the Blumhardts as the two polar forces which in this period powered Barth's theology as "impossible possibility."

18. Busch, *Karl Barth,* p. 99.

at the time—the liberal in theology and the socialist in politics—now seem to be far removed from each other. True, in his stirring exegesis of Romans 13 one reads suddenly: "[Your participation in the shaping of politics] can, depending on the circumstances, be very far-reaching and you will hardly be able to position yourselves anywhere but on the extreme Left." But he immediately added: "But in matters of detail, in this context, one must consult Ethics. . . . And your work as a *Christian* in any case does *not* consist in such participation. . . . The divine may not be politicized and the human may not be theologized, not even in favor of democracy and social democracy." It is significant that the commentary starts this line of thought at 12:16c and places it under the heading of *Überlegenheit* ("Superiority"). In keeping with the main theme of the entire commentary the controlling thought is: "In view here is the great work of building a new world which, though it can express itself in storms and catastrophes, must be realized inwardly and essentially through a peaceful process by which all people (in Christ!) jointly accustom themselves to the divine atmosphere and jointly begin to feel at home in the divine orders, and which may not be drawn into the external world by individual anarchistic outbreaks and disturbed."[19]

Barth's other world, the world of Marburg theology, was now very far away. But that is not saying it strongly enough. Without explicitly referring to it, he is constantly combating it. Over against its bloodless idealism Barth posited his realism; over against its individualism, he offered his organic way of thinking. He now firmly rejects its central concept of "personality." All this creates the impression as though, after a gradual process of preparation, he had now decisively turned his back on Herrmann.[20] Herrmann himself had already sensed this change ear-

19. Barth, *Römerbrief*, 1st ed., pp. 381, 380; cf. pp. 390, 388. Marquardt made an interesting attempt to prove that with his view of the state Barth consciously put himself in a dialectical position vis-à-vis Lenin's *Staat und Revolution* (1918) (*Theologie und Socialismus*, pp. 126-41). Despite an occasional allusion in Barth ("Christianity does not compete with the state; it ignores the state: its basis and its being. It is *more* than Leninism!" p. 379), Marquardt, in my opinion, has not succeeded in making his thesis stick. For that reason his conclusion—"In the second edition of his *Romans* a sensational antirevolutionary shift occurs" (p. 142)—is untenable. On this statement by Barth and the meaning of his phrase "the revolution of God," cf. E. Jüngel, *Barth-Studien* (Zurich: Benziger, Gütersloh: Gerd Mohn, 1982), pp. 114-26.

20. On Oct. 9, 1917, in Safenwil, in a brilliantly simple address to young teachers, Barth firmly repudiated Herrmann's concept of religion (determined as it was by privatization and inwardness) in the name of a broadly conceived concept of life. The Bible and life constitute an alliance against a bloodless ideal-

lier. In 1918 he once again sent his pupil a book of his with the inscription: "Nevertheless, with best regards from W. Herrmann." Two other Marburg men, the New Testament scholars Adolf Jülicher and Rudolf Bultmann, decisively rejected the commentary on Paul on scholarly grounds.[21]

Only a few years later, after the appearance of the second edition of *Romans* at the latest (1922), the interested *Umwelt* was able to perceive that Barth's sensational shift had been only a brief interim. When soon afterward a second edition was due, in 1920, Barth decided to rewrite the commentary from beginning to end, moving now "independently of old Württemberg theology and other kinds of speculative theology. Only now did my opposition to Schleiermacher become clear and quite open."[22] The material he had consulted was apparently not suited after all to giving adequate expression to what he had in mind. In Barth's work as a whole the first edition of *Römerbrief* remained an oddity.

GROPING AND ADVANCING

It was not the case, however, that now, after the interlude of the first edition of *Römerbrief*, a time of clarity followed. On the contrary, in the years 1919-1922 we encounter a theological and terminological searching and groping of a kind that makes it difficult even for today's interpreters to recognize the crimson thread that runs through it all.

On September 25, 1919, at the Conference on Religion and Social Relations held at Tambach (Thüringen)—substituting for Ragaz, who had been first choice as speaker—Barth gave a lecture on "The Christian's Place in Society," which at a single stroke made Barth both famous and notorious in Germany.[23] Upon reading it, one marvels that so shortly after the publication of his *Römerbrief* he should be moving

---

istic religion. Cf. "Religion und Leben," in *Evangelische Theologie* 11 (1951/52) 437-51 (in a commemorative issue for Günther Dehn).

21. Adolf Jülicher, "A modern interpreter of Paul," in *The Beginnings of Dialectic Theology*, ed. James M. Robinson (Richmond, VA: John Knox, 1968), pp. 72-81. Jülicher spoke of the "arbitrary adaptation of the Pauline Christ-myth." Coming out in favor of the book was the young Emil Brunner, who had been struck precisely by the anti-idealistic realism of the book (*Beginnings*, pp. 63-71).

22. Busch, *Karl Barth*, p. 114.

23. "The Christian's Place in Society" in English translation occurs in *The Word of God and the Word of Man*, pp. 272-327.

on such a different track. Not that he disavowed his book; there are passages in the lecture which breathe the same spirit.[24] Still, the key words are now different. Instead of "organism" and "growth," we now hear of "negation" and "position," of "affirmation and denial," of "analogy" and "parable," of "origin" and especially of the three-step "thesis-antithesis-synthesis." We shall single out a few characteristic sentences:

> The kingdom of God does not begin with our movements of protest. It is the revolution which is before all revolutions, as it is before the whole prevailing order of things. The great negative precedes the small one, as it precedes the small positive. The original is the synthesis. It is out of this that both thesis and antithesis arise. Insight into the true transcendence of the divine origin of all things permits, or rather commands, us to understand particular social orders as being caused by God, by their connection with God. Naturally, we shall be led first not to a denial but to an *affirmation* of the world as it is. . . . Only out of such an affirmation can come that genuine, radical denial which is manifestly the meaning of our movements of protest. The genuine antithesis must follow the thesis: it is through the thesis that it derives from the synthesis. (p. 299)

There is therefore a "general original knowledge of life's meaning and aim" (p. 302). Barth even cites Romans 1:19! There is a "penetrating through the object to its creative origin" (p. 305), because one "can recognize in the worldly the analogy of the heavenly and take pleasure in it" (p. 305). In this sense we must understand Jesus' use of parables. "Only from the standpoint of an antithesis which has its roots in the synthesis can one accept the thesis so calmly, as Jesus did" (p. 305). Structural grounds "will not allow us to overlook the truth that the antithesis is more than mere reaction to the thesis; it issues from the synthesis in its own original strength; it apprehends the thesis and puts an end to it and in every conceivable moment surpasses it in worth and meaning" (p. 311). Precisely "at the point where society becomes a mirror of the original thoughts of God, it becomes a mirror of our need and our hope. So the kingdom of God advances to its attack upon society" (p. 314). "We may deny ourselves the universal No no less than the universal Yes, for both are one; or rather *rebus sic stantibus*, we may deny ourselves the No even less than the Yes, for it follows after it" (pp. 316-17). "No relegating of our hopes to a Beyond can give us rest, for it is the Beyond itself stand-

24. For example, see ibid., pp. 296ff.

ing outside and knocking on the closed doors of the here-and-now that is the chief cause of our unrest" (p. 317). Finally, even the negation is again negated: "While it is God who gives us that rest and this greater unrest, it is clear that neither our rest nor our unrest in the world, necessary though both of them are, can be final" (p. 320). "For creation and redemption are possible only because God is *God*, because *his* immanence means at the same time his *transcendence*" (p. 322). "It is only in *God* that the synthesis can be found; but in God it *can* be found—the synthesis which is *meant* in the thesis and *sought* in the antithesis" (p. 322). Barth's exposition ends in the defense of a political middle course, with reference to Eccl. 4:16–5:3. "As a result, short circuits to the right and to the left will gradually become fewer" (p. 325).

Politically, the continuity with the first edition of *Römerbrief* is plain. The divine synthesis referred to here is another name for "Superiority" there. Behind this change in name, could there be theological continuity? The stress on antithesis indicates that there is a shift in emphasis: our reality is no longer, harmoniously and unproblematically, a cloak for divine life and operation. We did in fact hear Barth speak of "an absence in the earthly" of the divine Beyond. However, as the context shows, that must be understood dialectically, not absolutely. The Beyond is at the same time the sustaining ground and promise of the earthly that is estranged from it. Barth is here thinking of the relationship between God and the world, neither in harmonious, nor in antithetical, but in dialectical terms.

One senses how Barth was groping for philosophical concepts that could help him to give more exact expression to what he had more or less clearly in mind. Where did he get these notions and how does he apply them? In the spring Barth's brother Heinrich, the philosopher, educated in the Marburg Neo-Kantianism of Cohen and Natorp, had given a lecture at the Aarau Student Conference on "Gotteserkenntnis,"[25] which made a strong impression on Karl (as on Brunner and others), and caused him to see that "the 'wholly otherness of the kingdom of God' needed to be stressed over against all human conditions and movements."[26] It was Heinrich Barth's intent to liberate religion from the embrace of natural science or metaphysics for a relationship to the whole of life. Along with the transcendental idealism of Mar-

25. Printed in *Anfänge*, 1:221-55. All the quotations occur in section V, pp. 246-50.
26. Busch, *Karl Barth*, p. 109. Some reservations with regard to his brother's lecture come out in Barth's letter to Thurneysen dated Sept. 11, 1919, in *Briefwechsel*, 1:344.

burg he was seeking an Archimedean vantage point in the "epistemological principle of critical negation." Only in the formal autonomy of cognitive reason, beyond all content, the mind *(Geist)* becomes itself as the origin and source of knowledge, as "the transcendence of origin." Here we have the Platonic idea, which is the source of the creative powers of life. As presupposition and origin, the idea had to be divine. We human beings live in constant forgetfulness of this origin. Philosophy serves to remind us of that fact. We must return to our origin. "The soul belongs to God; not only its 'ought' but also its 'being' is infinite and eternal because it is original." "The being of the soul is indestructible and the faithfulness of God perseveres." "The being of man is being in God; in the coming of the Son of man, the Christ, the world became conscious of it." The self lies back behind all that we call occurrence. Its occurrence takes place in God; that is our salvation. "And its movement is manifest in the person who places himself in the light of the knowledge of God; that is the authentication of its faithfulness and creative power."

There is no doubt that Barth owed the use of the word *origin* in his Tambach lecture and shortly afterward in the second edition of his *Romans* to this lecture of his brother, who had in turn taken it over from his teacher Hermann Cohen. For us that raises the question what influence that other, the philosophical, Marburg (which for that matter had fundamentally a lot in common with Herrmann) could have had on the shape of Barth's theology in this decisive epoch.

It would be a mistake for us, for the sake of a historical answer, to turn to Hermann Cohen's main theological work *Religion of Reason out of the Sources of Judaism,* for it appeared only after Cohen's death in 1919.[27] Heinrich Barth proceeded in his thinking on the basis of the theory of cognition. And in fact in Cohen's *Logik der reinen Erkenntnis* (1902), the concept of "origin" plays a central role. Cohen criticizes Kant's postulate of an independent "thing-in-itself" which stands opposed to thought, and wants to return to Parmenides' identification of thought and being. "Only thought itself can give rise to what may be counted as being. And in the event that thought cannot dig up the final ground of being within itself, no means of perception can fill the gap." "For thought only *that* may be counted as given *which* it is able to discover by itself." "Thought is thought concerning origins." "To the origin nothing can be given. The principle here is laying the ground in the strictest sense. The ground must become origin. Otherwise, if thought

27. H. Cohen, *Religion of Reason out of the Sources of Judaism,* tr. Simon Kaplan (New York: Frederick Ungar, 1972).

has to discover being-in-origin, being can have no other ground than that which thought can lay. Only as thought concerning origin does pure thought become truthful."[28]

It is precisely this concept of origin which Heinrich Barth advances. But in order to make it useful for the knowledge of God he was forced, in an unclear way, to combine it with the then highly valued concept of "life," and that via the rhetorical question: "Where is life lived in the most fruitful, richest, and most original way?" From there he arrives at the Platonic idea of the Good as the ethical concept of primal origin, which is the source of creative powers. This idea, as the presupposition of all our action, is identical with the idea of a perfect creation (from which we have become estranged). In Heinrich Barth's lecture Cohen soon had to give way to Plato. The idea of origin became the idea of participation, and the latter in turn came close to crossing the border into pantheism.[29]

Karl Barth thus adopted the concept of "origin" from his brother; but in his thinking Cohen's epistemological access to it is completely concealed. He employed the word, as Heinrich Barth also did later, as synonymous with "creation." But in order not to lapse into an uncritical affirmation of existing reality or even pantheism (he nods in agreement toward Hegel's statement concerning the rationality of all that exists! p. 51) he had to make a further loan from Hegel and introduce the three-step theory of thesis-antithesis-synthesis. The concept of "origin," already unclear in Heinrich Barth, has now lost its semantic "carrying capacity" in Karl Barth.

Seven months later, as his brother had done the year before, Barth delivered a lecture to the Aarau Student Conference. The title of his paper was: "Biblical Questions, Insights, and Vistas."[30] One expects strong parallels, including terminological parallels, with the Tambach speech. The word *origin* occurs four times; the sequence thesis-antithesis-synthesis does not occur at all. The concepts "negation" and "affirmation," "No" and "Yes," now return as "death" and "life," "cross" and "resurrection." The second half of the paper is a revised Easter sermon. The philosophical terminology in which he cloaked his Tambach speech is now almost totally lacking; Barth used it to bring biblical insights up for discussion. But he soon demonstrated that he no longer needed it.

28. H. Cohen, *Logik der reinen Erkenntnis,* published as vol. 6 of the *Werke* (New York: Hildesheim, 1977). On the concept of origin(s) see esp. pp. 31-38, 79-93. The quotations are on pp. 81, 82, 36.

29. See H. Barth, *Anfänge,* 1:238-39, 244-47.

30. Printed in Karl Barth, *The Word of God and the Word of Man,* pp. 51-96.

More surprising—after the first edition of *Römerbrief* and the Tambach speech—is the concluding statement:

> One thing more remains to be said: resurrection is the *one experience of man*. . . . In God, however, the individual with his highly personal life discovers not only his duty but his right. . . . It is not the cosmos, not history in general, not even so-called humanity, organized or unorganized, not even the articulate or inarticulate masses of nations, classes, or parties; but it is always *the single man,* the suffering, working, and knowing subject of society . . . —it is the *God-fearing individual* who is the first to be touched.[31]

One wonders: after a brief crusade against individualism have we now landed back at Herrmann again? Or was the discontinuity between "before" and "after" less sharp than it seemed?[32] Or are we witnessing simply a passionate searching in different directions?

Let us stay for a moment with the problem of philosophical terminology. The index of the second edition of *Romans* does not refer to Cohen, and only rarely to Kant and Plato. But the names Dostoyevsky, Kierkegaard, Luther, and Nietzsche are prominent. Blumhardt is mentioned four times, Herrmann not at all. Of the philosophical apparatus from Tambach only the concepts "origin" and "analogy" (the latter significantly only under the biblical name "parable") are still left. "(Primal) origin" occurs in eight passages; of these, five, in relatively unaccentuated fashion, are synonymous with "creation" and three (to which we must return in a moment) are used in a more philosophical sense. More important, however, is the explanation Barth himself offers in the preface to the second edition (p. 10); I shall cite it in context:

> If I have a system, it is limited to a recognition of what Kierkegaard called the "infinite qualitative distinction" between time and eternity, and to my regarding this as possessing negative as well as positive significance: "God is in heaven, and thou art on earth." The relation between such a God and such a man, and the relation between such a man and such a God, is for me the

31. Ibid., pp. 94-95.
32. A subtle analysis of the notion of experience in the young Barth, with the emphasis on material continuity, occurs in H. J. Adriaanse, *Zu den Sachen selbst: Versuch einer Konfrontation der Theologie Karl Barths mit der phänomenologischen Philosophie Edmund Husserls* (The Hague: Mouton, 1974), esp. pp. 23-27. He comments: "The individualism of the second period [i.e., of the 2nd ed. of *Romans*] was stamped by Kierkegaard" (p. 211 n. 190).

theme of the Bible and the essence of philosophy. Philosophers name this KRISIS of human perception—the Prime Cause: the Bible beholds at the same cross-roads—the figure of Jesus Christ.

In my opinion these sentences are exceedingly weighty. The first sees an identity between the theme of theology and the primary concern of philosophy. The second statement, as proof for the first, refers to Cohen's critical concept of "origin."[33] And the third, also intended as support for the first, identifies this idea of origins with the message of the "cross-roads of Jesus Christ"; both speak of a "crisis" of the human. True, nowhere in his book does Barth equate origin and crisis and cross. He comes closest to it when, commenting on Romans 3:6, he explains:

> What are we then to make of the fact that the whole concrete world is ambiguous and under KRISIS? There is no object apart from our thinking of it; nor has an object any clear characteristics save when we are able to recognize them by some quick-moving previous knowledge. Therefore if God be an object in the world, we can make no statement about Him—for example, that He is capricious and tyrannical—which does not proceed from some previous superior knowledge. If, therefore, God were, as the objection in iii. 5 implies, an object among other objects, if He were Himself subject to the KRISIS, He would then obviously not be God, and the true God would have to be sought in the Origin of the KRISIS. And this is clearly the case: the objection in iii. 5 refers not to God at all, but to the No-God, who is the god of this world. The true God, Himself removed from all concretion, is the Origin of the KRISIS of every concrete thing, the Judge, the negation of this world in which is included also the god of human logic. (p. 82)

In the first half of this passage we hear an echo of Cohen; the second half may be conceived as giving expression to the way of the cross of Jesus Christ. The connection, however, is unclear and abrupt. We are not told where the *tertium comparationis* between the critique of knowledge and the message of the cross might lie. In the comments on 3:21, "origin" is suddenly equated, in a Platonic sense, with the "memory of our habitation" (p. 92). And in the explanation of 9:1 the message of sal-

---

33. Barth does not mention Cohen's name; he only refers to "philosophers." He may rather have had Plato in mind since on Nov. 23, 1920, his brother Heinrich had just delivered his inaugural lecture at Basel on "Das Problem des Ursprungs in der platonischen Philosophie" (see Busch, *Karl Barth*, p. 116).

vation is interpreted as the breaking forth, "like a flash of lightning," of the Primal Origin, "as the dissolution of all relativity, and therefore as the reality of all relative realities" (p. 331), the Beyond over the earthly as its hidden truth here and now. In my opinion these words indicate more precisely than the previous ones why for Barth the concept of origin was useful: it was because it expresses a transcendence which embraces both immediate nearness and critical distance. This is how he had used it in Tambach. From that point of view we must also understand the "way of the cross of Jesus Christ."

The index lists seventeen passages under the word *parable*. This concept is also intended, but now from the human side, to embrace in one notion both nearness and distance. The parable is therefore always only a pointer, a broken one but, on account of its relation to the Origin, a true pointer.[34]

Both "origin" and "parable" serve the same dialectic: the dialectic of the relationship between God and man. Whereas in the concept "origin" we still hear a confused undertone of philosophy, in the term "parable" there is only a faint echo of the philosophical concept of analogy.

Later on, the philosophical terminology totally disappears. In subsequent years Barth devoted his energies particularly to exegesis. In the instances where he still occupies himself with philosophy there is definitely no question any more of an identity of concern. And his brother Heinrich soon went in directions in which conversation no longer seemed possible between them.[35]

If at this point we now look back upon the approximately five tumultuous years after the publication of the first edition of *Römerbrief*, we cannot help noticing how intensely Barth searched for clarity in different directions. Hardly any two of his writings from this period move within the same terminological sphere. He employed side by side ideas from biblical theology, systematic theology, and philosophy. In the

34. Cf., e.g., *Romans*, 2nd ed., pp. 79, 333-34.
35. Even later Barth did not declare war on philosophy. He viewed theology and philosophy as hostile brothers working in the same cause. Basically he dealt unsystematically and eclectically with the results of philosophy. Cf. "Schicksal und Idee in der Theologie," in *Theologische Fragen und Antworten* (Zollikon, 1957), pp. 54-92 (the paper dates from 1929); and as the ripest fruit of his reflections about the relationship between the two: "Philosophie und Theologie" in *Philosophie und Christliche Existenz*, Festschrift for Heinrich Barth (Basel: Helbing und Lichtenhahn, 1960), pp. 93-106. About the relationship between the two brothers, cf. Busch, *Karl Barth*, esp. pp. 189, 269, 413.

process philosophical concepts played a subordinate role. Looking back on this period Barth later made this significant statement: "Was I deceived about the world and about myself? Am I after all merely one of those bad theologians who are no more than servants of public opinion? And are my readers also deceived in supposing a thing to be relevant to-day which was, in fact, relevant only for Paul and for Luther and Calvin? Have they been presented with what is really no more than a rehash, resurrected out of Nietzsche and Kierkegaard and Cohen?"[36]

I doubt that it was philosophical influences which helped Barth negotiate the great switch-in-subject which, initiated in the 1916 lecture about "the Righteousness of God" and following the detour via the theology of Württemberg (the 1st edition of *Römerbrief*), provisionally found its "final" form in the second edition of *Romans*. According to Barth's own sense of the matter, he owed the sudden shift in direction from the first to the second edition of *Romans* to an "inspiration" which at first even frightened himself. In this connection he thrice pointed, with gratitude, to Overbeck![37] If one nevertheless thinks here of extratheological influences, it makes more sense to look for them in the realm of the negative, in the disillusionments he suffered, especially after the war, from the liberal theology of experience on the one hand, and from social democracy on the other. These disillusionments drove him past all the relativities of human life to God—as the origin, the judge (crisis), and the hope of all that is human. In the contemplation of the absolute God the merely human was condemned and redeemed to the status of relativity and so made bearable. In the first edition of *Römerbrief* Barth still viewed the relationship between God and the world as harmonious, organic, more or less perceptible. In the second edition of *Romans* discontinuity and imperceptibility predominate. God is no less present than before, but his presence has fundamentally become "imperceptible," "lightning-like."

How, one may ask, could Barth, within the space of four years or less, read the same Pauline letter with such different eyes? I believe we must look for the reason, not in the domain of intellect, but in the depths of his *Lebensgefühl* (sense of life). We have seen earlier that in the Ritschlian school in which Barth had been educated theologically there had taken place, under pressure from the advancing secularization of the world, a retreat to an ever smaller base (Ritschl, Herrmann, or

36. From the author's preface to the 5th edition of *Romans*, p. 22.
37. Cf. *Briefwechsel*, 1:435ff., the letters dating from Oct. 27, Nov. 4, Dec. 3 and 6, 1920, Feb. 16 and April 7, 1921. See partial translations in *Revolutionary Theology in the Making*, pp. 53-58.

Troeltsch) from which they believed they could "still" cling to the absolute. In Barth this "base" is totally gone. "History" is completely secularized and the event of the word of God is now "verticalized." God's work in the world has lost its final vestiges of perceptibility. The retreat has become a clean break. This radical step is not conceivable without the experiences and disillusionments which the war occasioned in the lives of innumerable people, including Barth. For that reason—besides all the other things it means—the second edition of *Romans* is also a document of that cultural epoch and the *Lebensgefühl* which was part of it. From this point of view it must be placed in the same series as Rudolf Otto's *The Idea of the Holy* (1917), Franz Rosenzweig's *The Star of Redemption* (1921), Oswald Spengler's *The Decline of the West* (1918), Ernst Bloch's *Spirit of Utopia* (1918), and Paul Tillich's *Kairos* (1926). A new, intensely painful experience of the godless world and, on the basis of that experience, a new quest for the God of the Bible—these two factors determined Barth's groping progression during these years.[38]

DEPARTURE FROM HERRMANN?

Earlier we stated that after a gradual process of preparation, in 1919 Barth seemed to turn his back on Herrmann. This formulation intentionally contains an element of uncertainty, which the second edition of *Romans* should have totally removed. Precisely Rudolf Bultmann, however, the man who rejected the first edition, wrote a long and enthusiastic article about the second edition.[39] In the previous chapter we learned how Bultmann discovered in this new edition many similarities between Barth and Herrmann, their common teacher. He found a similarity particularly in Barth's concept of faith and in its rigorous object-relatedness. For Bultmann, however, this relatedness remained a relatedness of the human subject; human "existence" became for him the pivotal center of theology. But he did not realize the severity of the "switch-in-subject" in Barth and he therefore underestimated his distance from Herrmann. Still, there was a reason why he now observed a convergence which he had missed earlier. Barth himself, as we shall see, brought it out a few years later.

38. Here we differ from F. W. Marquardt and H. J. Adriaanse, who to my mind explain the shift too much in terms of Cohen's philosophy of origin. For the whole problem of the influences on Barth in this period, see C. van der Kooi, "De denkweg van de jonge Karl Barth," dissertation, Free University of Amsterdam, 1985.

39. Included in *The Beginnings of Dialectic Theology*, pp. 100-120.

Moltmann, too, has called attention to the important structural parallel between the Barth of that day and Herrmann: the "defenseless non-groundability of religious experience" in Barth becomes, in theologically consistent form, the "transcendental subjectivity" of the self-revealing God, a process in which the "self" still "retains all the attributes, all the relations and distinctions in which it had been formulated by Herrmann."[40]

In 1924, in a lecture entitled "The Principles of Dogmatics according to Wilhelm Herrmann,"[41] Barth brilliantly demonstrated what separated him from and what united him with his teacher. He did not repudiate him; on the contrary: "I should now like to show in what direction we should look for the really consistent conclusions to be drawn from Herrmann's theology" (p. 253). Herrmann tried to ground his theology on "experience," on "the facts we ourselves experience," but in the section cited by Barth he continues: "But its *beginning* and its end is none the less man's humbling of himself before the unsearchable" (p. 254). Therefore, if experience lives from that which transcends experience, and if this is its beginning even, then "the unabrogable subjectivity of God" has to become the starting point of our thinking, and it "becomes obligatory to ask whether dogmatics does not have to begin where Herrmann ends" (p. 256).

Barth then, in five points, demonstrates Herrmann's ambivalence: Herrmann emphatically suggests that he can derive the reality of God from religious experience and its object. But that is impossible. "What he does pass through and experience is certainly *not* that way" (p. 262). Nevertheless, Herrmann viewed it thus, presumably because in the back of his mind he presupposed and factored the divinely vertical in human experiences. If he had done this consciously and consistently he would have had to reintroduce concepts like "Word," "proclamation," "authority," and even the despised word "doctrine." At this point Barth attempts to draw out the implications of this hidden concern of his teacher. After that Barth did not again involve himself so explicitly with Herrmann's theology.[42] But that does not mean he had moved

40. J. Moltmann, *Theology of Hope*, tr. James W. Leitch (New York: Harper & Row, 1967), p. 54.

41. K. Barth, "The Principles of Dogmatics According to Wilhelm Herrmann," in *Theology and Church*, pp. 238-71. ["Die unaufhebbare Subjektivität Gottes," rendered "God is eternally subject," here became (for reasons which will become clear in the next chapter) "the unabrogable subjectivity of God" (cf. Moltmann, *Theology of Hope*, p. 53).—TRANS.]

42. In *Die Christliche Dogmatik* (Munich: Kaiser, 1927), Herrmann is mentioned only incidentally and in predominantly negative fashion. In the preface

farther away from Herrmann. And today, now that we can survey Barth's development as a whole from a much greater historical distance, the last word has to be not "break" but "ambivalence." The difference is clear and deep. As a rule, Herrmann remained confined within anthropological categories. But Barth rigorously built up his theology on the basis of "the unabrogable subjectivity of God." From this point, over a broad front, many differences followed: no point of contact in ethics; stress on the Word event; more space for salvation-historical facts, especially the cross and the resurrection; a wider use of scriptural witness, including the Old Testament; an emphasis on the priority and superordination of justification over sanctification and of faith as acknowledgment over trust; also, a higher valuation of the church, its offices, and its confessions.

In addition to these differences there are areas of agreement, in part a common inheritance from the school of Ritschl: negatively, rejection of natural theology and metaphysics, and positively, a rigorous Christocentrism. This second and very essential element of Herrmannian vintage only acquires its methodological centrality in Barth later—around 1930. The twin pillars of his mature thought as it comes to expression in his *Church Dogmatics* are this Christocentrism and, as its counterpart, the radical repudiation of natural theology. With these positions Barth was not in opposition to the nineteenth century but to the Ritschl-Herrmann line of thought within that century.[43] But when secularization advanced still more, Barth withdrew revelation even further from the world. It was not the "diastasis" which distinguished him from these predecessors but the degree of radicalism with which it was applied. Herrmann found final support in "the inner life of Jesus." Barth also gives that up and thus severs the connection between *Geschichte* and *Historie*. But is that a possibility if one wants to proceed on the basis of Jesus Christ, inclusive of his "historical" appearance? Barth could not do it even in the second edition of *Romans*, despite his dependence on Overbeck's Primal History *(Urgeschichte)*. The following statements are characteristic:

> In the Resurrection the new world of the Holy Spirit touches the old world of the flesh, but touches it as a tangent touches a circle,

---

Barth states: "I could only view the dogmatics of my respected teacher Wilhelm Herrmann as the final stage of a development with which, with all good will, I could only make a break" (p. VI).

43. Cf. Ch. Gestrich, "Die unbewältigte natürliche Theologie," *Zeitschrift für Theologie und Kirche* 68 (1971) 82-120.

that is, without touching it. And, precisely because it does not touch it, it touches it as its frontier—as the new world. The Resurrection is therefore an occurrence in history, which took place outside the gates of Jerusalem in the year A.D. 30, inasmuch as it there "came to pass," was discovered and recognized. But inasmuch as the occurrence was conditioned by the Resurrection, in so far, that is, as it was not the "coming to pass," or the discovery, or the recognition, which conditioned its necessity and appearance and revelation, the Resurrection is not an event in history at all.[44]

Later Barth tried to get past these contradictory lines. In his *Church Dogmatics* he attempted to bring *Geschichte* and *Historie* closer together in his thinking. But even there he failed to reach clarity on this decisive issue in modern theology. In regard to this problem Barth, with his base in the transcendental subjectivity of God, did not surpass Herrmann, who dealt with it on the basis of the transcendental subjectivity of the religious man. From either point of departure human history is merely a neutral instrument.

Barth decisively took his leave of the school of Herrmann; but even as one who had said his good-byes he remained a Herrmannian of a higher order.[45]

DEPARTURE FROM SCHLEIERMACHER?

As ambivalent as Barth's attitude toward Herrmann remained, his departure from Schleiermacher in the same period was to the same degree unambiguous. In 1922, to those who mentioned Schleiermacher in one breath with the Reformers (as in his article of 1912 he himself had also done), Barth declared: "The very names Kierkegaard, Luther, Calvin,

---

44. Barth, *Romans*, p. 30. In his review Bultmann wrote about the relationship between *Geschichte* and *Historie* in *Romans*, esp. the passage just quoted: "And here I confess that I simply do not understand him. Here I can discover only contradictions" (*Beginnings*, p. 115). Precisely at the one point where Bultmann fundamentally wants to go beyond Herrmann, Barth remains stuck in contradictions.

45. In *Programme der Theologie*, 2nd ed. (Munich: Kaiser, 1970), F. W. Kantzenbach attempted in vain, in my opinion, to make plausible a permanent social-ethical influence from Herrmann on Barth. His presentation of Herrmann under the heading "Der Entdeckung der konkreten sozialen Gestalt des christlichen Glaubens" seems to me distorted.

Paul, and Jeremiah suggest what Schleiermacher never possessed, a clear and direct apprehension of the truth that man is made to serve *God* and not God to serve man."[46] What he advanced in part against Herrmann he advanced in whole cloth against Schleiermacher: he who starts with man never arrives at God; man remains subject and God becomes his predicate. Barth believed that in Schleiermacher he could identify the source of the aberration of the theology of the nineteenth century and therefore devoted his lectures in the winter semester of 1923/24 in Göttingen to the theology of Schleiermacher. Starting with Schleiermacher's sermons, he ended with the *Christian Faith* and the *Speeches* (too briefly). Despite his great admiration for Schleiermacher's magnificent achievement, in general he found himself rejecting Schleiermacher's theology. This rejection went so far that he closed with the question: "How can the idea [the idea that Schleiermacher has brought us to a dead end] be squared with the providence of God which rules over his church?" and with the observation: "What remains is clearly—and I do not see how it can be avoided—the possibility of a *theological revolution* [Barth's italics], a fundamental No! to the entire body of Schleiermacher's teaching concerning religion and Christianity." That is the main line; but it is repeatedly crossed by other considerations; for example, where his Christology is called "the incurable wound in his system, simply because it is there," and where Barth observes that "Schleiermacher became and remained a Christocentric theologian with an intensity shared perhaps by only a few other theologians of name."[47] In keeping with this is the fact that in the same period Barth, aware of Schleiermacher's cultural and theological many-sidedness and superiority, defended him against Brunner's portrayal in "Mysticism and the Word."[48]

It is admirable how, just two and a half years later in a lecture delivered in Munster, 1926, Barth again treated Schleiermacher in a totally different way, with special emphasis on "the principle of the middle." Here he developed the points he made vis-à-vis Brunner earlier: "apologetics" and "cultural religion" are the vantage points from

46. In his paper "The Word of God and the Task of the Ministry" (Oct. 1922), in *The Word of God and the Word of Man*, p. 196.

47. K. Barth, *Die Theologie Schleiermachers*, ed. D. Ritschl (Zürich: Theologischer Verlag, 1978). The quotations, which occur on pp. 462, 196, 195 (cf. also pp. 189-96) of the original, are here taken from the English translation by Geoffrey W. Bromiley, *The Theology of Schleiermacher* (Grand Rapids: Eerdmans, 1982), pp. 259, 107, 106.

48. K. Barth, "Brunners Schleiermacherbuch," *Zwischen den Zeiten* 8 (1924) 49-64.

which one must understand and then also combat Schleiermacher—only Barth would consider the "war against this man and his work as a running battle." According to Barth, Schleiermacher "allowed himself to be forced into the fundamentally unworthy position of an apologist" because at bottom he was interested in Christianity "only for the sake of culture." "The Christian character of his theology would then be manifest in his refusal to swim with the current and be a modern man with no Christian reservation, and even more in his determination to know modern humanity as a humanity based upon and guided by Christianity."[49]

Much better known is Barth's brilliant presentation of Schleiermacher in *Protestant Theology in the Nineteenth Century* (Bonn lectures in 1932-1933).[50] Here a new perspective emerges: Schleiermacher's focus on the religious consciousness "*could* be the pure theology of the Holy Spirit" (p. 460). "The fact that Schleiermacher intended it as such (even if he did not perhaps execute it in this way) is revealed by the fact that he is very much aware of a second centre beside his original one, and seeks to grant it its full validity. In doing so he enters in principle into the course of Trinitarian thinking" (p. 460).

The following—italicized—sentence is also important and carefully formulated: *"The Word is not so assured here in its independence in respect to faith as should be the case if this theology of faith were a true theology of the Holy Spirit"* (p. 471).

Again, still different is Barth's view of Schleiermacher in his last colloquium (summer semester 1968, Basel) which became generally known by its incorporation in the famous "Postscript" to a Schleiermacher anthology. What we heard in 1922 can also be found now: "Until better instructed, I can see no way from Schleiermacher, or from his contemporary epigones, to the chronicles, prophets, and wise ones of Israel, to those who narrate the story of the life, death, and resurrection of Jesus Christ, to the word of the apostles—no way to the God of Abraham, Isaac, and Jacob and the Father of Jesus Christ, no way to the great tradition of the Christian church. For the present I can see nothing here but a choice."

Then, a few pages further, follows the reversal: "I am certain of my course and of my point of view. I am, however, not so certain of them that I can confidently say that my 'Yes' necessarily implies a 'No' to Schleiermacher's point of view. For have I indeed understood him correctly?" Then at four points he shows how differently and even contra-

49. K. Barth, "Schleiermacher," in *Theology and Church*, pp. 159-99; the quotations occur on pp. 198-99.
50. K. Barth, *Protestant Theology in the Nineteenth Century*, pp. 425-73.

dictorily Schleiermacher can be understood. He concludes by saying that he "would like to reckon with the possibility of a theology of the Holy Spirit, a theology of which Schleiermacher was scarcely conscious, but which might actually have been the legitimate concern dominating even his theological activity."[51]

Having embraced him with joy (1912) and rejected him with vigor (1922), Barth toward the end related to Schleiermacher with approximately the same ambivalent mix which marked his last word about Herrmann.[52] At the close of the chapter on Schleiermacher I believe I demonstrated the essential convergences in thought between these two theological giants. Barth seems increasingly to have sensed this agreement. But given our limitations as human beings, with our *theologia viae*, convergence does not necessarily lead to coincidence and not at all to the congruence of *theologia gloriae*. However much we may be able to feel the concerns of another along with him—Barth is right: one has to make a choice.

THE DISCOVERY OF DIRECTION

In the mid-1920s, after a period of searching and provisional positioning, Barth had the feeling he was sufficiently clear about his theological direction to set to work on the publication of a dogmatics of his own. Presumably he had no inkling at the time that he had still another shift ahead of him. Thus appeared *Die Christliche Dogmatik im Entwurf*, vol. I, which dealt with the prolegomena.[53] Despite the word *Entwurf* (sketch) in the title, here is someone who is sure of his intent. He has made a clean break with liberal German theology; among his ancestry he now counts largely "positive" theologians: Blumhardt, Dorner, Kohlbrügge, J. Müller, Vilmar (p. VI). "Prolegomena" no longer means

51. K. Barth, *The Theology of Schleiermacher*, pp. 271-72, 275, 278, respectively.

52. For that reason I cannot concur with Dietrich Ritschl when, comparing the lectures of 1923/24 with the Postscript of 1968, he finds a difference in tone and then concludes: "But the content of the argument is the same. Man has been made the subject of theology and Christ his predicate" ("Editor's Preface," in *Theology of Schleiermacher*, p. x). This does not accord with what Barth repeatedly said and wrote about a possible pneumatological interpretation of Schleiermacher.

53. K. Barth, *Die christliche Dogmatik im Entwurf*, vol. 1: *Die Lehre vom Worte Gottes: Prolegomena zur christlichen Dogmatik* (Munich: Kaiser, 1927).

the construction of *praeambula fidei;* in view of the prevailing uncertainty it signifies a "pre-understanding" about the meaning, possibility, and place of the dogmatic enterprise—"instead of speaking outright *from* the matter itself *about* the matter itself." But this can "only be done in the form of a provisional leap into the matter itself." "Our prolegomena will not only be controlled by but exclusively consist in a developed *doctrine of the Word of God*" (§ 2.2).

However, despite the three forms of this word (sermon, canon, revelation [§ 4]), the treatment of this doctrine remains strangely formal. We learn of the word of God as "revelation," "action and speech," "Deus dixit," and especially as Primal History *(Urgeschichte)*. This impression of formality is not really removed by the following expositions on the Trinity, the Incarnation, and the Outpouring of the Spirit. The reason for this is presumably that the consideration of the last two themes begins with "the objective possibility of revelation" (§ 14) and "the subjective possibility of revelation" (§ 17) respectively.

When in 1930 Barth looked forward to the appearance of the second edition of this book, conducting a seminar about Anselm of Canterbury (whom he already knew and appreciated at secondhand), he came into close contact with the clear methodology of this teacher. This experience became for him the occasion, not only to write a book about Anselm's theological method, but also to start once again from the beginning with his own dogmatics.

In the preface to the second edition of the book on Anselm (1958) Barth writes: "Most of them have completely failed to see that in this book on Anselm I am working with a vital key, if not the key, to an understanding of that whole process of thought that has impressed me more and more in my *Church Dogmatics* as the only one proper to theology."[54]

It is astonishing—and certainly a very rare phenomenon in the world of the humanities—that Barth produced two quite distinct versions of the greatest works he had written up to this time. It gives us a profound impression of the passionate intensity of his search for truth. The revision of his *Dogmatics*, however, was much less radical than that of his *Römerbrief,* of whose initial version "not one stone was left upon another." The new edition of the *Dogmatics,* which appeared in 1932 under the name *Church Dogmatics,* was partly an extension (in the English translation the material now covered 1,408 pages in 2 volumes!), partly a restructuring (particularly in the order of the material), and

54. K. Barth, *Anselm: Fides Quarens Intellectum,* tr. Ian W. Robertson (Richmond, VA: John Knox, 1960), p. 11 (preface to the 2nd ed.).

partly a new composition. The influence of Anselm shows in the restructuring of the old and in the new material.

In the first place, in his thinking Anselm proceeded concretely from the "credo" which in his case was totally embedded in the Credo of the apostles' preaching and the church's teaching. The title *Church Dogmatics* brings out, for Barth, the binding force of the faith which underlies all dogmatic thought. Connected with this in Anselm's thought is that reality precedes possibility, not vice versa. "I believe in order that I may understand" *(credo ut intelligam)*. The content of faith does not permit itself to be grounded by the human intellect but only to be unfolded by reflection. Theological thought, insofar as this is possible, brings out a posteriori the *ratio*, the inner coherence, of revelation. In this regard Barth followed Anselm. The priority of possibility over reality as it came to expression in the first edition in the headings of §§ 14 and 17 is now reversed: in the second half-volume reality is first discussed twice before the possibility of revelation comes up (§ 13 and § 16).

It was now inescapable that "the Word of God" could be addressed more concretely and fully than in the first edition. This Word is, in fact, a *concretissimum*, the Word become flesh. In Israel and in Jesus Christ God took "form"; he became an "Object" not only of our thought but also of our experience ("experience" now again has a positive meaning). Through Anselm—one can say—Barth again made the concrete presence and grace of God the all-controlling center of his dogmatic work. As a result, his concept of "the Word of God" was freed from the appearance of formalism and docetism which clung to it earlier. The vertical dimension of the Christian faith, which Barth had stressed so one-sidedly until then, now united much more naturally than in the second edition of *Romans* with the horizontal which is equally essential to the Christian faith. In the process Barth also came much closer again to his teacher Herrmann, for whom the person of Jesus Christ was the only object of faith and theology. To be sure, in sharp contrast with Herrmann, Barth did not defensively narrow down this concentration on Jesus Christ but rather extended it inclusively, relating it to the whole of creation, especially from volume 3, part 1 on (was he trying to get beyond the alternatives of Herrmann and Troeltsch?).

As a result of these new insights also other areas were treated afresh and more rigorously in volume 1, part 1: the prolegomena were understood more from within the content of dogmatics, and the Trinity as the basis of revelation and as expression of "the unabrogable subjectivity of God" was much more developed.

With that Barth had finally found his way for further thought. His *Church Dogmatics* became a grand development of the basic positions he had won over years of struggle. In the present context we need not go further into this matter. For us it is decisive to see how Barth gave up the goals of liberal theology and left its path behind him in order now to fall into line with classic theology as it was given its shape by Athanasius and Anselm, by Luther and Calvin. After the Enlightenment and after Schleiermacher, one can still do this with impunity? At no time in his life did Barth take this question lightly,[55] but after intense struggle he nevertheless answered it in the affirmative. His students adopted his answer as self-evident and repressed the question. However, the question must make itself heard again, despite or precisely because of Barth. In the next chapter we shall see how in the post-Barthian epoch that question again became the central problem of theology. We shall certainly not be able to leave it behind us.

Shortly after Barth's death in 1968 one heard it said from all directions that Barth's theology was now "obsolete." After a few years this superficial talk again died away. In theology, is anything ever obsolete? And how can one ever leave behind the radical switch-in-subject that Barth negotiated—this fundamental farewell to the presuppositions of an entire epoch? That, too, we ever have before us again both as a question and as an invitation. And we must take our positions.

---

55. In 1950, in a conversation with Barth, I asked him the question (which now strikes me as more than a little superficial) whether he could not express himself more succinctly and write shorter books. His answer took me by surprise: "You younger ones have no notion of how strong the nineteenth century still is. I continue to have to come to terms with it on a fundamental level ("Ich muss mich damit noch immer gründlich auseinandersetzen!").

CHAPTER XIV

The Controversy between Barthians and Post-Barthians

THE NECESSITY AND REALITY OF THE POST-BARTHIAN EPOCH

In the years 1930-1960 Barth exerted increasing, worldwide influence, although many theologians also rejected his fundamental stance. To the extent that this situation led to a reiteration of pre-Barthian liberal or conservative positions, such rejection was mostly a rearguard battle. Others, among whom Emil Brunner was perhaps the most important, took intermediate positions—and were condemned therefore to have less influence in the face of the profoundly thought-through and more consistent lines of thought engendered by Barth. A genuine, many-sided, and thoughtful alternative was offered by Barth's contemporary *Paul Tillich* (1886-1965). He narrowly defined Barth's methodology as "kerygmatic," to which he opposed his own "apologetic" theology. Materially this definition meant that he reciprocally related the problems of human existence and culture on the one hand, and the witness of the gospel on the other, as "Question" and "Answer," and rejected Pascal's contrasting of the God of the philosophers with the Father of Jesus Christ. In his three-volume *Systematic Theology* he delivered a grand and astutely structured (in Trinitarian terms) elaboration of his fundamental thesis. As an immigrant to the United States Tillich had more influence there than Barth, but in Europe, during the war and the post-war period, he exerted hardly any influence at all. Even more favorable external circumstances would have made little difference. Barth—with his consistent theo- and Christocentricity as well as his rejection of every anthropocentric orientation—presented the gospel in such a way that, to the highest degree, it inspired Christian resistance to the "neo-paganism" that was abroad. He offered, so to speak, the most suitable "ideology" for the "praxis" of the struggle. Tillich — with his method of correlation between the gospel and the world — would not have been able to put anything helpful alongside this. Not until after the conflict had become a thing of the past, in the years 1945-1965, did Tillich get attention and gain a following also in Europe. In a later chapter, "Paul Tillich: The Bridge of Correlation," we shall evaluate his alternative at some length.

In the 1960s Barth's influence suddenly subsided. As he himself said: "The nineteenth century came back." A generation grew up for whom the experiences of the church struggle against Hitler could no longer have the same fundamental significance it had for countless predecessors. Many people came to this realization for the first time when they read *Dietrich Bonhoeffer's* letters from prison which—immediately after their all-too-late publication in 1951—evoked a worldwide wave of recognition. This recognition concerned, in the first place, Bonhoeffer's prophetic insight into the culture of the post-war period. Bonhoeffer is at his most genial when in these letters he treated the system which imprisoned him essentially as part of the past and concentrated totally on the rise of the new, "mature," radically secularized, "religionless" man. When the Letters were published this secularized sense of life *(Lebensgefühl)* was fully on the march, and people even spoke of a second Enlightenment *(Aufklärung).*

Bonhoeffer (1906-1945) had not been a student of Barth directly, but at an early stage he had become a disciple. This led to a close, even a personal, bond between the older and the younger theologian. But when in prison Bonhoeffer saw "the religionless age" approach, this discovery brought with it as its counterpart a farewell to Barth's theology. Although he expressed himself—probably on purpose—only incidentally about this consequence, which was also painful to him, his words about Barth's "positivism of revelation" ("Take it or leave it")[1] struck like a bomb. These words were exceedingly painful to Barth. One can say that the post-Barthian period really starts with the publication of this position of Bonhoeffer. It arose directly from his analysis of the new cultural epoch. In the anthropocentric age in which Barth had sought his way as a theologian, his starting with God as the subject of faith and theology was a liberating new beginning. In Bonhoeffer's time this point had already become self-evident in theology. But in the period which he foresaw, such a starting point would be completely unintelligible. For

---

1. D. Bonhoeffer, *Letters and Papers from Prison,* ed. Eberhard Bethge, tr. Reginald H. Fuller (New York: Macmillan, repr. 1970), p. 168 (letters dated April 30 and May 5, 1944).

the people for whom the working hypothesis "God" would be a total re-dundancy, "the authority of the Word of God" would only constitute a double enigma: first, because they would accept nothing on authority any more and, second, because they could not handle the idea of a "speaking God." Since Bonhoeffer's time countless preachers, pastoral-care workers, and theologians experienced that they had to work under these conditions and—whatever they may have believed and thought for themselves—found themselves unable to start in their work where Barth did.

We used the word *experienced*, and for the time being we have to leave aside the question whether it is correct to build one's praxis on that basis. In order to determine the relative value of this experience we must first make an attempt to understand it in its broader cultural framework. How was it that all of a sudden this kind of person foreseen by Bon-hoeffer appeared on the scene of history? We had to raise this question once before when we sketched the mysterious, sudden shift from ideal-ism to materialism around 1830—in the form of a shift from Hegelianism to the Hegelian left. This change took place on the basis of a concurrence of internal and external factors. The rebound from the positivism and naturalism which prevailed since then was not so sudden and univer-sal. In Germany, however, a gradual, Kant-oriented countermovement took shape which began early and reached its culmination around World War I. Here, too, external factors must have played a decisive role; for many Germans the unification of Germany plus victory over France con-stituted visible proof of the superiority of the spirit over the lower forces. When during World War I this Germany collapsed, there arose a new desire to look for a basic foothold in a higher, supramundane, reality.

But when World War II and the early post-war years were past, the pendulum inexorably swung back. Again, in Europe "idealism" had to make way for "realism." Now, too, external and internal factors came together. For the internal theological reason one may consider the fact that Barth, with his starting point in the Word of God, never succeeded in making convincingly clear how, and how radically, "the Word" be-came "flesh." And in Bultmann also there was only a divorce—no link-age — between existence and the world. Many followers sensed a vacuum—from the side of one's experience of the gospel, existence, and faith, as well as from the perspective of one's understanding of reality.

With reference to the external causes of the shift, one must think especially of the enormous development of technology as it took place under pressure of the war effort and continued in the 1950s in the ser-vice of society. Electronics and nuclear energy, television and the pill transformed human life more in a relatively short period of time than had happened before over a period of centuries. Control over matter by *homo technicus* seemed to be the key to one's completed humanity. Life allows itself to be understood and shaped from below. Happiness and the future are exclusively in the hands of man the planner. If God exists at all, he is not a contributor to this decisive process; at best he has become marginal, an optional object of one's leisure time. In this kind of world, theology has to establish its relevance.

Till now the theologies of post-Barthians have been anything but uniform. In part they have also been too shallow and short-lived to rate special mention within the framework of this book. In all cases the methodological starting point was anthropocentric: a certain experience or inspiration became the vantage point from which the gospel had to come into view.

Usually, under these circumstances, only a small segment of life became visible; and that in turn appeared rather as a confirmation of human experience and wishes than as an independent, revealing, and redeeming power. From Barth's perspective much of what was offered now could be advanced as clear proof for the correctness of his break with an anthropocentric theology: to arrive at God one obviously has to start with him. Most of the theologies referred to here did not reach a level comparable to those of the nineteenth-century theologies with which Barth had to deal.

If we now look for examples, in connection with which the profoundest questions that are at issue in our epoch between Barthians and post-Barthians can be raised, only a few theologies fit the bill. I could refer here to the theology of Wolfhart Pannenberg. He rejects Barth's authoritative concept of revelation in favor of a revelation considered from below—from within history. He leaves the entire Herrmann school behind him and starts again with Troeltsch. He does not stop here, however, but attempts on this basis to involve the gospel much more deeply and broadly than Troeltsch himself ever succeeded in doing. He clearly wants to theologize, not in pre-Barthian but in the best post-Barthian terms. If nevertheless I do not choose him as an example, the reason is that the entire body of his thought (the affinity with Troeltsch already makes this clear) is so deeply rooted in the great late-idealistic German tradition that he could not really take into account the present positivistic and anti-metaphysical mood *(Lebensgefühl)*. This is not intended as an objection; the obligation to perform such a feat is not one which can be easily argued on theological grounds. Here, however, we need a paradigm in which such an assimilation is presupposed and which, besides this and on this basis, has led to a far-reaching confrontation with Barth's theology.

THE DISCUSSION BETWEEN KUITERT AND THE BARTHIANS

I am familiar with only one good example of this confrontation. It is the work of *H. M. Kuitert* and the discussion it triggered.[2] Dr. H. M. Kuitert is Professor of Ethics and Introduction to Dogmatics at the Free University in Amsterdam, founded by Abraham Kuyper as a Calvinistic institution of higher learning. He experienced the influence of G. C. Berkouwer, his teacher in dogmatics, and through him in an even greater measure that of Karl Barth. His dissertation, "De Mensvormigheid Gods" (1962), further developed Barth's thoughts concerning the humanity of God. His second and larger work, *Die Realität des Glaubens* (1966), beside Barth's influence shows a stronger leaning toward Pannenberg as Kuitert searches for a third way between biblicism and existentialism in the categories of history and tradition. Also in his later writings he often follows Pannenberg, especially in matters of the theory of science (e.g., verification as plausibility). Increasingly also the influences of British language analysis show up, especially in his third book, *Wat heet geloven?* (1977), and its explanatory subtitle: *Structuur en herkomst van de christelijke geloofsuitspraken.*

This last book constitutes a radical break with Barth, being an attempt to ground theological statements of faith from below, from an anthropological view. Both the departure from Barth and the new construct will occupy us here. Although Kuitert placed his break with Barth at the end, our plan requires that we begin with it. First we shall sketch Kuitert's arguments, together with those of his partners in discussion, insofar as they involve the interpretation of Barth. Because in the previous chapter I have myself offered a certain interpretation of Barth, I shall also take a position in the discussion. After that we shall turn our

2. H. M. Kuitert, *Wat heet geloven? Structuur en herkomst van de Christelijke geloofsuitspraken* (Baarn, 1977). In *Wending* (a monthly journal for gospel, culture, and society) student pastor Paul van Dijk reviewed the book and attacked its anthropological grounding of faith (Nov., 1977, pp. 472-82). Kuitert replied in the same issue (pp. 483-90). In the January issue another attack took place, this time with three participants: Paul van Dijk (pp. 38-42), Rochus Zuurmond (pp. 43-49), and N. T. Bakker (pp. 50-60). Kuitert's response was published in the February issue (pp. 116-23). In addition to this discussion H. J. Adriaanse devoted a lengthy article to Kuitert's interpretation of Barth in *Nederlands Theologisch Tijdschrift* (April, 1978) 145-60. Since then, and after the publication of the original edition of the book, appeared C. van der Kooi's dissertation, "De denkweg van de jonge Barth" (Free University of Amsterdam, 1985). In it, in a much more broadly based approach than that of the *Wending* opponents, he offers a critical alternative to Kuitert's view on Barth.

attention to the alternative approach which Kuitert develops, and to the counterarguments of the Barthians. Finally, we wish to try to define the fundamental contrast and to ask whether it can be resolved.

THE IMPORT OF "THE UNABROGABLE SUBJECTIVITY OF GOD IN HIS REVELATION" IN BARTH

To Kuitert the starting point both for his understanding of Barth and for his opposition to Barth is the latter's phrase "the unabrogable subjectivity of God." For his understanding Kuitert appeals to the work of Moltmann, Adriaanse, and Groll referred to in the previous chapter. His interpretation is: "For Barth revelation is an immediate occurrence; it is the speaking God himself. . . . That is the figure of the transcendental subjectivity in optima forma to which Barth adhered throughout his entire life" (p. 204).[3] With this concept he operated in the tradition of Kant and Herrmann. The difference is that Barth started with the transcendentality of God. This does not replace the transcendental subjectivity of man but grounds it, and that via the teaching concerning the Trinity developed in *Church Dogmatics*, 1/1. By this method Barth cut himself free from the attempt to ground the knowledge of God either in history or in religious experience. He had seen how these two ways had proved themselves to be dead ends. Such mediating entities do not lead to God but away from him. God mediates himself: his subjectivity grounds ours. This took Barth—as we saw from his Tambach speech and the second edition of *Romans*—to the idea of the union of man with God, almost to an identity of the divine and the human consciousness. According to Kuitert this solution is definitely no improvement over the cognitive paths of history and experience, because Barth identified his faith concept with the subjectivity of God. "God mediates himself via Barth's thesis concerning God's unabrogable subjectivity" (p. 214). By doing so Barth claims an exceptional position for his own theological approach. He bases this on the subjectivity of faith granted us and realizing itself within us. Thus he excused himself from all discussion and from the necessity of giving an account of his thoughts. To the legitimate question: How do you know? he has no answer. Accordingly, his thesis is an impossible one: "The thesis of the subjectivity of God cannot introduce God's subjectivity itself" (p. 217). "One cannot base a theory on given grace (granted where and when it pleases God!)" (p. 218).

Kuitert, to be sure, does point out that later Barth again softened

3. The page references will be to Kuitert's book *Wat heet geloven?*

this immediacy of the knowledge of God in two directions. First, Barth actually relied on appeal to the biblical witness (and the churchly tradition). His doctrine of inspiration, however, seeing that according to him the Bible *is* the witness of the Word of God and also, in our hearing and believing it, over and over *has to become* the Word of God, suffers from tension. The unanswered question is: Where did the biblical witnesses get their knowledge of God? The relationship between Scripture and the immediacy of the knowledge of God remains unclear. In view of Barth's unhistorical understanding of scriptural revelation and the lack of a hermeneutical method, Kuitert ascertains that *subjectivity* (in a double sense) remains predominant in him.

A second softening of this principle consists in the fact that later Barth assigned a positive role to history: God in fact acts and speaks in history. However, history does not itself participate in revelation. History is merely the locus, or stage, of revelation. In itself it is autonomous and godless as is the entire world of experience (here too Barth follows Kant). Theologically, it is not clear where history comes from. "That means: revelation is again [or rather, is still] God's act of breaking into a world that is alien to him and in that sense autonomous" (p. 228). Of course, if we link God with historical experience, the danger exists "that God is made totally into a predicate of our experience." But we cannot avoid the alternative: "Either the vocable God remains empty, or it receives an arbitrary content from within subjectivity, or it receives its content [i.e., we predicate] from within [historical] experience" (p. 229).

According to Kuitert, Barth has no answer to the legitimate question: How do you know? He even regards it as illegitimate. Thus, as the atheist Machoveč noted, he makes a virtue out of necessity. He does not want to offer proof, but he still wants to be right. In that way theology becomes a closed circle or (as Sperna Weiland characterized Barth's theology) "a house without doors." With its unreasoned appeal to revelation it withdraws from communication with the outside world and culture in general.

This sharp renunciation of Barth from one who had been akin to him earlier could not remain unanswered. In the monthly journal *Wending* three young Barthians not only rejected Kuitert's own approach (to which we shall return later) but also called his representation of Barth a caricature. This last charge came especially from *Nico T. Bakker*, who in his book *In der Krisis der Offenbarung* (1974), which deals with Barth's hermeneutics especially in the two editions of *Römerbrief*, had proved himself an authority on, and a follower of, the young Barth. He accused Kuitert of adducing hardly any material from Barth himself in support of his interpretation of "the unabrogable subjectivity of God." According to Bakker, Kuitert forgets that the correlate of divine subjectivity is not some "God-intimate" subjectivity of the believer ("a quite untenable construal of Barth's doctrine of revelation") but what Barth called the threefold form of the Word of God: the incarnate, the inscripturated, and the preached Word. In my opinion, Bakker is correct in the main line of this counterattack. I would add that I found the expression "the unabrogable subjectivity of God in his revelation" only twice in Barth, once in a letter to Thurneysen dated May 28, 1924, and again in his paper on Herrmann's theology.[4] These two occurrences belong chronologically together (both date from the year 1924). Barth had a habit of picking up certain expressions from philosophy, literature, and politics, using them for a brief period, and then dropping them. This practice is presumably related to the fact that in philosophy Barth called himself an eclectic. Therefore one may not canonize the passing uses of words like "life," "existence," "God's revolution," and the Neo-Kantian sounding term "unabrogable subjectivity." Nor can one on this basis interpret an entire theology. On the contrary: such expressions must themselves be interpreted in the light of the whole of a theology. Kuitert overestimated the import of the expression he used as an interpretative key.

In his interpretation of Barth, Bakker rightly championed the earthly forms of revelation in their objectivity. He referred to the positive use Barth made of the three mediating concepts: experience, Scripture, history. As he worked this out, however, Bakker became less convincing. He referred to the role played by the notion of "experience" in *Church Dogmatics*, 1/1, § 6. But that is another concept than that for which Kuitert searched in vain in Barth. For Kuitert "experience" denotes the common human experience of the world to which, in his thinking, he wants to see revelation in a close relationship. For Barth "experience" is a predicate of revelation itself; it indicates its power to shape human existence; it is the experience which human beings have with the Word-event. Hence this use of the word *experience* in Barth cannot serve to refute Kuitert's claim.

For Bakker the most important mediating concept is Holy Scripture, which, according to Barth, is the second form of the Word of God. Its introduction, to Bakker's mind, refutes Kuitert's verticalistic-subjec-

---

4. Cf. *Revolutionary Theology in the Making: Barth-Thurneysen Correspondence 1914-1925*, tr. and ed. James D. Smart (Richmond, VA: John Knox, 1964), p. 185, where the expression is translated "the inalienable subjectivity of God in his revelation"; and K. Barth, *Theology and Church*, tr. Louise Pettibone Smith (New York: Harper & Row, 1962), p. 256 (the paper on Herrmann given in 1924). [The phrase is unrecognizable in this translation; see also n. 41 in the previous chapter.—TRANS.]

tivistic misconstrual of Barth. Scripture in Barth is "the objective authority" by which every statement about God must be measured. On that basis Bakker responded to some of the arguments of Kuitert against Barth's doctrine of Scripture and use of Scripture (p. 55). In an appendix he rejected Kuitert's argument that Barth reads Scripture unhistorically, simply by saying that the Bible must not be read "historically" (nor fundamentalistically nor in the fashion of historical criticism) but "as an utterly unique history" (p. 60).

That takes us to the third mediating concept — that of history. Kuitert misses in Barth the view that history is an instrument and dimension of revelation. Bakker, who along with Barth favors a sharp disjunction between human history *(Historie)* and divine history *(Geschichte)*, cannot fundamentally deny Kuitert's charge. Still he wants to prove over against Kuitert that history does function as a mediating agency in Barth. "By his Word God posited a history [*Geschichte*], in a highly original, inimitably creative, and hence 'unhistorical' [*unhistorisch*] fashion, that is, one that cannot be subsumed under the same category as our so-called general history" (p. 53). At the same time he refers to "Scripture as the historical [*historischen*] embodiment of a unique history [*Geschichte*]" (p. 56), and writes: "When the Bible reports on revelation it does it in the form of a concrete historical narrative. The remarkable weight which the Bible attributes to chronological and topographical statements may serve to confirm this fact." The next sentence, however, reads: "This does not mean, according to Barth, that history in the biblical sense is identical with what we are accustomed to call history. That history is not open to neutral observation. The neutral observer does not hear what there is to hear or see what there is to be seen here." The section concludes with the words: "The mystery of revelation is as concrete as the world. It is precisely this concreteness which makes it so mysterious. We have the Word of God in no other way than in the mystery of its 'world relatedness' [*Welthaftigkeit*]." In this rather unclear back-and-forth movement of Bakker's line of thought one sees precisely reflected the embarrassment with which Barth adopted the legacy of the Herrmannian disjunction of *Geschichte* and *Historie* and then developed further with strong shadings of his own. Bakker is saying the same thing which Kuitert had said, except that what to the former is self-evident truth is proof to the second that revelation and experience *(Welterfahrung)* do not connect in Barth. In his reply Kuitert therefore objects to Bakker that in the occurrence of revelation God has to break into a world that is foreign to him, as One, moreover, whose work cannot be seen by neutral observers. In 1 Kings 18 the watching priests of Baal, however, did see God working! (p. 120).

Our own conclusion is that the difference in these two op

ponents' interpretation of Barth, though not unimportant, does not touch the core of the issue. At bottom it is not really the interpretation of Barth which produces the gulf between them but the personal decision which each of the participants in the discussion makes vis-à-vis Barth's approach.

Of a different nature is the discussion in which H. J. Adriaanse engages with Kuitert. In his dissertation, a comparison between Husserl's and Barth's development, entitled "Zu den Sachen selbst" (1974), in which in keeping with his theme he approached Barth from the side of philosophy, he had demonstrated toward the end a radical switch-in-subject in Barth and in that connection strongly emphasized the expression "the unabrogable subjectivity of God." In the process he struggled with the question whether and how the human subject could know this God at all. The relevant pages made a strong impression on Kuitert, which was one of the reasons why he shaped his rejection of Barth in the way he did. It turned out, however, that Adriaanse was not overly thrilled with the way Kuitert used his position. He pointed out that his book dealt only with the young Barth and that the projected second volume would show that later in life Barth deliberately introduced agencies of mediation for revelation. The identity of the divine and the human subject which Adriaanse saw threatening in Barth around 1920 disappeared in order to make way for the concepts of "analogy" and "relationship" (the concept of "analogy," as we saw earlier, already occupied a key position in the Tambach lecture). Adriaanse states that though Kuitert was aware of these later developments, including the epistemological function of the doctrine of the Trinity, he did not make enough use of them for his interpretation of Barth. One can say that in this view of Barth Adriaanse and Bakker were essentially in agreement—only that Bakker really wanted nothing to do with the notion of a development in Barth, or at least that he showed no interest in such "history."

More important, however, is that Adriaanse, in view of Kuitert's use of his interpretation of Barth, saw himself compelled to supplement and to concretize what he had written about "the transcendental subjectivity" in the young Barth. In distinction from Kuitert he does not understand this concept in the light of Kant, as referring to a "totally empty and formal Ego," but in the light of the concept of "life" and hence as expression of an experience—comparable to the notion of the "life of consciousness" in Husserl. Barth's discovery of the "unabrogable subjectivity" of God and the switch-in-subject connected with it presumably was not only an act of reflection but in the first place a faith experience. Differently than Kuitert thinks, this experience, "even if it was the experience of the abrogation of experience" (p. 153), must have played a decisive role in Barth. In addition it must be noted that the experience of the subjectivity of God may not, as Kuitert believes, be understood as a withdrawal from our reality. This seeming reduction expresses the conviction that the world must no longer be understood from within itself but in the light of God. Not *cogito ergo sum* (I think, therefore I am) but *cogitor, ergo sum* (I am thought, therefore I am) is the way to put it. The world as such is unmasked as an abstraction and hence "bracketed," excluded from consideration. Viewed in the light of God the world does not vanish; rather, our experiences are purified and newly illumined.

For that reason Barth could later assign the "lights of this world" to their place; no human being exists apart from God-in-Christ. Consequently a certain *theologia naturalis* is among Barth's theological possibilities. There is in him no nihilism, rather a universalism of grace. Kuitert is correct in saying that this experience is epistemologically ill-grounded in Barth, but on the issue itself Kuitert was perhaps closer to Barth than he himself knew.[5]

By introducing the notion of experience in the interpretation of the young Barth, Adriaanse dissociates himself essentially from the— virtual—common front between Kuitert and Bakker. At this front one understands Barth totally as a theologian who starts from the other side, from the side of God. For Bakker that is the only legitimate theological point of departure; for Kuitert it is, in the light of the human situation, a skipping of one's own position and a flight into pure subjectivism. Adriaanse believes that in Barth's switch-in-subject, man, world, and experience play their own roles. The fact that these roles are so totally different from what they were in the work of Barth's predecessors (and earlier in himself) must not be explained from within Barth's intellectual

5. As far as I know, Kuitert commented on Adriaanse's article only once in passing (in his second reply in *Wending* [Feb., 1979]). There he wrote: "A short while ago Adriaanse even defended the thesis that 'transcendental subjectivity' in Barth can be understood as transcendental experience, with the consequence that Barth would then have believed in a universal knowledge of God given to all men in virtue of their humanity. If that should be true it would in any case show beautifully the line of demarcation between my understanding and that of Karl Barth: in his construction of the cognitive process Barth does not need the outer world, but in my thinking the outer world is essential for the emergence of knowledge of God" (p. 118). I doubt whether this is correct. It is not correct if Adriaanse is right in saying that the theological reduction has a new understanding of the world as its counterpart. In that case the issue is not the significance or nonsignificance of the "outer world" but the question in what way— negatively or positively—the "outer world" mediates "God."

movement as such but in the light of something behind it: in Adriaanse that is the "switch-in-subject," a sort of code name for "conversion." By saying this Adriaanse, in my opinion, distances himself more or less from the closing pages of his dissertation "Zu den Sachen selbst." In the previous chapter we questioned the importance he and others attributed to philosophical influences in Barth. It seems to me that in his interaction with Kuitert Adriaanse has corrected himself. He even writes: "His [i.e., Barth's] theology can no more be captured cleanly in the theological reduction than in some philosopher. One may criticize this fact; nevertheless, this is the source of its attraction and, what's more, its authenticity" (p. 158).

Accordingly, the answer to the question concerning the place and historical significance of Barth's theology becomes (even) more difficult. The post-Barthian solution—"Barth thinks from the top down; let us start from the bottom up"—would then be too simple a contrast. One could perhaps extend Adriaanse's interpretation a little by saying: Barth also thinks from the bottom up. However, between Barthians and post-Barthians that "bottom" is not identical. Above I called Adriaanse's "switch-in-subject" a code name for conversion. He himself does not use this word, though with his word "life" or "experience (of life)" he comes very close to it. In that case both parties would take their starting point in man; however, each would start from a different human experience. Simply put, one might express that difference by speaking of "experience of the world" versus "experience of conversion." However, we do not want prematurely to reduce the problem to a simple set of opposites. We have not yet heard what alternatives to Barth are possible, or required, in our empiricistic epoch. We must first sketch Kuitert's blueprint for an alternative theology and present the objections of the Barthians. Only then can we determine whether, and how, we may have to choose between them.

KUITERT'S ALTERNATIVE TO BARTH'S THEORY OF REVELATION

What Kuitert attempts is what is called, in the technical jargon of dogmatics, "prolegomena." But Barth can only recognize the "prolegomena" as signifying "the first part of dogmatics rather than that which is prior to it."[6] To Kuitert this means self-enclosure in a closed circle and a refusal to render an account of our method to one who asks: "How do you know that?" To him the "prior" themes of dialogue must be dealt

---

6. *Church Dogmatics*, 1/1: *The Doctrine of the Word of God*, 2nd ed., p. 42.

with first, especially if we wish to speak about God. We must start with "man," on an "anthropological floor" which believers and unbelievers have in common. Thus Kuitert again picks up the theme of the "apologetic" theology which Tillich opposed to the "kerygmatic" theology of Barth. A half-century before, Barth had moved away from the increasing cultural "eclipse of God," replacing Herrmann's apologetic stance by a radical "switch-in-subject." As a result the classic type of dogmatician again emerged in the school of Barth. Now, as secularization advanced and became ever more manifest, even this posture was abandoned by many as inappropriate to the situation. In many circles, as it did a century before, attention reverted to the prolegomena. This meant that the dogmatician was replaced by the apologist (in Catholic theology the two have always lived side by side). In America, one can think in this connection of Lonergan and Gilkey; in Germany of Rahner and Pannenberg (to whom Küng joined himself in 1978 with his *Does God Exist?*); in the Netherlands, of Schillebeeckx and Kuitert. Let us take a look at the blueprint for prolegomena offered by Kuitert.

Faith, says Kuitert, always has to do with statements about facts, with "propositions," with "is"-statements, or whatever name one wants to give to them. All other statements, especially those which concern "praxis" or "engagement," always presuppose faith in certain God-related states of affairs. Must one accept such propositions as authoritative, as revealed truth? Many leading theologians are no longer willing to do this, nor ground such propositions, as did liberal theology, as though they were inherent in human consciousness. The result is that though they again make statements about God, they neither can nor want to subject them to a universal test. If theology still wants to claim status as a science, it has to do more than bear witness, even if, in the nature of the case, it cannot perform a "verification." Theology can scrutinize theological pronouncements only in terms of their "plausibility." "A proposition is plausible if and in the measure it makes its truth perspicuous to the largest possible number of people" (p. 60). That is possible only by reference to a certain state of affairs. Therefore theology must, in the first place, be descriptive in character: it examines religion and religions, and thus makes also God an object of its intellectual striving. The descriptive never totally excludes the subjective, and includes the normative and the possibility of choice. The phenomenon of faith can be described on three levels: (a) anthropological; (b) historical; (c) institutional.

(a) Following the example of Scheler, Gehlen, van Peursen, and Pannenberg, Kuitert describes the human being as "experiencing meaning" and "giving meaning" (in that order!). Man is not, like an animal, preprogrammed. Ever and again he has to make choices; he has to make his world intelligible and surveyable in order to talk about it and to intervene in it. In order to act meaningfully, people must have experienced their universe more or less as meaningful. In every act of intervention they assume or anticipate a larger context of meaning. Such an undertaking is always risky. A person trusts himself to what he cannot perceive as yet. Kuitert calls that "the primal faith" presupposed in every human act of cultural formation. This primal faith is always embattled and nevertheless ineradicable and always, in keeping with its nature, a "saving" faith, because it trusts the positive outcome of culturally formative action.

This primal faith, says Kuitert (following G. Ebeling's *Jesus und Glaube*), is present also in the New Testament, especially as the anthropological presupposition of the miracles of healing. From this point Kuitert infers the Christian-theological relevance of primal faith. This does not make theology into anthropology. Nevertheless, people, even in speaking about God, are bound to this "anthropological floor." One who skips over this fact allows theology to answer only such questions as it itself has first conceived. But in the Christian theological tradition this was never what happened, as the doctrine of general revelation, which deals with this anthropological floor, makes clear. We may never oppose the two kinds of revelation to each other, nor (as Barth does) incorporate the general into the special, and creation into redemption. "I would rather (like Schillebeeckx) reverse that order and assign redemption a place in creation conceived as history" (footnote, p. 112).

(b) In the historical section Kuitert turns to the phenomenology of religion. We always encounter primal faith only in a certain historical form. Religions are "networks of myths, rites, and mores which, each in its own way, (a) make explicit the inexplicabilities which threaten to destroy man with his ineradicable primal faith, and (b) give an answer to these inexplicabilities which simultaneously confirms and grounds this primal faith" (p. 122). All religions have "God" as their point of reference. This does not mean, however, that the differences between them are immaterial. It is often certain very distinct experiences which press people to pronounce the name "God" as an expression of meaning. Such experiences are only possible within certain frameworks of interpretation. One such framework is itself the result of longer, cumulative experience. Therein lies the possibility of testing the plausibility of a religion with the aid of the question whether the experiential conditions of such a framework of interpretation still exist or are obsolete. For: "Built into faith *(fides quae)* is an argument which makes an appeal to experience" (p. 139). "The grounds of faith therefore consist in that which religious people view as the footprints of God in our world of experience" (p. 142). Such a religious faith dies a slow death "when it is no longer possible to point out a footprint or signal of God as people pictured him" (p. 144). As an example Kuitert refers to the decline and death of fertility religions in the ancient Near East. When trade and industry, and finally artificial fertilizer, undermined the decisive role of the fertility of the earth, it turned out that what people took to be the footprints of God were not that at all. "If it is meaningful to speak of God, then God has to meet at least one condition: there cannot be an entity which surpasses him in power" (p. 145).

At this point Kuitert introduces a further concept to denote a religion in the sense of a complex of faith propositions. In Dutch he calls it a *zoekontwerp*, a word that is hard to translate: a construct or hypothesis which guides one in the search for God. By means of this term he seeks to express both the subjectivity as well as the verifiability of a religious conviction. Hence such a search-hypothesis is designed to help a person find "that God and that salvation which are prefigured in the hypothesis" (p. 150). "Without such a search-hypothesis we perceive nothing of God in the world, and conversely: what we do perceive of God is ever dependent on the search-hypothesis with which we are equipped" (p. 151). At the same time it is true that the search-hypothesis is not an end in itself; the goal is personal experience with God and his salvation, in which the preliminary character of truth is ever exceeded.

Search-hypotheses can die and they can survive. The latter may occur where such a hypothesis is regularly "readjusted" in accordance with the changed historical situation. We find such "adjustments," for example, in the Old Testament. And the New Testament as such can be viewed as a universalizing correction or adjustment of the Old Testament. Also Christianity, as a human search-hypothesis, "can only be built up from below. The appeal to revelation in no way changes that fact . . . because human beings cannot exist without an 'above' and at the same time can only speak about an 'above' from 'below'" (p. 155). The Christian hypothesis by itself can also be superseded. There are two elements, however, which protect it from that fate, when they are rightly maintained and emphasized: the first element is that it is history which is the real revelatory means of this God. "He is never superseded; he himself supersedes" (p. 157). The second element is love as that which, according to Christianity, constitutes the real being of God. Religious search-hypotheses fade away "because their God is too small, not sufficiently the God for all people, the God of universal salvation" (p. 158). In Christianity, which orients itself to the footprints of God, Jesus' way and work are the central footprints which cannot be superseded. However, this faith is also dependent for its confirmation on history, that is, the future "in which God and his salvation enter into our world" (p. 158).

(c) The third level is the institutional. The search-hypothesis of Christianity takes the shape of official church doctrine. In this context Kuitert especially points out that the coercion of faith tends to prevent the necessary historical "adjustments." The institutional may never suppress the personal decision of the individual. Conversely, such a personal decision can only find its mark against the background of a communal search-hypothesis. The tension between the institution and the individual can only be borne if the institution has the courage to be pluriform and is consequently willing to accept discord and disagreement.

THE CONFRONTATION BETWEEN KUITERT AND THE BARTHIANS

Of the several Barthian responses to Kuitert published in *Wending* (there were some also in other journals but Kuitert himself did not become involved), I essentially oriented myself to the contributions of Paul van Dijk, student pastor at the time, because they—and especially his first essay intended as a review article—were more comprehensive and to the point than those of the two other authors. Besides, van Dijk demonstrated great understanding of and sympathy for Kuitert's concern. What is more, Bakker concentrated on Kuitert's interpretation of Barth, while Zuurmond (another student-pastor) argued with Kuitert about the political implications of Barth's theology and the so-called materialistic exegesis. In fact, in his book Kuitert had polemicized in passing against "the Barthian left" which, in his view, combined Barth's dogmatism with a Marxist political dogmatism. All three of his opponents belonged to "the Barthian left"—but with a view to the focus in this book we shall now leave aside this element of the discussion.

Van Dijk's position comes out clearly in the following quotation.

> There is no question that I would advocate a process of cognition (faith is a form of knowing!) apart from insight and experience. For me the question is only whether the structure of faith (and all productive knowledge generally) is not captured better when insight and experience are not positioned as founding and selecting authorities at the beginning of the process of cognition but are looked for and expected as concluding authorities at the end. Or, to put it in the words of Anselm and Barth (whom Kuitert criticizes): *fides quaerens intellectum.* Faith is not so much

> validated by an appeal to insight and experience but it goes out
> in search of insight and experience. (p. 474)

That is the consistent thread of criticism in the responses of all three opponents: Kuitert again undoes Barth's Copernican revolution. In the
footsteps of Anselm Barth discovered that true theology starts with the
concretissimum of revelation in Christ and moves from there to the universal. "Kuitert chooses the opposite road: he wants to ground the
special knowledge of faith in the fact that it invokes the realities of experience that are universally accessible in nature and history" (p. 475). Or
as Zuurmond puts it in terms of the history of dogma: "the theological
line of Irenaeus (the Logos as predicate of Christ) can be extended to
Barth; the more or less philosophical line of his contemporaries (the
Apologists) can be extended to Kuitert" (p. 46).

　　We heard van Dijk use the word *grounding* for Kuitert's method.
In his response Kuitert scored this designation as a great misunderstanding: it was his aim not to ground the Christian faith but to make it dis-
cussable and examinable (p. 485). In their counter-replies both van Dijk
and Bakker say that this is a word game not substantiated by Kuitert's
own statements: "To test means to examine: to check whether a cognitive assertion is reliable, i.e., has grounds" (Bakker, p. 55). But Kuitert
countered (orally): "I mean the English word *argument*, which seeks only
to persuade, not to substantiate."

　　But van Dijk's objections are not only theological. He regards
Kuitert's anthropology as not very universal at all; if it were, faith would
appear as a special case, within a general category and a confirmation of
what was already known. In reality, however, the world is teeming with
contradictory meaning-systems and, on top of that, of experiences of
meaninglessness (Nietzsche). Kuitert's anthropological floor seems
covered from wall to wall with a Christian carpet! Van Dijk speaks of the
"voice" of the "irreducible other" within our horizontal history (philosophically he would like to orient himself to Levinas). He too wants to
speak of "experience": but "according to experience, that which is experienced does not itself stem from experience" (reply on p. 39). In short,
van Dijk is afraid that in Kuitert "revelation has become a predicate of
nature and history instead of the reverse; consequently, in Kuitert nature
and history determine what revelation is instead of letting revelation tell
me what nature and history may be" (pp. 40-41). To these lines of thought
Bakker adds that the "is-statements" of the Christian faith are but tenu-
ously related to the states of affairs of universal human experience, and
that, as a result of the manner in which the Word of God brings our existence into crisis, "the human search-model is so fundamentally dis-

ordered that one would do better to abstain from further attempts at correction [*Beistellung*]" (pp. 50, 52).

To all this Kuitert replies that for him the issue is how to account for faith and that he does not see how his opponents could not be of the same conviction. He vehemently rejects their immanentistic interpretation of his theology. He even writes: "A God who can be accounted for by human beings can never be the true God" (p. 118). In his first reply to van Dijk he had written: "Undoubtedly the knowledge of God is the fruit of God's self-revelation, and one cannot in turn account for this self-revelation which grounds our knowledge. On that point I am in agreement with Barth and with all the theologians and philosophers who have also said that before and after him" (p. 489). Bakker was unable to square this statement with other assertions of Kuitert (p. 55). But Kuitert asks his critics: Is revelation for you then an act of supernatural intervention? To this question van Dijk replies that what a person considers "natural" already presupposes an entire metaphysic and that God's act of making himself known is not felicitously captured in the term *intervention*. Kuitert would also like to know how van Dijk, on an Anselmian foundation, would account for his position over against his nonbelieving friends. I could not find an answer to this question in van Dijk. To the question about the reversal of *general* and *special* revelation Kuitert replies that there cannot be a special revelation without general revelation against the background of which it stands out. His example of the vanquished Baal-religion led van Dijk to remark that Israel's prophets did not reject Baal on the basis of an appeal to societal development but on account of a "nonreducible voice which set a certain event, the Exodus, in motion" (p. 477). Kuitert replied that Baal did not *become* a false god in the course of history; in later times it became clear that Baal *had* always *been* a false "construct." The prophets knew it; but their criticism had not yet been able to destroy the people's fascination with Baal.

Although Adriaanse dealt primarily with Kuitert's interpretation of Barth, he also devoted a section of his book to his objections against Kuitert's alternative. He stated: Every theological theory is a *petitio principii*, itself a construct of faith. Barth may have made a virtue out of necessity; Kuitert is in danger of underrating the necessity. "Can one ever advance a notion of history or nature which makes the legitimation of faith assertions from within history or nature anything other than a *petitio principii?*" (p. 159). True: primal faith is a necessary presupposition of faith in God; but the same is true of the rotation of the earth and the function of the heart-muscle! "How does one get from anthropological primal faith to faith in God? For that, is it not still necessary that in one way or another one's eyes or ears are opened?" (p. 159). And when that happens, what use is then the reference to experience rather than to revelation?

APPRAISAL OF THE DISCUSSION

In closing I should like to attempt, within the focus of the present book, to formulate my own position in this—paradigmatic and far-reaching —discussion, however difficult that may prove to be in the light of the weight of the arguments on both sides. The question I have to answer is: For the interpretation of the gospel in today's world, does Kuitert offer a better starting point than Barth? The weakness of Barth's position is well known: since he starts with God, he does not seem to reach real people. Kuitert starts "from below"; can he, from this direction, arrive at the God of the gospel, the father of Jesus Christ? He makes his ascent from below from a diversity of levels: the anthropological "floor" (primal faith); historical forms of primal faith; frameworks of interpretation and experience; "search-hypotheses" and their "corrections." Not until pp. 154-59 in his book does the question arise how from within these points of departure one reaches the "above" of revelation and what it looks like. The Christian faith orients itself to the footprints of God in the way and work of Jesus. These footprints can never be surpassed. How can one arrive at an assertion about them if even this faith ever has to be confirmed in history as it unfolds?

We learned of Kuitert's reference to the historicity of this God and to his assertion that God is love. Both, however, are assertions of a Christian; as such, as assertions of faith, no plausibility accrues among outsiders. The assertion that love is the highest value, in the sense of an antidiscriminatory universalism, is an idea of modern culture arising from within the Western Christian tradition. The same is true of the historicity of God. We are revolving here within a cultural circle whose origin is Christian—like Troeltsch, who looked in vain for an absolute point in the history of religion. Kuitert, who made his ascent from an anthropological floor, here reached the anthropological ceiling beyond which he cannot climb. In contrast with Troeltsch he does not want to go farther either. He is not looking for an absolute point but for that which in history has proven itself tenable. He only wants to unearth presuppositions and suggest a way of dialogue with "outsiders"—which explains the brief number of relevant pages. For the purpose of rendering an account of our faith we have then come no farther than that, exactly like the adherents of other religions, we have appealed to "experiences" which cannot be exchanged because they were called into existence by very different traditions (search-constructs) which "serve to help believers find that God and that salvation which were prefigured in the search-construct" (p. 150). For "what we perceive of God is always dependent on the search-construct with which we are equipped" (p. 151).

Hence what emerges is that we are led, also from below, into a closed circle in a way similar to that of which Barth was accused with his starting point "from above." It is of no help that this closed circle is presented as a concentration of experiences. For the people who have had no such experience themselves, these experiences are transformed into authorities (helpful authorities, to be sure). That too is structurally similar to Barth's construct: the authority of the inscripturated Word of God is the human precipitate of experiences, especially those of hearing the prophets and apostles, the witness to which aims to engender new faith experience in us. Over against this construct stands Kuitert's assertion that one day even Christianity may possibly fade away because its construct is no longer confirmed by experience. In that respect he is close to Schleiermacher and Troeltsch, who also envisioned that possibility. But like them, and partly for the same reasons, Kuitert rejects it. It remains an abstract noetic exercise which does not constitute a concrete contradiction of Barth.

The question then is: Does Kuitert essentially understand the Christian faith differently from Barth? He knows that our search-hypotheses only lead to certainty "when people themselves encounter this God" (p. 150). No one has such an encounter at his disposal. We already read earlier the astonishing assertion that "undoubtedly the knowledge of God is the fruit of God's self-revelation and one cannot in turn account for this self-revelation which grounds our knowledge. On that point I am in agreement with Barth" (p. 489). And in the second reply we read: "A God whom human beings can account for can never be the true God" (p. 118). These statements, as also the theory of plural search-constructs, negate the capacity of the anthropological floor to support an accounting for the faith in dialogue with outsiders. In one's belief one clearly has to do with a closed circle.[7]

---

7. Kuitert himself senses the lack of an authority able to break through the closed circle. According to him also, there has to be something like it. Otherwise it would be inexplicable that people should abandon their inherited search-hypotheses or exchange them. In an astute study, "Ervaring als toegang tot de godsdienstige werkelijkheid," *Nederlands Theologisch Tijdschrift* 32 (July, 1978) 177-96, he also assigns a certain limited role, alongside search-hypotheses, to experiences of totality and contingency which confirm religion rather than ground

Barth's insight that one who does not start with God will never get to him seems to be confirmed by Kuitert, positively, by outright affirmation, and negatively, by the failure of his alternative method. This does not mean that we are blind to the weakness of Barth's starting point (a revelation which seems to take place somewhere on a level "above" where we live our lives). Kuitert as well as other theologians simply had to attempt an alternative approach. The necessity of this attempt is only verbally recognized by van Dijk and not at all by the other critics—while one must nevertheless assume that all three (who at the time were chaplains at advanced schools of technology), however reluctantly, had to start again and again "from below" in their conversations with students! Both Barthians and post-Barthians live from the questions their counterparts do not answer. For the time being, however, as we consider Kuitert's construction, one which (also by comparison with other post-Barthian theologies) evidences great intelligence and critical acuity, we must note that the movement away from Barth after the 1960s occurred with undue haste.

---

it, serving in any case as a ground for negotiation and dialogue between search-hypotheses. In the symposium for Schillebeeckx, *Meedenken met Edward Schille-beeckx*, ed. H. Häring, et al. (Baarn: Nelissen, 1983), in an essay entitled "Offenbarung und Erfahrung: ein übel angebrachter Gegensatz," Kuitert writes "that though a circular line of thought must be avoided as long as possible, it cannot in the long run be avoided . . . in any discipline" (p. 46). The difference here between him and Barth is more a question of content than of method: as a Christian Kuitert opts for a quantitatively wider "search-construct" in which general and special revelation are brought together in one "cumulative experience" (pp. 44ff.).

CHAPTER XV

Immanent Transcendentality: The Catholic Bridge

CATHOLIC THEOLOGY IN THE MODERN AGE

As far as building a bridge between the church and the modern world is concerned, Catholic theology has a real advantage over Protestant theology because it acknowledges the authority of Thomas Aquinas. Thus it proceeds from the assumption of harmony between nature and grace, whereas the fundamental starting point of Reformed theology is the contrast between sin and grace. Indeed, the theology of Thomas Aquinas was itself designed in response to a secularizing framework of thought. Averroism, which was very influential at the newly established university of Paris in the thirteenth century, had led to a kind of immanentism in which Aristotle's philosophy, as the universal philosophy of nature, was placed in a superordinate position vis-à-vis the particularist thought arising from Christian revelation. In response to this secularizing framework Albertus Magnus and his pupil Thomas then incorporated Aristotle's truth in, and subordinated it to, the truth of revelation.

One might think that Thomas's adage "Grace does not negate nature but completes it" could have been made fruitful again and in a fresh way over against the challenge of Enlightenment thought. In general, however, that expectation has not been fulfilled. To be sure, many Catholic theologians have made attempts to do this, but they have always encountered suspicion and resistance from the side of the dominant curial theology in Rome, where the challenge of modern thought was felt much less strongly than by many Catholic thinkers in northwestern Europe. Fundamentally, the Roman hierarchy has continually sought, right into modern times, to rescue the validity of Thomistic thought, whereas the thinkers it mistrusted wanted to make Thomas's intent and motive operational again under changed conditions and with new, hence with non-Aristotelian, categories. The second group was prepared to undertake a struggle with the spirit of modernity; it was, however, again forced to engage in an intramural struggle with the spirit of the Roman hierarchy. In consequence, the struggle with the outside was paralyzed; and the inside battle was ever and again decided unilaterally by authoritarian means. Since 1800 the path of Catholic theology has been marked by impressive achievements, but it has even more been one of actual failure and personal tragedy.

This does not mean that in modern times Roman Catholic thought has proven unfruitful in every respect. Fortunately, Catholic theology had and still has a life and a domain of its own outside the Catholic hierarchy. Many priests and laypeople have let themselves be inspired by it in preaching, pastoral care, worldview, and action. In addition, Protestant theology has increasingly taken advantage of Catholic theology.

Not even curial thought was able in the long run to remain unaffected by the theologians it rejected at the outset. Not even Thomas was infallible, and new interpretations of his teaching were allowed. Often those who were originally condemned later (usually after their death) became authorities. Often, also, the condemnations led to stronger substantiation of the positions taken and more careful formulations. Much that was in full blossom was destroyed; but also much theology flourished, like a palm tree, under the burden of adversity.

In this chapter we have to exclude from our purview several persons and areas of thought. Many theologians—from Möhler to Guardini and beyond — have written original and influential books in which, while presupposing Catholic doctrine as a whole, they transposed it in a new and more modern key without necessarily aiming to confront and come to terms with modern secularity. Contrasting with them are other theologians, like Günther, Hermes, and the majority of modernists, who so accommodated themselves to the dominant ideas of their epoch that in their work no real encounter between modernity and Christian tradition occurred either. In this chapter we are in search of theologians who attempted to build a bridge between the two worlds. We have already found one: John Henry Newman (cf. chapter 7 above). By his conversion to Catholicism, he unwittingly introduced Anglo-Saxon theology (which was based on experience, existence, and conscience) into the domain of Catholicism in which Thomism, based on the primacy of the intellect,

held sway. The fact that Pope Leo XII elevated him to the cardinalate saved him from condemnation and kept the road clear for his influence on coming generations.

MAURICE BLONDEL

The Catholic bridge builders in the epoch after Newman should be viewed as his spiritual kin. Often they were also, to a large degree, under his influence. I consider as by far the most important member of this group the professor of philosophy from Aix en Provence, *Maurice Blondel* (1861-1949). We may say with Henri Bouillard that from the beginning of our century no one influenced French Catholic theology more powerfully than he did. One must remember in this context that French or French-language Catholic theology occupied a leading position in this period, similar to that of German-language evangelical theology in the Protestant world. Remarkably enough, Blondel's influence rests essentially on his two early works: his dissertation "L'Action" (1893, enlarged and published in 1895; not to be confused with his two-volume work of 1936-1937 which bears the same name) and his *Lettre sur l'Apologétique* (1896, intended as a clarification of "L'Action"). His later works are predominantly elaborations of his fundamental insights, either in a more defensive or a more polemical way.

In France, toward the end of the nineteenth century, the secularization of culture had progressed much more than in Germany. The French intellect regarded as unscientific and subjective, if not outright superstitious, any assertion which exceeded the boundaries of what could be empirically established, and therefore excluded it from discussion. Thus also the dissertation which the young philosopher Blondel presented to the Sorbonne initially encountered surprise and rejection. It was regarded as an attack upon "scientific" naturalism. Besides, "action" was not a philosophical concept and therefore no theme for a philosophical dissertation. In view of the originality and high intellectual level of the text, however, opposition disappeared. Nevertheless, for two years the Ministry of Education was able to prevent the young doctor from being appointed as a teacher of philosophy.[1]

Action, which in the translation of the second edition is almost

---

1. I derive these details from interviews conducted with Blondel by F. Lefèvre in 1927; they were published as *L'Itinéraire philosophique de Maurice Blondel* (Paris, 1966). The book as a whole is most helpful for an understanding of Blondel.

four hundred and fifty pages of tight print,[2] to this day reads like a modern book. In language and method it reminds us again and again of the later French phenomenologists, especially Sartre, and now and then also of Heidegger. With its method of analyzing human existence it anticipates existentialism. It seeks to gain access to life as human life in action. Man's being is being-in-act. His method of analysis is purely immanentistic. Blondel takes as his point of departure all the then-current dogmas of secularized culture: autonomy, determinism, immanence, rationality, etc. He *thinks* them through in a way such that he has to think *through* them. The question that guides him in his analysis comes to expression in the first sentence: "Yes or no, does human life make sense, and does man have a destiny?" (p. 3). Blondel looks for an answer to that question through an analysis of human volition and action. Like Kant, he calls his work "a critique": he searches for the transcendental presuppositions of volition and action in general, but links this search nevertheless with a broad phenomenology of human existence and action. At the same time he employs the empirical, bias-free method of the natural sciences. In this way he hopes to find out the meaning of human life. "It must be enough, for the most intimate orientation of hearts to be revealed, to let the will and action unfold in each individual. . . . It is into action that we shall have to transport the center of philosophy, because there is also to be found the center of life" (p. 13).

Next, Blondel gives a broad presentation and analysis of the several directions human volition and action take. Their ends are as diverse as reality, order, a person's own subjectivity and freedom, family, country and humanity, metaphysics and morality. This one will, which necessarily inhabits everyone, Blondel calls the "willing will" *(volonté voulante)*, from which he distinguishes the "willed will" *(volonté voulue)*, which is the freedom of a person to affirm or to deny the necessary will. The willing will has no rest until it finds rest in the absolute, the one thing needed *(l'unique necessaire,* "The One Thing Necessary," the title of Part IV, I, Third Moment). With his "willed will" man stands in danger of identifying this final reality with one of the many relative objects of his will. He then, in superstitious fashion, deifies the earthly *(l'action superstiteuse,* "Superstitious Action," the title of Part III, Stage 5, Chapter 3). He prematurely ceases to strive and surrenders himself to some "natural religion." "As much as every natural religion is artificial, the same expectation of some religion remains no less natural" (p. 299). Man must

2. Quotations are from the translation of the 2nd edition: M. Blondel, *Action (1893): Essay on a Critique and Science of Practice,* tr. Oliva Blanchette (Notre Dame: University of Notre Dame Press, 1984).

will not only the objects of his action; he must also will the totality, the origin, the creator of his willing. "He has to will, no longer what he wills, no longer life and the use he makes of it, but what in him produces it, criticizes it, and judges it" (p. 301). Hence the idea of God is not an intellectual corollary but a practical certainty inherent in, given with, our action. If nonbeing is impossible and our relative being is inadequate, then philosophy must conceive perfect being as that for which our being strives and that to which we wish to conform. The determination of our action drives us in the direction of our perfect freedom. Here philosophy has to stop. "As soon as we think we know God enough, we no longer know him" (p. 324). "He is the only one that we cannot look for in vain, without ever being able to find him fully" (p. 325). Only if it posits God at the end as a necessity of thought can philosophy remain scientific and preserve its inner coherence. But in virtue of its nature it cannot get past this necessity of thought. Whether God really exists and how he really is must be revealed to us from another source.

Christian revelation, however, starts precisely at the point where the philosophy of action has to stop; it confirms its insights and answers the questions which, to be sure, philosophy can pose but not answer itself. "It is not for human science to inquire whether it [the idea of revelation] is real, nor even whether it is possible: science has to show, in the name of determinism, that it is necessary" (p. 357). Man can and must posit the supernatural order as a necessary hypothesis, indeed as a scientific postulate (p. 446); but he cannot from within his own resources answer the question whether it exists. The closing words of this book read: "If it is permitted to add one word, only one, which goes beyond the domain of human science and the competence of philosophy, the only word able, in the face of Christianity, to express that part, of certitude, the best part, which cannot be communicated because it arises only from the intimacy of totally personal action, one word which would itself be an action, it must be said: 'It exists' [*c'est*]" (p. 446).

In this book Blondel fought on two fronts. On the one hand, he sought to show "its cultured despisers" that religion cannot be denied by philosophy but has to be thought through by it. On the other hand, he rejected the traditional categories of Catholic apologetics, replacing the Thomistic predominance of the intellect with one of the will. Blondel's thinking was not inspired by Thomas but by Augustine and Pascal; he was also conscious of his affinity with Newman.

Catholic theologians initially welcomed his book as fervently as the naturalists rejected it. They did not regard it, however, as a scientific treatise but rather as a psychological analysis with an apologetic purpose. As a result of this misunderstanding Blondel felt obliged to write a further explanation of his method. Three years after the appearance of his dissertation he published a treatise generally referred to as *La Lettre sur l'Apologétique*.[3] In this letter he made clear his position amidst the debates conducted at the time between secular immanentists and Catholic transcendentalists. According to Blondel, secularity and the supernatural determine each other. The method of immanence regards the supernatural as both indispensable and inaccessible to man. Conversely, in revelation this human desire "is itself, so to speak, the human sacrament that is immanent to the divine operation" (pp. 44-45). Here is a comprehensive quotation:

> Since philosophy only considers the supernatural insofar as its concept is immanent within us, and since it regards natural reality as transcendent in view of the knowledge it has of it, it prepares us for a deepening understanding of the reality that we can neither ignore nature nor end with it; that the human order participates in all things and is satisfied by nothing; that our natural being, though not able to perfect itself, is nevertheless indestructible in spite of the murderous demands of the supernatural which it misjudges; and that, even in its radical inadequacy, human action remains coextensive with the divine. (pp. 86-87)

As a result of this publication, a remarkable change took place among French philosophers. This time it was the immanentists who proved to be satisfied with Blondel's understanding of immanence whereas the transcendentalists noted with shock that Blondel's position did not agree with traditional Thomism.[4] They correctly sensed that in Blondel the *seculum* was conceived much more secularly than was the case in Thomas. It was much harder to build a bridge now, and the result was much less harmonious, than was possible in the Middle Ages. Now it could no longer be achieved by way of the intellect. The entire depth dimension of modern inwardness had to be considered. Opponents did not sense that precisely thus Blondel was following in the footprints of Thomas and giving new form to his concerns. For them the "analogy of being" and the adage "Grace does not negate nature but per-

---

3. The full title reads: "Lettre sur les exigences de la pensée contemporaine en matière d'apologétique et sur la méthode de la philosophie dans l'étude du problème religieux." It was published in the *Annales de Philosophie Chrétienne* (Jan.-July, 1896). I am citing the new edition (Paris, 1956).
4. I owe these and other insights in Blondel's position to the inaugural lecture given by G. E. Meuleman at the Free University in Amsterdam: "Maurice Blondel en de apologetiek," Kampen, 1959.

fects it" were only the expression of a rational disposition toward a natural knowledge of God, not a personal disposition toward the supernatural self-disclosure of the redeeming God-in-Christ.

Throughout his life Blondel remained faithful to his view of the immanent transcendence of human existence. We have to bring out one more element. In this voluntative thinker, the elevation of man to the God-likeness of the supernatural life, to *assimilari Deo*, as it is called in Thomas, is not a passive kind of intellectual contemplation which realizes itself harmoniously, but a second birth, both a mortification and a delivery in a single experience. We have to give up our autonomy in order to receive the grace of heteronomy. We must "submit the gift of nature to a new gift which can only be received if we return to God the egoistic use we have made of the gift received first." For Blondel the transition to the supernatural passes through a break, a crisis of the will. In this matter he knew himself to be strongly influenced by Paul.[5]

Not long after the struggle with the traditionalists had begun, Blondel was confronted with another group, the so-called modernists who themselves were partly influenced by him and hoped for his support. Blondel courteously but firmly rejected this partnership. He could not do otherwise.[6] In his view the modernists replaced an intellectualistic "externalism" in relation to nature and supernature by a vitalistic immanentism. "For me, on the other hand, the initial autonomy of our will has to accept and love the real and irreducible heteronomy of divine love; hence comes the annihilation, the submission, the mortification, all these frightful powers of the (divine) will which sovereignly establishes his kingdom in us."[7] Blondel never tired of distinguishing between immanence as a method and immanence as a doctrine. He firmly rejected the second because we can at no time bring forth divine truth from within ourselves.[8]

When Pope Pius X condemned the teaching of modernism in the encyclical *Pascendi dominici gregis* (1907), he did so at this point in part with the same considerations advanced by Blondel: in modernism

5. Cf. esp. *Exigences Philosophiques du Christianisme* (Paris, 1950), the article "De l'Assimilation comme aboutissement et transposition de la théorie de l'analogie," p. 231.

6. Cf. the correspondence, collected under the title "Immanence et Transcendence," as part V in *Lettres Philosophiques de Maurice Blondel* (Paris, 1961), pp. 251-301. The letters make it unlikely that in his rejection of modernism he had been affected by other — opportunistic — motives, as is suggested, e.g., by A. Vidler, *A Variety of Catholic Modernists* (Cambridge, 1970), pp. 80ff., 118ff.

7. *Lettres Philosophiques*, p. 258.

8. Cf. esp. *Lettre Apologétique*, pp. 38-51.

grace is viewed as nature.[9] Popes as diverse as Leo XIII and Pius X valued and protected Blondel. His deviation from the ruling Thomism of the day they permitted in the freedom pertaining to theological discussion.[10]

HENRI DE LUBAC

Most of Blondel's later ideas are elaborations of those found in *Action*. In his case one can hardly speak of development. It could be, however, that experience with his traditionalistic opponents made him cautious. A younger generation of French theologians had been deeply influenced by this philosopher. They were more radical than he in reaching beyond scholasticism to the church fathers and the Scriptures. This *nouvelle théologie* knew, however, what it owed to Blondel, and several representatives of it, especially Henri Bouillard, Henri de Lubac, and Yves de Montcheuil, expressly called themselves his disciples.

Important for our theme in particular is the way in which, following in Blondel's footsteps, de Lubac attempted a fresh interpretation of the theory of the relationship between the natural and the supernatural life. In classical Thomism the two were linked solely in an external fashion: Nature as created has its own natural final goal, one that lies outside communion with God; it is elevated beyond itself to the contemplation of God in virtue of an additional undeserved gift *(donum superadditum, indebitum)* of supernatural life. Blondel, for his part, linked the two internally, on the path of volition and action. As a result they complemented each other in human existence. This inner connection might have blurred their duality. In Blondel, as we noted, this was not the case because in him conversion stands as a break and a bridge between the two worlds. Nevertheless, he was accused of being a disciple of the Augustinian Michael Baius (Louvain), who had rejected the duality of the natural and the supernatural life (the latter also belongs to our created nature) and whose theses had been condemned by Pope Pius V in 1567; they seemed to be too similar to the Reformation doctrine of sin and grace.

9. Cf., e.g., H. Denzinger and A. Schönmetzer, *Enchiridion Symbolorum,* 33rd ed. (Freiburg, 1965), no. 3478: *affirmatio illa modernistarum perabsurda, qua religio quaelibet pro diverso aspectu naturalis una ac supernaturalis dicenda est. Hinc conscientiae ac revelationis promiscua significatio.*

10. About the attitude of the popes to Blondel, see Lefèvre, *Itinéraire,* pp. 58-61.

It was quite clear, however, that Blondel's reasons for entertaining another approach in this regard had a very different background. He did not wish to view human nature as such *(pura natura)* as godless and abandon it to the naturalists of the day. Man is by nature adapted for the message of grace.

Henri de Lubac, born in 1896, Jesuit, disciple and admirer of Blondel, professor at the theological faculty at Lyon-Fourvière, was involved as a soldier in World War I and as a resistance fighter in World War II. Hence the world penetrated deeply into his life in the monastery. In the French Resistance he fought alongside humanists and communists. This experience forced him to think deeply about the relationship between the grace of God and so-called outsiders; hence his publications on Proudhon, Nietzsche, Feuerbach, and *The Drama of Atheist Humanism* (1944; Eng. tr. 1966). These experiences also fed the great theme of his life: the relationship between nature and grace. On that subject he published his *Surnaturel* (1946) and *The Mystery of the Supernatural* (1965; Eng. tr. 1967). The first book was written almost entirely in the form of studies in the history of dogma, the subtitle reading *Études historiques.* In the book, however, it becomes ever more clear to the reader that this form serves the objective of reaching behind the traditional doctrine of the supernatural back to Augustine and of illuminating later developments afresh in the light of him.

Especially important for us is his new interpretation of the ideas of Thomas Aquinas. In distinction from Blondel he saw Thomas as being close to Augustine and the church fathers in general. In his opinion, in Thomas one cannot yet speak of two levels with two distinct final goals. "Holding to the main lines, one observes a direct kinship regarding the relationships of 'nature' and 'the supernatural' between the teaching of the church fathers and that of Saint Thomas of Aquinas." The church fathers make a distinction between the "image" and the "likeness" of God; the first relates to the (spiritual) nature of man, the second to the supernatural end of man. Between the two "there is an organic connection: man was made in the image of God in order that some day he might attain his likeness." De Lubac viewed this as the fundamental paradox of the human spirit: "Unabrogable duality as much as indissoluble unity." "Hence spirit [*Geist*] is desire for God. The whole challenge of the spiritual life will be to liberate this longing and then to transform it." But the aim of this desire is not to conjure up God as the object to which it is entitled. "The spirit does not actually desire after God the way an animal hungers for its prey. It desires him as a gift. It does not at all desire to possess an infinite object: it seeks free and undeserved communion with a personal Being." This is demanded both by his created being and by the sovereignty of God. This desire to see God as he is (the *desiderium naturale videndi Deum per essentiam* in Thomas) does not itself have anything to demand of God, but is the form in which God requires us to transcend the ontological order of our nature by way of the moral order of a free and personal surrender to him. "When this desire demands that it be fulfilled, the reason is that God himself, even if still 'anonymously,' is at the root of it. Natural desire for the supernatural: that is the constant action of God who creates our nature; just as grace in us is the constant action of God who creates the moral order, the order of 'nature' and the order of 'morality', these two orders, embrace all the conditions—the one the essential and necessary; the other the personal and free conditions—suited to allow us to attain our natural goal; both are inwardly held together in one and the same world, a unique world which, though it contains completely natural elements, one can call a supernatural world precisely for that reason."[11]

Hence nature and "super-nature" no longer constitute two separate levels, as they often seem to do in post-Tridentine theology. They constitute the two sides of what as a rule is called human nature: the "is" and the "ought," the structure given to us and the realization to which we are called. Indeed, on the Christian view, man is created for an (unmanipulable) encounter with God. This points to a tension which de Lubac describes as "paradox." This tension is lost when the inseparable unity of the two aspects, the ontological and moral, is resolved into a duality. Unremittingly de Lubac combated, as a pure abstraction, the scholastic doctrine of a pure nature with its possibilities. Also, he particularly defended himself against the suspicion that his teaching implied that revelation and faith are realities given with our nature or demanded by our nature. His real concern, however, was still something else. He saw that one could not master but only promote the growing secularism of European culture if one conceived—even if solely as an abstraction— a pure, autonomous human nature (in Thomas this was an intellectual autonomy) apart from revelation and surrender to divine love. De Lubac questioned whether one could appeal to Thomas for this position. At the same time he is convinced that the post-Tridentine Thomism of the Baroque period contributed significantly to advancing secularization and that we now need other lines of thought to bring about the subordination—which Thomas fought for—of the "secular" (the world in an Aristotelian sense) to revelation. A theory of two anthropological levels makes it far too easy for secularized man to settle down, comfortably

11. The quotations occur in *Surnaturel* (Paris, 1946), pp. 475, 483, 487; most are from the "Conclusion. Exigence divine et désir naturel."

and godlessly, on the ground floor. This kind of person should learn to see that "Thou hast created us for thyself and our heart is restless until it rests in thee" (Augustine). It is precisely with the "nature" in which modern man entrenches himself against God that his "un-naturalness" must be uncovered.

In 1950, in the encyclical *Humani Generis*, Pope Pius XII opposed a variety of teachings, mostly those of the French *nouvelle théologie* which was dominant at the time, teachings of which he believed, as the subtitle says, that they "threatened to undermine the foundations of Catholic doctrine." He called upon theologians to return to the basic principles both of Thomistic philosophy and of Thomistic theology. In this encyclical especially the replacement of the primacy of the intellect (Thomas) by voluntarist or existentialist ideas was sharply repudiated.

In *Humani Generis* the ideas of de Lubac's *Surnaturel* are only touched upon in passing, but at the same time clearly repudiated (§ 26): "Others destroy the gratuity of the supernatural order, since God, they say, cannot create intellectual beings without ordering and calling them to the beatific vision." It seems to follow from this sentence that curial theology wants to cling to the idea of a pure nature in order to be able to preserve the "gratuity" of grace. One is not shown how the subordinate clause relates to the main clause which precedes it. There is no attempt to respond to de Lubac's assertion that such a subordinate proposition does not at all lead to the inference of the main clause.

De Lubac took this remark deeply to heart. At the advice of the General of the Jesuit order he suspended his teaching activities that same year until, in 1958, Pope John XXIII rehabilitated him. This pope even appointed him, like so many other theologians previously under suspicion, an adviser to the Vatican Council (1961-1965). In this period de Lubac published his second book on the same theme under the title *The Mystery of the Supernatural* (1965; Eng. tr. 1967). Here the concept of paradox, used also earlier, is at the center. The main thoughts have remained the same. He continues to reject sharply what he calls "the dualist or, perhaps better, the separatist thesis." Especially telling is his warning against the practical implications:

> While wishing to protect the supernatural from any contamination, people had in fact exiled it altogether—both from intellectual and from social life—leaving the field free to be taken over by secularism. Today that secularism, following its course, is beginning to enter the minds even of Christians. They too seek to find a harmony with all things based upon an idea of nature which might be acceptable to a deist or an atheist: everything

that comes from Christ, everything that should lead to him, is pushed so far into the background as to look like disappearing for good. The last word in Christian progress and the entry into adulthood would then appear to consist in a total secularization which would expel God not merely from the life of society, but from culture and even from personal relationships.[12]

In the very next section, however, following the example of Blondel, he turns just as forcefully against a reviving modernist immanentism. Grace indeed is no part of nature; it is God's undeserved personal disposition of favor. It is fully undeserved—and still we have been created precisely for this purpose. That is the paradox one must be sure to cling to. In this connection de Lubac believes he is in accord with *Humani Generis,* although he concedes that the conclusion in *Surnaturel,* "at the request of various people," was sketched too rapidly and fragmentarily. In this new book he aims rather to stress the duality of the divine initiative and the divine gift and so amplify his first study without claiming to be complete. It should be completely clear, however, that the hypothesis of a "pure nature" is inadequate and not useful (p. 67). With equal emphasis de Lubac asserts the priority of the supernatural: "Thus, it is never nature which of itself has any call on the supernatural: it is the supernatural which, so to say, must summon up nature before nature can be in a position to receive it" (p. 124). Within this framework, he at the same time stresses the duality more strongly than before (to fend off gnosticism, Buddhism, and all naturalistic mysticism): "Between nature as it exists and the supernatural for which God destines it, the distance is as great, the difference as radical, as that between non-being and being: for to pass from one to the other is not merely to pass into 'more being', but to pass to a different type of being. It is a crossing, by grace, of an impassable barrier" (pp. 107-8).

If I understand de Lubac correctly, he does not, by saying this, in any way readmit "pure nature" through a back door but, in the manner of Blondel, thinks here of the mortification of the old man and of the regeneration without which sinful man cannot attain to communion with God.

One cannot avoid noting that the response of Catholic theologians to growing secularization is of a different nature from that of the liberal German theology of the preceding generation. Here resistance is

12. H. de Lubac, *The Mystery of the Supernatural,* tr. Rosemary Sheed (New York: Herder and Herder, 1967), pp. xi-xii. The concluding words of the preface are: *Fecisti nos ad te, Deus* (Augustine).

not to a church which allows too little space and freedom to the secular, but to a theological tradition which has made too much allowance for human autonomy and as a result has forgotten to call the world to Jesus Christ and to repentance. In that regard the *nouvelle théologie* is a parallel to "dialectical theology." It does not surprise us at all that precisely from its midst there came much understanding for the theology of Karl Barth. The accentuation of the relative independence of nature over against grace continued to separate it from Barth, who could see in it only "the accursed word 'and'"—nature *and* grace.[13]

KARL RAHNER

This theologian, certainly the most outstanding Catholic theologian in the third quarter of our century, is marked—despite and in his astonishing many-sidedness—by the fact that he made the principle of transcendentality the basis of his theology and applied it to all areas of dogmatic theology. He was born in 1904 in Freiburg/Breisgau and was admitted to the Jesuit order at the age of eighteen. Since 1948 he was professor of dogmatics and/or the philosophy of religion, first at Innsbruck, later in Munich (1964), and finally, up to his retirement, in Munster (1967-1971). He died in 1984.

The dynamic of his mature conviction was consciously anthropocentric. For "as soon—which is self-evident—as man is conceived as the being of absolute transcendence toward God, the 'anthropocentricity' and 'theocentricity' are no longer opposites but strictly one and the same (stated from two perspectives)."[14] For that reason Rahner cannot and need not go back behind Heidegger's analysis of human existence and the Copernican revolution of Kant. His point of departure is man as the subject of his world—and on the basis of this subject-status he pushed through to the transsubjective that is given with this status. This procedure reminds us of Blondel, though Rahner was barely influenced by him.[15]

13. B. Wentsel, *Natuur en Genade* (Kampen: Kok, 1970) (Dutch with a French summary), offers a broad overview on the theme of nature and grace in the Catholic theology of the last few decades.

14. I found this quotation in an essay on Rahner by J. B. Metz in *Tendenzen der Theologie im 20. Jahrhundert*, ed. H. J. Schultz (Stuttgart/Berlin: Kreuz-Verlag, 1966), p. 517.

15. As a student, however, he was profoundly influenced by the Belgian Jesuit J. Maréchal (1878-1944), who had affinities with Blondel. This "transcen-

The principle of subjectivity has for its counterpart that of transcendentality because "this subject is fundamentally and by its very nature pure openness for absolutely everything, for being as such." "This experience is called *transcendental* experience because it belongs to the necessary and inalienable structures of the knowing subject itself, and because it consists precisely in the transcendence beyond any particular group of possible objects or of categories. Transcendental experience is the experience of transcendence, in which experience the structure of the subject and therefore also the ultimate structure of every conceivable object of knowledge are present together and in identity."[16]

The words *structures* and *subject* may remind us of Kant and lead us to look for an understanding of transcendence in his direction. But transcendence as "experience" directs us toward phenomenology and the analysis of existence. Often Rahner's terminology is philosophically unclear.[17] He himself occasionally calls it deliberately unphilosophical. In any case it is certain that man does not in transcendence project himself but experiences "the infinite horizon of being making itself manifest."

> Whenever man in his transcendence experiences himself as questioning, as disquieted by the appearance of being, as open to something ineffable, he cannot understand himself as subject in the sense of an *absolute* subject, but only in the sense of one who receives being, ultimately only in the sense of grace. In this context "grace" means the freedom of the ground of being which gives being to man, a freedom which man experiences in his finiteness and contingency, and means as well what we call "grace" in a more strictly theological sense.[18]

The reader may be astonished at this rapid transition from the language of philosophy to that of theology—this "interlocking of philosophy and

---

dentalistic Thomist," with Kant, proceeded from subjectivity in order to show that Kant stopped halfway and that his method can only find its consequence and completion in a metaphysic of a Thomistic kind. Cf. his five-volume work *Le point de départ de la métaphysique* (Brussels, 1922-1926), vol. 4 (posthumous), 1947.

16. K. Rahner, *Foundations of Christian Faith: An Introduction to the Idea of Christianity*, tr. William V. Dych (New York: Seabury, 1978), p. 20.

17. On the obscurity and ambiguity of Rahner's terminology of transcendentality, see F. Greiner, *Die Menschlichkeit der Offenbarung: Die transzendentale Grundlegung der Theologie bei Karl Rahner* (Munich: Kaiser, 1978).

18. K. Rahner, *Foundations*, p. 34.

theology," as Rahner calls it, corresponds precisely with his purpose. Just as in him the notions of subject, person, responsibility, freedom, and spirit flow together and into the concept of transcendence, so the notions of mystery, holiness, love, grace, and God (as person) all spring from it.

> Hence when we reflect here upon transcendence as will and as freedom, we must also take into account the character of the term and source of transcendence as love. It is a term which possesses absolute freedom, and this term is at work in freedom and in love as that which is nameless and which is not at our disposal, for we are completely at its disposal. It is what opens up my own transcendence as freedom and as love. But the term of transcendence is always and originally the source of the mystery which offers itself. This term itself opens our transcendence; it is not established by us and by our own power as though we were absolute subjects. Hence if transcendence moves in freedom and in love towards a term which itself opens this transcendence, then we can say that that which is nameless and which is not at our disposal, and at whose complete disposal we exist, that this very thing is present in loving freedom, and this is what we mean when we say "holy mystery."[19]

Nor do we have to leave the matter at that.

> Insofar as this subjective, non-objective luminosity of the subject in its transcendence is always orientated towards the holy mystery, the knowledge of God is always present unthematically and without name, and not just when we begin to speak of it. All talk about it, which necessarily goes on, always only points to this transcendental experience as such, an experience in which he whom we call "God" encounters man in silence, encounters him as the absolute and the incomprehensible, as the term of his transcendence which cannot really be incorporated into any system of coordinates. When this transcendence is the transcendence of *love*, it also experiences this term as the *holy mystery*.[20]

Here the question arises whether, from a desire to fend off the neo-scholastic dualism of nature and grace and its abstract notion of "pure nature," Rahner himself does not imperceptibly let nature pass over into the domain of supernatural grace, as a result of which a sort of

19. Ibid., pp. 65-66.
20. Ibid., p. 21.

naturalization of grace threatens. Rahner's reply is that, on the contrary, what he advocates is a sort of supernaturalization of what we call "nature." For him creation and created human nature must be understood solely as the infrastructure of the grace-conditioned unity of the Creator and the created in the incarnation of God, and in the final goal of the beatific vision of God based on it. Since redemption in Christ has become a reality, since it is God's will that all human beings be saved, and since faith is the necessary condition for salvation, one must assume, says Rahner, that God makes himself known to every human being and enables him, in freedom through his moral actions, to accept or reject the offer of salvation. In the abstract, one has to separate nature and supernature, but:

> In the concrete actualization of existence . . . there is no knowledge of God which is purely natural. . . . In a subsequent theological reflection I can indeed specify elements in the concrete knowledge of God which I ascribe and can ascribe to nature, to the realization of man's essence as such. But the concrete knowledge of God as a question, as a call which is affirmed or denied, is always within the dimension of man's supernatural determination. . . . We call this orientation grace, and it is an inescapable existential of man's whole being even when he closes himself to it freely by rejecting it.[21]

To understand how Rahner arrived at this (seemingly or really) extreme counter-position, vis-à-vis the neo-scholastic "extrinsicism," we must consider his objection to de Lubac. De Lubac so directly aimed nature toward the supernatural that the sovereignty of God and the gratuity of grace seemed threatened. The encyclical *Humani generis,* as we noted, sounded a warning at this point. In his second book about the supernatural, de Lubac then sought to avoid this danger by developing the concept of paradox. Rahner viewed this as inadequate: If one so strongly orients nature to grace it must by that token acquire a claim on grace. "Thus if the ordination cannot be detached from the nature, the fulfilment of the ordination, from *God's* point of view precisely, is exacted. And, as all admit, just this is false, and so must the presupposition be."[22] He therefore approached the matter from the opposite direction: the disposition toward grace belongs to the supernatural order as much as grace itself. At the same time, like de Lubac, he wanted to see the secu-

---

21. Ibid., p. 57.

22. K. Rahner, *Theological Investigations,* vol. 1: *God, Christ, Mary and Grace,* 2nd ed., tr. Cornelius Ernst (Baltimore: Helicon, 1965), p. 306.

lar existence of man in all its depth and breadth in relation to the revelation of salvation.

The resultant of these two lines of thought became his theory of the "supernatural existential" which is present to every human being along with existence. "Here we must note something else, which should be borne more clearly in mind than is usually the case. Acts inspired supernaturally by grace are not confined to the justified" (p. 179).[23] "We may say that the supernatural transcendence is always present in every man who has reached the age of moral reason" (p. 180). "Our actual nature is *never* 'pure' nature. It is a nature installed in a supernatural order which man can never leave, even as a sinner and unbeliever. . . . And these 'existentials' of man's concrete, 'historical' nature are not purely states of being beyond consciousness. They make themselves felt in the experience of man. By simple reflexion on himself, in the light of natural reason, he cannot simply and clearly distinguish them from the natural spiritual activity which is the manifestation of his nature" (p. 183). In the light of this one has to ask how this supernatural "natural religion" relates to faith in Jesus Christ. The answer is: "The preaching is the express awakening of what is already present in the depths of man's being, not by nature, but by grace. But it is a grace which always surrounds man, even the sinner and the unbeliever, as the inescapable setting of his existence" (p. 181). In this context belongs Rahner's familiar theory of "anonymous Christianity."

These several lines of thought together form a fairly involved structure. Rahner has to distinguish at least three levels which he would prefer to link together closely. There is pure nature and there is the supernatural Word-revelation. But, to be distinguished from these two, there is also the so-called transcendentality of man which constitutes the "medium" between nature and grace; but because it is the counterpart of a universal revelation of grace and of a universal offer of salvation, it serves simultaneously for the "realization" of the gratuity of grace, and must therefore be viewed as itself belonging to the order of grace and hence as a "supernatural existential." One asks, What then is left of "pure nature" in man after being stripped of supernatural transcendentality? The answer is: " 'Nature' in the theological sense . . ., i.e. as the concept contraposed to the supernatural, is consequently a remainder concept *(Restbegriff)*. By that is meant that starting as we have done, a reality must be postulated in man which remains over when the supernatural ex-

---

23. These quotations have been taken from the well-known foundational essay "Nature and Grace," in *Theological Investigations,* vol. 4: *More Recent Writings,* tr. Kevin Smyth (Baltimore: Helicon, 1966), pp. 165-88.

istential as unexacted is subtracted, and must have a meaning and a possibility of existence even when the supernatural existential is thought of as lacking."[24] At the same time, however, Rahner emphasizes even more strongly that this pure nature can never be found in "a chemically pure" state, separated from its supernatural existential. Generally, in order not to lapse into the abhorred dualism, he wants to keep the boundaries between the anthropological domains as fluid as possible. Hence in his work statements occur like:

> The 'definition' of the created spirit is its 'openness' to being as such: as created, it is open to the fullness of reality; as spirit, it is open to absolute reality in general. It is not therefore surprising that the grandeur of the (varying) fulfilment of this openness (which does not of itself imply necessarily an absolute and unsurpassable fulfilment and yet, as absolute openness, still has a sense without such fulfilment) cannot be recognized at once as 'due' or 'undue.' And yet the basic essence of man, his nature as such openness (transcendence) can be perfectly well established. The initial elements of such fulfilment . . . are in fact tributary to that divine force which impels the created spirit—by grace—to an absolute fulfilment. Hence in them grace is experienced *and* the natural being of man.
>
> For the essence of man is such that it is experienced where grace is experienced, since grace is only experienced where the spirit naturally is. And vice versa: where spirit is experienced in the actual order of things, it is a supernaturally elevated spirit.[25]

In the end the reader is left with the impression that in Rahner the supernatural (in contrast with traditional church doctrine) is to such a high degree a self-evident and universal "existential" that in ordinary language it can really only be described as "nature." Had he used this language, however, he would have violated the official teachings of the church. Hence he had to design an intricate construction in which the boundary between nature and grace was moved downward and the word *nature,* having been emptied, became an abstraction. Thus the avoidance of the heresy of a grace that was "owed" to nature led to a much greater and graver one: the complete universalization of the supernatural. At this point Rahner, it seems to me, though he employs a

---

24. *Theological Investigations,* 1:313-14. For a good insight into Rahner's line of thought, cf. also the Dutch dissertation by B. Wentsel, "Natuur en Genade," esp. pp. 131-39.

25. Rahner, *Theological Investigations,* 4:183-84.

more orthodox idiom, comes very close to the (condemned) immanentism of the modernists.

As we said at the outset, Rahner not only used the principle of transcendentality as (anthropological) foundation for his theology but then proceeded to apply it to the entire content of dogmatics, on a scale and with a consistency that I have not seen in other Catholic theologians.

Characteristically, the principle of transcendentality even controls the three short formulas of faith Rahner proposed, of which the first, which he calls the *theological* one, reads as follows: "The incomprehensible point of reference towards which human transcendence is orientated, and which cannot, either absolutely or in the concrete conditions of human living, be attained to by speculation alone, or in merely conceptual terms, is called God. And it imparts itself to man in the concrete and historical conditions of his existence by an act of forgiving love as his true consummation. The supreme eschatological point of God's self-bestowal in history, in which this self-bestowal is revealed as irrevocably victorious, is called Jesus Christ."[26]

It is neither possible nor necessary to examine here all of Rahner's applications of the transcendentality principle. We shall restrict ourselves to three examples which we shall indicate briefly. They are Rahner's Christology, his theory of the non-Christian religions, and his view of death and dying.

(1) In virtue of his transcendental starting point Christology presented Rahner with special problems—problems of which he was fully aware. In his *Foundations* he refers in a subtitle (p. 81) to "The Tension Between a Transcendental Starting Point and Historical Religion." In the existential of his transcendence *homo religiosus* turns upward, toward the infinite and absolute, away from the finite and objectifiable (Rahner calls them the "categorical") conditions of our being-in-the-world. The Christian faith, however, directs our gaze precisely upon this world, upon history, the history of salvation, and especially upon the incarnation of God as the center of history. But how, for the transcendental eye, can the intra-mundane ever disclose the supra-mundane? At this point Rahner introduces the expression "mediated immediacy" (pp. 83ff.). The experience of the transcendent takes place after all by way of the categorical as an experience that is simultaneously given with, and distinguished from, the categorical. The two experiences are enclosed together as in a circle. Of course, this universal religio-philosophical idea cannot as such sustain faith in the incar-

26. Rahner, *Theological Investigations*, vol. 11: *Confrontations I*, tr. David Bourke (New York: Seabury, 1974), p. 238.

nation, but it is a necessary presupposition for a possible connection between transcendence and incarnation.

Rahner extensively and carefully developed this connection in a book on Christology which he published in collaboration with his New Testament colleague Wilhelm Thüsing, a work from which we glean the following lines of thought.[27] He proceeded from the assumption that our relationship to Jesus Christ is an absolute one. "Where this relationship is not realized and interpreted as absolute in history, (explicit) Christianity ceases to exist" (p. 19). But how can something so categorical as an event in history be absolute? The bridge is built by describing Jesus as "the absolute (eschatological) bringer of salvation" (p. 18). As transcendental being man is certainly he who (also) hopes that "the incomprehensible mystery" "bestows itself as the fulfilment of the highest claim of existence" (p. 22). "In any case . . . God can only be self-revealingly present in the domain of the categorical (without which there is no transcendental givenness of God for us!) in the mode of *promise*" as negating transcendence of the categorical "and of *death* as the most radical occurrence of that negation which belongs to the essence of every historical revelation and becomes absolute [in death], because nothing categorical can be hoped for anymore, so only the hope of 'everything' or mere despair is left" (p. 23). "Hence if man affirms his existence as permanently valid and worth saving . . . then in hope he affirms his own resurrection" (p. 39). "This transcendental hope of resurrection is the horizon of understanding for the faith-experience of the resurrection of Jesus" (p. 39) which simultaneously, as we heard, includes the transcendental necessity of his death. The unity found here of the transcendence-"postulate" and historical facticity at the same time implies a "resolution of the verification problem of Christology" (p. 47). The Christ-event, to be sure, is the answer to a universal understanding of existence which embraces within itself a "searching" or "anonymous" Christology because for its fulfillment it is on the lookout for three things: absolute love of neighbor, a radical readiness to

27. Karl Rahner and W. Thüsing, *Christologie—systematisch und exegetisch* (Freiburg: Herder, 1972). Rahner's systematic exposition comes first (pp. 18-78). On pp. 82-305 Thüsing develops (against Rahner) a biblical-theological alternative to Chalcedon, to which Rahner does not respond. But even apart from its relationship to Rahner's thesis, Thüsing's exposition deserves attention, though to the best of my knowledge systematic theologians have not dealt with it. [The English translation of this work is entitled *A New Christology*, tr. David Smith and Verdant Green (New York: Seabury, 1980). In it Rahner's systematic exposition is so different from the German original, however, that it cannot be viewed as a translation. The quoted sections here are my rendering of the German.—TRANS.]

die, and a well-founded hope for the absolute future of God. This can be summarized by saying that "man is on the lookout for the absolute bringer of salvation and affirms his having come or his future coming in every total act of his existence as directed (at least unthematically) by grace toward the immediacy of God" (p. 63). For that reason Rahner wants to supplement or correct Chalcedonian Christology which is "from above" by a transcendental or fundamental-theological one "from below" (without changing its material identity).

In one of the last lines of the "Conclusion" Rahner writes: "He who accepts his humanity totally and without reservation (and it remains unclear who really does this), that person has accepted the Son of man because in him God has accepted man" (p. 71). Here, as in the theory of the "supernatural existential," one senses how that which is Christian and particular threatens to be absorbed by what is human and universal.[28]

(2) According to Rahner, *the non-Christian religions* can only be understood in a correct *theologia religionum* if they can be conceived as expression of the supernatural existential of transcendence. In his article entitled "Christianity and the Non-Christian Religions," he offered a beginning in that direction which we shall trace here.[29] In this article he poses two theses alongside, and against, each other: (a) "Christianity understands itself as the absolute religion, intended for all men, which cannot recognize any other religion beside itself as of equal right" (p. 118). (b) "Until the moment when the gospel really enters into the historical situation of an individual, a non-Christian religion (even outside the Mosaic religion) . . . contains . . . supernatural elements arising out of the grace which is given to men as a gratuitous gift on account of Christ. For this reason a non-Christian religion can be recognized as a *lawful* religion (although only in different degrees) . . ." (p. 121). He bases the first part of this second thesis on the Christian certainty that God desires the salvation of everyone. Then he establishes the connection with the first thesis as follows:

> And this salvation willed by God is the salvation won by Christ, the salvation of supernatural grace which divinizes man, the salvation of the beatific vision. It is a salvation really intended for

28. From these lines of thought one perceives how difficult it was for Rahner to establish the link between anthropological transcendentality and the historicity of revelation. In the work of F. Greiner, *Die Menschlichkeit der Offenbarung,* the problematics of this relationship are sharply analyzed. Cf. esp. p. 279.

29. Rahner, *Theological Investigations,* vol. 5: *Later Writings,* tr. Karl-H. Kruger (Baltimore: Helicon, 1966), pp. 115-34.

all those millions upon millions of men who lived perhaps a million years before Christ—and also for those who have lived after Christ—in nations, cultures and epochs of a very wide range which were still completely shut off from the viewpoint of those living in the light of the New Testament. If, on the one hand, we conceive salvation as something specifically *Christian,* if there is no salvation apart from Christ, if according to Catholic teaching the supernatural divinization of man can never be replaced merely by good will on the part of man but is necessary as something itself given in this earthly life; and if, on the other hand, God has really, truly and seriously intended this salvation for all men—then these two aspects cannot be reconciled in any other way than by stating that every human being is really and truly exposed to the influence of divine, supernatural grace which offers an interior union with God and by means of which God communicates himself whether the individual takes up an attitude of acceptance or of refusal towards this grace. (pp. 122-23)

The absoluteness of the Christian revelation on the one hand and the universal will to salvation on the other together lead to the result of what is from then on described as "anonymous Christianity." Hence the third thesis is: "If the second thesis is correct, then Christianity does not simply confront the member of an extra-Christian religion as a mere non-Christian but as someone who can and must already be regarded in this or that respect as an anonymous Christian" (p. 131). From here the reasoning goes on to the relationship between nature and grace which we treated earlier. The conclusion follows directly from this fundamental position. In its elaboration and manifold progression of levels we need not follow it here.

(3) *Dying and death* are also themes which are freshly illumined by Rahner's transcendentality principle. As far as I can see, Rahner himself does not link these themes so explicitly with the transcendentality principle as he did in the case of the two preceding examples. Presumably the reason for this is that, fighting through a maze of exegetical, philosophical, and especially official doctrinal pronouncements, he had somehow to blaze a trail on which there was little room left for his own terminology. Nevertheless, the principle of transcendentality is fully present here and is applied in a way which has rendered Rahner's "theology of death" striking, fascinating, and controversial.[30]

30. K. Rahner, *On the Theology of Death,* tr. Charles H. Henkey (New York: Herder and Herder, 1961); idem, *Theological Investigations,* vol. 13: *Theology,*

Death for man not only has a passive side (as it does for an animal) but also an active. After all, man has not only "nature" but also "spirit." As spirit (i.e., freedom), man is made for self-realization. Even death, as nature, has to serve this goal. For the separation of the soul from the body in death does not mean that the soul becomes a-cosmic; rather it becomes all-cosmic, experiencing and codetermining reality as a whole.[31] "In other words, Adam could have brought his personal life to its perfect consummation in its bodily form through a 'death' which would have been a pure, active self-affirmation."[32] By sin, however, this goal has been undone and man estranged from God suffers death in a purely passive fashion as fate. Contrasting with this passive death is the dying of Jesus Christ in which the divine goal as active consummation is realized. Through this act Jesus himself becomes all-cosmic for the benefit of the whole of humanity. "Through Christ's death, his spiritual reality, which he possessed from the beginning, enacted in his life, and brought to consummation in his death, becomes open to the whole world and is inserted into this world as a permanent destiny of real-ontological kind."[33] By their union with Christ the death of believers becomes a liberating "dying with Christ." "The trinity of Faith, Hope and Charity makes death itself the highest act of believing, hoping, loving. . . . In so far as these fundamental acts become constituents of death as an act of man, death itself is changed; the dreadful falling into the hands of the living God, which death must appear as a manifestation of sin, becomes in reality: 'Into thy hands I commend my spirit.'"[34]

Thus death becomes the supreme act of freedom. "Eternal life is not the 'other side' so far as our personal history is concerned, but rather the radical interiority, now liberated and brought to full self-realization, of that personal history of freedom of ours which we are living through even now and which, once it has been fully brought to birth in death, can no longer be lost."[35] The passive element is now totally overshadowed by the active: "Death as final event is the absolute powerless-

---

Anthropology, Christology, tr. David Bourke (New York: Seabury, 1975), pp. 169-86. For a brief and helpful summary by Rahner himself, cf. *Sacramentum Mundi: An Encyclopedia of Theology,* 6 vols., ed. K. Rahner, et al. (New York: Herder and Herder, 1968-1970), 2:58-62.

31. Cf. esp. *On the Theology of Death,* pp. 21-39.
32. Ibid., p. 42.
33. Ibid., p. 71.
34. Ibid., pp. 79-80.
35. *Theological Investigations,* 13:175.

ness of man, in which we certainly also become too powerless to conceive of death or of God. But the dying man, who of his freedom possesses his own life, nevertheless inescapably confronts death with a demand that it must constitute the sum total of his life as an act of freedom in which the whole of life is gathered up. For the very nature of freedom and its claim to the absolute dignity of responsibility and of love belonging to it cannot give its assent to a mere empty draining away of life."[36] In the last two quotations this view is first grounded theologically, then essentially philosophically. For Rahner the two lines of thought are reciprocally supportive.

Is not the result a too titanic line of thinking? Rahner, however, sees it verified, so to speak, in the attitude of the martyrs toward death. For good reason he concluded his *On the Theology of Death* with an excursus, "On Martyrdom," "a moving and blessed event testifying gloriously to man's free belief and his entry through this act of total freedom of faith, born from grace, into the infinite freedom of God."[37]

THEOLOGICAL VALIDITY

With the anthropological-theological theory of the transcendental structure of human existence, the vanguard among Catholic theologians turned away from a wooden and sterile scholasticism and attempted to open up new roads for a genuine encounter between the (Catholic) church and the secularized world. Within the church, despite conservative and particularly curial resistance, this attempt has proved to be very successful. This success is evident also from the fact that even its opponents increasingly have to employ this more modern idiom to be still heard at all.

To many Protestant theologians, however, even this new tradition will feel strange. Through the surface of existentialist language one will always still see the old dichotomy of nature and grace. For Reformation theologians, as the reader knows, it is the contrast between sin and grace, instead of the two-story structure of nature and grace, which determines the structure of theology. That, at least, is how it is frequently put by the theologians of the Reformation. If that were the whole story, there would, from a Protestant point of view, be hardly anything of significance to be discerned in this Catholic change of concepts; the gap be-

36. Ibid., pp. 179-80 [with a minor alteration.—TRANS.]
37. *On the Theology of Death*, p. 127.

tween the Catholic and the Protestant mode of thought would be as wide after the change as it was before.

Still, it clearly emerged from our preceding reflections on the problematics of Protestant theology since Kant that, at least in their prolegomena, liberal and mediating theology had to appropriate a way of posing questions which came very close to that of Thomas Aquinas. These theologies looked passionately for convergences, transitions, and parallels between the post-Enlightenment way of thinking and the gospel—as Thomas looked for them with a view to the immanentism of the Averroistic Aristotelianism which fascinated the leading minds of the thirteenth century. It is not by accident that men like Schleiermacher and, in our time, Tillich also exerted strong influence on Catholic theology because it correctly recognized the interests and concerns of these men as its own. Nature—in other words, the created structure of human existence—is for all of them the infrastructure which persists despite and in sin, an infrastructure on which the grace of revelation builds and without which it would be unintelligible. The difference consists in the fact that Protestant theology is not burdened in this connection by inherited conceptual models and can therefore find its way much sooner and more effectively in this modern way of thinking.

If anyone should think that these observations apply only to liberal theology, he should consider the close proximity to the Thomistic pattern of Karl Barth's theology, at least after *Church Dogmatics*, 3/1. In him grace is not only God's response to sin but also, and from the very beginning, the fulfillment of the created and threatened world. The covenant of grace, indeed, is the inner ground of creation. The statement, "Eternal life as the continuance of man in fellowship with God Himself, in the *consortium divinitatis*, is not in any way assured to man simply because he is the creature of God," could have been by Rahner but it comes from Barth.[38]

From within the central perspective of Scripture one can regard the nature-grace problematic as a speculative area. But there are times in which people so strongly rebel against grace in the name of nature that theology sees itself obliged especially to testify that "all things were created through him [Christ] and for [with a view to] him" (Col. 1:16), and must therefore disclose their limitations and referential character in the light of him. In such times Catholic as well as Protestant theology, for all their differences in emphasis and conceptual idiom, share a common concern. These differences must not be covered up. Catholic theology will often (but not always) look for a solution to problems in an

38. Barth, *Church Dogmatics*, 4/1:72.

authentic knowledge of God even outside Christ, whereas Protestant theology will tend to think more rigorously in terms of Christ. It will therefore often (but not always) regard the "transcendence" terminology with distrust as a way of rendering "nature" innocuous.

In my opinion, Blondel is a model of the convergence of concerns, even in a context of different terminologies, precisely because in his thinking (influenced by Augustine and Pascal) the themes "nature and grace" and "sin and grace" remain interlocked. As a result both the world in its secularity and the gospel in its critical sovereignty are taken seriously and the one is not cheaply cancelled out by the other. Between the two there yawns a gulf which can be bridged only by the surrender of our autonomy, by "mortification" and second birth.[39]

In de Lubac these lines of thought are not as prominent because he tends rather to remain close to the structures and concepts of the Middle Ages. Nevertheless, his idea of "paradox" is fruitful; by this idea he wishes to express (whether happily or not I shall not judge) that on the one hand man is created for an encounter with God and on the other that this encounter cannot be staged or caused to happen at will. We are created with a view to an encounter which can only be brought about from the other side. In this concern he reminds us especially of Emil Brunner. In any event, Protestant theologians must not reject the concept of "gratuity" as such because it seeks to protect the sovereignty of God in the act of encounter.

Undoubtedly the apex of the theology of transcendence is formed by the wide-ranging thought of Rahner. In him one senses throughout that to a high degree it derives from his own authentic experience — from where he is in his own existence. He observes everywhere how man is driven past the limits of his secular and horizontal view (Rahner: "categoricality"), interpreting this experience predominantly in the sense of modern man's autonomous passion for freedom. This understanding, of course, entails far-reaching theological consequences. At the same time it leads in his thinking to an extrapolation from the transcendentality principle which must be felt to be hypothetical and artificial. Is man in fact essentially and everywhere a being driven

39. One can, with the Reformed G. E. Meuleman (cf. n. 4 above), adduce as criticism of Blondel that he puts far too much stock in apologetic proofs (op. cit., p. 28); behind this is concealed an optimism of reason which is more Catholic than Protestant. But in Blondel one must also acknowledge Pascal's concept of reason as an operative factor. For the rest, the question-answer methodology of the Protestant Paul Tillich is certainly not far removed from the Catholic theory of transcendence.

by the need for transcendence and the question of meaning?[40] Such a "universal" anthropology as Rahner's is conceivable only in a well-to-do and highly educated world. Objections multiply where, under the pressure of an incidental comment in *Humani Generis*, Rahner saw himself forced to construe the relationship between nature and grace in such a complex fashion that as a result the gain of his transcendentality principle was again largely lost. Rahner himself sensed the tension between his transcendentality principle and the historicity of revelation but was not able, it seems to me, convincingly to resolve it. In Rahner the theme of sin-and-grace remains incorporated in, and subordinated to, the theme of nature-and-grace. Blondel's view of "mortification" precisely in connection with the relationship between nature and grace is no factor in Rahner's too-harmonious construal of that relationship. A kind of Christian idealism, optimism, and imperialism ("anonymous Christianity"!) permeates all his work. All that is natural is so consistently elevated into the sphere of the supernatural that it can only create the impression of a grand naturalization of the supernatural. By means of a series of swift apologetic leaps, that which is "secular" is "baptized" into Christianity. Breaks, paradoxes, and discontinuities are never denied by this astute thinker; they are, however, all too quickly incorporated into the framework of his thinking. As a result this grand theological project seems to overshoot the goal of a confrontation between the gospel and the modern world. For the (restricted) application of the notion of transcendentality we should—presumably—not go beyond the boundaries set by Blondel.

40. In his *Foundations of Christian Faith*, Rahner underscores much more than before the non-self-evident character and repressibility of the sense of transcendence.

CHAPTER XVI

North America: From Social Gospel to Neo-Orthodoxy

THE THREE LEVELS OF AMERICAN CHRISTIANITY

When we dealt with Anglican theology, it became clear how far the Anglo-Saxon way of thinking was removed from that of the European continent. This observation applies still more to the cultural and ecclesiastical difference between the United States and Europe. To make this assertion we need not even bring into view the well-known fact that the United States is a melting pot of nations and cultures. We can simply proceed from the reality that the United States still, to a large extent, bears an Anglo-Saxon stamp. That is also true of its churches and theologies. Episcopalian, Presbyterian, Congregationalist, Baptist, and Methodist traditions and institutions are still the norm. Therefore, what we said earlier with regard to the English or British way of thinking applies here as well.

This similarity should certainly not be understood to mean, however, that these churches are still in the grip of traditions inherited from England. On the contrary: after they were transplanted to the soil of a young nation, which was still at the beginning of its growth and the formation of its culture, these traditions in time underwent a profound change. They were borne by pioneers and adapted to the frontiers of America. Of course, this development largely took place without their being aware of it and in part even against their will. It was unavoidable, however, that everything the United States inherited the United States transformed into something else.

This transformation means, in short, that the American mind has little time or inclination for theoretical problems and reflections. The question of "truth" which is so important in Europe has to take a back seat to a concern for "efficiency" in the United States. The typical focus is not on tradition, nor is it directed, speculatively or meditatively, toward what is "above," but toward plans for the future; its concern is with progress and renewal. For the intellectual traditions of Europe there continues to be a feeling of respect, if not a feeling of inferiority, but it is mixed in with the opposite feelings, as is evident from the saying: "Europeans do the wrong thing for the right reasons; Americans do the right thing for the wrong reasons."

The new American world was built on three successive intellectual-spiritual foundations. The first was a Puritan form of Calvinism (17th century); the second, a revivalism largely stamped by Methodism; the third was that of a moderately deistic Enlightenment. To this day these three layers lie on top of, or under, or next to, or in synthesis with, each other. Often it is hard to tell them apart because they tend to use a common language (in which the word *experience* plays a prominent role), and almost all of them are focused on "renewal." The five main traditions referred to (Episcopalian, Presbyterian, Congregational, Baptist, and Methodist) have gone through all three layers and, by a process of repulsion and attraction, have continually related to, and combined with, each other. For that reason the mainline churches in the United States were able to spawn the charismatic movement as well as the God-is-dead movement. They often embrace the entire spectrum from left to right: fundamentalists, evangelicals, conservatives, liberals, and modernists. In the United States "conservative" and "liberal" are less distinct notions than in Europe. Anyone professing loyalty to the classic tradition of Christianity may call himself "conservative," but anyone who is critical of that tradition is soon called a "liberal"—a practice which comes near to the German theology of mediation and is therefore sharply distinguished from "modernist." For many people the different views form an amalgam which easily degenerates into a "civil religion" held in common with Catholics and Jews. The majority have a distaste for a harsh "either-or." Whatever works is true. A typical illustration and parallel is the American relationship between church and state. On the one hand, there is a sharp separation inspired by the Enlightenment; on the other hand, state and society are shot through with numerous Christian elements reminiscent of the theocratic notions of Puritanism.

The United States was built by people who had escaped from the European wars of religion. Tolerance was a principal feature of the new society, a fact which at the same time linked it with the legacy of the Enlightenment. It therefore never came to a clear and conscious contrast between the gospel and modernity, nor could it, as long as the United

States wanted to be and remain itself. Of course, such sweeping observations must always be strongly qualified. Especially in the smaller
churches of a more homogeneous stamp there is often a strong awareness of contrasting spiritual alternatives between which one must take
a stand. In mainline churches this awareness is often repressed, not only
for the sake of survival but also from conviction. People tend to live less
by a conflict model than by one of harmony. The question of truth has
to yield precedence to that of action. Ethics is more valid than dogmatics, and "pragmatics" counts for more than metaphysics. To this observation must be added that the explosive melting-pot situation of American society makes conflicts much more dangerous than in old and
established Western European societies.[1]

   This fact explains why, by comparison with European theology,
American theology has far fewer highly elaborated alternatives and
clearly marked crossroads. Still, it is not devoid of such contrasting perspectives either, if for no other reason than that American theology has
always allowed itself to be strongly influenced by European models. In
the United States, in distinction from Europe, such crossroads-situations
are, however, as a rule bound up with the challenges of ethics. Ethics in-
corporates decision. In my opinion the best example of this phenomenon is the switch from "social gospel" to "Neo-Orthodoxy." But to see
this switch in proper perspective we must first take a cursory look at the
history of American theology.

FROM THE PREVIOUS HISTORY: EDWARDS AND BUSHNELL

American theology, it is agreed, begins with the thought of *Jonathan Edwards* (1703-1758). In the mind of this original thinker the three layers we
mentioned come together. We should rather say: Three distinct currents
issued from his faith and thought, and the synthesis they formed in his
mind dominated American theology for more than a century. Edwards
was first, and above all, a Puritan and a decidedly scholastic Calvinist.
The sovereignty of God was the alpha and omega of his thinking. The
doctrine of election and damnation from eternity was to him incon-
testable. His worst opponents, whom he fought tirelessly, were the

---

1. With these observations we are touching upon the sociological aspect
of the religious mind-set of Americans. To what extent are theological positions
and nonpositions to be explained in terms of sociopolitical or socioeconomic factors? H. R. Niebuhr's classic work *The Kingdom of God in America* (New York: Willett, Clark & Co., 1937), esp. the Introduction, offers a balanced view of this issue.

Arminians. Following the Leyden professor Jacobus Arminius (1560-1609), whose teaching had been rejected by the Synod of Dordt (1619), the Arminians attributed to the free will of man a certain influence on man's faith and salvation. The same Edwards, as pastor of a church in Northampton, played a leading role in several revivals, especially in "The Great Awakening" (1740-1742), in which he worked together with the Methodist George Whitefield. In numerous sermons and publications he entered deeply into the mental states of sinners in need of salvation, and laid down the true marks of a person's election and regeneration. Finally, there was a third Edwards, the philosopher who under Locke's influence designed an original theory of the will and human motivation and in his views on virtue ("benevolence to being in general") expressed himself in the idiom of deistic moral philosophers. In this context the sovereign God and human beings are subsumed under the same concept of "loving benevolence." Thus Edwards operated simultaneously with different norms: Scripture, the experience of the pious, reason, and common sense. Scripture continued to be the highest authority; Enlightenment elements in his thinking had to remain subordinate to it. For many of his followers it was not easy to see, however, how man could simultaneously be purely the object of divine predestination *and* the subject (agent) of his own will and virtues (if perhaps only apparent virtues). In eighteenth-century theology these anthropological elements began increasingly to lead a life of their own, with the result that the Arminianism which had been banished from the front door finally conquered the temple of theology through this back door. By his many-layered theological thought Edwards both advanced and held back this process, especially through the mediation of the so-called New England School (till about 1880).

Whereas Edwards was the great theologian of the eighteenth century, *Horace Bushnell* (1802-1876) was the most influential theologian of the nineteenth century. Much more deeply and decisively than was (and could be) the case with Edwards, he anchored truth in the experience of people (experimental theology). From metaphysical and dogmatic conceptual forms truth was transmuted into social, psychological, and historical forms. Bushnell attempted to realize this transmutation especially in the doctrine of original sin ("organic solidarity"), in Christology ("from below"), and in the doctrine of the Atonement (an inner process expressed in objective images), forming a certain parallel to the left wing of German mediating theology. Right into the present his anthropological interpretation has remained characteristic for American theology.

By 1880, with a few exceptions, the point of gravity had shifted in mainline churches from a (mostly Calvinistic) theocentric perspective to a liberal anthropocentric view. That was the way in which the majority of the leading theologians of America assimilated the problematics of European theology. The time was now ripe for the rise of a complex of themes deriving from American life and thought itself.

THE RISE OF THE SOCIAL GOSPEL MOVEMENT

The Social Gospel movement arose in the 1870s and 1880s. In the 1890s it experienced a breakthrough, and in the years 1900-1914 it climaxed. It did not drop from the sky but had its roots deep in American church life. The challenge of building a new society, the push of the pioneers westward, and especially the Civil War between North and South (1861-1865) continually demanded far-reaching ethical decisions. The church's role in the battle against slavery and for abstinence is well known. The impulse for this position came from all three layers of the young American tradition: from Calvinism with its activism and insistence on the holiness of the church; from Methodism with its "Arminianism" and its ideal of "Christian perfection"; and finally from the Enlightenment with its moral philosophy and respect for humanity. In the second half of the nineteenth century, however, these personal ethical norms weakened as the nation faced a great new ethical challenge: advanced capitalism. In the eastern states industrialization took giant strides forward and brought with it, as side effects, the pull to the large cities, the poor quarters, exploitation of women and children in labor, unemployment, alcoholism, disease, premature death, illiteracy, etc. At this point the ethical ideals of the past proved themselves powerless. They conveyed an ethic of inward virtue and were all essentially geared to the individual. Vis-à-vis the poor they called for the private initiative of compassion and benevolence but had neither conceptual nor practical means with which to combat or change economic structures themselves.

Here the Social Gospel movement pointed in a new direction, earlier and more radically than in Europe, and with much more support from the clergy and among church people. It discovered the social dimension of the gospel and from there arrived at a radically new interpretation of concepts originally religious. It not only had special, social-ethical relevance in American history, therefore, but also great theological significance in general. Visser 't Hooft correctly wrote: "The social gospel, therefore, in the sense in which we are going to speak about it, is more than an application of Christian principles to society;

it is also an application of social principles to Christianity; or to put it shortly: it is a form of interpenetration of religious and social thought."[2]

Much of the vast literature produced by this movement lies outside the perspective of this book. What interests us is the relationship which the social gospel establishes between the hard realities of the modern world and the gospel. A founder and the first theologian of the movement, *Washington Gladden* (1836-1918), as a Congregational pastor and a follower of the liberal theology of Horace Bushnell, committed himself to the social gospel when in 1866 he came into contact with the struggle between capital and labor in his church at North Adams (Massachusetts). He always remained simultaneously an apologist for liberalism in the spirit of Bushnell and a social prophet in the spirit of a socialism of cooperation. As a third element in his thinking the theory of evolution must be mentioned. It made a substantial contribution to the sense of progress and optimism of the Social Gospel movement.

WALTER RAUSCHENBUSCH AND HIS THEOLOGY

The social gospel is always linked, and rightly so, with the name of *Walter Rauschenbusch* (1861-1918), who became the leading theologian of the movement. His father was a German immigrant, missionary, and theologian, who as a Pietist turned from Lutheranism to the Baptist faith. Both father and son served as professors in the bilingual Baptist theological seminary at Rochester, New York, the son as church historian from 1902 on. From his youth Walter Rauschenbusch had strong attachments to Germany. He studied at the gymnasium of Gütersloh and for a time also at the University of Berlin. A study trip to Germany (1891) completed his conversion to liberal theology. From that time on he often made his appeal to Schleiermacher and even more to Ritschl. The background and influence of German theology helped to make him the real theologian of the social gospel. The inspiration for and content of his theology, however, he could not gain from Europe. Just as in the case of Gladden, so here the impetus came from his pastoral experience: in 1885 he became a pastor near a poor section in New York known as Hell's Kitchen. He discovered that his inherited pastoral ideal—to save souls for eternity—was not adequate. Liberal theology offered him, as it did

---

2. W. A. Visser 't Hooft, *The Background of the Social Gospel in America* (Haarlem: Tjeenk Willink, 1928), p. 16 (originally a dissertation at Leiden). This study—an attempt to convey American developments to European theologians—has lost little of its informational value and validity.

Gladden, room for a new understanding of the gospel (in his case also there was the influence of Bushnell), but this space too had to be extended before it could serve as an instrument for social-ethical action and the transformation of economic and political structures.

Concretely this need meant the gospel had to be thought through afresh in the light of the idea of the kingdom of God. His study trip (1891) also brought him to full clarity on that issue. He struggled with the problem of how he could combine the tradition he inherited with his new experiences:

> How to find a place, under the old religious conceptions, for this great task of changing the world and making it righteous; making it habitable; making it merciful; making it brotherly. Somehow, I knew in my soul that that was God's work. Nobody could wrest that from me. Jesus Christ had spoken too plainly to my soul about that. I knew that he was on the side of righteousness, and on the side of his poor brother. But how could I combine it with my old Christianity—with my old religion?
>
> Now that is the way the matter presented itself to me as a personal problem. And then the idea of the kingdom of God offered itself as the real solution for that problem. Here was a religious conception that embraced it all. Here was something so big that absolutely nothing that interested me was excluded from it. Was it a matter of personal religion? Why, the kingdom of God begins with that! The powers of the kingdom of God well up in the individual soul; that is where they are born, and that is where the starting point necessarily must be. Was it a matter of world-wide missions? Why, that is the kingdom of God, isn't it—carrying it out to the boundaries of the earth. Was it a matter of getting justice for the workingman? Is not justice part of the kingdom of God? Does not the kingdom of God simply consist of this—that God's will shall be done on earth, even as it is now in heaven? And so, wherever I touched, there was the kingdom of God. That was the brilliancy, the splendor of that conception—it touches everything with religion. It carries God into everything that you do, and there is nothing else that does it in the same way.
>
> And then, besides that, you have the authority of the Lord Jesus Christ. It was his idea. That is what he came and died for. The kingdom of God is a social conception. It is a conception for this life here of ours, because Jesus says: "Thy kingdom come, thy will be done" here. It is something that is here on this earth;

that quietly pervades all humanity; that is always working toward the perfect life of God. It cannot be lived out by you alone —you have to live it out with me, and with that brother sitting next to you. We together have to work it out. It is a matter of community life. The perfect community of men—that would be the kingdom of God! With God above them; with their brother next to them—clasping hands in fraternity, doing the work of justice—that is the kingdom of God![3]

We are reproducing these words at length because they are so characteristic for the shift and reorientation which many, especially young, Americans made in the decades before World War I. They show why it was not an otherworldly orthodoxy but only liberal theology with its accentuation of the historical Jesus and his message which could yield a foundation for the social gospel. They also make clear, however, that it was not Rauschenbusch's purpose to subordinate the gospel to some principle of sociality. His goal rather was to restore the catholicity of the gospel which had been so contracted and mutilated in pietism. From within the perspective of the kingdom of God he sought to hold together the divine and the human, as also the personal and communal.

Within the framework of our book great importance has to be accorded to the lecture series which Rauschenbusch gave at Yale a year before his death (April, 1917) under the title *A Theology for the Social Gospel*.[4] As we now turn to this volume we may not forget that certain ideas which occupy a central place in Rauschenbusch could hardly be reflected in these lectures. I shall mention only two: First, the religious importance which the scientific notion of evolution has for him as a second pillar, next to that of the kingdom of God: "Translate the evolutionary theories into religious faith, and you have the doctrine of the kingdom of God."[5] Second, he could only touch here the social-economic development of ideas which were central for him: his faith in democracy as the true expression of theocracy and his evolutionary, unpolitical, and nondoctrinaire socialism. Nevertheless, the reader will here find him, more than usually, looking at biblical revelation as the source of power for his thought and action.

3. From an informal autobiographical speech which Rauschenbusch gave on Jan. 2, 1913, before the Y.M.C.A. in Cleveland, published in *The Social Gospel in America 1870-1920*, ed. R. T. Handy, in the series *A Library of Protestant Thought* (New York: Oxford University Press, 1966).

4. W. Rauschenbusch, *A Theology for the Social Gospel* (New York: Macmillan, 1917).

5. Rauschenbusch, in Handy, ed., *Social Gospel in America*, p. 258.

Rauschenbusch struggled with the question whether his social gospel theology would be viewed as so new that it had to be considered an alien element in Christian thought. In the third lecture (entitled "Neither Alien nor Novel") he stated:

> The belief in the universal reign of law, the doctrine of evolution, the control of nature by man, and the value of education and liberty as independent goods,—these are among the most influential convictions of modern life and have deeply modified our religious thought. But they are novel elements in theology. They are not alien, but certainly they held no such controlling position in the theology of the past as they do with us. . . .
>
> On the other hand the idea of the redemption of the social organism is nothing alien. It is simply a proper part of the Christian faith in redemption from sin and evil. As soon as the desire for salvation becomes strong and intelligent enough to look beyond the personal sins of the individual, and to discern how our personality in its intake and output is connected with the social groups to which we belong, the problem of social redemption is before us and we can never again forget it. It lies like a larger concentric circle around a smaller one. It is related to our intimate personal salvation like astronomy to physics. Only spiritual and intellectual immaturity have kept us from seeing it clearly before. The social gospel is not an alien element in theology. (pp. 23-24)

Having made this point Rauschenbusch immediately takes the next step:

> Neither is it novel. The social gospel is, in fact, the oldest gospel of all. It is "built on the foundation of the apostles and prophets." Its substance is the Hebrew faith which Jesus himself held. If the prophets ever talked about the "plan of redemption," they meant the social redemption of the nation. So long as John the Baptist and Jesus were proclaiming the gospel, the Kingdom of God was their central word, and the ethical teaching of both, which was their practical commentary and definition of the Kingdom idea, looked toward a higher social order in which new ethical standards would become practicable. (p. 24)

For centuries, however, this real gospel was darkened by Hellenism and individualism. "What would Jesus have said to the symbol of Chalcedon or the Athanasian creed if they had been read to him?" (p. 25).

One who knows the social gospel only from hearsay may think

that Rauschenbusch's evolutionary optimism will leave no room for a true doctrine of sin. However, the contrary is the case. He speaks of sin at greater length and in more detail than most dogmaticians do. Of the nineteen chapters of his series of lectures no fewer than six are devoted to this theme. This part of his work is still impressive and relevant. Persuasively he discusses how badly we underestimate sin when we view it only as a personal or individual matter. He stresses that we can only gain a correct view of the *negativum* of sin in the light of the *positivum* of the kingdom of God. If the kingdom of God must be viewed as "the realm of love," hence as the realm of service, "the commonwealth of cooperative labor," then sin, as a social force, must be regarded as a "realm (of evil)." Hence the chapter headings of this book: "The Transmission of Sin" (VII); "The Super-Personal Forces of Evil" (VIII); "The Kingdom of Evil" (IX). Rauschenbusch is aware that he is offering an incisive revision of the doctrine of sin. He draws on the Pauline teaching of the powers and gives a new interpretation of the doctrine of original sin: man is especially manipulated and seduced into evil by social and institutional forces. A characteristic quotation is the following:

> Those who do their thinking in the light of the Kingdom of God make less of heresy and private sins. They reserve their shudders for men who keep the liquor and vice trade alive against public intelligence and law; for interests that organize powerful lobbies to defeat tenement or factory legislation, or turn factory inspection into sham; for nations that are willing to set the world at war in order to win or protect colonial areas of trade or usurious profit from loans to weaker peoples; and for private interests which are willing to push a peaceful nation into war because the stock exchange has a panic at the rumour of peace. These seem the unforgivable sins, the great demonstrations of rebellious selfishness, wherever the social gospel has revived the faith of the Kingdom of God. (p. 54)

The personal side of sin and grace may certainly not be forgotten. For Rauschenbusch, too, the personal constitutes the beginning and the source. His definition of sin (sin is selfishness) is therefore personal. However, the personal and the social are the two sides (front and back) of the same thing. "At any rate, any religious experience in which our fellow-men have no part or thought does not seem to be a distinctively Christian experience" (p. 97). "Salvation is the voluntary socializing of the soul" (p. 99). Hence it is what the classic dogmatics call "sanctification" or "regeneration." Although Rauschenbusch praises Ritschl's doctrine of the ellipsis with the two foci, he, like the majority of liberal theologians, has no appreciation for justification. Salvation is the cure of self-ishness. Like sin, it is essentially focused on one's fellow human beings; but in the kingdom of God, God and neighbor constitute a single whole. Faith is primarily future-oriented; it is confidence in the possibility and establishment of a totally different world from the one we now see before our eyes. The present — the Christian's fellowship with God — is not thereby excluded. The warrior may lean, in prayer and meditation, on God. "But what we get thus is for use" (p. 105). The main issue remains "The Salvation of the Super-Personal Forces" (the title of ch. XI). There are unsaved organizations (the autocratic and mammonistic ones) and there are saved ones (the democratic and cooperative).

> The salvation of the super-personal beings is by coming under the law of Christ. The fundamental step of repentance and conversion for professions and organizations is to give up monopoly power and the incomes derived from legalized extortion, and to come under the law of service, content with a fair income for honest work. The corresponding step in the case of governments and political oligarchies, both in monarchies and in capitalistic semi-democracies, is to submit to real democracy. Therewith they step out of the Kingdom of Evil into the Kingdom of God. (p. 117)

The church should really be the alternative to the unsaved organizations. But as a church historian, Rauschenbusch knows too much about the evil role the church has often played. His ecclesiology is not very nuanced. "The church grows old; the Kingdom is ever young. The Church is a perpetuation of the past; the Kingdom is the power of the coming age. Unless the Church is vitalized by the ever nascent forces of the Kingdom within her, she deadens instead of begetting" (pp. 129-30).

In the following chapters he deals at length with the marks of the kingdom of God. We cite as characteristic the following:

> Since Christ revealed the divine worth of life and personality, and since his salvation seeks the restoration and fulfilment of even the least, it follows that the Kingdom of God, at every stage of human development, tends toward a social order which will best guarantee to all personalities their freest and highest development. This involves the redemption of social life from the cramping influence of religious bigotry, from the repression of self-assertion in the relation of upper and lower classes, and from all forms of slavery in which human beings are treated as mere means to serve the ends of others. (p. 142)

Now Rauschenbusch has to define his Christology. In a chapter title Christ is called "The Initiator of the Kingdom of God" (p. 146). Old Testament prophets, to be sure, announced the kingdom, but "Jesus experienced God in a new way. The ethical monotheism which he inherited from the prophets was transformed within his spirit and through his experiences into something far lovelier and kinder" (p. 154). God became for him a Father and the loveliness of this experience in his life left room only for righteousness and love. "This is the highest idealistic faith ever conceived, and the greatest addition ever made to the spiritual possessions of mankind" (p. 154). Jesus therefore cannot have been an ascetic, a man from heaven, or an apocalyptic, although he may have employed the language appropriate to the corresponding groups in his environment. The professional theologians of Europe who all belonged to the bourgeoisie and hence had no affinity for revolutionary ideas had to reinterpret Jesus' ideas into ascetic and apocalyptic ones. The real Jesus is the Jesus of the parables which portray the kingdom of God both as a present and as a future reality and as involved in process. For that reason Jesus was no pessimist but "a religious optimist." But he had to bear the sins of the world; that is, because of his attitude he became the victim of the six main social sins: superstition, corruption, injustice, the madness of the masses, militarism, class-consciousness. Though assaulted by all of them, Jesus remained obedient. He acted as God acts. Thus his death became the highest revelation of love and the greatest leap forward in the direction of the kingdom of God.

The resurrection of Jesus is not mentioned at this point and hardly occurs elsewhere. Obviously this theme is too difficult or too delicate for Rauschenbusch to handle. One is inclined to regard this silence as the great weakness of his theology. At the same time, one has to say that faith in the resurrection indirectly permeates all his thinking. He sees the world involved in one great resurrection. Christ lives in the Spirit and the Spirit creates resurrections in the United States and everywhere. H. R. Niebuhr could be right: "Gladden, Rauschenbusch, and their colleagues carried with them a vision and a promise which had been written not on stone or paper but on fleshly tables of the heart by a fresh and nation-wide experience of the resurrection."[6]

Rauschenbusch treats the doctrine of God in close association with Christology. In the social gospel there is no room for a "natural theology"; such a theology always entails a despotic conception of God, because "God" then becomes the reflection of the autocratic relationships of society. "The worst form of leaving the naked unclothed, the hungry

---

6. Niebuhr, *Kingdom of God in America*, pp. 162ff.

unfed, and the prisoners uncomforted, is to leave men under a despotic conception of God and the universe; and what will the Son of Man do to us theologians when we gather at the Day of Doom?" (p. 174). God is not autocratically transcendent but democratically immanent. One may not, therefore, trace undeserved suffering back to God. It is, in the first place, the consequence of capitalistic exploitation: "The bourgeois theologians have misrepresented our revolutionary God. God is for the Kingdom of God, and his Kingdom does not mean injustice and the perpetuation of innocent suffering. The best theodicy for modern needs is to make this very clear" (p. 184). In agreement with this statement is the fact that the Holy Spirit advances, as the most important gift, prophecy as a declaration of war against the sinful world order.

In his interpretation of New Testament eschatology he stresses the development idea as he finds it in the parables of Jesus over against the catastrophic-apocalyptic theme. It is only this interpretation which agrees with faith in God's immanence. But this interpretation also implies that there will be no final consummation. God created us for never-ending progress, not for the tedium of immutability. Also, humanity will come to an end for astronomical reasons, but not the individual. Belief in survival after death may be supported by science, philosophy, or psychical research, "but its main supports are the resurrection of Christ, his teachings, and the common faith of the Christian Church, which all embolden the individual. Further, the sense of personality, which is intensified and ennobled by the Christian life, and rises to the sense of imperishable worth in the assurance that we are children of God" (pp. 228-29). That assurance is a great comfort when we think of the numerous lives which ended prematurely. Rauschenbusch, having expressed a number of personal ideas about eternity, summarized what he regarded as certain as follows: "That the love of God will go out forever to his children, and especially to the neediest, drawing them to him and, where necessary, saving them; that personality energized by God is ever growing; that the law of love and solidarity will be even more effective in heaven than on earth; and that salvation, growth, and solidarity are conditioned on interchange of service" (p. 238). Thus, finally, Rauschenbusch's future expectation is much more otherworldly and individual than the main thrust of his theology would lead one to expect.

DECLINE AND TRANSITION

A year after he gave these lectures, Rauschenbusch died at the age of only 56. Three weeks earlier his great predecessor, Washington Gladden, had died at age 82. These incidental facts at the same time marked a spiritual state of affairs. World War I ended the heyday of the social gospel. After 1918 a period of searching and confusion ensued, but it was not the same as in Europe. In the United States the war undermined the idealism of the people much less than it did in Europe—just think of the idealistic president Woodrow Wilson and the response he evoked. People fostered the hope that this war would end all wars. The immanentism and the idea of progress of the Social Gospel movement even led many in the direction of a humanistic modernism. Others, however—and their numbers grew—sought a better foundation for their ideals and became increasingly critical of the movement: must not the transcendent sovereignty of God and human sin be considered far more deeply if one is to confront squarely the demonic forces at work in society?[7] Had not the movement as a whole remained too utopian and too much a movement of the middle class? People looked for new directions and to that end often had to position themselves against the social gospel and its advocates; the word *liberalism* acquired the connotation of a superficial optimism. When in 1925 the first World Conference for Practical Christianity was held in Stockholm—a conference attended by many American followers of the social gospel—the European delegates who had experienced the collapse of their continent were shocked at the self-assured speeches of their American counterparts. What emerged there was a gulf which has not been bridged to this day. Thus the expression "social gospel" acquired a bad meaning in Europe. No sensible theologian would or will describe himself in these terms. And in the United States the years between 1918 and 1940 meant the gradual decline of this movement. We shall see in a moment what alternative ways were explored.

Still, if we look back on it from our present perspective, we can see that the law of the grain of seed (John 12:24) was fulfilled in the Social Gospel movement. Much that has happened in the United States or

---

7. It is most interesting to see what the young W. A. Visser 't Hooft (in his dissertation, 1928) criticizes and in what direction he points. He especially criticizes the movement's immanent conception of God by which, in his opinion, God threatens to become a projection of human ideas and ideals. He continues: "It is only before a God Who is different from us, because He is Holy and we are sinful, that man begins to realize his calling. There is no calling unless there is one who calls. Where God is not believed to be the eternal 'Thou,' man necessarily falls back on his own human reality. And even the best of that reality is finally self-love, egotism, sin" (*Background of the Social Gospel*, p. 183). His verdict, "Their God is more akin to the impersonal God of pantheism than to the dynamic God of Christian theism" (p. 180), is not fair, at least to Rauschenbusch.

in Christianity generally would not be at all, or be as it is, if the social gospel had never existed. More than other personalities and movements it rendered people conscience-bound to criticize capitalism and to assume the prophetic and social task of the church. Apart from the social gospel the work of the National Council of Churches of Christ (NCCC) in the United States is unthinkable. To a lesser degree the same is true of the social divisions of the World Council of Churches. If we read the social-theological views of Rauschenbusch today we are surprised by their similarity with many ideas which we hear expressed now and seem so provocative (negatively or positively) to us, because we prematurely shoved the social gospel aside and therefore never worked through it. Not only to understand the United States better but also to be able to discern our task as Christians and as churches more clearly, we cannot ignore a theologian like Rauschenbusch—and all the less because he, being deeply influenced by German theology, drew new conclusions from it. From our perspective, his naiveté concerning the essence of the gospel as well as the possibilities of modern society is evident. This observation can only mean, however, that with much more sophisticated methods and far less optimism than he we must nevertheless repeat his conceptual and practical initiative. Anyone attempting such a new start will discover that many of the details of his theology (I am thinking especially of his doctrine of sin) will perhaps still prove to be helpful.

H. RICHARD NIEBUHR

The challenge mentioned at the close of the preceding section was answered in the following epoch of American theology especially by two brothers, Reinhold and Richard Niebuhr, minister's sons who had their roots in the immigrant church of the Prussian union (the Evangelical Synod of the United States). The father had left behind his harsh Prussian training and environment by emigration. In his day the little German church was still quite isolated. This changed when in 1934 it merged with the Swiss Reformed Church to become the Evangelical and Reformed Church, and even more when in 1956 it strove for union with the Congregational Christian Churches. This process brought into being the United Church of Christ. Far earlier, however, the two theologians we mentioned had already broken through the bounds of language and culture, especially by their study at Yale. Like Rauschenbusch before them, they remained in close touch with European (German-language) theology, while their thinking belonged totally to the young American tradition.

It is natural from our point of view to start with the younger of the two, *Helmut Richard Niebuhr* (1894-1962). Except for two years in the ministry, his career was purely academic. He wrote his doctoral dissertation at Yale about Ernst Troeltsch's philosophy of religion (1924), and from 1931 on served as professor of Christian Ethics at Yale. Troeltsch, with his all-relativizing historicism, both occupied and fascinated Niebuhr throughout his life. More than an ethicist, he was, like Troeltsch, a sociologically oriented cultural historian. His best-known and classic book, *Christ and Culture* (1951), can be viewed as the American counterpart of Troeltsch's *Social Teaching of the Christian Churches*.

At this juncture we wish to direct our attention to an earlier book which, on account of its high qualities and influence, deserves the attribution "classic" as much as the other: *The Kingdom of God in America* (1937). Both its theme and the way it is developed make clear, more sharply than his other writings, the precise shift in American theology which engages us here.

Niebuhr turned against theological liberalism with extreme sharpness: "It established continuity between God and man by adjusting God to man" (p. 192). "A God without wrath brought men without sin into a kingdom without judgment through the ministrations of a Christ without a cross" (p. 193). Still, for the greatest among the liberals Niebuhr immediately had to make an exception: "The temper of evolutionary optimism did not prevail in all parts of the liberal movement. There were mediators who shared the protest against static versions of divine sovereignty, salvation and Christian hope but sought nevertheless to retain the critical and dialectical elements in Protestantism. Of these Horace Bushnell was the greatest" (p. 193). "Washington Gladden and Walter Rauschenbusch represented the same mediating tendency in the social gospel movement, and the latter did so more than the former" (p. 194). Hence in the case of Richard Niebuhr the shift was not without continuity; but a shift had to be made if the concept of the kingdom of God was to have any relevant content at all. It cannot be merely a projection of our ideas and ideals. The kingdom of God is much more the kingdom that is founded by God and of which he is the center. The sustaining idea in this book, which is historical in form, is the conviction that "the instrumental value of faith for society is dependent upon faith's conviction that it has more than instrumental value. Faith could not defend men if it believed that defense was its meaning. The godliness which is profitable to all things becomes unprofitable when profit rather than God comes to be its interest" (pp. 265-66). At the end of these expositions Niebuhr refers to certain renewal movements and then, in his last sentence, he writes: "And it was significant that such movements manifested increasing interest in the great doctrines and traditions of the

Christian past, as though they were aware that power had been lost because the heritage had been forgotten, or that there was no way toward the coming kingdom save the way taken by a sovereign God through the reign of Jesus Christ" (p. 198).

From such sentences one can see why this kind of thinking was given the name "Neo-Orthodoxy." Less understandable, but typical for the theological polarization that took place, was the fact that liberals frequently decried this thought as "biblicism" and even "fundamentalism." For Richard Niebuhr these tags were even less true than for Reinhold Niebuhr; Richard stayed, or came, much closer to liberalism than Reinhold. During these years his position was strongly reminiscent of that of the young Barth in the second edition of *Romans*. Troeltsch and Barth were the two theologians by whom he was most influenced; they were complementary for him. Whereas Troeltsch taught the absolute relativity of earthly history, Barth taught the absolute sovereignty of God as the ground of all earthly relativity. This "theocentric relativity" in which the historical is grounded is the only possibility of avoiding relativism and of conducting an active struggle against all absolutizations of the relative, also against all the idols of modern society.

Soon he worked out these insights into *The Meaning of Revelation*.[8] As almost always in Niebuhr, so here the foreword is of great importance. In this book he refers to Troeltsch and Barth as his teachers and adds: "These two leaders in twentieth century religious thought are frequently set in diametrical opposition to each other; I have tried to combine their main interests, for it appears to me that the critical thought of the former and the constructive work of the latter belong together. If I have failed the cause does not lie in the impossibility of the task. It is work that needs to be done" (p. x).

Niebuhr points to three convictions which underlie the book:

The first is the conviction that self-defense is the most prevalent source of error in all thinking and perhaps especially in theology and ethics. I cannot hope to have avoided this error in my effort to state Christian ideas in confessional terms only, but I have at least tried to guard against it. The second idea is that the great source of evil in life is the absolutizing of the relative, which in Christianity takes the form of substituting religion, revelation, church or Christian morality for God. The third conviction, which becomes most explicit in the latter part of this essay but

8. H. R. Niebuhr, *The Meaning of Revelation* (New York: Macmillan, repr. 1962) (lectures from the years 1938-1940).

underlies the former part, is that Christianity is "permanent revolution" or *metanoia* which does not come to an end in this world, this life, or this time. Positively stated these three convictions are that man is justified by grace, that God is sovereign, and that there is an eternal life. (pp. viii-ix)

The sovereignty of God, which Niebuhr regarded as so decisive for human action, cannot, however, embrace the whole of faith. The sovereign God is simultaneously he who comes down to us in Jesus Christ; the transcendent is he who makes himself immanent and historical. Though Niebuhr does not deny this point, it remains in the shadow of his confession of the sovereignty of God.[9] For that reason he could not join Barth on his journey to a Christocentric perspective. Jesus, indeed, is precisely the revelation of God because with his life and trust in his Father he was a unique pointer to monotheism and to the sovereignty of God. For that reason we may not interpret revelation solely from within the person of Jesus. He is past. Nor dare we locate the presence of God in the church. Revelation is present only where God discloses himself to us in personal encounter. Psalm 139 was one of Niebuhr's favorite texts. Certainly we do not know this God apart from Jesus. But: "The God who reveals himself in Jesus Christ is now trusted and known as the contemporary God, revealing himself in every event; but we do not understand how we could trace his working in these happenings if he did not make himself known to us through the memory of Jesus Christ; nor do we know how we should be able to interpret all the words we read as words of God save by the aid of this Rosetta stone."[10]

In this way, however, not only Jesus Christ but also God himself

---

9. Niebuhr, giving a personal statement of faith, emerges impressively as a "Christian existentialist" in the closing chapter (VII: "Concluding Unscientific Postscript") of his *Christ and Culture* (New York: Harper & Row, 1951), pp. 230-56. One should read this credo in connection with his equally impressive views concerning the radicality of Jesus on pp. 11-29.

10. *Meaning of Revelation*, p. 154. Other statements from this chapter on "The Deity of God" include: "A definition of revelation in terms of the person of Jesus is manifestly inadequate" (p. 148). "Unless we have another certainty prior to the certainty about Jesus' personal value the latter is very tenuous and uncertain" (p. 149). "Revelation means the moment in our history through which we know ourselves to be known from beginning to end, in which we are apprehended by the knower; it means the self-disclosing of that eternal knower" (pp. 152-53). "Revelation means that in our common history the fate which lowers over us as persons in our communities reveals itself to be a person in community with us" (p. 153).

is impoverished. An unworldly or super-worldly existential conduct seems to be the only thing that comports with the sovereignty of God. At this point Niebuhr became aware that his way was diverging from that of Barth, and he began therefore to charge Barth with a unitarianism (of the second Person of the Trinity) while he viewed himself as the complete Trinitarian. He saw in Barth an "overcorrection" of liberalism and hence began to lean more strongly toward Bultmann. The personal "wholly other" of the sovereign God fades away behind the existential relationship and can now be described as "the ground of all being." Especially for the last years of his work as a theologian it is difficult to determine his place in the shift of "Neo-Orthodoxy." Perhaps one might rather say that Niebuhr anticipated the coming epoch of "Neo-liberalism."[11]

REINHOLD NIEBUHR

Karl Paul Reinhold Niebuhr (1892-1971) was almost two years older than Richard. He regarded his brother as the greater man, though he regretted that as a genuine academic Richard did not share in his political interests and activities. I cannot agree with his judgment; in my opinion Reinhold is doubtlessly the greater of the two. Over against the greater subtlety of Richard stand the power and scope of Reinhold's thought. In his day Reinhold profoundly influenced the theology and culture of the United States in general. In distinction from Richard, Reinhold was a pastor no fewer than thirteen years (1915-1928), and that in Detroit, the large and

11. Cf. esp. his last book, *Radical Monotheism and Western Culture* (New York: Harper & Row, 1960). Even if one takes account of the secular context in which the majority of these lectures (the Montgomery Lectures on Contemporary Civilization at the University of Nebraska) were given, it still remains hard to understand that the one God is consistently referred to as "the universe of being," "the realm of being," and (in connection with the faith of Israel!) as "the principle of being." "Yet insofar as the Christ event elicits radical faith, it is seen as a demonstration of Being's loyalty to all beings and as a call to decisive choice of God's universal cause" (p. 44). Cf. esp. ch. III, in which, however, there is an attempt to incorporate the notion of personality in the concept of God (pp. 44-47). This development is not new in Niebuhr, as is evident from the essay "Faith in God and in gods" (1943), where God is called "the void" and "the great X" (pp. 122-23). Here Niebuhr's appeal to Whitehead is striking (pp. 123-24). For a thorough existentialist interpretation of these difficult lines of thought of Niebuhr, cf. two articles by H. W. Frei in the collection *Faith and Ethics: The Theology of Richard Niebuhr*, ed. Paul Ramsey (New York: Harper & Row, 1957), pp. 9-116. Niebuhr's last book cannot be considered further in this volume.

swiftly growing city of Ford's automobile industry. What the experiences in North Adams and Springfield (Massachusetts) meant for Gladden, and what Hell's Kitchen in New York was for Rauschenbusch, Detroit became for Niebuhr: the theater of murderous conflict between capital and labor, or rather (we are still completely in the epoch of high capitalism) the murderous exploitation of workers by the acquirers of capital. The seriousness of the situation was masked by Henry Ford's social policies. Ford was, in a sense, an idealist. He paid his employees far more than many other factory owners and, accordingly, was often presented as an example. Niebuhr, however, soon saw through the fine veneer: for Ford, too, laborers hardly counted as human beings: the unfit and the exhausted were ruthlessly thrown away as people without rights. Labor unions were regarded as natural enemies. Here Niebuhr also saw the ambiguity, as he called it, of idealism with its fine solutions. This perception made him a lifelong enemy of all churchly and theological liberalism, a mind-set he accused of utopianism, romanticism, and sentimentality.

His congregation was not, as is often assumed, a poor parish; it consisted predominantly and originally of German members of the middle class. A year after Niebuhr's arrival the language used in worship changed from German to English. This congregation, as a whole, did not abandon its revolutionary pastor. A wealthy member of his church even provided the salary for an assistant, so that Niebuhr could set aside time for the spread of his ideas through lectures, particularly in the academic world.[12]

Niebuhr's thinking was less influenced by World War I than by the labor situation in Detroit. Initially, it is true, the war made him, like so many others, a pacifist; more important is the fact that as a result of the great influx of black laborers to Detroit, and by his appointment to the chairmanship of the city's Committee on Racial Relations, Niebuhr now linked the social question with the race issue. That was something that had hardly ever happened before.

In 1928 he moved from Detroit to New York and became professor of "Applied Christianity" (Christian Ethics) at Union Theological Seminary. There his revolutionary ideas were soon reinforced by the

12. Even the article in *Religion in Geschichte und Gegenwart*, 3rd ed., s.v., calls him "a pastor of a church of laborers in Detroit." Many details from Niebuhr's career have been assembled by J. Bingham in her Niebuhr biography entitled *Courage to Change* (New York: Scribner's, 1961). On Niebuhr in Detroit, see ch. IX. Another valuable biography, more focused on Niebuhr's responsiveness to the social and political problems of his time, appeared in 1985: R. W. Fox, *Reinhold Niebuhr: A Biography* (New York: Pantheon Books).

crash of the stock market in 1929. For a time his explanation of this event ("Capitalism is dying and it ought to die") brought him close to Marxism. Did not the solution lie in a power takeover by the oppressed? Still, Niebuhr turned away from this "solution" in the belief that this power, too, would soon be abused. The power of the diverse groups in society had to be reciprocally limited. Thus Niebuhr became a revisionist socialist, something he remained till 1940, after repeatedly faulting the Communist Party for its pacifism and isolationism. At this point, more clearly than before, he devoted himself to theology as his real calling and task. In this respect his career is strikingly parallel to that of Karl Barth.

Niebuhr had long been acutely aware how rotten the two pillars were on which the Social Gospel movement and liberalism generally rested; namely, faith in social and cultural progress and the confidence that the gospel proclaims the kingdom of God as an optimistic and moral entity which can and ought to be realized by human beings. These two convictions had reinforced each other for decades. But now this harmonious synthesis collapsed. Reinhold Niebuhr's "Neo-Orthodoxy" also rested on two pillars which supported each other. The first is insight into the world's powerlessness to redeem itself: every liberation leads sooner or later to new idolatry and oppression. The second is the discovery that it is the gospel which tells the exact truth about the world, and, by the offer of a higher reality, that of grace, enables us to uphold ourselves and always again to find a way. It is impossible to tell which of these discoveries was primary for Niebuhr and which came later; presumably they went hand in hand. He himself spoke of a "circular relation" between the two[13]—a conviction which linked him with Brunner and separated him from Barth. As we learned, his great enemy was and remained American liberalism with its optimism. He devoted much less time to combating the Social Gospel movement as a variety of this liberalism; indeed, in its ranks he had found many fellow combatants against capitalism. Like his brother, despite occasional criticism, he had a positive view of Rauschenbusch, even though he rarely mentioned him.[14] It

13. These words are characteristic: "The centuries of historical hope have well nigh destroyed the Christian faith as a potent force in modern culture and civilization. We do not maintain that the period of disillusionment in which we now find ourselves will necessarily restore the Christian faith. It has merely reestablished its relevance. There is always the alternative of despair, the 'sorrow of the world' to the creative despair which induces a new faith" (R. Niebuhr, *The Nature and Destiny of Man*, 2 vols. [New York: Scribner's, repr. 1949], 2:206-7).

14. In the preface to his "Rauschenbusch Memorial Lectures" delivered in Rochester, he writes: "I venture to hope that they [these lectures] are an exten-

took a fairly long time, however, before these groups discovered what really animated Niebuhr. Liberals regarded him as a biblicist or even a fundamentalist; followers of the conventional social gospel viewed him as a pessimistic preacher of social passivity.

Niebuhr the theologian viewed himself particularly as an apologist. It was his purpose to show the secularized intelligentsia of the eastern seaboard of the North American continent that the gospel alone is the answer to the contradictory experiences under which they labored. But it is an answer! Its relevance to us lies not, as liberalism believed, in its conformity with us but in its nonconformity.

In keeping with the American tradition, Niebuhr preferred to take his starting point in the realm of anthropology. Central in his thinking is "the transcendental self"; that is, man in his unique capacity to raise himself above the two components of his being, namely, nature and reason. That is his freedom and at the same time his responsibility. In this freedom man becomes conscious of his finitude and searches for its fulfillment. But he keeps looking for it in false directions. The self is split. "For I do not do the good I want, but the evil I do not want is what I do" (Rom. 7:19). The self seeks a value beyond itself which it then, however, ever and again hopes to find within the range of its own narrow interests and which it pursues within these interests. This idle hope characterizes entire nations as well as individuals; for that reason "the responsible self is also the guilty self."[15] The creative capacities of the self work themselves out destructively. "The self must lose itself to find itself in faith and repentance; but it does not find itself unless it be apprehended from beyond itself."[16] "We cannot, therefore, escape the ultimate paradox that the final exercise of freedom in the transcendent human spirit is its recognition of the false use of that freedom in action."[17]

Here, in Niebuhr, a "natural" anthropology runs into his understanding of the relationship between creation and sin. Man is called to submit to God and to strive for his goal in love for him and his neigh-

---

sion and an application to our own day of both the social realism and the loyalty to the Christian faith which characterized the thought and life of one who was not only the real founder of social Christianity in this country but also its most brilliant and generally satisfying exponent to the present day" (R. Niebuhr, *An Interpretation of Christian Ethics* [New York: Harper & Brothers, 1935], p. 7).

15. Niebuhr, *Faith and History* (New York: Scribner's, 1949), p. 97. See further pp. 93-97.

16. Ibid., p. 151.

17. Niebuhr, *Nature and Destiny of Man*, 1:260. See also pp. 12ff., 255ff.

bor. "The fact that man can transcend himself in infinite regression and cannot find the end of life except in God is the mark of his creativity and uniqueness; closely related to this capacity is his inclination to transmute his partial and finite self and his partial and finite values into the infinite good. Therein lies his sin."[18]

Sin is the action of exceeding the finite bounds set for human freedom. Man wants to deify himself; sin is essentially pride. In terms of creation, freedom and finitude belong together. The highest exercise of freedom is seeing its limitations. "The real evil in the human situation . . . lies in man's unwillingness to recognize and acknowledge the weakness, finiteness and dependence of his position, in his inclination to grasp after a power and security which transcend the possibilities of human existence, and in his effort to pretend a virtue and knowledge which are beyond the limits of mere creatures."[19] In a manner that is unusual in systematic theology, Niebuhr dealt extensively with this doctrine of sin in the second half of the first volume of his *Nature and Destiny of Man,* especially in chapters VII-IX. Many readers had the impression that the main emphasis of his theology lay here. In any case, for the second time in this chapter, we must now speak about new developments in the doctrine of sin.

It gives us pause that American theology, which in Europe is generally considered superficial and optimistic, precisely in this respect achieved something which has no equivalent—apart from Barth—in European theology. One must also note in this connection that Niebuhr did not in the first place advance the doctrine of sin from within sociology, like Rauschenbusch, but deepened it, psychologically and existentially, with the help of Kierkegaard.[20]

Still, one cannot regard the doctrine of sin as the central focus of Niebuhr's theology; it is rather the bridge which links reality and faith. If one is to speak of a central focus it should rather be sought in his Christology. When he comes to Jesus and his work, he repeatedly quotes Matthew 21:42: "The very stone which the builders rejected has become the head of the corner." By this he means to say that the message of Jesus Christ does not fit the categories with which we attempt to explain and control the world; nevertheless, we discover that, if we put the ill-fitting stones of our ideologies together, they acquire their place, coherence, and

18. Ibid., 1:122.
19. Ibid., 1:137.
20. In ibid., 1:246, Niebuhr raises a gentle objection against Rauschenbusch to the effect that, given his understanding of sin, the bias toward evil is always outside and never inside a particular will. This is dealt with under the heading of "Pelagian doctrines."

meaning only in the Christ-event. Hence, in his great Christological presentation in the second volume of his *Nature and Destiny of Man* (and not only there), Niebuhr orients himself to 1 Corinthians 1:18 ("For the word of the cross is folly to those who are perishing, but to us who are being saved it is the power of God") and to 1:23-24 ("we preach Christ crucified, a stumbling block to Jews and folly to Gentiles but to those who are called, both Jews and Greeks, Christ the power of God and the wisdom of God)." All the emphasis falls on the work of Christ, on reconciliation on the cross.

This emphasis is not, however, at the expense of the life of Jesus. The Sermon on the Mount and the cross belong together. In Jesus Christ we see the possible impossibility of a loving eternity in the rebellion of our time. Therefore Niebuhr does not separate the work of Christ from his person. The paradoxical unity of the divine and the human is essential to him; but that is an account of the work accomplished by it amidst all our ambiguities. "The only adequate norm is the historic incarnation of a perfect love which actually transcends history, and can appear in it only to be crucified."[21] "The content of the revelation is an act of reconciliation in which the judgment of God upon the pride of man is not abrogated, in which the sin of man becomes the more sharply revealed and defined by the knowledge that God is Himself the victim of man's sin and pride. Nevertheless the final word is not one of judgment but of mercy and forgiveness."[22]

In our world God can only suffer. He enters into our contradictions and resistances. In them he maintains himself with his judgment and love. These two, in their oneness, become manifest on the cross. Forgiveness presupposes justice. Justice is the form in which God resists the violation of his order. If we ignore this justice we will "sentimentalize" the love proclaimed in the gospel. Conversely, justice without love degenerates into legalistic harshness. Man can only live with the unity of these two. However, this unity lies outside himself and above him in Christ. He can only grasp it in the unity of faith and repentance. He can only appropriate it fragmentarily. The "Christ for us" far exceeds the "Christ within us."[23] We live still in the interim between the revelation and the fulfillment of the meaning of life. We cannot endure on the basis of our own ever-sinful achievements. Only in the power of the forgive-

---

21. Ibid., 2:147.

22. Ibid., 2:147-48; cf. idem, *Faith and History,* ch. IX.

23. In his distinguished article "The Christology of Reinhold Niebuhr," P. Lehmann sees Niebuhr's leitmotif in the tension between these two (in *Reinhold Niebuhr: His Religious, Social, and Political Thought,* rev. ed., ed. C. W. Kegley (New York: Pilgrim Press, 1984), pp. 327-56.

ness and hope promised us can we take new steps which aim at making visible the love of God in our fallen world. For in Christ not only "the wisdom of God" is present but also "the power of God," and as such "a power of God over man" and at the same time (and here "the Christ in us" appears) "a power of God in man" which breaks our pride and arrogance, frees us from illusion and despair, and fills us with serenity and creativity.

Therein, despite the offense and folly, lies a wisdom and a power which can have a convincing effect on man. One might speak of a certain verification of the gospel. Niebuhr uses the word *validation*. "A limited rational validation of the truth of the Gospel is possible. It consists of a negative and a positive approach to the relation of the truth of the Gospel to other forms of truth, and of the goodness of perfect love to historic forms of virtue. Negatively the Gospel must and can be validated by exploring the limits of historic forms of wisdom and virtue. Positively it is validated when the truth of faith is correlated with all truths which may be known by scientific and philosophical disciplines and proves itself a resource for coordinating them into a deeper and wider system of coherence."[24]

Here the tasks and insights of the apologist and the ethicist flow together. A discussion of the various ethical problems which occupied Niebuhr lie outside our framework. It is simply astonishing to note the numerous individual problems on which he expressed himself, especially in his influential journal *Christianity and Crisis*. In this connection he combined precise social and political data with a sharp eye for the human essentials. He was able to point out everywhere how pride, despair, and complacency threatened to lead people into false directions, and to point to ways of sobriety and humility on which justice could be realized, which in turn pointed to the goals—never attainable on earth —of God's love for his world. One must bear in mind that also as a theologian Niebuhr was a typically American figure: to a degree much greater than is the case with the majority of European theologians, thought for him stood in the service of action. The truth of reconciliation and justification was so dear to him precisely because he saw it confirmed in so many choices and decisions in society.[25]

Niebuhr could not, of course, construct such an ethically oriented theology without a firm hope in a final victory of the love of God, that is, without an eschatology. The "eschaton," however, remains for him a limiting concept. The problem of human existence cannot be

24. Niebuhr, *Faith and History*, p. 152; see the whole of ch. X.
25. One may wonder why in *Nature and Destiny* the cross should be so central as evidence of God's love while the resurrection is not mentioned. Was

solved within the limits of history. The resolution, though not without continuity with history, occurs beyond history. This paradoxical relationship between eternity and time can be expressed only in symbols. Before the great fulfillment in the future we live, in our ambivalent history, only by facets of meaning.[26]

In order to define Niebuhr's position in theology somewhat further, we should compare him with two other great theological contemporaries. The first of these is Karl Barth. We already mentioned the striking parallels between them in their course of development. When they met, on the occasion of the founding of the World Council of Churches (Amsterdam, 1948), it became clear that there was a deep gulf between them.[27] In his address Barth had turned sharply against the tendency of the (mostly Anglo-Saxon) pre-conference preparatory papers to expect the salvation of the world from human —Christian— effort, "as though man were the Atlas appointed to carry the canopy of the heavens on his shoulders." Unfortunately, however, he expressed himself so one-sidedly (from the perspective of the whole of his theology) that even Niebuhr, who had always warned his fellow Americans against pride and illusion, charged that Barth tended "to rob the Christian life of its sense of responsibility" and that "the real weakness of this unvarying emphasis upon what we cannot do and upon what Christ has already done is that it tempts the Christian to share the victory and the glory of the risen Lord without participating in the crucifixion of the self." Over against this tendency he asserted: "Freedom over law cannot mean emancipation from the tortuous and difficult task of achieving a tolerable justice." Barth, on his part, could not recognize in this attack the positive image he had of Niebuhr and certainly not the thrust of his own theology. With his speech at Amsterdam he had meant to call the churches, in humility and courage, "to approach the problems which confront us when we descend from the

---

there no room in his thinking for such a "happy end" in the midst of our history? Or did he sense historical-critical objections here? Also in *Faith and History* (pp. 147-50) he shrank from "this type of miracle" (namely, the empty tomb) as "in opposition to true faith": "It is the revelatory depth of the fact which is the primary concern of faith," but Niebuhr does not further explicate this "depth."

26. For his eschatology, cf. *Nature and Destiny*, II, ch. X; *Faith and History*, chs. XIII, XIV.

27. This exchange was originally published in *The Christian Newsletter* (London, 1948), nos. 323 and 326, from which all quotations in this paragraph are taken.

heights into the depths and encounter the distresses and problems of our daily life." But, he adds, there is actually a profound contrast between Anglo-Saxon and continental theology, namely, in "the different attitude to the Bible." Anglo-Saxons prefer "to theologize on their own account" and "quote the Bible according to choice." This "non-committed attitude to the Bible" threatens to obscure the crucial dimension of God's action. For that reason people separate into camps called "liberalism" and "fundamentalism" and miss the possibility "that the questions raised from the side of the left or the right are corrected from the center and that questions which are meaningless become meaningful."

One would think that in these words Niebuhr's own concerns were approximated, and one must therefore strongly regret that these two great theologians, who were so close to each other in what each had to say to his own audience, could only see each other as caricatures. Barth cautiously ended the discussion with the words: "Perhaps it may be a good thing that in the first instance the caricatures should be brought to the light, and that then they should from one side or the other be designated as such and repudiated. After that the real discussion can begin." Unfortunately this hope was not fulfilled. Soon the supposed theological distance was reinforced by a political difference. Niebuhr increasingly adopted an anti-communist stance (as did Brunner), whereas Barth was a strong opponent of anti-communism.[28] The alienation in theology between Europe and America which existed at least since the World Conference at Stockholm (1925) and which was close to being bridged to a certain extent shortly after World War II, therefore continued and, despite all mutual inspirations and borrowings, continues to this day.

The second person with whom we shall compare Niebuhr is Paul Tillich. Through Niebuhr's efforts Tillich had escaped persecution by Hitler and been called to Union Theological Seminary. The two men were bound by ties of friendship and mutual respect. Still, they were divided by something deeper. To the superficial onlooker this division was not always clear because they occupied themselves with the same themes and not infrequently expressed themselves in a similar terminology. They themselves, however, were conscious of the difference. To state it in the briefest possible formula: Tillich as a theologian was an ontologist, Niebuhr an ethicist. The ethicist is ever obliged to oppose action to being; he thinks in concepts like freedom, decision, break, leap,

28. Cf. R. Niebuhr's article in *The Christian Century* (1957) 108-10, under the title "Why is Barth silent on Hungary?" and the references to Niebuhr in *Karl Barth: Letters, 1961-1968*, ed. J. Fangmeier and H. Stoevesandt, tr. G. W. Bromiley (Grand Rapids: Eerdmans, 1981) (see the index of Names, p. 373).

conversion. The being that is common to all remains a distant or speculative horizon which is the presupposition, not the goal, of his thought.
The ontologist can and must also think ethically but is always concerned
to understand action as a variety of being and to channel it into being.
He too knows of bridges and shifts but only as elements within the en-
closure of being. From Tillich's vantage point Niebuhr courted the
danger of supernaturalism, whereas Niebuhr feared that Tillich was
moving toward a static monism and a kind of "gnosticism." Tillich criticized Niebuhr especially because the latter did not in any way wish to
understand the self ontologically, because by his preference for paradox
and the grace of revelation as an "impossible possibility" tended toward
irrationalism, because he could only conceive of ontology as being static,
and because he failed to relate freedom dialectically to destiny, etc. For
his part, Niebuhr objected to Tillich that in his thinking the personhood
of God threatened to be absorbed in "Being itself" (Tillich's definition of
God); that sin instead of being an abnormality becomes a tragic ontological necessity and that its character as guilt is therefore cancelled.[29]

Summarizing his views he wrote:

> I do not believe that ontological categories can do justice to the
> freedom either of the divine or of the human person, or to the
> unity of the person in his involvement in and transcendence
> over the temporal flux or that the sin of man and the forgiveness
> by God of man's sin or the dramatic variety of man's history can
> be comprehended in ontological categories. If it is "supernatu-
> ralistic" to affirm that faith discerns the key to specific meaning
> above the categories of philosophy, ontological or epistemologi-
> cal, then I must plead guilty of being a supernaturalist. The
> whole of the Bible is an exposition of this kind of supernatural-

29. Niebuhr expressed his criticisms of Tillich in C. W. Kegley and R. W.
Bretall, eds., *The Theology of Paul Tillich* (New York: Pilgrim Press, 1952), under
the heading "Biblical Thought and Ontological Speculation in Tillich's Theology" (pp. 216-27), in which he attacked statements by Tillich (from the section
"God as creating" in Tillich's *Systematic Theology*, vol. 1), such as: "fully developed creatureliness is fallen creatureliness" (p. 219), to which Tillich briefly replied (pp. 338-39, 342ff.). In the second volume of this series, *Reinhold Niebuhr*,
the roles were reversed. Tillich wrote "Reinhold Niebuhr's Doctrine of Knowledge" (pp. 37-43), to which Niebuhr replied briefly (pp. 432-33). Tillich defended
the relationship between his doctrine of sin and his ontological doctrine of alienation against Niebuhr in *Systematic Theology* (Chicago: University of Chicago
Press, 1957), 2:44. Man "affirms the state of estrangement in acts of freedom
which imply responsibility and guilt."

ism. If we are embarrassed by this and try to interpret Biblical religion in other terms, we end in changing the very character of the Christian faith.[30]

For fifteen years following World War II Niebuhr and Tillich were the two great authorities for wide circles of people both inside and outside the United States. In Tillich's thought people found an answer to the question concerning life's meaning; in Niebuhr's thought they found an answer to the question concerning right action, socially and internationally. Niebuhr's influence extended to the State Department in Washington and to the World Council of Churches in Geneva (where the Department of Social Studies was vigorously and successfully led by his and John Bennett's pupil Paul Abrecht). Soon there were theologians, ethicists, and politicians everywhere who were guided by Niebuhr's basic ideas and concrete proposals. The power of his influence can be measured by the prayer which Niebuhr uttered in a worship service in 1943 and which has since been repeated a million times:

O God, give us
Serenity to accept what cannot be changed,
Courage to change what should be changed,
and Wisdom to distinguish the one from the other.[31]

THE END OF NEO-ORTHODOXY

Still, today we look back upon the period of Neo-Orthodoxy as a closed epoch. Why closed? There are several reasons. First, there was, of course, the fact that the Niebuhrs, like so many great theologians, were especially effective because they were impressive personalities, and this direct influence ended with their death. Second, in my opinion, neither the abstract subtlety of Richard nor the way Reinhold Niebuhr brought

---

30. Quoted in Kegley and Bretall, eds., *Reinhold Niebuhr*, p. 509.

31. Motto in J. Bingham, *Courage to Change*, and in *Justice and Mercy* (New York, 1974), a collection of sermons and prayers edited by his wife Ursula Niebuhr. The latter dates the prayer in 1943; J. Bingham mentions 1934. The problem of the authorship of this widely circulated "Serenity Prayer" is too long to be told here. In Germany, where it circulated during the war, it was purposely ascribed to a former German theologian, and that pseudonymity lasted several decades more. In the United States, for quite different reasons, Niebuhr's authorship was contested. See Fox, *Reinhold Niebuhr*, pp. 290ff. Perhaps Niebuhr had used unconsciously what he had read or heard from others.

disparate realities together could in time satisfy the hunger for a more practical and direct ideology. Even Reinhold's understanding of justice in society remained for many people too complex, too intangible, and insufficiently a stimulus to direct action. In addition, in their thought and action Americans are generally oriented to the present and the near future, to modernity and renewal, to ever new lines of thought and action. The manner in which especially Reinhold Niebuhr sought to resolve the ambiguities of modernity in the light of Scripture and the Reformation did not appeal to many. The American mind with its bent toward experience and renewal will always be disposed to favor a short-lived liberalism over a view which radically questions its post-Enlightenment situation or seeks to be strongly rooted in the great tradition of earlier centuries and the biblical message. This last statement is not true for the majority of church-related theological seminaries, but it is for the majority of the great interdenominational training centers, and for the rapidly increasing departments of religion at the secular universities. There Reinhold Niebuhr is regarded as much too "orthodox" and "conservative"; people remain susceptible to optimistic and utopian views even when reality contradicts them. Also, the American mind is more open to the immanent than to the transcendent side of God and leans more to empiricism than to metaphysics. In the case of Richard Niebuhr we observed a shift from transcendence toward immanence, a shift he validated with an appeal to Whitehead. At this moment, as I am writing these pages, Neo-Orthodoxy is being shouldered aside in many quarters by varieties of process theology.[32]

No less important and perhaps decisive for the disappearance of Neo-Orthodoxy is the fact that since the 1960s theology has no longer been the privileged domain of a small group which attempted to wed the gospel to its "sense of life" *(Lebensgefühl)*. Other life views outside this dominant group sought expression, linking the gospel with its very

32. Especially to be mentioned are John B. Cobb, Jr., Schubert M. Ogden, T. W. Ogletree, Norman Pittenger, and D. D. Williams, while Langdon Gilkey establishes a link between process theology and Richard Niebuhr's and Tillich's thinking. They all welcome process theology as a new and dynamic variety of natural theology which is well suited as a *praeambulum fidei* for a modern understanding of the Christian faith. For a discussion of process theology in a European context, cf. the thorough study by M. Welker, *Universalität Gottes und Relativität der Welt: Theologische Kosmologie im Dialog mit dem amerikanischen Processdenken nach Whitehead* (Neukirchen-Vluyn: Neukirchener, 1981). Welker, while viewing process thought as a deepening of Christian cosmology, rejects it as an attempt to enrich the doctrine of God.

different and often very negative experiences. What comes to mind for the United States is especially black and feminist theology. Such new theologies, arising as they do from the experience of oppression, can only develop from below. They start with experienced realities which they then recognize also in the Bible. What the two Niebuhrs accused liberalism, and to some extent the social gospel, of doing—namely, that it read its own views into the Bible—now repeats itself in another way. With a certain inherent necessity present-day theologies of emancipation must remain deaf to the call to open themselves up to divine contradiction and judgment as the only way to salvation. Neo-Orthodox ethics, which relativizes all human choices, is hard to combine with the conviction of oppressed groups of the rightness of their cause and with their inclination to think in terms of black and white.[33]

Still, as it passes through one unsettling experience after another, everything in this dynamic country remains in rapid flux. One can hardly imagine that numerous experiences of failure will not again lead to a new discovery of the liberating strangeness of the gospel. Should this discovery be made, people could again link up with the living legacy of Neo-Orthodoxy still present below the surface. The first signs of this happening are already visible.[34] Both Jonathan Edwards and Reinhold Niebuhr, though in different ways, achieved a synthesis of the three religious-cultural layers present in America. One may expect new such attempts in the future. If they are not to lead to a powerless amalgam, however, they must not fall behind the biblical power of Reinhold Niebuhr.

33. In the framework of this book I can only touch upon the contrasting views concerning the relation or contradiction between the pre-war radical and post-war more conservative or pessimistic political stance of Reinhold Niebuhr. Fox, *Reinhold Niebuhr,* beginning with the Introduction, gives a good impression of this hermeneutical controversy. See also the review of Fox's book by R. W. Lovin in *Religious Studies Review* (April, 1988): 97-102. From my more theological angle I am inclined to seek the solution in what for Niebuhr was the heart of the gospel: the paradox of man's sin and God's grace, which led him to a realistic ambivalence.

34. I have in mind particularly L. Gilkey, *Reaping the Whirlwind* (New York: Seabury, 1977); and D. J. Hall, *Lighten our Darkness: Toward an Indigenous Theology of the Cross* (Philadelphia: Westminster, 1976). For a careful and typical appreciation of R. Niebuhr in the present generation, cf. D. Tracy, *Blessed Rage for Order* (New York: Seabury, 1975), pp. 213-14.

CHAPTER XVII

Paul Tillich: The Bridge of Correlation

TILLICH'S THEOLOGICAL CAREER

We shall now devote a separate chapter to Paul Tillich, even though he also figured expressly in the previous chapter on American theology in general. But why could we not deal with him in that chapter as we did, for example, with his great friend Reinhold Niebuhr? The answer is that somehow Tillich does not quite fit within the framework of American theology. Like Rauschenbusch and the Niebuhrs, he too was of German extraction. But he was unlike them, externally, in that he was not born in the United States; he was 47 years old when he came to America. Though grateful for his new homeland, he himself often stressed how long it took him and how difficult it was for him to establish roots in the United States. Tillich also differed from them internally: though his immigration clearly brought with it a shift in his thinking, in many respects he remained a European or German thinker. The extraordinary thing in his case is that he fascinated American intellectuals with his books and lectures not in spite of, but because of, his European orientation and focus, and that in the 1950s and 1960s he again found a hearing in broad European circles, even more than in his first German period. Obviously, after World War II his thinking came as a welcome answer to a general question in the Western world. This phenomenon has to do with the precise problem which occupies us in this book.

    Paul Johannes Tillich (1886-1965) was born as the son of a conservative pastor in Starzeddel, a small town in eastern Germany. When his family moved to Berlin in 1900, the broad and free education for which he had so eagerly yearned became a possibility. He breathed in the air of classic idealism. Ritschl with his Kantian dichotomy between nature and morality could not satisfy him. By contrast, his nature mysticism, not unlike romanticism, allowed him to experience more freely the wholeness of reality. This explains why in this period he oriented himself especially to Schelling (particularly his philosophy of nature). Schelling's "positive philosophy," however, moved him away also from Hegel's harmonious system in the direction of a beginning existentialism. In 1910 he gained his doctorate in philosophy (in Breslau) and in 1912 in theology (in Halle), both times on themes in Schelling. During World War I he served as a chaplain in the German army. His war experiences demolished the idealistic foundations of his thought. He became a socialist and soon a leader of the religious-socialist movement. The philosophical and theological problems associated with this position constituted the most important themes of his German writings (1919-1933).

He worked as a theological instructor *(Privatdozent)* in Berlin (1919-1924); for a brief period as associate professor in Marburg (1924-1925); then as a full professor in Dresden and Leipzig (1925-1929); and from 1929 on, succeeding Max Scheler, as a professor of philosophy at the University of Frankfurt. There he especially liked to work in the border area between theology and philosophy. His opposition to the rise of the national socialists led to his dismissal immediately after Hitler's takeover. Reinhold Niebuhr, who was in Germany in the summer of 1933, invited him to come to Union Theological Seminary in New York. There, in the same year, he began his second theological career, being appointed to a chair in "philosophical theology," as it was called to his delight. He remained there until his retirement in 1955. After that he worked at Harvard (1955-1962), and then, until his death, at the Divinity School of the University of Chicago.

His natural giftedness allowed him to be active in many different directions: theological, philosophical, literary, esthetic, homiletic, social, etc. But it has surprised many people that in the United States he hardly pursued his earlier interests in religious socialism. People have sought to explain this in a variety of ways. It is better, however, to hold to Tillich's own explanation: his socialism, so he wrote in 1952, "is still a reality, although mixed with resignation and some bitterness about the division of the world into two all-powerful groups between which the remnants of a democratic and religious socialism are crushed. . . . After the Second World War I felt the tragic more than the activating elements of our historical existences, and I lost the inspiration for, and the contact with, active politics."[1]

1. Thus Tillich in his "Autobiographical Reflections," in *The Theology of Paul Tillich*, ed. by C. W. Kegley and R. W. Bretall (New York: Macmillan, 1952),

To this factor may be added the fact that in the United States socialism played a much less significant political role than in Europe. In any case, especially after World War II, Tillich encountered in his new homeland another kind of quest, one which especially suited his philosophical-theological bent: the quest for the meaning of life and for a place to stand in the shattered existence of the post-war world. As a Christian and a thinker Tillich had always lived and thought in the context of the polarity between question and answer. In his case it became the foundation of his mature theology. As a result he became for many the bridge builder between their personal problems and the gospel. We shall now see how this bridge was constructed—what Tillich's "method of correlation" looked like.

For this purpose we shall turn to his three-volume *Systematic Theology*. Not only is it constructed rigorously and consistently on this principle of correlation; it is also the only place where he expressly reflects upon the concept of correlation, mainly in the Introduction to the first volume (esp. pp. 18-28, 59-66), and also, to refute misunderstandings which have arisen in the meantime, in the Introduction to the second volume (pp. 13-16).[2] The latter section begins with the following words:

> The method used in the theological system and described in the methodological introduction of the first volume is called the "method of correlation," namely, the correlation between existential questions and theological answers. "Correlation," a word with several meanings in scientific language, is understood as "interdependence of two independent factors." It is not understood in the logical sense of quantitative or qualitative coordination of elements without causal relation, but it is understood as a unity of the dependence and independence of two factors. (p. 13)

But is God in his self-revelation then dependent on man? "God in his self-manifestation to man is dependent on the way man receives his manifestation. . . . The 'divine-human encounter' (Emil Brunner) means

---

pp. 3-21. This is the source also of other details I am citing. The quotations occur on pp. 12 and 19.

2. The three volumes of *Systematic Theology* were published simultaneously by the University of Chicago Press (Chicago) and James Nisbet & Co. Ltd. (London) in 1951, 1957, and 1963. However, the pagination in these two editions is not identical. The references here are from the American edition.

something real for both sides" (1:61). For theology this means: "Theology formulates the questions implied in human existence, and theology formulates the answers implied in divine self-manifestation under the guidance of the questions implied in human existence" (1:61).

THE METHODOLOGICAL CORRELATION OF QUESTION AND ANSWER

In order to understand precisely what is meant here we first have to consider the two components of this correlation. We learned already that to ask questions is part of the essence of human existence, but we are not now talking about multiple and disparate questions. In English we speak both of "question" and of "quest." Tillich favors "quest" because it expresses a strong concern, an existential search. "The question, asked by man, is man himself. He asks it, whether or not he is vocal about it. He cannot avoid asking it, because his very being is the question of his existence. In asking it, he is alone with himself. He asks 'out of the depth,' and this depth is he himself" (2:13). Hence the quest is fundamentally singular. It is aimed at one's "ultimate concern," at the absolute and eternal to which we stand in a relationship and which decides about our finite being or nonbeing. This quest is therefore genuinely religious. It is the abstract translation of the "first and great" commandment. Whether man knows and wants this quest is not decisive. What is essential is that in all areas of life he is in search of that which concerns him unconditionally: in his religions, worldviews, and political ideologies; in art and literature, in myth and science, and in a special way in philosophy, because it inquires into reality itself (and is therefore mainly understood by Tillich as ontology).

This quest of man arises from the depths of his predicament, the predicament of his experienced self-alienation. He is not really at home with himself—hence his dread, brokenness, and despair. From within his inner dividedness he is in search of integration, harmony, reunion with his true self. To fathom all this and to perform the right analysis of human existence is the task of philosophy. Every human being, Christian or otherwise, must be able to fathom the final questions of life. If he does so with the necessary acuteness and the requisite courage, he will be able to uncover the gap in his existence. Then he will also discover that it cannot be bridged. He discovers a question without an answer. He does not know what lies beyond his question. He only recognizes his human, that is, his difficult, situation or predicament. For that reason both natural theology and humanism have to be rejected as misleading because they view humanness as such not as a question but as an answer.

Tillich's analysis of existence is strongly reminiscent of that of Heidegger. Hence he is often viewed as a Christian existentialist. However, the label "existentialist" can only be partially applied to him because in his thinking everything stands within an ontological framework—as it does for that matter in Heidegger after his "shift" (his *Kehre*). In his short period in Marburg Tillich did come into close contact with Heidegger, but one can hardly speak of dependence. Such lines of thought were in the air at the time. Besides, both thinkers were strongly influenced by Kierkegaard. The main thing, however, is that Heidegger was a philosopher and Tillich a theologian, and therefore the same concepts were illumined by these two men from very different angles. About his meeting with Heidegger Tillich himself said: "It took years before I became fully aware of the impact of this encounter on my own thinking. I resisted, I tried to learn, I accepted the new way of thinking more than the answers it gave."[3]

More important than the source of his understanding of the human quest is its theological value. Is modern existentialism the first and only system to disclose the essence of man? Or is it the case that in other epochs the quest had a different content? Tillich's answer to these questions is not unambiguous. On the one hand he asserts that in different epochs the quest assumes different forms: in the time of the church fathers it was the quest for immortality; in the time of the Reformation it was the quest for the justification of the sinner, etc. On the other hand he believes that all ultimate questions circle around the opposition between "finite" and "infinite," "human existence" and "absolute being," and that this theme has only fully come to expression in modern existentialism (cf. esp. 2:27-28). Hence on the one hand he believes that every dogmatics constructed on correlation is time-conditioned; on the other hand he leans toward seeing the earlier formulations of the quest as fundamentally oriented to the relationship between existence and essence.

The answer does not lie within the question; it comes from without. As man himself is the question, God himself is the answer which man can therefore not give himself. At this point Tillich sounds almost like Barth. "For God is manifest only through God" (2:14). Here lies the truth of supernaturalism. Its untruth consists in the fact that it does not see the Word of God as answer, hence as fundamentally related to our quest. Question and answer are mutually independent and mutually dependent. How that can be will be seen the moment we turn from methodology to ontology. Here we note the image of the ellipse with which Tillich explains his view:

3. In *The Theology of Paul Tillich*, p. 14.

The theologian as theologian is committed to a concrete expression of the ultimate concern, religiously speaking, of a special revelatory experience. On the basis of this concrete experience, he makes his universal claims, as Christianity did in terms of the statement that Jesus as the Christ is the Logos. This circle can be understood as an ellipse (not as a geometrical circle) and described in terms of two central points—the existential question and the theological answer. Both are within the sphere of the religious commitment, but they are not identical. (2:14-15)

Two elements in this quotation deserve special attention. First: "Both are within the sphere of the religious commitment," since both have the same theme: our ultimate concern. Philosophy, in the attitude of objectivity, is preoccupied with the question; theology is existentially involved in the answer. The stated thesis thus holds the problematics of the question and that of the answer together like an accolade in music. Second: theological formulation, be it cursory, of this bifocal view (*Zusammenschau*) is given when Tillich indicates that, on the one hand, Christ as "the concrete expression of man's ultimate concern" is the content of the divine answer; and on the other, Christ as the universal *Logos* somehow indwells the whole of earthly reality.

The latter statement implies that Tillich wants to develop his theology in terms of the centrality of Christ. This intent often escapes the critical reader because of his manifold philosophical analyses of human existence. One is then in danger of viewing Tillich only as the exponent of a natural theology. But that would be to misunderstand him completely. "The question does not create the answer. The answer, 'the Christ,' cannot be created by man, but man can receive it and express it according to the way he has asked for it" (2:16). "The theologian . . . must look where that which concerns him ultimately is manifest, and he must stand where its manifestation reaches and grasps him. The source of his knowledge is not the universal *logos* but the Logos 'who became flesh,' that is, the *logos* manifesting itself in a particular historical event" (1:23). The center of this theology is the paradox that universal being manifests itself in a historical person. This unity of the absolute and the finite, which is foolishness to philosophy, is for Tillich the great miracle in the light of which he can live and think. For only in Christ (he always speaks of "the Christ" to indicate his supra-individuality), who offers his finite life for the sake of union with God, is the fate of our estrangement abolished and access to "new being" opened. The paradox is possible and actual through love. Tillich's entire second volume is devoted to this thesis.

THE ONTOLOGICAL BACKGROUND

Only after this introduction are we in a position to glance at the broad ontological context of this historical center, as it is developed especially in the first volume. Apart from this background, one cannot completely understand the structure of correlation. For in Tillich epistemological theory and content, method and ontology, are bound together very closely. The fact that man is fundamentally a question and cannot reach his ultimate concern is the expression of his ontological position: he is estranged from his essential being because he is estranged from "the ground of being" or from "being itself." This estrangement is necessity as well as guilt (for the discussion of his doctrine of sin which Tillich conducted with Reinhold Niebuhr, see the preceding chapter). As long as man is secure in his pure essence, he exists in a state of "dreaming innocence" or potentiality and is not actual. He becomes actual when he grasps his finite freedom and so begins to ex-ist, that is, to stand out from pure potentiality, in order in his finiteness to stand in absolute nonbeing and at the same time to stand out from nonbeing (cf. 2:20ff.). That is the ambivalence of human existence. With his finite freedom man lives at the boundary between two worlds. He lives under threat of nonbeing, of death; so he is full of anxiety. Out of this arises the question: Where do I get the courage, despite my anxiety, to affirm my existence? Only "that which determines our being or non-being, and therefore concerns us ultimately" can give my life meaning and provide the "courage to be."[4] To this question God as the ground of being and the power of integration and union is the only answer. Unfortunately, in volume 1 the doctrine of God is so abstract that it seems to offer only a philosophical statement. This impression is reinforced by Tillich's rejection of the personhood of God. "He is not a person but he is not less than personal" (1:245). In this connection one must bear in mind not only his theory of symbol but also what he wrote earlier about "the final revelation" and later about "existence and the Christ."

The extent, both ontologically and methodologically, to which the correlation determines his entire work can be seen from the familiar division in five questions and answers: Reason and Revelation; Being and God; Existence and the Christ; Life and the Spirit; History and the Kingdom of God (for a defense of this division, cf. 1:66ff.). In the subsections of the five main parts, the correlation is often recognizable in still

---

4. Tillich's *Courage to Be,* written for a wider circle of readers, is probably his most read work and, in my opinion, an excellent introduction to his thought.

another way: everywhere Tillich starts with an analysis of the question and uncovers the "ambiguities" on which it rests. Then follows the presentation of the answer. Especially in Pneumatology the line of thought then curves back to the ambiguities to show how they change under the influence of the answer (esp. 3:162-282). This tripartite division occurs also elsewhere in Tillich. Compare, for example, the headings in *The Eternal Now* (1963): 1. The Human Predicament; 2. The Divine Reality; 3. The Challenge to Man. All this can obviously lead to a dry schematism. If that is usually not the case in Tillich the reason is that the schemata are filled over and over both with biblical *chokmah* and human wisdom which makes the content—which is not easy even apart from the schematism—rewarding.

Tillich presents his doctrine of faith as "answering theology" and opposes it to a "theology of proclamation" as it occurs in Barth. He also speaks of "apologetic" versus "kerygmatic" theology. But the two are not mutually exclusive. The first kind also aims to be kerygmatic, to relate the message and the human situation to each other. On Tillich's view, in Barth the message either stands unrelated next to the situation or floats above the situation. According to Tillich, the apologetic theory of correlation is more comprehensive than the kerygmatic and can also do justice to the latter. Besides, it has the great tradition of classic Christian thought on its side: the church fathers, Thomas, even (Tillich believes) Calvin.

QUESTIONS AND RESERVATIONS

As one can imagine, Tillich exerted a great deal of influence in the 1950s and 1960s on all those who sighed under the burden of Barth's rigorous theology of the Word, unable to relate it to their own needs and questions. Here they had an alternative that at first glance was both simple and convincing. This certainly is how it should be: man asks questions, God answers. The principle of correlation proved fruitful not only for theology, but also for preaching, church education, adult education, etc.[5] One could view Tillich's theology simultaneously as a vindication of and a reflection on a methodology that was widely followed in the modern churches.

5. Perhaps this point applies even more to Catholic than to Protestant circles, especially in church instruction. Cf. *A New Catechism*, commissioned by the bishops of the Netherlands (New York: Seabury, 1967, 1969), which starts with "Man the Questioner."

Still, upon closer scrutiny questions and objections multiply. Tillich himself was aware of them and, as we shall see, attempted to answer them. To begin with: Did Tillich correctly understand man's existential quest (if we may speak of it in such general terms)? Is not giving answers as essential to human beings as asking questions? Were and are the great thinkers, poets, scholars only important for the questions that may be derived from their answers? They themselves would rather think the opposite to be true. Therefore, their self-understanding cannot be captured under the word *quest*. That is especially true of philosophers to whom Tillich attributes the work on the question side of the correlation. We also heard him say, however: Theology formulates the questions inherent in the human situation. He explains this statement in the following fashion: Philosophy and many other expressions of culture make available the material for an analysis of existence.

> The theologian organizes these materials in relation to the answer given by the Christian message. In the light of this message he may make an analysis of existence which is more penetrating than that of most philosophers. Nevertheless, it remains a philosophical analysis. The analysis of existence, including the development of the questions implicit in existence, is a philosophical task, even if it is performed by a theologian, and even if the theologian is a reformer like Calvin. . . . This does not make the philosophical work of the theologian heteronomous. As a theologian he does not tell himself what is philosophically true. As a philosopher he does not tell himself what is theologically true. But he cannot help seeing human existence and existence generally in such a way that the Christian symbols appear meaningful and understandable to him. His eyes are partially focused by his ultimate concern, which is true of every philosopher. Nevertheless, his act of seeing is autonomous, for it is determined only by the object as it is given in his experience. (1:63-64)

From these laborious and almost contradictory statements one can tell how Tillich had to struggle to make his discussion of the correlation logical. In the second volume, in response to attacks and misunderstandings, he again explains his method. Here we read: "The material of the existential question is taken from the whole of human experience. . . . All this, as far as it reflects man's existential predicament, is the material without the help of which the existential question cannot be formulated. The choice of the material, as well as the formulation of the question, is the task of the systematic theologian" (2:15).

Essentially the explanation in the second volume is a condensed repetition of what was said in the first volume. Presumably it is inherent in the matter itself that it cannot be explained any further. Tillich operates within a circle, and he knows it; in fact, he wants it. Immediately at the outset of his prolegomena he introduced the concept of the theological circle. Like all the humanities, theology is based on "mystical experience" and rests therefore on a "mystical a priori." Besides, it works with the norm of the Christian message, and so its circle is narrower than that of the philosophy of religion (1:8-11). This difference presupposes a "leap" (into the circle), although Tillich, who regards the problem from a merely epistemological point of view, as a rule avoids the word. But even then the notion of a circle serves the apologetic nature of this theology. Tillich attempts to narrow the gap between philosophy and theology (a gap that is given with the concept of the circle) by referring to the Christian stamp of modern philosophy. In this connection one encounters a number of strong assertions: "In this sense [in the sense of a philosophy 'whose existential basis is historical Christianity'] all modern philosophy is Christian, even if it is humanistic, atheistic, and intentionally anti-Christian." "The modern vision of reality and its philosophical analysis is different from that of pre-Christian times, whether one is or is not existentially determined by the God of Mount Zion and the Christ of Mount Golgotha." The marks of the Christian tradition "cannot be erased; they are a *character indelebilis*" (1:27). This reference, though intended as explanation, can hardly diminish the sense of distance between the human question and the divine answer—on the contrary.

Our conclusion has to be: in Tillich the answer shapes the question—as a rule by selection from given materials. Only the person who already knows the answer knows wherein the true question consists: the question from within his anxiety, estrangement, and guilt (fundamentally Tillich's anthropology is reformationally pessimistic) is for healing, salvation, and reconciliation and therein for the meaning of life and the courage to be. But can one view this question as a universally human question (since after all modern existentialism is a post-Christian phenomenon)? Over the years Tillich must repeatedly have had second thoughts about this point. A few years after the appearance of volumes 1 and 2 he expressly wrote about this in a concluding review added to a selection of articles under the title *Theology of Culture*. He knows that in Asiatic religions anxiety about death plays no role, that modern man does not recognize his guilt but his neurotic guilt feelings, that Marxism traces the feeling of tragedy back to a situation of economic alienation, and that many other people alongside these groups deny that there is such a thing as a universal human nature and view only man's infinite capacity for change as essential. Tillich's answer is that indeed we cannot prove anything but that nevertheless we must hold before all these groups the "mirror" of human misery, show them "the structures of anxiety, of conflict, of guilt," because these structures mirror what we are, and if we are right, they are in other people also, and they will be able to concur with our analysis. Of course, whether we shall succeed "nobody knows. This is the risk we must take." In this context Tillich unexpectedly turns to the realm of pedagogy and takes one more step:

> There are two principles we should follow in the religious education of our children. The first is that the questions which are really in the hearts of the children should be answered and the children should be shown that biblical symbols and the Christian message are an answer to just these questions. And secondly, we ought to seek to shape their existence in the direction of the questions which we believe are the more universal ones. This would be similar to what we do with primitive peoples in the mission field. We seek to answer *their* questions and in doing so we, at the same time, slowly transform their existence so that they come to ask the questions to which the Christian message gives the answer.[6]

This also means that on his own account man asks questions which are pointers to the big question to which the Christian educator or preacher or theologian must first lead him.

In view of all this one is led to ask whether Tillich has offered a genuine alternative to kerygmatic theology, whether he has made credible the claim to an answering theology. In any case it is clear that the gap between the two forms of theology is less wide than Tillich and Barth thought at the time. We are reminded of what we said above in the chapter on Schleiermacher about his concerns in comparison with those of Barth. As in Schleiermacher, so in Tillich human self-understanding is not identical with the question to which revelation gives an answer; it is only the "place" (Schleiermacher) at which man finds himself and at which the gospel "calls" on him. Nevertheless, like Schleiermacher and differently than Barth, Tillich avoids—as long as possible—presenting the transition to faith in the God-given answer-and-question as a break with the presupposed human understanding of existence.[7] God is at

---

6. P. Tillich, *Theology of Culture* (New York: Oxford University Press, 1959), pp. 202-3, 205-6.

7. "As long as possible," for in volume 3 of his *Systematic Theology*, concerning the work of the Spirit, he also attempts to do justice to the vantage point

work everywhere, and hence there is a "latent Christianity" everywhere, which can, however, only be discovered in the light of Christ. Barth also asserts that the creation is "the external ground of the covenant" and that there are therefore many "lights of the world"; indeed, Jesus Christ, precisely in his exclusiveness, is universally inclusive. While Tillich would say that the right question is selected from the given situation in the light of the gospel, Barth would say that the gospel itself first creates in man the question appropriate to it. In Tillich the classic doctrine of "common grace" regains the place it had lost in Barth. Under the pressure of secularization, however, it is much more modest than would appear at first sight. Even so, from Barth's perspective it still plays a dangerous role. For as long as Tillich speaks of correlation and ellipse he has to provide a place of its own for the analysis of existence if he is not to return totally to a theology of the Word. For that reason Tillich must also be criticized in the opposite direction from that given above, namely, that in his theology the answer of the gospel remains caught in the grip of a nonevangelical formulation of the question and is therefore distorted.

Usually Tillich's critics appeal, with reason, to the doctrine of God in which all of God's attributes are explained by the ontological assertion "God is being itself" and the link with Christ is only established at the very end. But if one were to bring into consideration, beside the doctrine of God, Tillich's Christology and Pneumatology, then the resulting picture might be very different. In the case of Tillich, however, one remains fundamentally caught in a finally unresolvable oscillation which leaves room for various interpretations of his theology.[8]

This reality makes it impossible to view Tillich's theology as a genuine bridge between the gospel and modernity. However, this conclusion does not in the least diminish the significance of this great theologian. On the contrary: from one who has attempted with such exceptional constructive power to build that bridge one can learn in a decisive way. But those who have come after him, beginning with the God-is-dead theologians, apparently have not seen precisely this decisive element.

---

of the break, esp. in Part IV, section III: "The Divine Spirit and the Ambiguities of Life."

8. A good introduction to the main problem of Tillich's method may be found in G. Thomas, "The Method and Structure of Tillich's Theology," in *The Theology of Paul Tillich*, pp. 86-105.

CHAPTER XVIII

Backward Glances and Conclusions

WHAT REALLY HAPPENED?

Many readers of these chapters will have been left with a feeling of confusion. That fact by itself need not depress us. After all, theology is not a heavenly enterprise but a form of the human scholarly quest, and subject like every other discipline to the laws of trial and error. If theology were one of the natural sciences it would, despite its complexities, be able to show clear progress. Every scholarly researcher builds, in accordance with the same method, upon the achievements of his predecessors. In the humanities, to which theology largely belongs methodologically, the situation is different. No one would hold that Heidegger, because he lived in a later period than Leibniz, had a better insight into the fundamental questions of being, or that Leibniz, in virtue of the centuries which separated him from Plato (who may therefore be denominated "primitive"), surpassed him in thought. And if today we read Shakespeare differently than he was read in the Sturm-und-Drang period, that does not mean we understand him better. The arts and humanities *(Geisteswissenschaften)* know no progress because the laws which govern man and his achievements are infinitely complex and, if not theoretically then practically, incapable of being brought into a single perspective and synthesis. Here one does not progress but moves continuously in a circle around one's object, ever and again viewing it from a different angle—and the angle changes with the experiences and predicaments of every given cultural epoch. For that reason the great cultural historian Johan Huizinga could say of the science of history that it was the form "in which a culture gives account of its own past." This is not to say that here a pure, be it a culturally collective, form of subjectivism prevails; but it does mean that we are talking about a search, a questioning, an encounter, an interaction. Here neither subjectivism nor objectivism but intersubjectivity is, in many cases, the highest attainable measure of objectivity.

Translated into theological methodology, this idea means that systematic-theological conceptions are the ways in which the Christian community gives an account of the gospel as its source and norm. Especially in the Western world, which until now has been in the lead, this community lives in the midst of a culture which is estranged from this gospel. This is the culture for which the Christian church would like to reinterpret the gospel so as to make it a vital option again. Therefore the task of "giving an account of" (1 Peter 3:15) the gospel is performed in constant interaction, a process in which theology is the intermediary which from within its experience of the world interrogates the gospel and then translates the results of this interrogation back to the world. Thus theology constantly finds itself in a steady feedback situation. In this connection the mediating theologian does not stand outside his world but directly in the midst of it. He participates, consciously or not, in its presuppositions and experiences. As a result he finds himself in an encounter situation which is more complex as well as more existential than most encounters which occur in the arts and humanities. In theology more than elsewhere in these disciplines intersubjectivity is threatened by subjectivism. A counterweight is that the gospel is not only an object of scholarship but authoritative for faith. It constantly forces the theologian to raise more and different issues than he would be inclined to do from within his own subjective and narrow horizon of understanding. Precisely because of his existential relationship to the gospel as a normative message, however, the theologian is especially vulnerable to the danger of reinterpreting it for his own protection and profit. To illustrate this point as well as the preceding statement, one could cite a great many examples. The best theologian is not the person who knows how to escape the dangers inherent in this process of encounter, for such people do not exist; the best theologian is the person who is most aware of these dangers and hence practices modesty and caution in what he says.

With reference to the cultural situation we mentioned two things: "presuppositions" and "experiences." In my opinion, the intellectual presuppositions of the epoch after the Enlightenment have essentially remained the same since then. Man has become his own law, so he objectivizes and manipulates nature and marginalizes God. He views himself as the only responsible subject, and responsible only to himself. Within these confines one can fit almost all the utterances of the leading intellectual circles in this epoch; however, within the same confines this epoch is full of contrasts. They have less to do with the presuppositions than with the experiences. Great technical achievements, wars, revolutions, environmental exhaustion, etc., can change people's views and conduct and force them to modify (not, however, to abandon) the presuppositions. The theologian will sense all this and in his feedback situation and mediating activity question the gospel from changing points of view. Schleiermacher did it from within the perspective of German idealism, Ritschl in the light of the realism of the technical-industrial world, the young Barth on the basis of the general sense of failure during and following World War I. This dynamic situation need not mean a surrender of the gospel to the spirit of the times. In the first place it has something to do with the theological "command of the hour" *(Gebot der Stunde).* On outsiders, to be sure, it has to make a chaotic and subjectivistic impression. This impression is reinforced when a succeeding generation of theologians accuses the preceding one of having interpreted the gospel falsely. But was the interpretation of the previous generation really false? And did the succeeding generation then do it right? Against their better knowledge many theologians still seem to proceed from a static, unhistorical, freely available "truth" and to believe that it is most safe within their keeping. That has created the impression of a boundless subjectivism and given theology a bad reputation. In contrast, my journey has taught me that the basic concerns and aims of the several schools, modalities, and generations have much more in common than concentration on all the larger and smaller differences (as this occurs especially within universities) would ever lead one to suspect. In the prolegomena, where questions of method are central, this fundamental commonality of concern is generally concealed, but when the material issues of dogmatics are discussed, and even more in preaching, it comes more clearly to the fore. Usually, however, this commonality is only granted to a degree when a new and common foe forces the formation of a new front. However this may be, for me as an observer the journey has been an exercise in tolerance.

WAS IT LEGITIMATE?

The things we said above may create the impression that in the darkness of relativization all cats are equally gray. A greater degree of commonality of purpose—greater than the participants realize—is no guarantee, however, that the articulations of it will be of equal value. As soon as the commonality has been recognized, there is room from within the common purpose for mutual criticism and correction. Then the legitimacy of the different designs is open to discussion and debate.

The question of legitimacy must even be raised earlier and more radically: Is this common concern to be viewed as legitimate at all in the light of the gospel? By raising this question we are back where we were on the opening pages of the introduction; there we asked ourselves whether an understanding was at all possible between the gospel and the presuppositions of our modern culture. This culture after all rests on presuppositions which in the Old and the New Testament are simply described as sinful. The constant effort to relate these two worlds to each other seems to be a hopeless enterprise.

Still, there is—seemingly or in reality—something common, something central to both these worlds: man and his salvation. One can even go further and say: this theme comes up in both the Old and New Testaments in such a way that in the process the presuppositions of the modern world also come up. Already in Genesis 3 man appears as a creature who wants to be like God: the absolute subject of his knowledge of and control over the world. This man is punished by God, that is, God drives him further down that self-chosen road. In the New Testament—in the parable of the wicked tenants (Mark 12:1-9)—there is a similar view of man: people renounced their allegiance to their master in order to conduct and enjoy their lives in autonomous freedom. The same picture emerges in the parable of the prodigal son (Luke 15:11-32), where man with his given endowments dissociates himself from the Father in order to lead and enjoy his life in accordance with his own pleasure—there where God is far away and cannot disturb him. Many other statements in the Bible, especially in the prophets and in the epistles, cast a similar light on the human situation.

Now this man who breaks his ties with God because he suspects his salvation is there where God is not is nevertheless not abandoned by God, as all three stories show. God pursues this wayward human being with his judgment and grace. And judgment stands in the service of grace. Though man wants to live without God, God does not want to live without man, and therefore man is never God-less. That is the first thing that needs to be said with a view to modern man. This situation implies that—whatever may have motivated the theologians not to take the godlessness of modern man with total seriousness—in the light of the gospel this attitude must at least in part be regarded as legitimate. The Christian church must, in the name of its Lord, be where the wayward are. And theology, as scholarly reflection on the movement of God toward his lost world, must mirror this movement in its themes.

This movement of God, however, is one of disturbance, of calling back, and of invitation. This aspect, too, theology must mirror. In all solidarity with the world it must conduct a dialogue with it; but because of its solidarity with God it must do this in the form of a dispute. It cannot cover up the gap; it has to uncover it in order to bridge it. That is true not only of theology; it is true of the church in the world in general; but it is true of theology in the manner of an intellectual struggle. For that reason its work entails enormous tension.

The apostle Paul brought out this tension with exceptional clarity. I have in mind particularly two passages in 1 Corinthians. One instance occurs in 9:19-23, where Paul very emphatically brings to expression the external and internal necessity of solidarity:

> For though I am free from all men, I have made myself a slave to all, that I might win the more. To the Jews I became as a Jew, in order to win Jews; to those under the law I became as one under the law—though not being myself under the law—that I might win those under the law. To those outside the law I became as one outside the law—not being without law toward God but under the law of Christ—that I might win those outside the law. To the weak I became weak, that I might win the weak. I have become all things to all men, that I might by all means save some. I do it all for the sake of the gospel, that I may share in its blessings.

The seventh and last purpose clause is surprising: it breaks the parallelism. By it Paul draws the reader's attention to the fact that behind his solidarity with human beings there is another solidarity; his own participation in the gospel and his self-denying ministry to his fellow human beings are two sides of the same movement. His solidarity with and service to people aims at making many others participate in the gospel. For that reason the word *solidarity* does not cover everything, not even the essential thing, that needs to be said, for the goal of solidarity is the conversion of the other.

That takes us to another passage in which Paul reflects on the relationship between the gospel and the world, 1:22-25 (within the context of vv. 18-31 in which it resonates):

> For Jews demand signs and Greeks seek wisdom, but we preach Christ crucified, a stumbling block to Jews and folly to Gentiles, but to those who are called, both Jews and Greeks, Christ the power of God and the wisdom of God. For the foolishness of God is wiser than men, and the weakness of God is stronger than men.

Here the emphasis is on the other side: solidarity with the gospel over against mankind. It casts a new light on solidarity with mankind: this solidarity occurs with a view to participation in the gospel of the Crucified and therefore in contradiction and struggle. Paul places himself alongside all people, not to stay there even for a moment, but to draw them all away from where they are and to lead them on a new road.

We referred to "enormous tension"—tension which over and over surfaces in Paul's letters. He, the diaspora Jew from the south of Asia Minor, did not feign solidarity with Jews and Greeks. He, himself a Jew, lived in a Greek world. Literally and intellectually he could express himself in two distinct languages. In the letters to the Romans and Galatians we observe him writing as a Jew, struggling with Jews about Jewish concepts. In large parts of the Corinthian letters and in Colossians he expresses himself in the idiom of religious Hellenism. However, the two worlds cannot be simply divided among the different letters. Consider the doctrine of the "elemental powers" *(stoicheia)* in Galatians 4 and the Stoic language in Romans 1:18-25 and 2:12-16. Consequently I consider the depiction of Paul's preaching to the Greeks in Acts 17:16-34 to be essentially correct. It illustrates the double solidarity, the mutual contradiction, and the conflict.

From this evidence one can infer that the relationship between the gospel and the world is dialectical, ever swinging back and forth between yes and no. The question concerning legitimacy can then be answered with the observation that everyone is justified in his theological methodology provided that when he says yes or no he bears in mind the counterpart and brings it to his audience in one way or another. Before we go that far, however, we must first attempt to describe more precisely the relationship between no and yes which we have sketchily indicated with the polyvalent term *dialectic*.

For this purpose too we find support in a section of Paul's letters, Philippians 3:4b-14:

> If any other man thinks he has reason for confidence in the flesh [i.e., some external mark], I have more: circumcised on the eighth day, of the people of Israel, of the tribe of Benjamin, a Hebrew born of Hebrews; as to the law a Pharisee, as to zeal a persecutor of the church, as to righteousness under the law blameless. But whatever gain I had, I counted as loss for the sake of Christ. Indeed, I count everything as loss because of the surpassing worth of knowing Christ Jesus my Lord. For his sake I have suffered the loss of all things, and count them as refuse, in order that I may gain Christ and be found in him, not having a righteousness of my own, based on law, but that which is through faith in Christ, the righteousness from God that depends on

> faith; that I may know him and the power of his resurrection, and may share his sufferings, becoming like him in his death, that if possible I may attain the resurrection from the dead.
>
> Not that I have already obtained this or am already perfect; but I press on to make it my own, because Christ Jesus has made me his own. Brethren, I do not consider that I have made it my own; but one thing I do, forgetting what lies behind and straining forward to what lies ahead, I press on toward the goal for the prize of the upward call of God in Christ Jesus.

Here Paul is not, as is usually thought, looking back on his pre-Christian period under the law as on a period of darkness and despair. On the contrary: that was a good time in which he believed he lived in harmony with God by keeping his law. But when he learned to know Christ he was offered a new, far better, indeed a surpassing (Gr. *hyperechon*) way to God. In the light of the preceding biographical remarks, these words suggest that, in surpassing the offer of the law, Christ's offer based on faith stood in a certain continuity with it, in line with which the "gain" of the one now has to be viewed as "loss" by comparison with the greater "gain" of the other. But then the language suddenly changes drastically. The two sets of saving benefits which initially seemed comparable in quantitative terms of "more" and "less" are now contrasted qualitatively. In the light of the righteousness of faith the righteousness based on law proves to be as "refuse." At this point one would expect a sort of antithesis, say, between "refuse" and "treasure." Because the treasure still lies in the future, however, Paul now introduces the image of the race and thus a road to run on. A few verses later he exhorts the congregation: "Only, we must let our steps be guided by such truth as we have attained" (v. 16, Moffatt).

Paul is on the way, and from the point he has reached he first looks back and then forward. The road began in Jewish righteousness, the righteousness of the law. On this road he discovered a new possibility of gaining the salvation promised through the law. But when he turned to it, he realized that by pursuing it he had left the original road behind. Looking back he saw that the first part of his "road" had been a detour, no, a wrong road altogether.

The theologians we studied in this book differ from Paul, since for the most part they want to be Christians from the beginning. But they also want to be modern people—and in fact they are. On that basis they want to start their intellectual journey, traveling in the direction of the gospel. What unites the beginning and the end of that journey is the theme of man and his salvation. In the course of that journey it has to become apparent sooner or later, however, that the road is not at all as innocuous as it seemed at the beginning. The wanderer is thrown off course. He experiences the transvaluation of his values. Gain becomes loss and what he prided himself on turns to "refuse." But the crisis does not mean the end of the road. After the crisis there awaits him a road that does not end within our world and time, one on which large differences of opinion can and do arise among travel companions, on which all sorts of lapses and aberrations are possible. It is a road on which the travelers must stop at regular intervals to look back and to look ahead and to determine jointly what the direction should be.

It seems to me that for nearly two thousand years now the history of theology has been that kind of journey. In Paul's lifetime and later, upon their conversion the Jews first and then the Greeks started their journey, still tied to their culture. Every epoch, in fact every person, must time and again start from the beginning. One can never appropriate more than a small part of the experiences of those who have gone before. One often marvels at how the insights of Paul were almost completely hidden from view in the apostolic fathers and the apologists by Stoic, Platonic, and Gnostic conceptions. But that was necessary. The truth of the gospel is a very different one from the truths of the natural sciences because in them people start at the point where their predecessors left off. In contrast, the truth of the gospel is a road everyone must travel by himself. This road is itself the truth. One does not "stand" in the truth but "walks" in it on the way toward the goal that is not attainable this side of eternity.

Of course—and fortunately—one must not understand this imagery in a totally individualistic way, although analogies emerge in the life of every dynamic theologian. Theology in particular has always known intensive interchange within a broad community. The journey proceeds through development, differentiation, and confrontation among schools and trends. First there were the Apologists, then came Irenaeus; first came Origenism, then Athanasius; first Cyprian, then Augustine; first the Christ-hero in the German *Heliand* poem, then the Crucified One of Bernard of Clairvaux. First there is early scholasticism with its rational optimism; at the end of the road there is Occamism with reason and faith as opposites. Apart from the wave of enlightenment that came with Averroism Thomas Aquinas is simply inconceivable. A figure like Luther could only emerge against the background of late medieval moralism. Just as the Spirit finds the individual, so the Spirit also finds theological reflection where it is initially at home, however "carnal" that home may be. The Spirit then leads us toward a crisis in our thinking. After the crisis our thought has to and is allowed to proceed under the guidance of the motto "I believe in order that I may understand." However, just as our thinking *before* the crisis is threatened by an uncritical modernity, so *after* the crisis there is the danger of scholastic sterility. The gospel is the great non-self-evident factum which is ever threatened by betrayal on our theological journeys. Where it is turned into a mirror image of our modernity, there protest in the name of the true gospel has to arise. And where people have gone to sleep with their heads on the pillow of the "true gospel," a new generation which has turned away from it because it seemed to have no bearing on its own experience has to be found where it is at home. Thus the journey proceeds over and over from a stage of being "before" the crisis to a stage of being "after" the crisis.

Let us now return to the issue of legitimacy. By this time we can, we hope, put more content into the rather inexpressive word *dialectical*. I now venture to say: the measure of legitimacy belonging to a given theological method or system corresponds to the measure in which it is involved in the double movement toward the crisis and away from the crisis. From this vantage point it is clear that there have always been, also in the past two hundred years, theologians whose work had little theological validity: liberal theologians who in their movement toward the gospel stopped long before they came to the crisis; and orthodox theologians who detached the gospel from its arena of struggle and began the process of thinking it through at a point beyond the crisis. Between these two extremes there is a large number of theologies in which one senses, to a smaller or greater degree, the tension evoked by the crisis. The "usefulness" of a given theology also depends, of course, on the stage a person has reached in his or her own theological journey.

The greatest theologians would be those who most deeply and consistently plumbed and pondered the double movement: the one toward the crisis and the one following the crisis. But do such theologians exist? Can this double movement be executed with equal power and from every angle by one and the same person? I find it happening in the case of Paul. But are there examples of it in the theology of the last two hundred years? One would like to think first of all of the two greatest theologians of this time span: Schleiermacher and Barth. We have already indicated that there is much less opposition and much more convergence and complementarity between them than is usually assumed. Schleiermacher constructed his theology much more in opposition to the prevailing idealism than seems at first glance to be the case. Still, he allowed himself to be guided by a desired harmony between the church and the intellectual culture of the time to such a degree that the crisis only occasionally flashes out on the horizon. Barth is a person who in his own life traveled the road from the spirit of the time *(Zeitgeist)* to the crisis; when the crisis was past and he started afresh, he no longer wanted to remember the road that brought him to that point. From fear of a point of contact he abstained from making the crisis itself a theme of reflection. This explains the passion with which the younger theologians after him now everywhere return to the first stage of his journey. There they themselves are also able to make a new beginning! Whether a person can ever think on some level beyond such one-sidedness has become a major question for me. What he gains in comprehensiveness he will probably lose in power. It seems to me that Kierkegaard, in his theological dispute with his own culture, a dispute he conducted in the thought forms of that culture, came closest to what we are groping for here. For the current period I am thinking of Helmut Thielicke's *The Evangelical Faith,* vol. 1 (German, 1968; Eng. tr. 1974), *Prolegomena: The Relation of Theology to Modern Thought Forms,* in which the author takes the reader on a road leading from Descartes *(cogito ergo sum)* to the gospel *(cogitor ergo sum).* Another question is whether a comprehensive presentation is really the form in which the bridge between the gospel and modernity can best be constructed. Would it not perhaps be better if in the various stages of our journey we were accompanied now by one theologian, now by another—as it usually happens in our experience anyway?

DID IT MEAN ANYTHING?

Here I am using the word *mean* in the conventional and almost trivial sense of "succeed." This question must not be avoided. The men with whom we occupied ourselves here sought to achieve something. They were pained by the ever growing gap between their church and their culture—the liberal theologians definitely no less than the orthodox. And they wanted to make the gospel understandable in their world—the orthodox just as well as the liberal. Was that goal achieved?

Unfortunately, the answer has to be negative. Liberals hoped by means of their accommodation to gain a hearing among the cultured. But this hardly ever occurred. They were not taken very seriously because they were not regarded as being in solidarity with the spirit of the time and were suspected of trying, by apologetic means, to save a lost cause. Even those who were more sympathetic toward their efforts viewed their work rather as spectators. The reader may recall how in his own culture Schleiermacher remained a—mostly ignored—stranger. Liberal theologians allowed themselves to a high degree to be instructed by contemporary philosophers. Conversely, however, these philosophers did not let themselves be taught, let alone converted, by the theologians. They took but little notice of their efforts. I know this generalization is dangerous, and to the best of my knowledge the history of theology has never been explored from this perspective. In the personal realm there have presumably also been other experiences. In general, however, secularized culture manifested polite indifference if not outright intolerance.

What is true for the liberal theologians is even more true for the orthodox. Occasionally they enjoyed somewhat more regard among outsiders because people saw in them the exponents of genuine historic Christianity. As a result they seemed to be subjectively more honest but at the same time objectively even less credible than their liberal colleagues. If some theologians nevertheless exerted a certain influence within their culture—I have in mind here Adolf von Harnack and Karl Barth—this had nothing to do with their theological message but rather with their cultural endowments and achievement or their political insights.

A certain exception has to be made here for Anglo-Saxon, and particularly American, theology. In the United States the boundaries between church and world are indefinite and fluid. Theologians as theologians can still get a hearing in wider cultural circles, as evidenced by Reinhold Niebuhr and Paul Tillich. One imagines that this fact is not unrelated to the greater proximity of these theologies to ethical issues.

Therefore the negative answer must be qualified. But even then it is only half the total answer. The other half is that, though these theologians and theologies may hardly have found a response outside Christianity, within the churches they have often been very important. They may have brought few people to the gospel from the outside; they did enable many who were brought up as Christians to remain loyal to the gospel amidst the temptations of secularism, or to bring them back to the gospel. They instilled fresh courage for the ministry in the hearts of many pastors, and so they indirectly served the upbuilding of the church. With their efforts at making the gospel intelligible they exerted great influence in Christian student movements, and in wider circles they made an impressive contribution to the formation and preservation of a Christian mind. They have been useful, if not for the penetration of the light of the gospel, then for the presence of the gospel in the intellectual world. That applies as well to liberal as to mediating and conservative personalities and schools. The only difference was and is that they exerted this preserving influence on different groups, presumably depending on the degree of threatening secularization in these groups. I have the impression that many a searching young theologian was initially more attracted to liberal conceptions in order subsequently to process these views in a more conservative fashion. Of these developments and cross-connections we also know little. What does seem to me to be certain is that all attempts at doing theology within the culture of modernity were and are much more effective at conserving the faith than at recruiting people from the outside.

NOW WHAT?

Today what theology offers on a world scale is more confusing than ever. This negative observation is the reverse side of a very positive one: suddenly, following the end of the 1960s, large groups of people who till then had hardly shown any interest in theological reflection became theologically active. This is especially true of the third world: marginalized blacks in so-called white countries; Christians in young African and Asiatic states who are exploring anew their pre-Christian culture and religion; exploited masses in Latin America who, under the guidance of theologians and clergy, are discovering that the Bible is not the book of the exploiters but of the helpless. A parallel to all this in the Western world is the feminist theology developed by women who experience themselves in our culture as the oppressed half of the population. Everywhere large groups are joyfully discovering that they themselves, each in their own uniqueness, are known and called by God. In all these new theologies the word *experience* serves as a point of entry, a *praeambulum fidei*. Depending on their *Sitz im Leben* these experiences are very diverse, as are the theologies developed in terms of these experiences. In the 1970s one often had the feeling that in the multiplicity of experiences and the demand of "contextuality" arising from them, the oneness of the object, the universal cause of the gospel, threatened to disappear from sight and that only a tower of Babel was left. Should that be the case, that would be the end of theo-logy in general, for on account of the oneness of God (theo-) and that of science (-logy), it can never be content with such pluralism. This objection came especially from the side of Western, so-called academic theology. At work here, however, is an optical illusion which is being increasingly discovered and conceded also in the West: we too, though we believe we are doing purely academic work in theology, actually think contextually, proceeding from our own cultural *Sitz im Leben*. Are concepts like conscience, self-understanding, existence, ambivalence, border situation, basic trust, hope, self-realization, selftranscendence, process thinking, openness to the world, meaning of life, encounter, rationality, etc., legitimate, while concepts like oppression, liberation, black self-affirmation, feminity, etc., are illegitimate? The real difference lies in the cultural, social, and political climate from within which people are trying to discover the gospel and to which people want to communicate it. In the third world it is the rugged climate of struggle to establish the most elementary conditions of humanity; in the first world it is the mild climate of a prosperous pluralistic culture in which people can afford the luxury of reflecting on the so-called ultimate questions of the meaning of life.

From a theological viewpoint, therefore, this difference is a penultimate matter. It is the material counterpart of a profound methodological agreement on the task of theology to mediate between a strange gospel and the situation estranged from it. Within this unity there are also methodological differences, however, which need to be noted and which are related to what we wrote earlier about the "journey" of theology. Recently the "younger" theologies have started their journey from within their own experiences. In distinction from Western theologies, they regard "contextualization" as their primary task. They have become "a Greek to the Greeks." The fact that they have something to offer which must seem "foolishness to the Greeks" is, for the time being, another story. For the sake of the gospel and theology, however, they must sooner or later push their own experiences toward the crisis of the gospel and walk a road on which they do not harden into an ideology but let their experiences be criticized, corrected, deepened by the crucified and risen Lord, and placed in *his* context.

The "older" theologies of the West, with their centuries-long march through numerous experiences, know that one cannot stop there. In the final analysis they want to theologize on the basis of the gospel. Consequently they tend not to see their own contextuality or to reflect on it critically. Thus as the younger theologies are threatened by a tendency to ideologize the gospel, so these are threatened by a tendency to scholasticize it. The two groups can, however, correct and enrich each other, and bring their own regionally conditioned but legitimate understandings into the universal context of the one gospel, out of reverence for Christ in whom "all the treasures of wisdom and knowledge are hidden" (Col. 2:3). In theology we must love our regional neighbor as ourselves but we must do so from within the light of the one God whom we together love with all our heart and mind. The fact that a fruitful convergence of contextualities is possible is manifest from the rapprochement between J. Moltmann and J. Miguez Bonino which did not occur until after they had sharply told each other "the truth."

Only now can we take up the question whether the two hundred years of Western theology, which coincide with the heyday of Western bourgeois culture, constitute an epoch on its last legs. For two related reasons I am inclined to say no to that question. The first is that, as we noted, the fundamental problematics of post-Enlightenment theology are, on closer scrutiny, essentially identical with the problematics in the Old and New Testaments and in earlier epochs of church history. The second is that, as we noted a moment ago, non-Western theologies display the same structure and tension (experience–revelation) as the Western ones. That similarity is already the case today though now the different *Sitze im Leben*, here and there, still lie far apart. This situation will be even more evident when also in the third world the theme of secularization will come to the fore as being of the same weight as the themes of exploitation and national development.

However, Western theology will soon lose its predominance. Buenos Aires, Lagos, Bangalore, and Tokyo (let us say) will play an equal role alongside Tübingen, Edinburgh, and Chicago. Western theology will die in its Western-ness in order to rise again in globalness. Pluralism will then be far more extensive. But this multiplicity will be held together through numerous dialogic relationships within a framework of an essentially unified structure and method.

All will have to learn from one another what is entailed in the question of the fate of all theology before and after the Constantinian era. That applies not so much to the elaboration of our current horizons of experience as to the road to be taken from this point on, the road which has to lead us all into the crisis of revelation, that we may learn in that crisis to make our experiences take part in a new experience. As long as the pressure of secularization continues, or even increases in many places, we shall be tempted (a temptation to which many of our predecessors succumbed) to let the projected audience of the message prescribe to us the presuppositions of theological thought and to present the gospel as an affirmation and reinforcement of our own ideas and ideals. In any case, on the road of experience we must encourage each other to leap over the gap which takes us into the new circle of revelation in which our thoughts, far from being imprisoned and isolated, are judged, extended, and consecrated. We must again and again start within our respective contextialities in order then to fuse our context increasingly with the context of the gospel, in a way such that the message gains superiority over all that which emerges from our situational analyses. No matter where one goes, it often looks as if a great many theologians lack the courage to travel the road of theology to the end. Anyone who spends so much time in the *praeambula fidei*, be it of a sociological, linguistic, philosophical, or political nature, is in danger of losing the chance to enrich his *Umwelt* with the great and new experience of the Word of God.

Theology should not shy away from the alienating nature of its task. It is only as "alien" that it can be relevant and fruitful in the world. Only "the theologian of the cross," said Luther at the Heidelberg disputation, "calls things by their right names."

INDEX